Forensic Mental Health Nursing

Capabilities, Roles and Responsibilities

edited by

The National Forensic Nurses' Research and Development Group
Alyson Kettles (Chair), Phil Woods and Richard Byrt
on behalf of the Group

Chapter reviews by Mary Addo, Richard Byrt, Michael Coffey, Mike Doyle, Alyson Kettles and Phil Woods

QUAY BOOKS

Quay Books Division, MA Healthcare Ltd, St Jude's Church, Dulwich Road,
London SE24 0PB

British Library Cataloguing-in-Publication Data
A catalogue record is available for this book

© MA Healthcare Limited 2008
ISBN-10: 1-85642-362-X
ISBN-13: 978-1-85642-362-5

Printed in the UK by Ashford Colour Press, Gosport, Hants

Contents

List of contributors

'Algy', *'Bede'*, *'Colm'*, *'Dirk'*, *'Ezra'* and *'Ferg'*, among many other roles, have been service users on Cannock ward, Arnold Lodge medium secure unit, Leicester.

Mick Adams, RMN, BSc, CertEd(FE), is a Practitioner-Tutor at the School of Health Science, Swansea University; and a Community Mental Health Nurse, Assertive Outreach Service, Abertawe Bro Morgannwg University NHS Trust.

Mary Addo, PhD, MEd, MA Soc Sci, DMS, PgCertTLT, RMN, EN(G) is a Lecturer in Mental Health Nursing/Practice Education at the School of Nursing and Midwifery, Robert Gordon University and NHS Grampian (Mental Health), Aberdeen, Scotland. She teaches pre- and post-registration nursing students, and contributes to the teaching of post-graduate taught Master's degree module(s) at the Centre for Advanced Studies in Nursing, University of Aberdeen. She is involved in nursing research, has published on forensic nursing and related issues, and her interest lies in promoting positive acceptance of people with mental illness and supporting nurses in clinical practice.

Gillian Kay Archibald, Bsc (Hons), SRD is a senior dietitian, based at Royal Cornhill Hospital, Aberdeen, Mental Health Hospital. This includes the Blair Forensic Unit for Acute, Long-Stay and Rehabilitation services. She now specialises in the areas of acute mental illness, forensic mental illness and eating disorders after gaining experience in the specialities of diabetes, stroke care and orthopaedics. Gillian contributes to the training of dietitians, nurses and other allied health professionals visiting Royal Cornhill Hospital.

Stuart Bowness, BSc (Hons), RN is a senior staff nurse, Arnold Lodge medium secure unit, Leicester.

Paul Burberry, RMN, DipCogTh co-ordinates the Sex Offender Treatment Programme for the Adult Forensic Mental Health Services Directorate, part of Greater Manchester West NHS Foundation Trust. He is also a Cognitive Behavioural Therapist with the Directorate's Forensic Psychotherapies Department providing CBT for both inpatients and outpatients with a range of mental health concerns and personality disorders.

Richard Byrt, RMN, RNLD, RGN, PhD, BSc (Hons) is Lecturer-Practitioner, Nursing, at Arnold Lodge medium secure unit, Nottinghamshire Healthcare NHS Trust and the School of Nursing and Midwifery, De Montfort University, Leicester. He also has experience as a service user and carer.

Michael Coffey is Lecturer in Community Mental Health Nursing at Swansea University. He previously worked as a community mental health nurse in both generic and forensic mental health services. His research focuses upon aspects of community mental health nursing and particularly people's experiences of receipt of these services. He has co-edited, with Chris Chaloner, the textbook *Forensic Mental Health Nursing: Current Approaches* and, with Ben Hannigan, *The Handbook of Community Mental Health Nursing*.

Graham Durcan, Research and Development Manager, Criminal Justice Programme, Sainsbury Centre for Mental Health.

Leah Evans is Forensic Community Mental Health Nurse, Caswell Clinic, Bridgend.

Gavin Garman, PhD, Msc, BA (Hons), RN is Head of Forensic Nursing for the Thames Valley Forensic Mental Health Service in England. He also lectures in Forensic Psychology at Reading University, from where he obtained his PhD. He is the senior manager for over 250 nursing staff across three English counties. His interests include mindfulness and cognitive therapy, service user involvement, research and clinical governance.

Linda Hart is a writer, artist and campaigner. She is the author of, among other works, the MIND Book of the Year: *Phone at Nine, Just to Say You're Alive*, based on her experience as a service user.

Linnette James-Sow, RN, BSc(Hons) is a staff nurse working in an acute mental health setting. Linnette is also a poet and song writer during her spare time.

Richard Jones is Team Leader, Carmarthen and Towy Valley Crisis Resolution and Home Treatment Team, Pembs and Derwent NHS Trust

Alyson M. Kettles, PhD, MSc (London), BSc (Dundee), RMN, RGN, RNT, PGCEA (Surrey), Dip Crim, ILTM, FHEA, FRSM is Research and Development Officer (Mental Health) for NHS Grampian and is based at the Royal Cornhill Hospital in Aberdeen, Scotland. She is also Honorary Senior Lecturer for the Centre for Advanced Studies in Nursing at the University of Aberdeen where she co-ordinates and teaches on modules for the post-graduate taught Master's degrees. Her personal portfolio of research has had a forensic focus for more than the last decade, as a result of being the Link Tutor with Broadmoor Hospital while a nurse teacher at the Frances Harrison College of Nursing in Guildford and the University of Surrey. She is a well known author of mental health and forensic nursing articles and books. Her research interests include assessment and interventions, such as risk and observation.

Mohammed Khoshdel, RMN, BSc, is a facilitator for the Sex Offender Treatment Programme as well as being a forensic nurse on a male acute ward. Both roles are held within the Adult Forensic Mental Health Services Directorate (the Edenfield Centre), part of Greater Manchester West Mental Health NHS Foundation Trust.

David Langton, BA(Hons), Dip Sy Practice, Cert Ed, RCNT, RMN, RNMH is Nurse Consultant for the Forensic Network in Scotland. Until being promoted to his current role in 2005, David had worked exclusively in High Security Hospitals having commenced work in the NHS in 1975 at Rampton Hospital, moving to the State Hospital in Scotland in 1998 as a Senior Nurse.

Lauren Mason, BSc (Hons), MSc is an Assistant Psychologist, Arnold Lodge medium secure unit, Leicester.

Romanus Ngeh, BSc (Hons), RN is a staff nurse, Arnold Lodge medium secure unit, Leicester.

Cindy Peternelj-Taylor RN, BScN, MSc, PhD(c) is Professor at the College of Nursing, University of Saskatchewan. Much of Cindy's career has focused on professional role development for nurses who work with vulnerable populations. In this role, she has had many opportunities to assist students and nurses with clinical and ethical concerns that emerge in practice. She is a member of the Editorial Board of the *Journal of Psychiatric and Mental Health Nursing,* and is an Associate Editor of the *Journal of Forensic Nursing.* She is currently completing a doctoral dissertation in Nursing at the University of Alberta, where she is exploring the experience of engagement of forensic clients from a nursing perspective.

Fomayi Saliki, MSc (Management in Health and Social Care), RMN, Dip Ed is a Forensic Community Mental Health Nurse with the Thames Valley Forensic Mental Health Service. He has worked for the service for seven years, working in both inpatient and community settings. Interests include contemporary mental health issues and diversity in patient management, engagement and quality of care.

Penny Schafer RN, BSN, MN, PhD(c) is currently completing a doctoral dissertation in Educational Administration at the University of Saskatchewan. The focus of her doctoral work is a postmodern discourse analysis regarding the research literature on bullying in elementary and high school students. She has a long history in forensic psychiatric and correctional nursing. Work with individuals diagnosed with personality disorders has been the focus of the majority of her career. The challenge of establishing and maintaining therapeutic relationships and facilitating psycho-educational groups are areas where Penny has developed clinical excellence.

Ian Smith is currently a lecturer in mental health nursing at Robert Gordon University in Aberdeen, Scotland. He worked in learning disabilities for many years prior to coming into teaching. He then taught for 16 years in this area. Ian is involved in nurse education research projects within the School of Nursing and Midwifery although most of his work is concerned with teaching. He has recently developed a distance learning module in communicating with people with learning disabilities.

Helen Walker, BEd, RMN, BSc, MSc (in CBT) is currently acting Senior Nurse for practice development at the State Hospital, Carstairs, Scotland. She qualified as a mental health nurse in 1991 and has experience of working in a variety of mental health settings, predominantly community, acute admissions and a high secure forensic unit. Throughout most of her career she has been actively involved in research and many posts she has held have been evenly divided between clinical and research activities.

Phil Woods, RMN, RPN, PhD is an Associate Professor at the College of Nursing, University of Saskatchewan. He has an extensive personal portfolio of forensic-related research. He is a well-known author of mental health and forensic nursing articles and books. His specific research interests are risk assessment and management, and violence prediction.

Cathy Wray, RMN, EN(M) is ward manager, Cannock ward, Arnold Lodge medium secure unit, Leicester.

CHAPTER I

Introduction

Alyson McGregor Kettles, Phil Woods and Richard Byrt

This book is about issues related to the role and function of the forensic mental health nurse. We hope that you will find it enjoyable and relevant. The book originated from the determination of the National Forensic Nurses' Research and Development Group to contribute to the development of forensic and other aspects of mental health nursing. It is aimed at helping nurses to understand the changing nature and multiplicity of roles of the forensic mental health nurse, in order to enable the provision of appropriate care to patients, their carers, families and significant/relevant others, including the person harmed (the victim or survivor of an offence). It is also aimed at enabling a greater understanding to develop between professions and is designed to give examples of how professionals can work together. Much of the content of this book is relevant to forensic learning diability nursing; and to other forensic and prison mental health professionals, and to service users and organisations representing their rights and interests.

While 'forensic' can have different meanings for different people, in this book the following definition is used:

> *Forensic means of the law, and is based on the Latin word 'forum', meaning 'what is out of doors'... The Ancient Romans met outside in...[forums] for public meetings, political debates and public legal hearings to try offenders... In the United Kingdom, forensic mental health nurses work with the relatively small proportion of individuals whose mental health problems are associated with offending behaviour.*
> (Kettles et al, 2007:1, quoting Soanes, 2002 and citing Parker, 1985)

Forensic mental health nursing and forensic learning disability nursing are small but growing branches of nursing practice that occur in a wide range of settings, and continue to extend to other areas. The latter include hospitals and units offering low, medium and high security, 'court diversion schemes (e.g. in magistrates' [sheriff and high] courts), prisons, young offender institutions, police stations' (Kettles et al, 2007:1), community settings, and accident and emergency units (McClelland et al, 2001; Rowe and Lopes, 2003; Wix and Humphreys, 2005). Forensic mental health nurses also work with a greater variety of professionals than, for example, nurses working in acute mental health care.

The forensic mental health nursing role: Then and now

According to Kettles et al (2007:2) 'there is an increasing need for forensic knowledge' and understanding about the role of the forensic mental health nurse in all settings and with all groups of patients. Patients' problems and needs, and consequently, nurses' roles, are growing in complexity (Dale et al, 2001:19; Chaloner and Coffey, 2000; Kettles and Robinson, 2000). As has been noted in an earlier book in this series: 'the majority of general mental health nurses work with individuals with histories of offending in (non-forensic) settings, including acute admission wards; services for children and young people and older people; therapeutic communities; and facilities for treatment and recovery, as well as individuals with problematic substance use' (Kettles et al 2007:1, citing Kettles et al, 2002a, Woods, 2004). From this, it can be seen that the forensic mental health nursing role is not limited in relation to particular client groups or settings. Provision of safety and security for patients in high security care is no longer enough, and has not been enough for some time. In many respects, the current forensic mental health nursing role is 'out of doors' because it is no longer solely in the purview of high security care.

Fortunately, forensic mental health nursing has matured over the past 30 years in order to meet need and to accommodate the political, legal, social and professional necessity that has been part of development in the health services in a 'modern' world (Woods, 2004).

We have come a very long way from being 'keepers' (the forerunners of forensic mental health nurses) in Broadmoor Criminal Lunatic Asylum (Roberts, 2006) which was founded in 1863 (Kirby 2000). Until well into the 19th century, keepers, both in institutions and in the care and confinement of people in their homes, were seen as uneducated and of lowly status (Nolan, 1993), and this is reflected in some of the fiction of the time. One example is Grace Poole, the keeper caring for Mrs Rochester in *Jane Eyre*, first published in 1847 (Bronte, 1994). Neither Mrs Rochester and her mental illness nor Grace Poole, are described very sympathetically, and indeed, Grace Poole is found to have attempted murder, so she can hardly be viewed as a good early role model for forensic or other mental health nurses (Literature Organisation, 2007). Although forensic mental health nursing has travelled far since the founding of the first high security hospital, the profession faces some formidable challenges in the future.

Kirby (2000:300) states that:

Most mental health professionals are familiar with the term 'forensic psychiatry' but they are perhaps less likely to have a clear conception of the forensic mental health nurse. Unlike many specialities, there is little understanding of what forensic nursing represents.

This was written a few years ago, but the truth of this statement has not significantly changed. Although the profile of forensic mental health nursing has risen within forensic care, it is still, in the experience of the authors, not particularly well understood within general mental health. This is further compounded by the move towards genericism and the general taking up of such materials as the 10 Essential Shared Capabilities (10 ESCs; Sainsbury Centre, 2004). Although these initiatives are important in themselves, and intended to be of wide relevance, they make it harder for forensic mental health nurses to raise the profile of their work in the general arena. For example, there can be a general assumption that all forensic patients are the same and that they should be where they are, i.e. in secure facilities. Forensic nurses spend considerable time and effort with various groups and individuals to show that there are specific diversity issues and that offenders are individuals who require even greater understanding than those with either a single or dual diagnosis in mental health. This does fit with the 10 ESCs but it makes it seem as if the role and work of the forensic mental health nurse is the same as every other mental health nurse, when there is much more to it. Forensic mental health nurses deal with a multitude of issues, interventions, skills and capabilities that start with specifics such as the 10 ESCs but which go much further. This will be explained in more depth later in this chapter.

With the commissioning of an increased number of forensic units and an increase in the number of forensic patients receiving community care, it is likely that new roles and extensions to current roles will become the norm for forensic mental health nursing services (Coffey et al, 2007; Kettles and Hall, 2007). There are already many new roles, such as the nurse consultant and specialist forensic community mental health nurses (FCMHNs). These nurses deal with crisis situations or use particular therapies and modalities, including psychosocial interventions (PSI) and dialectical-behaviour therapy (DBT) (Coffey et al, 2007). Other forensic nurses are involved in diversion from custody (Hillis, 1999:191). ' Not only this, but substantial demands are being made on ... inpatient services by [patients with] challenging symptoms' (Kettles et al, 2007:2), which may be complicated by problematic substance use and more serious index offences (Kettles and Woodally, 2006). This means that forensic mental health nurses require a clear fundamental route into forensic care, with specialist practice courses available at postgraduate level. Currently, forensic mental health nurses can take only a very small range of courses that are specific

---

Box 1.1: Components of the forensic role

- Characteristics
- Features
- Knowledge
- Skill
- Skills
- Conceptualisation

- Competence
- Competencies
- Issues
- Definitions
- Evidence

---

to forensic mental health nursing, although there are other courses focused on specialist practice, such as clinical masters and doctorates (Watson and Kettles, 2007). However, there is recognition (Forensic Network, 2006) that something more substantial is required, for example, there are plans to establish a multidisciplinary forensic school in Scotland.

Argument for a forensic mental health nursing role

The forensic mental health nursing role has never been, and is not now, a single entity. The forensic mental health nursing role comprises many components as shown in *Box 1.1*.

Chaloner (2000:1) states that:

The role of the forensic mental health nurse has expanded and there is a growing number and range of practice areas to which 'forensic' nurses make an active contribution... The expansion of the role has naturally extended the range of skills required by forensic mental health nurses and contributed to an expanding knowledge base relating to the diverse requirements of practice... The diverse range of publications generated by forensic nurses has contributed to the recognition of this 'specialism' and enabled a nursing 'voice' to be heard within the varied and complex debates relating to the treatment, care and management of mentally disordered offenders. (Box 1.1)

Burrow's (1993) case for forensic mental health nursing was based on the following six premises:

1. 'The client category consists overwhelmingly of offenders with psychiatric pathology.'
2. 'Nurses contribute towards the therapeutic targeting of any mental disorder or offending behaviour related to psychiatric morbidity.'
3. 'These care strategies are largely incorporated within institutional

control and custody of patients.'
4. 'The configuration of patient pathology, criminal activity, therapeutic interventions and competencies, court/legal issues and custodial care creates the need for a formidable and accelerating knowledge base.'
5. 'The advocacy role is different from that in other nursing specialities, embracing both the destigmatisation and decriminalisation of the patient group.'
6. 'Clients' potential for future dangerousness requires the formulation of risk assessment strategies.'

Burrow (1993:903)

However, Burrow's six premises need to be revised to reflect current use and an updated version follows:

1. The client group consists mainly of people with a mental illness who have offended or been diverted from custody.
2. Nurses care for the client population in the various settings in which they live, and contribute to the therapeutic care and treatment of the person and his or her illness and offending behaviour.
3. The care strategies follow the patient journey through detention/secure care to community-based services, in the variety of settings in which patients can find themselves.
4. Forensic mental health nurses have specific roles which differ from other mental health nurses. These differences relate to the following areas:
   - The complexity of patients' multiple pathologies.
   - Individuals' criminal behaviours and recidivism in social/cultural systems.
   - Specific therapeutic/clinical competencies.
   - Specific issues related to forging therapeutic relationships/ interpersonal skills/boundary issues.
   - Avoiding negatively custodial care, but working safely in the reality of secure settings or measures to ensure safety in the community.
   - Roles related to the criminal justice system and its workings.
   - Legal issues such as the multitude of new laws, and ethics and rights-based practice.
   - Responsibility to and protection of the public.
   - Probability/risk, offence-specific assessment and care.
   - Meeting varying safety security needs applied through differing security levels.
5. Both advocacy and the delivery of culturally competent care differ from other areas of nursing, in view of the need to both de-stigmatise and de-criminalise the client group.

6. There are also specific needs to defend and maintain staff morale, as well as ensuring clinical supervision and other means to deal effectively with the emotional impact of caring for this client group.

7. The client group continues to have the potential for future dangerousness and requires staff to have coherent and consistent risk assessment, management and probability measurement.

8. Future challenges include:

   • Care that is increasingly holistic in relation to the individual's safety, and psychological, physical, interpersonal, spiritual, cultural, psychosexual, social, legal, advocacy, economic and other needs.

   • The provision of forensic services which both increasingly recognise individuals' shared humanity, and are sensitive to and meet the needs of individuals related to their diversity, including gender, age, culture, ethnicity, spirituality, varying intellectual, physical and sensory ability, sexual orientation and gender identity, in line with the Equality Act 2006 and related policy (Byrt and Hardie, 2007).

   • Provision of new services for specific groups, such as women; adolescents; and services that are gender and culturally sensitive, and which cater for specific groups of people such as survivors/victims of domestic violence; and facilities for people who are sex offenders.

   • New and/or extended roles, e.g. related to influencing relevant Government policy and 'public education and prevention' (Kettles et al, 2006:230).

   • Other challenges include the search for new knowledge and evidence through appropriate research, audit and assimilation.
     (Burrow, 1993; Robinson and Kettles, 1998; Kettles and Robinson, 2000; Woods et al, 2002; National Forensic Nurses' Research and Development Group, 2006, 2007)

The evidence for the forensic mental health nursing role is not of a high level, but what there is, does provide the basis for both discussion and further research. The research evidence goes back to Phillips (1983), who provided the first study which addressed some issues of the forensic nurse's role through examination of the attitudes of forensic mental health nurses. However, Phillips (1983) did not examine the role of the forensic mental health nurse per se, did address some issues of the role through examination of the attitudes of forensic mental health nurses. Other well-known studies include Niskala (1986), Kitchener and Rogers (1992), Kitchener et al (1992), Scales et al (1993) and Kettles and Robinson (1998).

Besides research evidence, conceptual evidence is also beginning to emerge, with nurses undertaking relevant concept analysis (Kettles, 2004; Kettles and Woods, 2006).

Argument against a forensic mental health nursing role

Much of the argument against forensic mental health nursing, as a separate, specialised area of nursing, is based on Whyte's (1997, 2000) idea that forensic mental health nurses do nothing different to general mental health nurses. Whyte (1997) argued that, although nurses working in forensic areas desired to be seen as having a unique and distinctive role, their actual duties were the same as those of general mental health nurses. Interestingly, Whyte (2000: 24) shifts his position slightly in a later publication to state that:

> *Rather than focusing upon the professional development of a role that, if established, is established on tenuous principles, nurses working within secure environments might be best served by 'going back to the basics of nursing work'.*

There are several problems with Whyte's (2000) premise, not least the idea that 'forensic' nursing only goes on (if it goes on at all) within high security and other secure environments.

Whyte is not the only critic of role development. Barker (2006: 387) in his editorial states that:

> *Many...have reverted back to 'role analysis'; developing 'minimum data sets', which describe what nurses **do**, much as Cormack did 30 years ago, with little consideration of whether this represents what they **need to be doing**. I fear that the idea of a 'mental health' nurse makes no more sense than the idea of a 'physical health' nurse. Trapped by the history of psychiatry, mental health nurses in almost every country worldwide, continue to tinker with their inherited roles, rather than conducting a radical appraisal of their possible core function... Why not diverse groups of nurse – catering for different needs, in differing contexts – united by a single ethical imperative: to provide the conditions necessary for people to grow and develop as persons, **and to do these persons no harm**.*

In some ways, Barker is describing the way in which forensic mental health nursing is, in fact, developing. As described earlier, there are many nurses practising in different contexts who are already trying to provide the conditions necessary for people to grow and develop; and who are endeavouring to do these persons no harm, but with the added caveat that these persons do no harm to themselves or to others.

However, forensic mental health nurses certainly do have the same roles as other nurses, in terms of the provision of care and interventions through the core skill of developing appropriate nurse–patient relationships (Collins, 2000:41).

In addition, we would argue that forensic mental health nurses often apply a range of other skills applicable in other areas of mental health nursing. These include, for example, skills used in the admission and assessment of clients and patients, and in their continued treatment, rehabilitation and recovery. Skills in the administration and monitoring of psychoactive medication, and in the application of psychosocial interventions, therapeutic community principles and other specialised interventions have been demonstrated to have applicability in both forensic and other mental health services. Examples of this wide applicability across areas of mental health nursing are given, for example, in Gamble and Brennan (2006), Kettles et al (2002), and the National Forensic Nurses' Research and Development Group (2006, 2007).

The forensic mental health nursing role as different from other nursing roles

Nevertheless, forensic mental health nurses work in ways that other nurses do not. For example, the most obvious differences include security levels, levels of dangerousness, types of risk assessment and management, and practice and related training and education in a variety of particular issues. The latter include security management, safety, searching, escort duty, hostage-taking and management, detention and legal issues.

However, there are also less obvious features of forensic mental health nursing that make it different. These include diagnostic or other categories of patients, including 'psychopath', 'dangerous and severe personality disorder', 'antisocial personality disorder', 'sex offender' and 'paedophile'. Forensic mental health nursing is different not only because of this diagnostic and public labelling of individuals, but also as a result of the high media profile of many of the patients, and the Government's actions in relation to offenders. This means that the staff have to deal with all the social, cultural and political consequences that ensue (Byrt, 2001; Byrt with Dooher, 2006; Kettles et al, 2006).

Additionally, the complexity issue makes forensic mental health nursing different. For example, dual diagnosis is becoming much more common in acute, community and substance misuse services. However, in forensic services, there are more usually multiple diagnoses, including combinations of two or more categories, such as mental illness, personality disorder, learning disability and substance misuse; and now the 'sociopolitical' diagnosis of dangerous and severe personality disorder can also be applied (Byrt with Dooher, 2006). It is common for triple diagnoses to be the norm, with people experiencing complex legal, psychological, social, diversity, emotional and cultural problems in their clinical presentation (Wix and Humphreys, 2005; National Forensic Nurses' Research and Development

Group, 2007). In addition, there is some evidence that forensic mental health nurses have more problems concerning patients' transference, their own counter-transference and other strong feelings than staff in other areas, and have to be constantly on their guard against this particular problem (Bowers, 2002; Mercer et al, 1999; Schafer, 2002).

The legal situation is usually complex as well, as forensic mental health nurses have to understand much more in terms of the legislation that affects each individual patient and the legal freedoms that each patient is allowed under the terms of that legislation. A few examples of the legislation that forensic mental health nurses must now be familiar with includes the following (Byrt and Hardie, 2007; Kettles et al, 2007):

- The respective Mental Health Acts applicable in their place of work, such as the Mental Health (Care and Treatment) (Scotland) Act (2003) and the Mental Health Act (2007) for England and Wales.
- The Police and Criminal Evidence Act (1984).
- The Health and Social Care Act (2001).
- Adults with Incapacity Act (2000).
- Disability Discrimination Act (2005).
- Human Rights Act (1998).
- Equality Act (2006).
- Civil Partnership Act (2004).
- Gender Recognition Act (2004).

All of the above Acts have some requirements relevant to forensic services, and which forensic mental health nurses have to know and may have to carry out in the course of their duties.

Risk assessment and management is also much more in-depth in forensic services with nurses conducting a variety of assessments, including nursing assessments and others such as the Behavioural Status Index (Reed and Woods, 2000); Health of the Nation Outcome Scales (HONOS; Wing et al, 1996) and HONOS-secure v.2 (Sugarman and Walker, 2004); the Hare's Psychopathy Checklist – Revised (PCL-R; Hare, 2003); and the HCR-20 (assessing historical, clinical and risk management issues: Webster et al, 1997) (Doyle and Coffey, 2007; Woods and Kettles, 2007).

Another of many possible considerations here, is the length of time forensic mental health nurses spend with their patients. In many instances, even with new ideas and ways of working, forensic patients are still longer term patients than many others. A person with recurring bouts of depression may be known to staff in an acute ward over a period of years as the person comes in and out of hospital, but forensic patients are often in hospital for years and face long-term input from a variety of multidisciplinary staff when they are finally repatriated and rehabilitated to community care. The course of care is different and so the level of care is also different, with the forensic patient facing a long-term care programme approach (CPA) and risk management monitoring and intervention, for example, involving the Risk Management Authority (RMA) in Scotland. In contrast, the depressed patient may see a community nurse for a specified period of time and is more likely to attend an outpatient clinic or see the consultant psychiatrist, followed by general practitioner care in the primary care setting. Thus, the overall course of care also tends to be different because of the nature of the index offence and other identified problems (Coffey et al, 2007).

There are many reasons why forensic mental health nursing roles are different to those of other mental health nurses; and there is no need to revert back to role analysis to justify the differences, as they are quite obvious, given the patient population and the varying environments in which forensic mental health nurses find themselves.

Forensic mental health nurse: A developing, evolving species

The current situation is that there are many roles and contexts in which forensic mental health nurses find themselves and this text seeks to explain, clarify and understand some of them. These are indeed evolving roles and contexts, as care and practice are constantly developing, and do not stand still for long. Where appropriate, research and future directions are discussed in each chapter.

Topics covered in this book

The following is a summary of the contents of this book.

- Helen Walker deals with the educational issues in *Chapter 2*.
- David Langton, in *Chapter 3*, highlights the role of nurse consultants in forensic mental health care (in Scotland).
- In *Chapter 4*, Mary Addo and Ian Smith discuss equality and diversity in relation to respecting the person with a learning disability.
- Through *Chapter 5*, Richard Byrt introduces power and participation in forensic services.
- Richard then goes on to discuss various perspectives related to power in *Chapter 6*.
- Patient empowerment and participation: barriers and the way forward are examined by Richard Byrt, Linda Hart and Linnette James-Sow in *Chapter 7*.

- Gillian Archibald, in *Chapter 8*, introduces the role of the forensic mental health nurse as nutrition provider, nutritional screener and food choice supporter in recovery.
- In *Chapter 9*, Paul Burberry and Mohammed Khoshdel discuss the forensic mental health nursing role in the assessment, management and treatment of sex offenders.
- The forensic mental health nurse's role in risk assessment, measurement and management is highlighted by Phil Woods in *Chapter 10*.
- Through *Chapter 11*, Stuart Bowness, 'Algy', Richard Byrt, Romanus Ngeh, Lauren Mason and Cathy Wray give an overview of managing anger creatively on Cannock ward.
- This is followed on in *Chapter 12*, where 'Bede', 'Colm', 'Algy', 'Dirk', 'Ezra', 'Ferg' and Richard Byrt outline patients' views and experiences of managing anger creatively on Cannock ward.
- *Chapter 13* by Mick Adams and Leah Evans deals with co-morbid mental health and substance misuse problems within contemporary forensic mental health practice.
- Michael Coffey and Richard Jones discuss forensic community mental health nursing in *Chapter 14*.
- In *Chapter 15*, issues in managing a forensic mental health organisation are highlighted by Gavin Garman and Fomayi Saliki.
- Graham Durcan informs in *Chapter 16* about prison mental health nursing, and how this is a time for change in the role of prison nurses in caring for prisoners with mental health problems in English and Welsh prisons.
- Cindy Peternelj-Taylor and Penny Schafer examine the management of therapeutic boundaries in *Chapter 17*.
- Finally, the conclusions are presented by Richard Byrt, Phil Woods and Alyson McGregor Kettles in *Chapter 18*.

References

Barker P (2006) Mental health nursing: The craft of the impossible. *J Psych Ment Health Nurs* **13**(4) 385–387

Bowers L (2002) *Dangerous and Severe Personality Disorder: Response and Role of the Psychiatric Team*. Routledge: London

Bronte C (1994) *Jane Eyre*. Penguin Books: Harmondsworth

Burrow S (1993) An outline of the forensic nursing role. *Brit J Nurs* **2**(18) 899–904

Byrt R (2001) Power, influence and control in practice development. In: Clark A, Dooher, J, Fowler J (eds). *The Handbook of Practice Development*. Quay Books: Dinton, Salisbury

Byrt R, Dooher J (2006) The social consequences of a 'personality disorder' diagnosis.

In: National Forensic Nurses' Research and Development Group: Woods P, Kettles AM, Byrt R, Addo M, Aiyegbusi A, Coffey M, Collins M, Doyle M, Garman G, Watson C (eds). *Forensic Mental Health Nursing: Interventions with People with 'Personality Disorder'*. Quay Books, MA Healthcare Ltd: London

Byrt R, Hardie T (2007) Cultural competence and patients' rights. In: National Forensic Nurses' Research and Development Group: Kettles AM, Woods P, Byrt R, Addo M, Coffey M, Doyle M (eds). *Forensic Mental Health: Forensic Aspects of Acute Care*. Quay Books, MA Healthcare: London

Chaloner C (2000) Characteristics, skills, knowledge and inquiry. In: Chaloner C, Coffey M (eds). *Forensic Mental Health Nursing: Current Approaches*. Blackwell Science Ltd: Oxford

Chaloner C, Coffey M (eds) (2000) *Forensic Mental Health Nursing: Current Approaches*. Blackwell Science Ltd: Oxford

Coffey M, Morgan J, Gronow T (2007) Forensic aspects of crisis intervention team working and acute mental health care. In: National Forensic Nurses' Research and Development Group: Kettles AM, Woods P, Byrt R, Addo M, Coffey M, Doyle M (eds). *Forensic Mental Health: Forensic Aspects of Acute Care*. Quay Books MA Healthcare: London

Collins M (2000) The practitioner new to the role of forensic psychiatric nurse in the UK. In: Robinson DK, Kettles AM (eds). *Forensic Nursing and Multidisciplinary Care of the Mentally Disordered Offender*. Jessica Kingsley: London

Dale C, Woods P, Thompson T (2001) Nursing. In: Dale C, Thomson T, Woods P (eds). *Forensic Mental Health: Issues in Practice*, Chapter 3. Baillière Tindall/Harcourt Publishers: London

Doyle M, Coffey M (2007) Forensic aspects of acute inpatient assessment. In: National Forensic Nurses' Research and Development Group: Kettles, AM, Woods, P, Byrt, R, Addo, M, Coffey, M, Doyle, M (eds). *Forensic Mental Health: Forensic Aspects of Acute Care*. Quay Books, MA Healthcare: London

Forensic Network (2006) *Forensic Managed Care Network*. Available from: http://wwwforensicnetworkscotnhsuk/documents/SDC%20part%203%20FMHS%20Business%20Case%20@%20MARCH%202006pdf [Accessed 16 October 2007]

Gamble C, Brennan G (eds) (2006) *Working with Serious Mental Illness: A Manual for Clinical Practice* (2nd edn). Baillliere Tindall/Royal College of Nursing: Edinburgh

Hare RD (2003) *Hare Psychopathy Checklist Revised*. Multi-Health Systems: Toronto

Hillis G (1999) Diverting people with mental health problems from the criminal justice system. In: Tarbuck P, Topping-Morris B, Burnard P (eds). *Forensic Mental Health Nursing: An Evidence-Based Approach*. Whurr: London

Kettles AM (2004) A concept analysis of forensic risk. *J Psychiat Ment Health* Nurs 11 484–493

Kettles AM, Byrt R, Woods P (2006) Conclusions: Themes, action and research for the future. In: National Forensic Nurses' Research and Development Group: Woods P, Kettles AM, Byrt R, Addo M, Aiyegbusi A, Coffey M, Collins M, Doyle M, Garman G, Watson C (eds). *Forensic Mental Health Nursing: Interventions with People with Personality Disorder*. Quay Books, MA Healthcare Ltd: London

Kettles AM, Byrt R, Woods P (2007) Introduction. In: National Forensic Nurses' Research and Development Group: Kettles AM, Woods P, Byrt R, Addo M, Coffey

M, Doyle M (eds). *Forensic Mental Health: Forensic Aspects of Acute Care*. Quay Books, MA Healthcare: London

Kettles AM, Hall P (2007) Forensic aspects of crisis intervention team working and acute mental health care. In: National Forensic Nurses' Research and Development Group: Kettles AM, Woods P, Byrt R, Addo M, Coffey M, Doyle M (eds). *Forensic Mental Health: Forensic Aspects of Acute Care*. Quay Books, MA Healthcare: London

Robinson DK; Kettles AM (1998) The lost vision of nursing. *Psychiatric Care* **5**(4) 126–129

Kettles AM, Robinson D (2000) Overview and contemporary issues in the role of the forensic nurse in the UK. In: Robinson D, Kettles AM (eds). *Forensic Nursing and Multidisciplinary Care of the Mentally Disordered Offender*. Jessica Kingsley Publishers: London

Kettles AM, Woodally J (2006) Observation and engagement with people with personality disorder. In: National Forensic Nurses' Research and Development Group: Woods P, Kettles AM, Byrt R, Addo M, Aiyegbusi A, Coffey M, Collins M, Doyle M, Garman G, Watson C (eds). *Forensic Mental Health Nursing: Interventions with People with Personality Disorder*. Quay Books, MA Healthcare Ltd: London

Kettles AM, Woods P (2006) A concept analysis of 'forensic' nursing. *Brit J Forensic Pract* **8**(3) 16–28

Kettles AM, Woods P, Collins M (eds) (2002) *Therapeutic Interventions for Forensic Mental Health Nurses*. Jessica Kingsley Publishers: London

Kirby S (2000) History and development. In: Chaloner C, Coffey M (eds). *Forensic Mental Health Nursing: Current Approaches*, Chapter 15, pp 288–305. Blackwell Science Ltd: Oxford

Kitchener N, Rogers P (1992) Gearing up to work in a secure unit. *Nursing Times* 88, 51

Kitchener N, Wright I, Topping-Morris B (1992) The role of the forensic psychiatric nurse. *Nursing Times* **91**(25) 11–12

Literature Organisation (2007) Available from: http://www.literatureorg/authors/bronte-charlotte/jane-eyre/chapter-16html [Accessed 3 May 2007]

McClelland N, Humphreys M, Conlon L, Hillis T (2001) *Forensic Psychiatric Nursing and Mental Disorder in Clinical Practice*. Butterworth-Heinemann: Oxford

Mercer D, Mason T, Richman J (1999) Good and evil in the crusade of care. *J Psychosoc Nurs Ment Health Services* **37**(9) 13–17

National Forensic Nurses' Research and Development Group: Woods P, Kettles AM, Byrt R, Addo M, Aiyegbusi A, Coffey M, Collins M, Doyle M, Garman G, Watson C (eds) (2006) *Forensic Mental Health Nursing: Interventions with People with Personality Disorder*. Quay Books, MA Healthcare Ltd: London

National Forensic Nurses' Research and Development Group: Kettles AM, Woods P, Byrt R, Addo M, Coffey M, Doyle M (eds) (2007) *Forensic Mental Health: Forensic Aspects of Acute Care* Quay Books, MA Healthcare: London

Niskala H (1986) Competencies and skills required by nurses working in forensic areas. *Western J Nurs Res* **8**(4) 400–413

Nolan P (1993) *A History of Mental Health Nursing*. Chapman and Hall: London

Parker E (1985) The development of secure provision. In: Gostin L (ed). *Secure Provision*, Chapter 1. Tavistock Publications: London

Phillips MS (1983) Forensic psychiatry-nurses' attitudes revealed. *Dimensions in Health Services* **60**(9) 41–43

Reed V, Woods P (2000) *The Behavioural Status Index: A Life Skills Assessment for Selecting and Monitoring Therapy in Mental Health Care*. Psychometric Press: UK

Roberts A (2006) *Mental Health History Timeline*. Available from: http://wwwmdxacuk/www/study/mhhtimhtm [Accessed 16 October 2007]

Robinson D, Kettles A (1998) The emerging profession of forensic nursing – Myth or reality? *Psychiatric Care* **5**(6): 214–18

Robinson D, Kettles A (eds) (2000) *Forensic Nursing and Multidisciplinary Care of the Mentally Disordered Offender*. Jessica Kingsley Publishers: London

Rowe D, Lopes O (2003) People with learning disabilities who have offended in law. In: Gates B (ed). *Learning Disabilities: Towards Inclusion* (4th edn) Chapter 14. Churchill Livingstone: Edinburgh

Sainsbury Centre for Mental Health (2004) *The Ten Essential Shared Capabilities: A Framework For the Whole of the Mental Health Workforce*. Sainsbury Centre for Mental health/ Department of Health, London

Scales C, Mitchell J, Smith R (1993) Survey report on forensic nursing. *J Psychosoc Nurs Ment Health Services* **31**(11) 39–44

Schafer PE (2002) Nursing interventions and future directions with patients who constantly break rules and test boundaries. In: Kettles AM, Woods P, Collins M (eds). *Therapeutic Interventions for Forensic Mental Health Nurses*. Jessica Kingsley: London

Soanes C (ed) (2002) *Paperback Oxford English Dictionary*. Oxford University Press: Oxford

Sugarman P, Walker L (2004) *Health of the Nation Outcome Scale for Users of Secure and Forensic Services: HoNOS – Secure (Version 2)*. St Andrew's Group of Hospitals: Northampton

Watson C, Kettles AM (2007) Forensic educational aspects of acute mental health care: Policy, characteristics, skills and knowledge. In: National Forensic Nurses' Research and Development Group: Kettles AM, Woods P, Byrt R, Addo M, Coffey M, Doyle M (eds). *Forensic Mental Health: Forensic Aspects of Acute Care*. Quay Books, MA Healthcare: London

Webster CD, Douglas KS, Eaves D, Hart SD (1997) *HCR–20. Assessing Risk for Violence. Version 2*. Mental Health, Law and Policy Institue: Vancouver

Whyte L (1997) Forensic nursing: A review of concepts and definitions. *Nurs Standard* 11(23) 46–47

Whyte L (2000) Educational aspects of forensic nursing. In: Robinson D, Kettles AM (eds). *Forensic Nursing and Multidisciplinary Care of the Mentally Disordered Offender*. Jessica Kingsley Publishers: London

Wing J, Curtis RH, Beevor AS (1996) *HoNOS: Health of the Nation Outcome Scales: Report on Research and Development, July 1993–December, 1995*. Royal College of Psychiatrists: London. Wix S, Humphreys M (2005) *Multidisciplinary Working in Forensic Mental Health Care*. Churchill Livingstone: Edinburgh

Woods P (2004) The person who uses forensic mental health services. In: Norman IJ, Ryrie I (eds) *The Art and Science of Mental Health Nursing: A Textbook of Principles and Practice*. Open University Press: Maidenhead

Woods P, Collins M, Kettles AM (2002) Forensic nursing interventions and future directions for forensic mental health practice. In: Kettles AM, Woods P, Collins M (eds). *Therapeutic Interventions for Forensic Mental Health Nurses*. Chapter 15 pp 240–245. Jessica Kingsley Publishers: London

Woods P, Kettles AM (2007) Measurement of health and social functioning. In: National Forensic Nurses' Research and Development Group: Kettles AM, Woods P, Byrt R, Addo M, Coffey M, Doyle M (eds). *Forensic Mental Health: Forensic Aspects of Acute Care*. Quay Books, MA Healthcare: London

CHAPTER 2

The role of education

Helen Walker

Introduction

Continuing education and development of staff are central to the success of any service. Amidst all the current developments in the structure of forensic services, there is a real opportunity for personal and professional development of staff. The time is ripe for reflection on previous practice and a real opportunity is emerging to consider a new direction. Working in partnership with service users and promoting patient-centred care is achievable across the spectrum of forensic services, if the climate is right. Achieving educational qualifications in parallel with other disciplines and appropriate to the level of practice remains a challenging agenda.

Policy and legislative development

There have been a number of events leading to the development of new policy and legislative change, all of which come with associated educational requirements. An example of this is the *Report of Inquiry into the Care and Treatment of Mr L and Mr M* (Mental Welfare Commission, 2006), that made recommendations for training and provision of education programmes. Some recommendations were directed at community psychiatric nurses, and focused on a few key areas. One recommendation was to review the functions of the community psychiatric nurse caring for people perceived to be of high risk, especially those subject to restriction orders. Another was to improve the training of forensic community psychiatric nurses, to ensure that they had the required competencies to carry out their functions in relation to people who had been discharged from inpatient forensic services, with conditions attached to their discharge (NHS Education for Scotland, 2007a).

The Scottish Executive Health Department (2006b) published a new policy on forensic mental health services which set out the national and regional need for high, medium and low secure beds for men and women and those with mental disorder and learning disability. One of the other recent policy developments is the NHS HDL (2007) publication on Sections 10 and

11 of the Management of Offenders (Scotland) Act 2005, which describes the implementation of the multi-agency public protection arrangements (MAPPA) in Scotland. In addition statutory guidance on how the care programme approach should operate for patients subject to the provisions of the Management of Offenders (Scotland) Act 2005 has been offered in the Scottish Government (2007) and will support better discharge planning and risk management. All staff need to be made aware of this new guidance in order that their practice reflects the new standards.

The new Mental Health (Care and Treatment) (Scotland) Act 2003 also has implications for the training of nurses working in forensic settings. Of particular importance are the changes to the act itself; working in a way that reflects the principles of the Act; the use of advanced statements; provision of information on the named person and the skills required for preparation for and attendance at tribunals. All aspects have been incorporated into the new Development Framework for Forensic Nurses (NHS Education for Scotland, 2007a).

Role of NHS Education for Scotland in forensic education

Over the years, NHS Education for Scotland (NES) has played an important part in the development of many services. Latterly, forensic services have seen some real benefits from this continuing support. NES has not only helped increase the profile of forensic services, but ensured that all disciplines are involved in any key initiatives. Financial support has been offered to establish key roles across many services, for example, practice education facilitators and practice education co-ordinators. NES has also led on the introduction of Nursing and Allied Health Professions Consultant Succession Planning and more recently Early Clinical Career Fellowships. Due to close working relationships with forensic services, staff within all settings have been able to take advantage of all of these important developments.

Workforce planning

NES involvement in workforce planning initiatives, such as the working group to develop the *Report on the Forensic Mental Health Workforce* (Forensic Mental Health Services Managed Care Network, 2005), led to funding some of the actions arising from the recommendations. A secondment was made available to enable the creation of a new initiative and update an existing framework, namely, the *New to Forensic* introductory education programme (NHS Education for Scotland, 2007b) – similar to that developed for the child and adolescent service (*New to CAMHS*; NHS Education for Scotland, 2006) – and the *Development Framework for Forensic Nurses* (NHS Education for

Scotland, 2007a). NES also played an active part in the Forensic Organisational Development Group in Glasgow (2005–2007), both offering advice and financial support to set up a service-user network, during the re-development of their services. The workforce planning group in Perth, Scotland is an ongoing piece of work until the new medium secure unit opens in or around 2012.

Wider issues

NES was actively involved in the development of the national standards for the Prevention and Management of Violence and Aggression training, via membership on the Peer Audit and Benchmarking Steering Group between 2006 and 2007. These standards have not been set for forensic areas alone, but they do have implications for staff working across areas where there is a forensic population. NES also has a central role to play in the development of many new initiatives associated with the recent mental health nursing review, *Rights Relationships and Recovery* (Scottish Executive Health Department, 2006a). The action plan attached to this review identifies NES as having a lead role in 12 different areas. Many have implications across all mental health services, such as the focus on introducing the 'recovery approach' and the provision of training in 'values-based practice'. Staff working across forensic settings will be actively involved in these initiatives, alongside their colleagues in the generic services.

The introduction of the 10 Essential Shared Capabilities training materials (NHS Education for Scotland, 2007c), which form the basis for values-based practice across all mental health settings, offers a real opportunity to reflect on and change current practice. The materials promote partnership working i.e. 'doing with' rather than 'doing for'/'doing to', which will mean a considerable shift in practice for some forensic practitioners.

Relationship between practice development, practice, research and education

Practice development is not a new concept, yet in reality, there still exists some confusion around the definition, the clarity of role and the relationship with research. Confusion arises with the introduction of different job titles and vague job descriptions. An attempt will be made to clear up the confusion.

Practice development

Practice development is a term that has been used to describe particular approaches to supporting change in health care (predominantly nursing) for over 20 years. It is said to be a continuous process of improvement towards increased effectiveness in patient-centred care (Garbett and McCormack, 2002). This is achieved by enhancing the skills of clinicians through education, learning, mentoring, coaching and supervision. In doing this, practice development examines and develops current practice and supports the development of all nursing staff. The aim is to improve practice and develop evidence-based practice. This enables nursing staff to become more competent in their work.

Practice

In practice settings, the success of practice development is dependent upon many things. One particular element to consider is the infrastructure to support it. The work of Shortell et al (1995) demonstrates the need to address multiple dimensions, namely: strategy, culture, technical support and structures/systems when introducing a new development. All four areas need to be addressed fully if a lasting impression is to be achieved, see *Table 2.1*.

Links to research and evidence base

Practice development can be achieved by all nurses maintaining their own knowledge of current theory and best practice, including learning from students. Key to this is nurses questioning current practice, both good and not

Table 2.1: Moving from concept to implementation (From Shortell et al, 1995)

Strategy	x Culture	x Technical support	x Structures and systems	= Result
0	1	1	1	No significant result on anything really important
1	0	1	1	Small temporary effects, no lasting impact
1	1	0	1	Frustration and false starts
1	1	1	0	Inability to capture the learning and spread it throughout the organisation
1	1	1	1	Lasting organisation-wide impact

so good, and also encouraging others to question and reflect on their current practice. Taking evidence from what is already published (research evidence) and putting it into practice is one way of developing practice. An example of getting research into practice in forensic services is the introduction of the Behavioural Status Index (BEST-Index; Woods et al 1999).

Following an earlier attempt in one English special hospital (Rampton), the Scottish High Secure service (the State Hospital) is currently training all registered nurses in the use of the BEST-Index as a new nursing assessment tool. It is anticipated the entire workforce will be using the new system by the summer of 2008. Unfortunately, not all good practice has been subject to research, so taking evidence of good practice from one area and applying it in another (unpublished evidence) is another way of developing practice. This then creates an opportunity to use the research process to establish the effectiveness of the change.

Links to education

Education is one of the central components of practice development and there are many opportunities for practice development to take place: opportunistic, informal teaching moments as well as formal, planned teaching, coaching, mentoring and individual innovation. Opportunities need to be made available to all nurses to share knowledge and information and to support and encourage others to seek out information/knowledge which can be shared in respect of best practice.

There are clear advantages for service in having close links with Higher Education Institutes (HEI), for example, enabling the development of lecturer-practitioner posts. Practitioners accepting these types of posts enable useful exchange of information in order that both sides (service and HEIs) understand each other's position and competing demands. The introduction of practice education facilitators is a good example of an initiative that can make a significant impact on bridging the gap between HEIs and services. There is also a need for continued and improved collaboration at the pre-registration stage. The move to include and promote increased awareness of forensic issues at the earliest opportunity, i.e. pre-registration, is welcomed. It is hoped that this will diminish fears and reduce speculation around future forensic placements.

School of Forensic Mental Health (SoFMH)

Partly due to the limited number of forensic courses in Scotland, there has recently been a drive to develop a School of Forensic Mental Health (SoFMH). In 2002 *The Right Place, The Right Time: Improving the*

Patient Journey for Those Who Need Secure Mental Health Care (Scottish Executive, 2002) recommended the setting up of a school of forensic research and development. The Scottish Executive subsequently requested that the Forensic Mental Health Services Managed Care Network (Forensic Network) take forward the issue of a forensic school and it established the Working Group for Teaching, Training and Research in June 2004. Joint funding of a formal needs assessment was agreed between NHS Education Scotland (NES) and the Forensic Network in September 2004. This work was carried out by the Scottish Development Centre for Mental Health (SDC) between April and September 2005, under the supervision of the Working Group and NES. A formal option appraisal arising from the work of the SDC was carried out by the Working Group between January and February 2006 and a full business case developed for the preferred options. The result of this was to establish a virtual school.

At the present time, the SoFMH works within the Forensic Network and has formal links with the universities of Edinburgh, Stirling and Glasgow Caledonian. It offers teaching and training to all professional groups and staff involved in the assessment and care of mentally disordered offenders and others requiring similar services. The emphasis of the school is to be proactive in the development of its teaching and research. It is a focus for supporting, developing and delivering multi-disciplinary and multi-sector initiatives. Its unique characteristic will be the multi-disciplinary approach to education and research delivery, as well as its focus on forensic mental health.

The success of this initiative is dependent upon support from potential partners in service, HEIs and further education, as well as additional funding from national bodies. It is anticipated that the SoFMH will provide a series of short courses, postgraduate diploma and masters degree courses.

Proposed changes to basic forensic education for nurses

It is anticipated that there will be tailored education programmes delivered in a flexible manner with a multi-disciplinary focus, via the SoFMH. This initiative has been welcomed across the service and both promotes and emphasises the specialist nature of forensic nursing. The creation of the *Development Framework for Forensic Nurses* (NHS Education for Scotland, 2007a) highlights the educational qualifications desirable at each stage in the clinician's career, see *Table 2.2*. The embedding of proposed education requirements is where the real challenge lies. The framework can potentially serve a number of functions for a variety of people. It aims to:

- Set out the core developmental capabilities needed to deliver an aspirational whole systems model of forensic care.
- Assist practitioners and managers in personal development planning and personal development reviews (in keeping with the Knowledge and Skills Framework process), highlighting developmental needs and supporting the planning of training and education needed to aid and support workforce and service development.
- Communicate and inform people who use forensic mental health services and their friends, families and carers what knowledge skills and attitudes they should expect mental health nurses working in these settings to demonstrate.
- Complement the existing forensic competencies outlined in the Skills for Health website.

In order to optimise the use of the Development Framework, it could be incorporated into the Knowledge and Skills Framework by writing the relevant knowledge and skills into the clinician's Performance Development Plan and monitoring this as part of the annual Performance Development Review.

Table 2.2: Development framework for forensic nurses

Scottish Credit and Qualifications Framework		Career framework	Knowledge and Skills Framework
Doctorate 11–12	9		Level indicators
Masters working towards doctorate	8	Consultant practitioner	Mostly 4
Postgraduate Diploma	7	Advanced practitioner	Mostly 3/4
	6	Senior practitioner	Mostly 3
8–9 Diploma/ ordinary degree 7	5	Practitioner	Mostly 2/3
HNC 6	4	Pre-registration	Mostly 1/2
SVQ 5	3		
SVQ2	2		

Proposed changes to basic forensic education for non-nurses

The focus of educational developments is not restricted to registered nurses and although non-nurses/nursing assistants/health care assistants seem to have been neglected in recent years, a very different picture is beginning to emerge. A number of educational opportunities for non-nursing staff now exist. The first initiative started a few years ago in response to difficulties with recruitment and retention of registered nurses in forensic settings. The Scottish Executive Health Department (SEHD) responded to the potentially hazardous situation by providing opportunities for nursing assistants already working in forensic settings. The SEHD engaged with health board partners, further education and higher education institutes to encourage the creation of tripartite agreements and promote alternative routes into registered nursing, crudely know as 'grow your own'. The initiative has provided an excellent opportunity for existing nursing assistants to enlist for a Higher National Certificate (HNC) in Health Care and follow on to year two of the Diploma in Mental Health.

Healthcare support worker standards

Another more recent Scottish Government initiative to improve the standards of health care workers is currently at the pilot stage. It is anticipated that the initiative driven by Scottish Government will also impact on nursing assistants currently working across forensic settings, effectively bringing them up to Scottish Vocational Qualification (SVQ) 2 standard. Involvement in the SVQ seems to act as a catalyst for further learning and is used as leverage for promoting future involvement in the HNC/Diploma in nursing.

A gap in the education provided for non-nurses was highlighted in the *Nursing Workforce Planning Report* (Scottish Executive Health Department, 2006a). This resulted in the recommendation to create an introductory programme for clinicians starting a career in forensic settings.

The 'New to Forensic' introductory education programme (NHS Education for Scotland, 2007b) was developed for all staff working across the spectrum of forensic care, albeit the initial consideration was for non-nurses. The programme offers new staff (from all disciplines, including non-clinical staff) an opportunity to learn the fundamentals about people who use forensic services as well as information on various elements of the services themselves. The programme is designed to promote self-directed learning and is multi-disciplinary and multi-agency in approach. It includes case studies of patients in a variety of settings, from the community to high secure psychiatric care. The workbook is not designed to be a stand alone text, rather it should be seen as an introduction to forensic mental health. Individuals may wish to supplement the material by using appropriate published material as fits their needs, and suggestions are highlighted in the workbook. An agreement has been reached across all forensic services to adopt this programme as part of the basic introduction to working with people in the forensic field.

Future developments

Over the past 10 years or so, there has been a steady increase in the variety of roles available to nurses across the different forensic settings. Formerly, the options were limited to clinical work on wards up to charge nurse level, passing through the hierarchical system leading to management roles; and a severely limited number of research opportunities, usually via a fellowship or branching off to work as a lecturer in a higher education institute. Today, the market is more competitive and services have had to be more creative in their attempts to attract nurses into the forensic arena. The broader options have made forensic nursing a more viable option for a wider group. Forensic nurses have the opportunity to engage in a wide range of psychological interventions, ranging from cognitive-behavioural therapy and psycho-education for drug and alcohol dependence, anger treatment, therapies to prevent fire raising, dialectical behavioural therapy or sexual offending treatment. There are a substantial number of community forensic psychiatric nursing posts, some attached to local health boards others to police departments or Court Liaison schemes. The management structure remains similar to that in the recent past, but the clinical research and education posts are more varied, e.g. clinical nurse specialist, lecturer-practitioner, practice development facilitator, practice education facilitator and advanced practitioner.

Development of consultant nurses and their role in education, practice development and research

Nurse consultants have a major role to play in influencing service development, challenging existing practice, and providing strategic direction and focus for nurses. It is anticipated they will be the catalysts of change and will quite probably guide practice development. Most (but not all) consultant nurses are expected to spend a proportion of their time on research-related activity and all have an educational role to play.

In conclusion, the future of practice development within the forensic context looks promising. It is hoped the changing face of forensic services, including the development of community services and the creation of more low secure units, will have a positive influence on practice. The new job opportunities may well prompt an increased focus on specialist practice, encourage the active application of psychosocial interventions across the broad spectrum of care and promote increased incidence of sharing expertise and protocols. The resultant effect is a more consistent approach and improvement in care provision. The approaches used to deliver learning opportunities also need to be creative, e.g. e-learning programmes and education has to be tailored to the needs of the service. The final note to make is that every practitioner needs to recognise practice development is everyone's responsibility and is an integral component of our day-to-day work.

References

Forensic Mental Health Services Managed Care Network (Forensic Network) (2005) *Report of the Forensic Nursing Workforce Project Group.* Available from: http://www. forensicnetwork.scot.nhs.uk/publications.asp [Accessed 27 November 2007]

Garbett R, McCormack B (2002) Focus: A concept analysis of practice development. *Nursing Times Res* **7**(2) 87–100

Mental Welfare Commission for Scotland (2006) *Report of Inquiry into the Care and Treatment of Mr L and Mr M.* Mental Welfare Commission for Scotland: Edinburgh

NHS Education for Scotland (2006) *New to Child and Adolescent Mental Health Service (CAMHS).* NHS Education for Scotland: Edinburgh.

NHS Education for Scotland (2007a) *Development Framework for Forensic Nurses.* NHS Education for Scotland: Edinburgh

NHS Education for Scotland (2007b) *New to Forensic Training Programme.* NHS Education for Scotland: Edinburgh

NHS Education for Scotland (2007c) *Educational Solutions for Workforce Development, Values Based Practice. The 10 Essential Shared Capabilities for Mental Health Practice, Learning Materials (Scotland).* NHS Education for Scotland: Edinburgh

NHS HDL (Scottish Government, Health Care Policy and Strategy Directorate Mental Health Division) (2007) *19 – Guidance for Forensic Services.* The Stationery Office: Edinburgh

Scottish Executive Health Department (2002) *The Right Place, The Right Time: Improving the Patient Journey for Those Who Need Secure Mental Health Care.* The Stationery Office: Edinburgh.

Scottish Executive Health Department (2006a) *Rights, Relationships and Recovery – Report of the National Review of Mental Health Nursing in Scotland.* The Stationery Office: Edinburgh

Scottish Executive Health Department (2006b) *48 – Forensic Mental Health Services.* The Stationery Office: Edinburgh

Scottish Government (2007) CEL 08; JD/3/2008 Sections 10 and 11 of the Management of Offenders etc (Scotland Act) 2005: Implementation of the Multi Agency Public Protection Arrangements (MAPPA) in Scotland. The Stationery Office: Edinburgh

Shortell SM, O'Brien JL, Carman JM, Foster RW, Hughes EFX, Boerstler H et al (1995) Assessing the impact of continuous quality improvement/total quality management; concept versus implementation. *Health Serv Res* **30**(2) 377–401

Woods P, Reed V, Robinson D (1999) The Behavioural Status Index: Therapeutic assessment of risk, insight, communication and social skills. *J Psychiatr Ment Health Nurs* **6**(2) 79–90

CHAPTER 3

Nurse consultants in forensic mental health care in Scotland

David Langton

Introduction

This chapter describes the work undertaken by the nurse consultant appointed to the Forensic Mental Health Services Managed Care Network (Forensic Network) in December 2005. The emergence of nurse consultant posts in the UK is detailed, as well as the approach taken to appointing posts by the NHS in Scotland. The context of the post in Forensic Mental Health Services in Scotland is described, followed by examples of how the postholder has worked with a variety of services throughout the country. Finally, future developments of consultant nurse posts in forensic services in Scotland are explored.

Nurse consultant posts

Consultant nurses were first appointed in England and Wales in 1999 as a result of a Health Services Circular (Department of Health, 1999a) which described the process for establishing posts and making appointments. In Scotland, the Minister for Health and Community Care announced the development of nurse and midwife consultant posts in the spring of 2000. The Strategy for Nursing in Scotland (Caring for Scotland) developed the concept further, stating that the advent of the role would offer a real opportunity for nurses to continue in their field of practice while at the same time developing their skills in leadership, research and education (Scottish Executive Health Department, 2001). Scottish Executive Health Department guidance states that all consultant nurse posts are to be built around four key performance areas:

- Professional leadership and consultancy.
- Expert practice.

- Education and research.
- Service development.

In reality, according to Fyffe (2004), nursing officer at the Scottish Executive Health Department addressing a workshop on the role, the post is primarily concerned with strategic leadership and strengthening the clinical nursing voice at the highest level. Fyffe contends that the process of introducing the new role will also bring back into clinical roles expert nurses who had moved away to management and education, thus significantly influencing clinical practice.

Forensic mental health care in Scotland

Forensic mental health care is delivered 'through a systemic structure incorporating mental health and criminal justice systems' (Mason et al, 2002: 563). Within a Scottish context, forensic mental health care is at a time of major change with the introduction, in October 2005, of the Mental Health (Care and Treatment) (Scotland) Act 2003, the creation of new medium and low secure facilities, the re-provisioning of high security care, the development of community forensic mental health services, and the proposed development of further services for women, people with learning disability, adolescents and individuals with personality disorder. An overview of forensic services and proposals for future service development can be seen on the website of the Forensic Mental Health Services Managed Care Network (Forensic Network) (www.forensicnetwork.scot.nhs.uk). *Figure 3.1* provides an illustrative example of this.

The Forensic Network was established in September 2003 when Scottish Ministers invited the Chief Executive of the State Hospital to lead its development. The Network is multi-agency, with strong links with the Scottish prison service, social work services, the police, criminal justice agencies, the Scottish Executive, and carers among others. In its first three years of development, the Forensic Network established several short-life working groups to inform policy for the future; this culminated in the publication of new policy and guidance as part of HDL (2006) 48 (Scottish Executive Health Department, 2006). An HDL is a Health Department Letter issued by the Scottish Executive Health Department to NHS Scotland organisations with advice and guidance in respect of health care policy in Scotland. As well as outlining the configuration of forensic mental health services for Scotland, the establishment of a national overview group to monitor patient flow and appeals against excessive security, the paper also outlines the need for the establishment of regional sub-groups. The HDL provides policy for secure care standards, conflict resolution and liaison between NHS Boards and the Scottish prison service. There is also

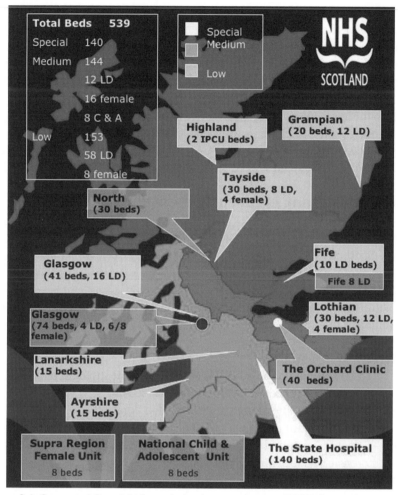

Figure 3.1: Proposed Scottish forensic beds as at August 2007 (reproduced with kind permission of the Forensic Mental Health Services Managed Care Network).

guidance on services for women, services for learning disabled people and definitions of levels of security. The HDL also describes further work being taken forward by the Network and the Health Department, such as services in the community; care programme approach for restricted patients; extension of secure care standards to high, low and community services; revision of the critical incident review guidance; the development of a Forensic School for Scotland; as well as services for children and adolescents and people with personality disorders. The full paper can be viewed on the Forensic Network website.

Currently, forensic mental health care in Scotland is delivered through a high security hospital (the State Hospital), a medium secure clinic (the

Orchard Clinic), low secure facilities in most Health Boards, some of which are closely linked to intensive psychiatric care units, and an emerging forensic community system. The independent sector provides 33 low secure beds for men and women. The forensic mental health care system also interfaces closely with the prison system, with some forensic mental health care being delivered within prisons.

Two further medium secure clinics (Rowanbank for Glasgow and the West, opened 2007, and Schiehallion for Tayside and the North, due in 2012) will complete the estate for medium secure services in Scotland. As these services develop, the State Hospital will be re-built and reduced to 140 beds by 2012.

Nurse consultant in forensic mental health care

Currently there is one nurse consultant post within forensic mental health care in Scotland. The postholder was appointed in December 2005 by the Forensic Network. The post was a newly created position which it was anticipated would be a resource for all of Scotland's forensic services. The following nurse consultant objectives for 2006/2007 (summarised in *Box 3.1*) reflected that aspiration:

1. Service development
   - To be actively involved in the development of strategic planning for national, regional and local forensic services.
   - To use expert knowledge to develop and contribute to the development of treatment protocols for nurses and other disciplines.
   - To actively support the work of individuals and groups in developing forensic services throughout Scotland.
2. Workforce planning
   - To offer support and advice on service redesign with reference to national guidelines and policies.
   - To be an invited active member of workforce planning groups in respect of forensic services development throughout Scotland.
3. Expert practice
   - To provide expert and high quality nursing care advice for those individuals who have been referred, and constitute part of the caseload.
   - To closely work with the psychology director (and other relevant directors) to identify and specify areas for development in respect of interventions for patients in forensic services.
   - To provide a consultancy service to clinical teams in local services, prison health centres and the courts.
   - To provide clinical supervision for nominated practitioners.

Box 3.1: Nurse consultant objectives 2006/2007

- Service development
- Workforce planning
- Expert practice

- Research and education
- National perspectives
- The State Hospital

---

4. Research and education
    - To be actively involved in the development of the Forensic School and the forensic curriculum.
    - To provide specialist nursing teaching and advice to students both in practice and in higher education institutes (HEIs).
    - To explore the relationship between the applied literacy and numeracy skills of forensic patients, and their emotional intelligence, in particular with reference to how levels and ability impact on the patient's capacity to both engage with therapies, and to cope when in community forensic secure services.
5. National perspectives
    - To work closely with NHS Education Scotland in respect of forensic competencies developments.
    - To provide reports, advice and information on emergent issues to the Forensic Network Board.
6. The State Hospital
    - To lead investigations as a trained investigating officer.
    - To be an on call incident commander.
    - To co-lead the project to implement the Prevention and Management of Violence and Aggression (PMVA) policy.
    - To lead fortnightly action learning sets for nominated ward managers.
    - To be a nursing representative for the Care Programme Approach.
    - To provide support and supervision for nominated staff.
    - To be an active member of the practice development team.

The postholder's work over the past 18 months has attempted to deliver the objectives; the following section illustrates how that has been done, using the twin themes of service development and developing practice, with examples of work undertaken to illustrate this.

Service development

The literature suggests that multi-disciplinary team (MDT) working is the preferred model for the delivery of health care in the UK (Mandy, 1996;

Mason and Carton, 2002). The reason for this generally accepted belief is that through this approach, a more efficient and effective service will evolve for the benefit of patient care. Within a mental health context, the view expressed by the Royal College of Psychiatrists supports the notion of MDT working:

> *A lot of different skills can be needed to help someone with a mental health problem. No single professional, however well trained, can possibly be expert in all these skills. This is why different mental health professionals work in teams. The team should have workers from different professions, who understand each others' different skills and ways of approaching problems.*
>
> (Royal College of Psychiatrists, 2006)

Within the forensic mental health care system, anecdotal information is that MDT working, while verbally supported, is not delivered in practice. The first piece of empirical support for this view was found in a research project carried out in 2000 for the English High Security Psychiatric Commissioning Board by Whyte and Brooker (2001). They reported inter-team tensions, that individuals identified with both their team and their profession, and that teams were generally struggling to be effective due to a lack of particular factors being present in their organisation which supported MDT processes. Mason et al (2002) also carried out a small research project into MDT working in a forensic setting; they found decision making in teams was complex due in part to differing ethical dimensions at play among professionals.

Example 1: Supporting MDT working at the State Hospital

It was in the above context and against a backdrop of a wider organisational redevelopment of the State Hospital that the nurse consultant was asked to support the launch of a new approach to developing MDT working. A small group was established, with the nurse consultant as lead, to agree the development of a model that would engage all of the MDTs at the State Hospital in developing (and auditing) their practice against standards developed in consultation with them.

The role of the nurse consultant was to chair the group, make contact with MDTs, obtain 'buy in' from MDTs, and facilitate the working of the newly appointed organisational development (OD) postholder who would continue this work once the project had been established. *Box 3.2* describes the task and membership of the group

The nurse consultant convened the team, agreed the brief with the other

---

Box 3.2: A standards-based approach to delivering effective multidisciplinary working at the State Hospital

Team members
- Forensic nurse consultant – lead
- Organisational development manager
- Training and development manager
- Clinical effectiveness department manager
- Workforce and planning manager
- Clinical nurse specialist – research

Floating membership
- Chief Executive
- General Manager
- External facilitator

Task
- Develop draft core standards which describe effective MDT working.
- Refine and produce a final set of agreed standards in consultation with all MDTs in the State Hospital.
- Develop an audit tool to measure current performance of individual MDTs against the agreed standards.
- Work with individual MDTs to develop, implement and evaluate improvement plans to address any shortfalls identified in the audit.
- Conduct an annual audit of the standards of MDT working in the State Hospital.

---

team members and supported the process during the first two months of development. The work was handed over to the OD lead once 'buy in' had been obtained from the MDTs. Currently the work is continuing through a pilot phase with one MDT with a view to producing a workable audit for more generalised use in the hospital.

Example 2: Developing a multi-agency approach towards exit pathways from low secure services in Tayside

The nurse consultant was approached by a senior manager from Tayside Health Board to assist in planning services for patients discharged from low secure settings. The work involved was to prepare the ground for the development of medium secure services in 2012, ensuring that bed blockages were avoided by bringing health authorities and the three Tayside local authorities together to plan how services should evolve. The work had been ongoing for over a year. It was difficult for all involved due to the nature of the work, which required discussions in respect of resources and

---

Box 3.3: The initial brief for Tayside community services work

Outcomes required
1. Mapping the current situation
    • Who are the clients/client group?
    • Where are the client group currently living?
    • What resources do they have access to?
2. A 5-year plan in broad terms
    • What services are required?
    • What types of staff will be needed to deliver the services?
    • How many places are required?
    • Where will services be located?
3. Developing a mechanism for joint planning and commissioning
    • Between forensic and general psychiatry
    • Between local authorities, housing and criminal justice
4. Risk management and public health protection issues described
5. Funding issues explored
    • Consideration of any need for new monies to be found
    • Agreement about NHS funding role
6. Mapping a patient's journey
    • From high secure setting to community
    • Treatment and care
    • Risks and management
7. From discussion and debate to *action*
    • Clarity over outcomes
    • Sign up and commitment
    • Nailing down the differences and agreeing a way forward

---

how to manage the development of new services that would require close partnership between all of the parties involved. It had been agreed that a 'fresh pair of eyes' with 'no baggage' would perhaps be a way forward; therefore the nurse consultant was approached.

A preliminary meeting took place between the nurse consultant and the two commissioning managers from the Tayside Health Board, following which the brief for facilitation was agreed as stated in *Box 3.3*.

The first meeting took place in February 2006, 24 key players from health and local authorities were invited. The nurse consultant used two particular techniques designed to engage the group which proved successful. The first was a technique called 'claims, issues, concerns'. This is a technique that asks individuals to provide their views on the work in hand, structured around three questions. Individuals then share their thoughts with the rest of the group, the rationale being that a working agenda can be generated out

---

Box 3.4: The claims, issues, concerns technique

Claims

A claim is any favourable assertion about the workshop

Example: 'Spending the session discussing issues will help me clarify my role within this development'

Issues

Issues are questions that reflect what any reasonable person might be asking about the workshop

Example: 'What will be the outcomes of the workshop'

Concerns

A concern is any unfavourable assertion about the workshop

Example: 'My ability to contribute to the discussion during the workshop'

---

of the views, which will be addressed during the day. *Box 3.4* illustrates the questions which provided a basis for the day.

The second technique, called values clarification, is a way of bringing together differing views and achieving a consensus. Individuals are provided with open value-based sentences and asked to complete the sentence. Once all of the comments are gathered, a consensus exercise takes place until a final agreed statement emerges. The questions posed to the group are reproduced in *Box 3.5*, together with sample answers to one of the questions which illustrates the effectiveness of the technique.

A further two meetings took place during 2006 at which the focus remained discussion around the development of community services to which patients in the Forensic Unit at Murray Royal Hospital, Perth could be discharged. The agenda mainly focused on accommodation and support. *Figure 3.2* illustrates how this thinking developed.

At the meeting in August 2006, it was agreed the work should be brought to a conclusion in the form of a commissioning agreement to which it was hoped that all parties would sign up. Part of this would be to establish a Tayside-wide commissioning group to oversee the onward movement of forensic patients from a variety of perspectives and services. It was agreed that such a 'joined up' approach would be essential if it was to work well. A secondee with a mental health nursing background, who understood the issues being discussed, was brought into the Health Board to develop a draft commissioning plan, which it was proposed would go to the regular joint meeting between the Chief Executives of Health and the three local authorities for their sign off and support.

As a result of this work, a further piece of work emerged for the nurse consultant in the form of describing exit pathways from secure care in the

---

Box 3.5: Values clarification exercise

Original questions posed to the group
- I believe the purpose of developing community services for forensic patients in Tayside is…..
- I believe this purpose can be achieved within Tayside by….
- I believe my role and purpose in respect of developing community services for forensic patients in Tayside are…..
- I believe the factors that will enable Tayside to develop community services for forensic patients are….
- I believe the factors that will inhibit Tayside in developing community services for forensic patients are…..

The following are actual answers provided to the question: I believe the factors that will enable Tayside to develop community services for forensic patients are….
- Decide who funds what (responsibility)
- Clearly identify how many people fit into which solutions (models of care support and accommodation)
- Specify need and respond collectively
- Understand each other's roles/responsibilities
- Ownership by all partners of a model and pathway of care
- Agreement to address needs and issues in each locality
- Improved relationships and respect between specialist forensic services and community-based services (health/social care/housing/social work)
- Understand patient and resource flows
- Will find a solution
- By working together cohesively, by mutual understanding of each area's roles and responsibilities
- Clarity of purpose/task
- Consistent forms
- Adequate resources
- Failure to reach a common understanding across agencies because we are stuck in different camps
- Agreement between parties

---

new North of Scotland (NOS) secure service. A new group was established from the planning team in the NOS; they invited the nurse consultant to be part of this new group and support their work. The work on exit pathways continues and it is hoped will provide examples for use in other forensic services in Scotland.

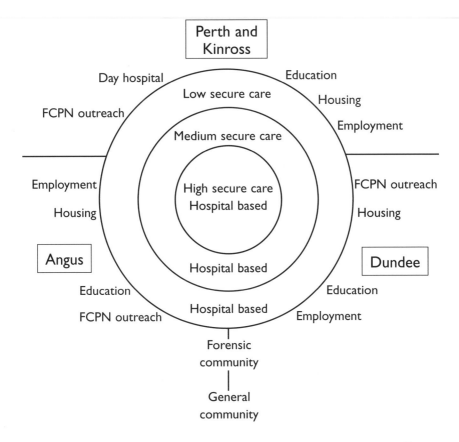

Figure 3.2: Mapping the interface between health and local authorities in Tayside (thanks to Neil Fraser, Tayside Health Board for his kind permission to reproduce).

Supporting the role of practice development

There is a growing literature about practice development; however, according to Carradice and Round (2004), it provides limited guidance to those working in the field day to day. They suggest that further research needs to be done to evaluate, for example, what works, in which setting, how and with whom.

In a recent research study evaluating the work of nurse consultants, Redwood et al (2007) concluded that the nature of practice development undertaken by nurse consultants is carried out at 'a level that crosses professions and agencies, and reflects a wider national or international perspective' (p.38). They also found that a major feature of the work is concerned with 'significant change and improvement to service delivery' (p.38). This is certainly consistent with the approach taken by the author. The following examples provide further evidence.

Example 3: The New to Forensic Programme

Forensic mental health care in Scotland is at a time of major change. Significant to this is the introduction of the Mental Health (Care and Treatment) (Scotland) Act 2003; the creation of new medium and low secure facilities; the re-provisioning of high security care; the development of community forensic mental health services; and the proposed development of further services for women, people with learning disability, adolescents and individuals with personality disorder. Workforce planning has estimated the need for 300 new staff to satisfy the demand of these new services (Forensic Mental Health Services Managed Care Network [Forensic Network], 2005); it is therefore likely that many staff entering the forensic mental health care system in Scotland in the future will have little prior knowledge of this area of work. Indeed, non-clinical staff may have little knowledge or understanding of mental disorder yet be required to engage with patients on a daily basis.

According to NHS Education for Scotland (2006), major change at such a pace will require a significant educational initiative to ensure staff are skilled at an appropriate level to provide proper care for patients within the forensic mental health care system and to ensure public safety. They argue that an adequate and competent workforce is fundamental to the successful delivery of mental health services for forensic clients, and there is therefore a need for a common shared core module of knowledge, skills and attitudes that all workers 'new to forensic' would need to undertake, which can then be built upon, depending on the role and remit of the individual group of staff.

NHS Education for Scotland (NES) appointed a senior nurse for practice development at the State Hospital on a one year secondment, as project lead for forensic mental health, with a remit to convene a 'New to Forensic' Development Group, made up of a cross-section of representatives from forensic services in Scotland. This group met on several occasions through 2006 working to identify the key elements of the proposed education programme. They were also involved in a collaborative one-day workshop in December 2006 which provided an opportunity for all key stakeholders to discuss and debate issues around the proposed new programme. Delegates included a range of all disciplines: members of the steering group, representatives from low, medium and high secure forensic settings, staff working with forensic clients in the community, carers, staff working in the private sector and representatives from NES and various HEIs.

Following this work, NES produced a project specification which they put out to tender to commission the design of a 'new to forensic' educational programme, and an accompanying training pack. It was anticipated that the training would be carried out over a six month period and the programme would include the use of case scenarios, following the patient journey from community to low secure, on to medium secure and ultimately ending up in high secure, then the return journey back through to the community.

The tender was won by a multidisciplinary team put together by the Medical Director, Forensic Network. The team consisted of:

- Lindsay Thomson, Medical Director, Forensic Network, and Reader in Forensic Psychiatry, University of Edinburgh.
- David C. Langton, Nurse Consultant, Forensic Network.
- Ed Finlayson, Team Manager, State Hospital, South Lanarkshire Council.
- Lisa Marshall, Lead Consultant Forensic Clinical Psychologist, State Hospital, and Senior Lecturer in Psychology, Glasgow Caledonian University.
- Cheryl McMorris, Head Occupational Therapist, NHS Greater Glasgow and Clyde, Directorate of Forensic Mental Health and Learning Disabilities.
- Louise Robinson, Lecturer in Forensic Psychiatry, University of Edinburgh.

The writing team discussed the requirements of the package and produced the 'New to Forensic' Programme. The team approached the writing of the package with the following model in mind.

Individuals new to forensic mental health care will come from a wide variety of backgrounds; both clinical and non-clinical, and will have diverse roles. The programme was designed to meet the entry needs of all new employees, who will be able to use the material at their own pace, supported by a mentor, gradually developing the skill set required for reflective practice. The overall aim of the programme is to encourage the development of reflective thinking in respect to the issues individuals will face when working in forensic mental health care. The programme is designed to promote self-directed learning and is multi-disciplinary and multi-agency in approach. It includes case studies of patients in a variety of settings, from the community to high secure psychiatric care. The programme is not designed to be a stand alone text; rather it should be seen as an introduction to forensic mental health care. It is envisaged that it will take most staff at least six months to work through this programme (some may take up to a year). This will include meeting the individual learning objectives associated with the programme, as well as other learning outcomes identified during regular meetings with the mentor. A reflective diary is included to assist learning and to help the employee get the most out of their sessions with their mentor. Completion of the programme should enable the employee to engage more effectively and safely with patients and/or in the development or delivery of services in this field.

Box 3.6: Table of contents of the new to forensic programme

Chapter 1   Aims and teaching methods
Chapter 2   Understanding mental disorder
Chapter 3   Definitions, principles and policy for mentally disordered offenders
Chapter 4   Civil mental health legislation
Chapter 5: Forensic mental health services
Chapter 6   Attitudes to mentally disordered offenders and ways of dealing with personal emotions and boundaries
Chapter 7: Forensic mental health services and the criminal justice system: Understanding the relationship
Chapter 8   Psychiatric defences and legislation for mentally disordered offenders
Chapter 9   Assessment, treatment and management of mentally disordered offenders
Chapter 10: Multidisciplinary working, communication and managing difference
Chapter 11 Safety and risk
Chapter 12 Users and carers

The use of mentors was seen as crucial to the success of the programme. Mentors are useful at any stage in a person's career but particularly at times of rapid development or major change. They are people who will listen, challenge and help review the progress of their mentees in order to encourage them to make the most of the programme. Mentors may have completely different backgrounds from those of the people they are mentoring, and the mentoring relationship will last for the duration of the programme, comprising several meetings. The content of the programme is shown in *Box 3.6*.

Example 4: A competency framework for the Glasgow Forensic Mental Health Directorate

As part of the Glasgow Forensic Directorate's move to the new Rowanbank Medium Secure Unit and the Directorate changes associated with this, a Forensic Organisational Development (OD) Group was established. The group's purpose was to identify changes around staffing and staff development which needed to occur to ensure that whatever systems and structures were put in place, they would be both supportive of staff and sustainable. The nurse consultant was invited to become a member of the group undertaking this work.

The group agreed that regardless of role and seniority in the Forensic Directorate, all staff must be competent to effectively and efficiently fulfil

Figure 3.3: Approach to competencies taken by Glasgow Forensic Directorate (with thanks to Greater Glasgow Forensic Services Directorate, for their kind permission to reproduce).

their role. A mechanism to achieve this would be through the development of a competency framework which would describe what is expected of all staff working in the Directorate. This work was informed by previous work undertaken by the National Board for Scotland (2000) that published a set of forensic nursing competencies, and work undertaken by Bell College and the Forensic Community Psychiatric Nurses group who described competencies for practice as part of a higher degree in forensic nursing awarded by the College. *Figure 3.3* illustrates the approach.

As the terms 'being competent' and 'showing evidence of competency' are used differently by different people to convey a similar meaning, it was important for members of the group to demonstrate clarity when doing their work. They therefore spent time differentiating between the two and their conclusions are reproduced directly from the final document below:

Competencies have been defined by the National Board for Scotland (NBS), the precursor for NHS Education Scotland (NES) as 'the knowledge, skills and attitudes necessary to practise safely and effectively'. This is distinct from the term competence, which is used to define minimum occupational standards (Chartered Institute of Personnel Development 2004). The distinction between competence and competencies reflects the reciprocal clinical governance responsibilities of the employee and the organisation, represented by the ability to perform tasks; the availability of training, support and facilities; and actual performance. **Competencies can be described as articulating what the organisation needs from its employees, both in terms of the manner in which they do their job (input) and what the employee produces (output).**

> *Core competencies will enable the Forensic Directorate to articulate what is absolutely necessary to function safely with our patients in the Rowanbank Clinic and elsewhere within the service. These competencies will also communicate the key features that differentiate forensic mental health workers from those in other mental health services.*
>
> (Glasgow Forensic Mental Health Directorate, 2006)

Both 'Core Competencies' and 'Core Clinical Competencies' were written to describe the minimum requirements which staff would be expected to have and be able to demonstrate in their everyday practice. The final document was presented by the general manager of the Forensic Directorate, to the Glasgow Project Board meeting in May 2006 where it received unanimous approval and was complimented by all present. The outline of the competencies are reproduced in *Box 3.7*, mapped onto the knowledge and skills (KSF) framework for the non-clinical version. Once the approval of the Board had been achieved, further work commenced on each of the competency statements to include examples of how they could be applied in the context of care.

A local perspective

As can be seen from the above, the core business of the nurse consultant role is to support and facilitate the work of forensic mental health care services in Scotland. The examples illustrate how the nurse consultant has worked with different parts of the forensic estate to support their development at a strategic level. Work has also been undertaken in the following areas, with a more local focus, still retaining the principle of supporting services and their development:

- Standards work in the East region, co-working with senior clinicians at the Orchard Clinic to develop performance indicators for medium secure services.
- Teaching in the West region, on the new Rowanbank Clinic Medium Secure Care Induction course for Glasgow Forensic Services in respect of MDT working.
- Standards work with senior clinicians at the Covenant Churchill Clinic (a low secure service from the independent sector) based in Ayr, to develop an audit tool for low secure services.
- Workforce planning at the State Hospital, facilitating a sub-group of the Organisational Development Group to plan the workforce for the new high secure hospital.
- Occupational therapy service review at Her Majesty's Prison (HMP) Cornton Vale, part of a team assisting the health centre manager to review the occupational therapy service

---

Box 3.7: Glasgow organisational development group work on competency development

Forensic Core Non-Clinical Competencies
(Applicable to all staff working within the Directorate)

Competency 1: Communication	(KSF – Level 2)
Competency 2: Personal and People Development	(KSF – Level 1)
Competency 3: Health, Safety and Security	(KSF – Level 2)
Competency 4: Service Improvement	(KSF – Level 1)
Competency 5: Quality	(KSF - Level 2)
Competency 6: Equality and Diversity	(KSF – Level 1)

Forensic Core Care Competencies

Competency 1: Risk Assessment and Risk Management: Assessment, analysis and management of risk with client groups within forensic mental health settings and other environments

Competency 2: Clinical Governance: Corporate responsibility for clinical practice.

Competency 3: Professional, legal and ethical aspects of care: Areas of clinical practice in which legislation/national policies/professional standards will have an impact on the care of the mentally disordered offender

Competency 4: Working with Service Users and Carers: Engagement with service users and carers in discharging professional roles and responsibilities

Competency 5: Clinical Interventions: Demonstration of knowledge and skills in relation to therapeutic approaches in a forensic environment

---

- The Prevention and Management of Violence and Aggression (PMVA) policy development at the State Hospital, a project co-managed by the nurse consultant and the risk manager to supervise two seconded ward-based members of nursing staff and implement a new family of policies around the prevention and management of violence and aggression.
- Providing weekly clinical supervision to nursing staff on a ward in the State Hospital.

Forensic Network work

The final element of the nurse consultant work is conducted on behalf of the Forensic Network itself. This work ranges from representing the Network at events, speaking about the Network at conferences, being a member of working groups established by the Network or the SEHD to develop advice or policy, attending Network board meetings and representing forensic nursing within the nurse consultant group in Scotland and the wider UK.

Characteristics of an effective nurse consultant in forensic mental health in Scotland

Normally one would expect the characteristics of a role to emerge through research into the impact of successful practitioners, however, as the nurse consultant role emerged as a policy initiative throughout the UK (Department of Health, 1999b), this has not really been the case with this role. Within Scotland the SEHD have maintained close scrutiny over posts, requiring them to be approved as consistent with the four key performance areas stated at the beginning of this chapter. This has had the effect of proportionately fewer posts being appointed in Scotland than in England. Currently there is one forensic nursing consultant and one other mental health nursing consultant, although there are plans for several new posts in mental health in the near future. There are also three nurse consultants with a learning disability portfolio. This is in stark contrast to figures from England where there were 120 nurse consultant posts by September 2005 in psychiatry (Information Centre, 2006).

There are no studies to date that contrast the approaches to appointment of nurse consultants between the different countries of the UK, but, clearly there is a significant difference in approach between Scotland and England. Anecdotally, there is a view that many clinical nurse specialists in England were appointed to nurse consultant posts and not replaced. This may well have been the case, perhaps due to a recognition that the postholders were functioning at the level of a nurse consultant. This approach has not been used in Scotland to date.

Few studies currently exist on the impact of the role; within Scotland, McIntosh et al (2002) found that the added value of consultant nurses included developing practice, improving standards of care, achieving service development and providing leadership at local, regional and national level.

At a UK level, in a larger study, Woodward et al (2005) found four themes emerged during their research into the role; 'characteristics of the postholder, role achievement, support systems and NHS influences' (p. 848). A major theme influencing the success or otherwise of postholders was their characteristics, these are discussed in detail in the paper, contrasting the characteristics of self-reporting successful consultants with those who self-reported lesser successes.

The literature therefore, while sparse, is beginning to illustrate the type of person and the role he or she is taking in successful appointments. This

---

Box 3.8: Characteristics of a successful nurse consultant

- Background prior to appointment: Most successful postholders have significant experience in education, practice or management
- Academically: Most successful postholders are studying towards or are at Masters level
- They are an expert in the field: Most successful postholders are acknowledged by their peers as experts
- They take a Leadership role: Most successful postholders have a leadership role in their everyday work
- Other qualities: Most successful postholders seek to empower those around them, they challenge the status quo, and they are self-confident, determined and collaborative

(From Woodward et al, 2005)

---

is summarised in *Box 3.8* to indicate what employers may consider when making appointments.

The future for nursing consultants in forensic mental health care in Scotland

Despite the fact that there is currently only one nurse consultant post in forensic mental health services in Scotland, there is a need, in the author's view, to develop posts in many areas. As the forensic estate continues to develop there will be opportunities for new posts to emerge. It is however important that the principles underpinning the appointment of nurse consultants should be applied with the same rigour in the future as has been the case to date. The key functions are:

- Professional leadership and consultancy.
- Expert practice.
- Education and research.
- Service development.

It is in the area of expert practice and the need for 50% of time to be involved in patient care which tends to cause most difficulty when trying to describe new nurse consultant roles. However, given the experience of the author who does not carry a direct case load at this time, this criterion can be easily satisfied. All of the examples above are designed to improve patient care, thus the postholder exceeds the 50% criterion by providing indirect care-assisting services to improve care (including nursing care) for their patients.

The possibilities described below are the opinion of the author as to how some posts would probably be developed.

Within the Forensic Network

As can be seen above, the work of the current nurse consultant is both complex and varied, covering the whole of Scotland. The nurse consultant is a 'free asset' to other services and is working towards supporting service development and standardisation of practice across the country. The work is not limited to forensic nursing, and in the opinion of the author, should not be in the future; instead, working collaboratively and supporting all parts of forensic services and influencing their development, in line with Scottish Executive policy, is the main component of the role.

Regionally it would make sense for the three regions to each appoint a nurse consultant to the Forensic Network, with the three postholders forming an alliance with the Network nurse consultant, thus embedding the concept of collaboration, support and development across the whole country. These posts could be part-time, linked for the other part of the role into one of the posts detailed below

Within forensic services

Patients within forensic services represent some of the most disturbed and difficult to manage patients in psychiatric services. They have complex, multi-faceted needs and problems which require sophisticated treatment regimes. The evidence base in terms of 'what works' is emerging; key to this being the development of psychological therapies. Nurses are currently well placed within this area, developing and delivering protocol-based psychological therapies in many problem areas; they are usually employed within psychology services, trained to British Association for Behavioural and Cognitive Psychotherapies criteria in cognitive behavioural therapy, and employed as Band 7 Clinical Nurse Specialists. This therefore is an area where nurse consultant posts could evolve, with nurses assuming greater responsibility as leads of programmes, or for the development of new protocols.

An example of this in general psychological therapies could be developing new evidence-based treatments for forensic populations such as family therapy. Examples of this in specific psychological therapies could be as below:

- Substance misuse.
- Violence and aggressive anger.

- Offending behaviours.
- Psychosocial interventions.
- Sex offender treatment.

Specialist community liaison

Community forensic teams are developing throughout Scotland; the evolving ones tend to be developing along parallel lines, mostly managed operationally by a senior forensic community practice nurse. The opportunity to enhance these roles into nurse consultant should be fully explored

Other potential areas

Within the forensic estate there are opportunities to develop posts which have a specific focus for a nurse consultant. These posts would probably be part-time, linked to distinct clinical roles in the regions. Potential posts could be developed in the following areas:

- Violence management.
- Women's services.
- Learning disability.
- Risk assessment and management.
- Prison health care.

This chapter has not discussed the outcomes of Agenda for Change and the impact of some nursing posts being graded at nurse consultant levels, when the postholder is functioning in a completely different type of post. The author believes that this is a corruption of the nurse consultant grade which should be resisted.

If a nurse is functioning at a significantly high level in for example, areas such as nursing research, nursing policy, or a senior nurse role in a special health board, then the banding they attract should reflect their value as per the spirit of Agenda for Change. A job profile should be developed with a title suiting the role and banded accordingly. Simply fitting individuals to nurse consultant profiles as they function at a high level is not satisfactory and de-values the nurse consultant profile.

In summary, while forensic services have not yet developed nurse consultant posts in Scotland at the pace or rate of English services, there are many opportunities to do so. Part of the author's role is to encourage services in Scotland to consider developing posts as their services evolve, through his work on behalf of the Forensic Network.

References

Carradice A, Round D (2004) The reality of practice development for nurses working in an inpatient service for people with severe and enduring mental health problems. *J Psychiatr Ment Health Nurs* 11(6) 731–737

Chartered Institute of Personnel Development (2004) *Factsheet*. Available from: http://www.cipd.co.uk/subjects/perfmangmt/competnces/comptfrmwk.htm?IsSrchRes=1 [Accessed 14 August 2007]

Department of Health (1999a) *Nurse, Midwife and Health Visitor Consultants: Establishing posts and making appointments. HSC 1999/217.* The Stationery Office: London

Department of Health (1999b) *Making a difference: Strengthening the Nursing, Midwifery and Health Visiting Contribution to Health Care.* NHS Executive: Leeds

Forensic Mental Health Services Managed Care Network (Forensic Network) (2005) *Report of the Forensic Nursing Workforce Project Group.* Available from: http://www.forensicnetwork.scot.nhs.uk/publications.asp [Accessed 6 August 2007]

Fyffe T (2004) The consultant role and strategic leadership. In Henry M (ed) *Nurse Consultants. Existing Roles and Potential Developments.* Scottish Centre for infection and Environmental Health. Available from: http://www.documents.hps.scot.nhs.uk/general/nurse-consultants.pdf [Accessed 9 August 2007]

Glasgow Forensic Mental Health Directorate (2006) *A Competency Framework for the Glasgow Forensic Mental Health Directorate.* Glasgow Forensic Mental Health Directorate: Glasgow

Information Centre (2006) *NHS Hospital and Community Health Services: Qualified Nursing, Midwifery and Health Visiting Staff.* Available from: http://www.ic.nhs.uk/statistics-and-data-collections/workforce/nhs-numbers/nhs-staff-1995--2005 [Accessed 9 August 2007]

Mandy P (1996) Interdisciplinary rather than multidisciplinary or generic practice. *Brit J Therap Rehab* 3(2) 110–112

Mason T, Carton G (2002) Towards a 'forensic lens' model of multidisciplinary training. *J Psychiatr Ment Health Nurs* 9(5) 541–551

Mason T, Williams R, Vivian-Byrne S (2002) Multi-disciplinary working in a forensic mental health setting: Ethical codes of reference. *J Psychiatr Ment Health Nurs* 9(5) 563–572

McIntosh J, Tolson D, Wright J (2002) *An Evaluation of Three Nurse Consultant Posts in Scotland.* Glasgow Caledonian University: Glasgow

National Board Scotland (2000) *Continued Professional Development Portfolio. A Route to Enhanced Competence in Forensic Mental Health Nursing.* National Board for Nursing Midwifery and Health Visiting for Scotland: Edinburgh

NHS Education for Scotland (2006) *Development of a 'New to Forensic' Education Programme for Staff in Forensic Settings: Project Specification.* NHS Education for Scotland: Edinburgh

Redwood S, Lloyd H, Carr E, Hancock H, McSherry R, Campbell S, Graham I (2007) Evaluating nurse consultants' work through key informant perceptions. *Nurs Standard* 21(17) 35–40

Royal College of Psychiatrists (2006) *The Mental Health Team – Fact Sheet.* Available from: http://www.rcpsych.ac.uk/mentalhealthinformation/thementalhealthteam.aspx [Accessed 9 August 2007]

Scottish Executive (2005) *Mental Health (Care and Treatment) (Scotland) Act 2003*. The Stationary Office: Edinburgh

Scottish Executive Health Department (2001) *Caring for Scotland*. The Stationary Office: Edinburgh

Scottish Executive Health Department (2006) *Directorate for Service Policy and Planning. NHS HDL (2006) 48, Forensic Mental Health Services*. St. Andrew's House: Edinburgh

Whyte L, Brooker C (2001) Working with a multidisciplinary team in secure psychiatric environments. *J Psychosoc Nurs Ment Health Services* 39(9) 26–34

Woodward VA, Webb C, Prowse M (2005) Nurse consultants: Their characteristics and achievements. *J ClinNurs* 14 845–854

CHAPTER 4

Equality and diversity: Respecting the person with a learning disability

Mary A Addo and Ian Smith

Introduction

Nurses working in secure environments are expected to engage with diverse client groups in the course of their practice, regardless of their own personal beliefs and values, and irrespective of any conspicuous differences between them and the particular clients (Nursing and Midwifery Council, 2008). The complexities of the interpersonal issues present in the context of forensic mental health nurses' work with clients placed in secure environments have been well documented (Kettles et al, 2002). Not only do they have to provide for the physical well-being, but also they must offer the client emotional containment, leading to issues of role conflict (Burrows, 1993a, b) due to working in such an emotionally charged environment (Cox, 1994). For any meaningful connections to occur, forensic mental health nurses will need to deal with their own prejudices first, be self-aware, and be able to cross barriers in terms of beliefs, religion, age, gender, social class, ethnic grouping, disability and education (Department of Health, 2005; Addo, 2006; Byrt et al, 2007).

More recently, the continuing change taking place within the delivery of health and social care to meet the diverse needs of clients requires nurses who are knowledgeable, pragmatic and capable of being critical and reflective in their attempts to help fellow humans, despite any differences that exist, to connect with their own humanity (UKCC, 1999; Department of Health, 2004, 2005; Scottish Executive, 2006a). The argument for this is based on the realisation that the objectives of service provision in health and social care for any group of clients cannot be achieved without a highly trained and skilled workforce. This workforce must be capable of positively embracing difference in the client groups they engage with and able to work positively with the concepts of equality and diversity. These qualities are emphasised in the values-based approach to service provision and delivery to clients, as reflected in the National Review of Mental Health Nursing in Scotland (Scottish Executive, 2006a).

If nursing can be construed as an interactive process, then the context of the nurse's work with people with learning disability implies that being affected by and affecting others are fundamental aspects of this kind of work. Tschudin (1987) asserts that in order to care, one must be able to relate to others. The giving of unconditional positive regard to clients is strongly advocated in the practice of nursing. Rogers (1957) defines unconditional positive regard as having and showing a warm acceptance of the client's experience, without conditions or judgement, which in some way could be perceived as caring. However, it is questionable whether all forensic mental health nurses can work with the range of diversity that exists in a positive manner and promote equality, since individual nurses' personal and professional values can come into conflict with each other.

This chapter explores the concepts of equality and diversity in relation to people defined as having a learning disability related to forensic mental health nursing. It examines briefly what learning disability is and identifies resulting needs in relation to how forensic mental health nurses can work with people with a learning disability, with reference to a broad range of literature and policies.

This chapter cannot capture every aspect of equality and diversity issues with reference to persons with a learning disability, nonetheless, recognising and valuing difference, promoting choice and involvement in decision making are discussed within the equality and diversity debate. It is hoped that this chapter offers a contribution to managing equality and diversity, in valuing people with a learning disability that places the focus on the person, rather than the disability.

People with learning disability and issues of equality and diversity

The Department of Health (2001) defines learning disability as 'a significant reduced ability to understand new or complex information, to learn new skills (impaired intelligence) with a reduced ability to cope independently (impaired functioning) which started before adulthood with a lasting effect on development'. This impairment of intelligence and functioning varies from person to person and results in very diverse needs and abilities; some people can live semi-independently and work in open employment and others require help with every aspect of living. The United Nations *Declaration on the Rights of Disabled People* (1975) states that whatever the origin, nature and seriousness of learning disabled people's handicaps and disabilities, they

---

Box 4.1: Unhelpful perceptions of people with learning disability

- A menace to society
- As sub-human
- Idiot

- A child in an adult's body
- As an object of ridicule
- An object of charity

(From Wolfensberger, 1975)

---

have the same fundamental rights as their fellow citizens of the same age, which implies first and foremost, the right to enjoy a decent life, as normal and full as possible.

People with learning disability are human beings; they are not a homogenous group. They are unique individuals with their own history, world views, aspirations and dreams. They have the right to feel safe, respected and included in society just as any other person who does not have a learning disability (Royal College of Nursing, 2006). Issues of equality and diversity are pertinent to working with people with learning disability in any care setting (Fern, 1994a; National Health Service Quality Improvement Scotland, 2006). However, within forensic mental health nursing care environments, clients are faced with a range of prejudices stemming from a combination of individual forensic mental health nurses' value systems, service design and delivery. Byrt et al (2007) argue that one's ethnicity, disability, criminal history, psychopathology, culture, religion, sexual orientation, gender, and the nature of interactional issues can discriminate against the individual client in these settings.

Historical overview of developments

To see how we have arrived at this, we need briefly to consider the history of the treatment and care of people with learning disabilities in society. This client group have variously been marginalised from our society or treated as a full member, according to the views and beliefs of the community in which they lived at the time. For example, in some communities in the past, people with learning disabilities were regarded as holy innocents who were without sin (Wolfensberger, 1975). They were treated well by the society in which they lived and had some esteem and standing within these communities.

However, Wolfensberger (1975) outlines a number of unhelpful perceptions (see *Box 4.1*) that have traditionally led to poor treatment of this client group.

These perceptions have led to the frequent dehumanisation of this client group within our society. Other unhelpful views were that these people were sick, which led them to be institutionalised in large hospitals and the medical model applied. The result of this was that the person with a learning disability was a passive recipient of care and received this care in a paternalistic system where the professionals knew best (Brown and Rennie, 2003).

Their autonomy was overridden and their individuality to express their views on issues that matter to them was denied in the institutions of the past, showing some of the inequalities that people with learning disability still face in their utilisation of services. The relationship between the professionals and the clients was characterised by a power imbalance where the professionals had the power to control the lives of these people (Brown and Paterson, 2003). Clearly, in these settings, equality and diversity was hard to achieve. However, from the 1960s onwards, there have been substantial changes in the models of care provision for people with learning disability (see Brown and Rennie, 2003, for detailed information). There was a gradual de-institutionalisation in the 1970s which gathered pace in the 1980s and 1990s.

The philosophy of normalisation was developed and applied to people with learning disability in health and social care settings. This encouraged unconditional societal acceptance of them (Bank-Mikkelsen and Nirje, 1969) but, conversely, in Wolfensberger's (1983) later social role valorisation version, we were encouraged to enhance the social image of these people so as to increase their value status.

More recently, health and social policy has centred on the concept of social inclusion for people with learning disabilities and other disadvantaged social groups. Social inclusion is concerned with encouraging society to change in such a way that socially disadvantaged groups move from the margins of our society into its mainstream. The Scottish Executive's (2002) *Promoting Health, Supporting Inclusion* highlights the national review of the contribution of all nurses and midwives to the care and support of people with learning disabilities. In addition, the Scottish Executive (2000) *The Same as You Campaign,* in the review of services for people with learning disability, also highlights the rights of individuals in service delivery. Implicit within this idea of social inclusion and 'Same as You' are the notions of equality and diversity.

Another driver to promote the concepts of equality and diversity is the recent Report on the Review of the Mental Health (Scotland) Act 1984, more commonly known as the Millan Report (Scottish Executive, 2001) which identifies certain principles (see *Box 4.2*) as relevant in the provision of care to individuals with learning disabilities and mental health problems.

It is evident that over time in the development of services for people with learning disability, efforts have been made to ensure that they have the same fundamental rights as fellow citizens (United Nations, 1975; Human Rights Act, 1998).

Legislative requirements in the provision of services and protection of people with disabilities have changed dramatically over the last decade (Human

---

Box 4.2: Millan principles

- Non-discrimination
- Equality
- Respect for diversity
- Reciprocity
- Informal care

- Participation
- Respect for carers
- Least restrictive alternatives
- Benefit
- Child welfare

(From Scottish Executive, 2001)

Rights Act, 1998; Department of Health, 2001; Disability Discrimination Act, 2005; Royal College of Nursing, 2006). Brown and Rennie (2003) give a detailed historical account of the policies into practice in care provision for people with learning disability. These legislative policies now place the onus on a holistic view of the composition of the diversity of individuals in society and the need to work positively with others in the provision of goods and services for people with learning disability.

The Disability Discrimination Act (2005) introduced changes to society's perception of disability and for the first time, provided protection against being discriminated against on grounds of having a disability in any given circumstances. The Disability Discrimination Act (2005) promotes and advocates the philosophy of positive attitudes to be demonstrated towards disabled people. This implies that, as forensic mental health nurses working with people with a learning disability in secure care environments we have to take positive steps to recognise the diverse needs of this client group in the context of our work and to practise in professional ways that do not discriminate against them because of a disability. The Disability Discrimination Act (2005) needs to be applauded for helping to create a culture of promoting positive changes in which fixed mindsets held about people with learning disability in any given health or social care context can be challenged, with forensic mental health nurses acting as advocates, to ensure this client group is treated with respect and as persons with rights. In so doing, the Act serves to contribute to dismantling many of the barriers that people with learning disability encounter in their daily lives in secure care environments, hence respect for diversity and promoting equality for their rights to be acknowledged and worked with, irrespective of differences.

Equality and diversity

Equality can be defined as 'being equal in person, status, size, in value as a person and having the same rights as another person' (*The Oxford Popular Dictionary and Thesaurus*, 1998). This definition implies the fair treatment of all people regardless of any differences that exist. It relates to each and every person gaining access to opportunities for self-development through having a fairer society/community where everyone, regardless of difference, participates fully and fulfils their potential through opportunity of access. Yet this cannot be claimed to be the reality for some people living with a learning disability (Fern, 1994a).

Owing to difficulties with stereotyping, stigma and discrimination in society, the concept of equality is heavily backed by legislation and various policies designed to address unfair discrimination in any form based on any perceived differences that are present (Race Relations [Amendment], 2000; Department of Health, 2001; Disability Discrimination Act, 2005; Equality Act, 2006). Equality, according to Millan principles (Scottish Executive, 2001), means there should be no direct or indirect discrimination on the grounds of physical disability, age, gender, sexual orientation, language, religion or national, ethnic or social origin.

Nonetheless, we cannot talk about equality without taking into account the issue of diversity within the context of determinants of health and well-being. This is because equality and diversity raise issues about distributive and procedural justice, ethics and social responsibility (Brown and Paterson, 2003). Evidence shows that people with learning disability have complex health needs and experience poor health and inequalities in health care delivery (Brown and Paterson, 2003). People with learning disability in secure care environments have health needs too and an interest in forensic mental health nurses who deliver their care. They have expectations of outcomes that they want from these nurses, that of respect for persons and involvement in decision making about their care. These expectations should be met by forensic mental health nurses in accordance with legislative requirements, best practice guidelines, professional ethics and standards in nursing practice (Scottish Executive, 2000; Nursing and Midwifery Council, 2008; National Health Service Quality Improvement, 2006). In short, people with learning disability are stakeholders and have the same rights as others to complain when their needs have been ignored by forensic mental health nurses in providing care for them, and to demand for a redress when their views on matters important to them are ignored. This is reflected in the Millan principles of participation listed in *Box 4.3*.

According to Thompson (2003:10) diversity refers to 'social variety across and within groups of people'. In other words, diversity could refer to the range of differences that exist among individuals such as age, gender, religion, race, ethnic grouping, nationality, capabilities, disabilities, sexual orientation and socio-economic background.

However, it needs to be borne in mind that diversity as a concept is complex to define, as it encompasses the notions of respecting and accepting

---

Box 4.3: Millan's principles of participation: Ensuring equality

- Full involvement in care
- Past and present wishes taken into account
- Provided with support and information to enable full participation

(From Scottish Executive, 2001)

---

others, to include the uniqueness of each human being and recognising differences along the dimensions of ethnicity, race, religion, gender, sexual orientation, beliefs, physical abilities, political beliefs, cultural practices and world views (Addo, 2006; Byrt et al, 2007). The embracing and examination of these differences in a safe, positive and nurturing manner by forensic mental health nurses is what leads to understanding the person with learning disability placed in a secure care environment, and moving beyond the mere tolerance of learning disability clients we care for, to achieving a meaningful understanding of the diversity embedded within each unique individual. In the context of forensic mental health nurses' work with clients with learning disability, it is this understanding of the client in a positive manner that brings out the valuing of the person, regardless of context (Scottish Executive, 2000; Department of Health, 2001).

Forensic mental health nurses working with people with learning disability in secure environments, can demonstrate equality and diversity by creating a culture of work practices that recognise, acknowledge, value, respect and treat the person with learning disability as an equal, irrespective of his or her disability. In such a working culture, forensic mental health nurses can facilitate the development of the person with learning disability charged to their care, a major part of the learning disability nurse's role (Aldridge, 2004). When we work in this fashion, it fulfils the ethos of the nursing profession while meeting the needs of the learning disability client as recipient of that service (Royal College of Nursing, 2006; National Health Service Quality Improvement, 2006).

Achieving equality and diversity through forensic mental health nurses' work practices in secure environments with people with learning disability, requires a person-centred focus in order to ensure a holistic engagement. Brown and Paterson (2003: 34) assert that a vision that seeks to promote equity for all, must be set within the context of the wider determinants of health and well-being, and must take account of core issues, such as poverty, employment, education, lifestyles, the physical environment, and the provision of effective health systems and health care.

Various factors come into play, such as the social standards that members of a particular society have adopted in interacting with each other as fellow

---

Box 4.4: Respecting the person with learning disability

- Receive nursing care and support that shows respect for individual qualities, abilities and diverse backgrounds
- Consider age, ethnic group, social, cultural and religious backgrounds
- Place valuing of individual at centre of care planning and delivery
- Give time to listen to client's points of view
- Do not make decisions based on assumptions
- Make the effort to see the whole person rather than the disability
- See the person as the 'expert' in his or her disability experience
- Recognise strengths and build on limitations

(From Scottish Executive, 2001)

---

humans. These social interactions are based on the values, roles, norms, and rules embodied in the laws and norms informing members of the particular society on how to behave in the context of equity of health care access and involvement with clients (Austin, 2001; Brown and Paterson, 2003; Baillie and Strachan, 2006). Therefore, as forensic mental health nurses, we need to be aware of these determinants of health for people with learning disability that we engage with in the course of our work, to ensure fairness in how they are treated.

Nonetheless, the challenge in meeting equality and diversity needs of any given group of people in society is fraught with difficulties due to differences in how different societies deal with ethical issues with reference to equity. For example, in some countries, the ill-treatment of people with learning disability is the norm. Such relativism is not in keeping with the moral absolutism inherent in the Human Rights Act (1998) and the United Nations Declaration on the Rights of Disabled People (1975). The implication for forensic mental health nurses working with learning disability clients is that we are witnesses of their experiences in relation to equality and diversity and the difficulties they encounter in getting their needs met in our daily work with them. To remain silent on this issue is to deny both its existence and its impact on clients with learning disability.

Respecting diversity within the context of forensic nursing work with people with learning disability requires forensic mental health nurses to conduct their engagement with this client group in an ethical manner in order to avoid ignorantly appearing maleficent in their acts. This is because fundamentally, forensic mental health nursing, regardless of the psychopathology and any differences that are apparent in the client group, is a humanistic and relational enterprise. It is about caring for and spending time with clients and about helping them to gain control over their circumstances (Kettles et al, 2002). Respect for diversity is another Millan principle, which is shown in *Box 4.4*.

Box 4.5: The 10 essential shared capabilities for mental health work

- Working in partnership
- Respecting diversity
- Practising ethically
- Challenging inequality
- Promoting recovery
- Identifying peoples' needs and strengths
- Providing service user-centred care
- Making a difference
- Promoting safety and positive risk taking
- Personal development and learning

(From Scottish Executive, 2006b)

Omissions and failures by forensic mental health nurses working in secure care environments, to act in ways that reflect equality in engaging with people with learning disability, can lead to accusations of unlawful discrimination against the nurses in failing to promote equality, and to respect particular diversity that exists, with resulting huge emotional and financial cost in cases of alleged negligence (Tingle, 2002; Nursing and Midwifery Council, 2008).

Promoting equality and diversity for people with learning disability cared for in secure care environments, is about forensic mental health nurses demonstrating social responsibility through practices that nurture, protect and enhance the well-being of people with learning disability as members of the communities they live in, and society as a whole (Human Rights Act, 1998; Department of Health, 2001; Nursing and Midwifery Council, 2008; Department of Health, 2005; Royal College of Nursing, 2006). Where individual forensic mental health nurses providing care at the frontline for people with learning disability feel ill-prepared to take on board the equality and diversity challenges inherent in their practice, then the expectations of this client group may remain unfulfilled, which can lead to grievances and complaints. At times, the nursing response may be defensive and attempts made to act within the law, but with less interest by way of promoting further acts of social responsibility. It is such concerns about standards of practice that makes the 10 Essential Shared Capabilities, the minimum set of competencies for mental health workers, so pertinent (Scottish Executive, 2006b) (see *Box 4.5*).

However, if equality and diversity are to be championed to give a fair and equal treatment to people with learning disability cared for in secure care environments, then there is a need for forensic mental health nurses to be more accommodating in balancing the range of perspectives from all stakeholders. This calls for a proactive response from forensic mental health nurses through having a critical dialogue and reflection, in order to learn from individuals with learning disability, and seek their involvement in a meaningful manner, in working together to meet their needs. Such an approach is necessary as forensic mental health nurses have an obligation to ensure that culturally sensitive care is provided, regardless of the diversity dimension presented by the individual client (Papadopoulos et al, 2001; Addo, 2006; Byrt et al, 2007).

Recognising and valuing differences

In order to respect and value differences that exist in the course of forensic mental health nurses' engagement with people with learning disability, it is important for them to understand the nature of learning disabilities, the learning problems these people commonly have and the processes resulting in the social devaluation of this client group (Scottish Executive, 2000; Addo, 2001; Royal College of Nursing, 2006; NHS Quality Improvement Scotland, 2006; Registered Nurses' Association of Ontario, 2007).

Forensic mental health nurses would then be ready to learn how to create an environment within the secure setting, where valuing of the person with learning disability and his/her learning needs are met in an ethical and humane manner deserving of every human being, irrespective of any differences (Human Rights Act, 1998; Department of Health, 2001; Addo 2001, 2006; Scottish Executive, 2000, 2006a; Byrt et al, 2007). Clearly, having access to good education and continuing professional development would help in achieving this aim. However, the process of valuing people with learning disability begins with the recruitment and selection of forensic mental health nurses who have the necessary training and education to work with people who have a learning disability, in addition to the positive qualities of being respectful and caring in nature, being open and broad minded and able to engage with different perspectives, coupled with a desire to make a positive difference in the clients' lives (Scottish Executive, 2000, 2006a; Addo, 2006).

Forensic mental health nurses can engage with people with learning disability in a positive manner with their knowledge, skills and attitudes. However, at the same time, they can also at times knowingly or unknowingly disengage with them through negative attitudes that they bring to the interaction process (Hammer, 2000; Scottish Executive, 2000). Such nursing behaviours do nothing to progress the equality and diversity agenda in the context of forensic mental health nursing and the nursing profession's contribution to care provision for people with learning disability. The attributes needed for forensic mental health nurses to prevent such situations arising are presented in *Box 4.6*.

Box 4.6: Attributes needed for the nurse to champion the equality and diversity agenda for people with learning disability

- A body of knowledge that is theoretical, practical and clinical in relation to learning disability work and ability to apply that knowledge to underpin practice
- Being open-minded and having the desire to explore new knowledge to enhance care and treatment
- Accountability in recognising personal capabilities, knowledge base and areas for development.
- Becoming aware of barriers and constraints that interfere with one's autonomy and seeking ways to remedy the situation
- Advocating for the client by understanding the client's perspective and assisting with any learning needs
- Being innovative and visionary by showing initiative for new ideas and being involved through taking action to make a difference
- Promoting collegiality and collaboration through partnership within a professional context
- Being knowledgeable about ethical values, concepts and decision making, identifying ethical concerns, issues and dilemmas, and applying knowledge of nursing ethics to make decisions and act on these

(Adapted from Registered Nurses' Association of Ontario, 2007)

Paying attention to recruiting appropriately qualified forensic mental health nurses with the right attributes for the job should be supported with robust induction and continuing professional development programmes that emphasise the ethos of care in working with people with a learning disability within secure care environments (Department of Health, 2001; Royal College of Nursing, 2006). For this to be effective, forensic mental health nurses working with this client group should give thought to exactly what they think their understanding of their work with people with learning disability is trying to achieve, and the processes that they need to ensure clarity of views, as lack of this will create disharmony.

So how do forensic mental health nurses encourage positive acceptance of difference? Part of diversity is recognising the person with learning disability as an individual (Human Rights Act, 1998; Department of Health, 2001, 2005; Royal College of Nursing, 2006). Individuality can be encouraged by forensic mental health nurses adopting a positive attitude in their everyday work with people with learning disability, by observing and celebrating important milestones in the clients' lives such as birthdays and other rites of passage, in the same way as people would with their own family and friends (Fern, 1994a). The living environment should also reflect the individuality of the client. For example, clients should have their own space containing items of their own choice, therefore personalisation of personal space and possessions to enhance a sense of self and value should be encouraged.

As forensic mental health nurses working with learning disability clients, we need to emphasise these differences if we are to encourage client growth, as envisaged by Aldridge (2004). To do so, we may need to talk about our own lives and the differences within them, thereby engaging in mutuality, which Turnbull (2004) believes is an essential element of the learning disability nurse's role. Seeing clients change in response to their input may, in turn, change the nurses involved and, in turn, this may change their future response to clients in a positive way, leading to a closer, more nurturing relationship where everyone's development is enhanced. However, self-disclosure within a secure care environment is not without its dangers and nurses must judge what, how much and to whom they can safely disclose to aid client development, keeping in mind the need to maintain professional boundaries (Nursing and Midwifery Council, 2008).

Traditionally, parents and carers have controlled the relationships people with learning disabilities have had with others, often encouraging friendship with other disabled clients and the use of segregated services. While clients may be happy with this, they also may not be, and opportunities to develop positive relationships with other members of the wider community should be provided to foster a feeling of social inclusion (Fern, 1994a; Scottish Executive, 2000, 2002). To enable this, the networking and supportive elements of the role of the learning disability nurse (Aldridge, 2004) would be emphasised.

More generally, when encouraging individuality it is important to recognise that people with learning disability have varied needs and wants and that individuality can be encouraged by providing care which is flexible and tailored to the individual. Involving individuals with learning disability in the planning of their day-to-day activities shows sensitivity to their needs and an understanding of their world views, history and identities (Fern, 1994a; Papadopoulos, 2001; Narayanasamy and White, 2005; Royal College of Nursing, 2006; Addo, 2006).

Another way in which individuality can be promoted is by the avoidance of labelling. Labelling causes us to interpret the client's behaviour purely in terms of their learning disability and prevents us from seeing the whole person with all the many facets of their character. It may also cause us to view clients as limited individuals with a narrow repertoire of behaviour caused by their learning disabilities, which in turn will lead to the provision of a restrictive learning environment (Wolfensberg, 1975).

Curtice (2003) argues that language has a huge importance within the politics of disability, as it becomes the weapon by which people's identity and legitimacy are taken away from them, weakening their power base and their ability to participate fully in society. It is therefore important that forensic mental health nurses are careful and judicious in how they choose words and use language in their interaction with people with learning disability within the secure care environment. The choice of words that professionals have used to describe the client group they work with, such as 'feeble-minded', 'imbecile', 'defective', 'sub-normal' or 'idiot', also contributes to this power imbalance (Wolfensberger, 1975).

These can all impact negatively on how individuals with a learning disability are made, by forensic mental health nurses, socially to construct their identity. Therefore, forensic mental health nurses working with this vulnerable client group, need to be aware and careful of the relationship between power and language use (Wolfensberger, 1975; Fern, 1994b).

Like anyone else, people with learning disabilities have a need to grow and develop by engaging in a wide variety of activities. Indeed, Aldridge (2004) has already indicated that promoting client development is a major part of the learning disability nurse's work. It could be argued that to become a unique human being, we need, as humans, to engage in a blend of activities individual to us, any of which may involve some element of risk. Yet, in the past, people with learning disabilities have often been prevented from engaging in even mildly hazardous activities, perhaps because nurses believed that their duty of care involved ensuring clients never came to harm. Even in modern services with a liberal philosophy, the fear of litigation may cause clients to be overprotected. This issue of positive risk taking is recognised as one of the 10 Essential Shared Capabilities needed by professionals working with clients in mental health (Scottish Executive, 2006b).

While forensic mental health nurses should ensure that all reasonable precautions are taken to protect clients, it should not exclude individuals from activities that would be challenging and stimulating through the application of overprotecting and limiting rules. Activities should be interesting for the client with learning disability in a secure care environment and take account of their attention span and physical capabilities. Clients should also be offered a range of activities to choose from (Fern, 1994a). In these days of evidence-based nursing one might ask where is the evidence for spending forensic mental health nurses' time trying to develop the client with a learning disability?

The evidence was provided by Marc Gold in the 1960s when he demonstrated that clients with moderate and severe learning disabilities could master quite complex activities if staff had a positive attitude to their development. He thought that if clients do not learn, then the trainers/teachers need to change their approach so that the client does learn (Perske, 1987). This approach worked then and it works today.

Promoting choice

As we have seen, part of encouraging equality and diversity for people with learning disability is offering a choice of activities. Indeed, informed choice is an essential element in promoting both equality and diversity (Department of Health, 2001; Scottish Executive, 2000, 2001, 2006a). However, it can be argued that the conditions have to be right before forensic mental health nurses working with people with learning disability can effectively offer informed choice. For example, if one accepts, as Marc Gold did, that the self-fulfilling prophecy has a role to play in our social interactions, then in this situation forensic mental health nurses would need to have a positive belief that people with learning disability have a right to choice and would benefit from choice. If forensic mental health nurses do not have such positive belief and do not value the person with a learning disability, then it is likely that they would not behave in ways that would encourage the client to make informed choices (Royal College of Nursing, 2006; Byrt et al, 2007).

For example, some forensic mental health nurses might not make every effort to communicate choices to those people who have communication difficulties. In addition, many clients need help to choose. For learning disability clients who are unused to choice forensic mental health nurses may need to offer simple, contrasting choices, initially followed by more similar and complex choices as the client's abilities develop (Randle, 2006).

An issue that is not often considered in the literature is the idea of teaching the consequences of choice. If the client makes a choice to do or not to do something, then there will be a consequence of making that choice which he/she has to live with. Taking responsibility for one's behaviour is part of one's development as a person, yet people with learning disabilities have often been denied the right to take responsibility for their behaviour because of unhelpful beliefs, such as, 'They don't understand what they are doing.' Such behaviours, based on assumptions, can lead to discriminatory practices and disrespect for people with learning disability, and undermines the promotion of equality for them, despite inherent diversities.

Such beliefs were intended to protect the person with learning disability but had the effect of stifling the client's development as a person, a problem recognised by the 10 Essential Shared Capabilities for Mental Health Practice (Scottish Executive, 2006b). For forensic mental health nurses who champion the equality and diversity agenda in their work, a more positive belief might be 'Let us give the client with a learning disability the opportunity to learn and take responsibility'. This might allow us to more effectively support clients with learning

---

Box 4.7: How nurses can promote choice for learning disability clients

- Teach about options, choices and responsibilities
- Work with client in ways that support choice and decision making
- Share relevant information to client's understanding
- Promote individual advocacy for the client
- Encourage full participation in activities of interest
- Create opportunities to make choices
- Use language that is meaningful and easily understood by the client

(Adapted from Fern, 1994a)

---

disability in their decision making and step in where they are clearly having difficulty. This more positive belief characterises the progressive approach to client development pioneered by Marc Gold in the 1960s and also fits with the equalising and empowering approach favoured today (Millan, 2001; Department of Health, 2001; Scottish Executive, 2001; 2006a). For examples of actions, see *Box 4.7*.

Nonetheless, respecting diversity is also about recognising and accepting that sometimes people do not want to learn or have great difficulty in learning, no matter how much support they get. In this case, diversity is not about encouraging client development, come what may, simply because it happens to be part of the service provider's mission statement. Diversity in this case is about accepting the client's differences in relation to ourselves with respect to motivation, wishes, desires and world views (Department of Health, 2001; Addo, 2001, 2006; Scottish Executive, 2006a). However, forensic mental health nurses must be careful not to use diversity as a justification for a lack of action and input in the delivery of health care to clients with a learning disability. They need to show that they have done all they can within their professional efforts to aid the learning disability client's development and to overcome any de-motivation created by previous institutional care through participative involvement of the client. This calls for the role of the consultant nurse in helping to take forward the equality and diversity agenda in working with people with learning disability within forensic nursing contexts.

In nurse consultants' capacity as change agents, they can contribute a great deal in advancing these concepts in practice. This can be done both by influencing policy at a strategic level and by providing an excellent role model at an operational level. Nurse consultants must spend a minimum of 50% of their time working directly with clients, ensuring that NHS clients continue to benefit from the expert skills of these nurses.

Involvement in decision making

Aldridge (2004) states that, in addition to promoting client development, another major role of the learning disability nurse is to plan, deliver and evaluate health care programmes designed to meet individual health needs. As part of promoting choice in developmental activities and in health care programmes, clients need to be involved in the decision making process. This requires that people with learning disability are given information in a form they can understand, which might involve trying several means of communication (Randle, 2006). This means that forensic mental health nurses must listen to what the client wants and avoid making assumptions without checking. Nursing actions based on assumptions can only make a fool of the recipient of that assumption, which is disrespectful to the person. Indeed, effective communication will involve forensic mental health nurses checking that clients with learning disability understand the information which is given to them. However, Bartlett and Bunning (1997) found that staff frequently overestimate the comprehension of service users. The reason for this may be that clients with learning disability may have learned that the use of certain phrases or non-verbal behaviour, such as nodding, pleases the nurses and may fool nurses into thinking that clients understand more than they actually do.

There are other issues that affect nurse–client communication. In forensic care settings where the ethos is one of containment versus therapy, one might find a power imbalance which, if not managed sensitively, can lead to neglect of particular needs of the individual person with a learning disability (Fern, 1994a; Gallop, 1998). One consequence of such an imbalance may be that there are inequalities in communication. For example, McConkey et al (1999b) found that nurses in institutional settings preferred to use the verbal mode of communication regardless of the client's preference.

In an equal relationship in the context of respecting diversity and promoting equality for people with learning disability in secure care environments, forensic mental health nurses need to find out what the client's preferred mode of communication is and learn to use it in all situations (Scottish Executive, 2000; Royal College of Nursing, 2006). When forensic mental health nurses work in this way with people with learning disability, it brings out the professionalism of the nurses and nursing practice (Registered Nurses' Association of Ontario, 2007), values the person with learning disability (Department of Health, 2001), and shows the humanistic and relational enterprise of forensic nursing.

Diversity requires that nurses communicate with clients about a range of events important to the client, yet research by Markova et al (1992) shows that in institutions, functional interactions are more prevalent than social interactions and research by McConkey et al (1999a) found that most staff communications with clients with learning disability are of a directive nature. The controlling nature of staff–client communication is also found in settings where clients use signs and symbols to communicate. Basil (1992), as cited by Ferris Taylor (2003), found that non-disabled people tend to dominate the interaction by initiating communication more frequently and taking more turns in the interaction.

The implications of these findings are clear. Forensic mental health nurses working in secure care environments need to encourage equal turn taking in communication and should make every effort to encourage communication by giving time, and indicating to the client the nurse's willingness to listen. Only then can an equal relationship be promoted and respect for diversity honoured.

Yet according to Fitzsimmons and Barr (1997) and (Brown 2001) nurses feel unprepared in their role to work with people with learning disabilities, relating this to issues of communication, which highlights the need for further continuing professional development. This shows that working in partnership with all stakeholders will not only promote shared learning to enhance the promotion of equality and managing diversity for people with learning disability, but also has the potential to improve the quality of life of this client group (Department of Health, 1999). Furthermore, working in partnership with other agencies contributing to the care of this client group can lead to better understanding of people with learning disabilities. Aldridge (2004) highlights the important role learning disability nurses play in liaising with these other agencies.

Arnold and Boggs (2003) contend that an essential component of the successful implementation of the therapeutic relationship between nurses and their clients requires self-knowledge, which they argue is the precursor to professionalism. This means that as individuals, we are what we have become in terms of our personalities and the world views that we hold, which is a product of our early socialisation and other experiences encountered in life.

Therefore, how nurses relate to the person defined as having a learning disability in the care situation is influenced by the perception of the self of the nurse. Without this self-awareness and the recognition of personal and cultural beliefs, and an understanding of intrapersonal strengths and limitations, it will be difficult for the nurse to attend to the client's needs and maintain a therapeutic relationship (Boyd, 1998). Thus, forensic mental health nurses' self-concept, their personality, and how self-aware they are, can all impact on how they engage and interact with learning disability clients (Hammer, 2000). Ways that forensic mental health nurses can promote involvement to empower the person with learning disability are listed in *Box 4.8.*

Box 4.8: Promoting involvement to empower the person with learning disability

- Promote easy access to information in a language that is understood
- Seek clients' views on support and care they will like
- Make an advance statement to enable clients' wishes to be upheld
- Get an independent advocate for the client
- Provide clients with what they need to be involved in their care
- Make available options and choices known to them
- Feel free to express views and wishes
- Get clients views listened to
- Make clients feel understood and that their views are respected
- Be able to influence the decision making process on things that matter to clients

(From Scottish Executive, 2000)

Having knowledge of what an individual is dealing with, it can be argued, empowers that individual, and, in the context of nursing work, it is nurses' knowledge that gives them self-confidence in their role, that they translate into their interaction with clients. When that knowledge is not present, it means the interaction with people with learning disability will not be based on sound professional knowledge and judgement, because the nurse does not possess the requisite understanding. When this understanding is lacking, nurses' interactions could be influenced by their personal beliefs and values, and the wider public and media portrayal of people with learning disability.

To guard against this requires continuing personal and professional development in order for nurses to enhance their self-awareness, since nursing involves the application of knowledge to practice to promote clients' health and well-being. Clinical supervision can offer forensic mental health nurses an educative process which is committed to value ends, helping to value the person within the nurse as a professional, and the nurse in turn being able to demonstrate the valuing of the person within the client with a learning disability through how they relate to the client. This process will enhance the therapeutic competence of the nurse, improve interpersonal functioning and ultimately meet the needs of learning disability clients entrusted to their care (Addo, 2000; Nursing and Midwifery Council, 2001).

Corporate and individual accountability require that forensic mental health nurses working at the frontline with people with learning disability in secure care environments, must have the relevant education, training and support for such work identified, and the appropriate development of educational strategies that are dynamic, to promote life-long learning to enhance their competence for practice. This, in turn, prepares them to engage effectively in their role in promoting equality and respecting diversity in their work with people with learning disability. Working with difference in a positive manner is about empowering individuals to take control of their circumstances, which is an aspect of the forensic mental health nurse's role.

However, forensic mental health nurses' professional role means that it is not possible for them to offer any kind of meaningful nursing care if they do not or cannot respect the personhood of the other (Swinton and Boyd, 2000; Nursing and Midwifery Council, 2008). Austin (2001) maintains that, within the nurse–client relationship, ethical issues of non-maleficence, beneficence, autonomy and justice require nurses to use these to guide their moral practice within the professional encounter with clients. These require that forensic mental health nurses do no harm in any way to the person with learning disability; that they promote good and do good towards their clients;promote respect and give the right to choose and make decisions; and are fair (Hammer, 2000; Millan, 2001; Department of Health, 2001; Royal College of Nursing, 2006).

So what?

There are benefits to be gained by society through forensic mental health nurses' work in responsibly promoting equality and diversity through demonstrating social responsibility and distributive and procedural justice in their work with learning disability clients in secure care environments. Such actions will impact positively on the well-being, sense of worth and valuing of improving the quality of life for learning disability clients cared for in secure care environments. Achieving this means that forensic mental health nurses must seek continuously to make good ethics part of their working culture in providing care and working with people with learning disability in a valuing manner (Department of Health, 2001; Royal College of Nursing, 2006).

Forensic mental health nursing work requires a level of emotional intimacy in order to see and feel what it is like for clients in their human condition, even if it is only imaginary. We need to be positive about differences that exist among human beings; as such diversity reflects the very existence of humanity. We are all different and and if we cannot learn from and about others who are different from us, because we choose to remain unconcerned about the injustices facing them in society, then achieving the noble aim of equality and diversity for all human beings, including people with a learning disability, will remain thwarted.

To adopt this stance will stifle the advancement of society and forensic mental health nursing practice, and the strife of committed forensic mental health nurses to understand their overall view on human diversity of existence will be hindered in the context of their work. This is because when all members of society, regardless of difference, have equal opportunity (McCarthy, 1996) everyone benefits and society benefits too. This way, the issues of inequality and its related negative impact on individual's stability and growth due to discriminatory experiences can be managed and the manifestation of feelings of oppression can be prevented (Fern, 1994a). The forensic secure care environment is a community as well. We are all different but we are all the same (Scottish Executive, 2000); in other words, having a learning disability should not make that person less of a human being in any given social context in society. What we see of the learning disabled person is another dimension of the complexity of what it is to be a human being, and our vulnerability (Addo, 2001).

Diversity needs to be embraced positively by forensic mental health nurses as it encourages reflection on the issues faced by people with learning disability from many perspectives, and gives us the opportunity to examine our own values and beliefs and how as individuals we fit into the wider system of forensic nursing work with learning disability clients and society (Human Rights Act, 1998; Department of Health, 2001; Addo, 2006). What nurses need to guard against is any tendency of bias in using information in ways that give an inaccurate perception of people with learning disability in society and devalues them. This is an area where forensic nursing research, within the nurse consultant role in learning disability work, can move forward the nursing frontiers for this client group and for forensic nursing.

In the 21st century managing diversity has become important as society battles to understand diversity in its entirety and how it impacts on the quality of life for various groups, as evidenced in the number of legislative changes and policies advocating the need to respect diversity and promote equality of person, gender, and inclusion (Race Relations [Amendment] Act, 2000; Department of Health, 2001; Disability Discrimination Act, 2005; Equality Act, 2006).

A priority therefore for forensic mental health nurses is a continuous increase in knowledge and awareness of the changes in diversity issues that are emerging in society and for people with learning disability, and an awareness of their personal hidden biases in how they work with marginalised groups in society and the need to focus on the person and to respect his/her personhood (Swinton and Boyd, 2000). The implication of this for nurses, and in particular for forensic mental health nurses working with people with learning disability, is to be aware of these changes and attempt to incorporate the positive values embedded in the various legislative changes and use them to demonstrate forensic mental health nurses' professionalism in helping to give a stronger voice to support people with a learning disability on issues of equality and diversity pertinent to their enjoyment of life.

Box 4.9: Cultural competence

Cultural awareness
  Self-awareness
  Culture identity
  Heritage adherence
  Ethno-centric

Cultural knowledge
  Health beliefs and behaviours
  Barriers to cultural sensitivity
  Ethno-history
  Stereotyping
  Sociological understanding
  Similarities and variations

Cultural competence
  Assessment skills
  Diagnostic skills
  Clinical skills
  Challenging prejudice
  Discrimination and inequalities

Cultural sensitivity
  Empathy
  Interpersonal communication skills
  Trust
  Acceptance
  Appropriateness
  Respect.
(From Papadopoulos et al, 2001)

In addition, understanding cultural differences and their impact on forensic service utilisation by people with learning disability from diverse cultural, ethnic and socioeconomic backgrounds is important if equality of access, involvement, opportunity, respecting and promoting ethical practice is to be the norm in service provision (Addo, 2006; Narayanasamy and White, 2005; Papadopoulos et al, 2001; Byrt et al, 2007). There is evidence that individuals and their families can experience what is described as double discrimination because of ethnic background and having a learning disability (Grant et al, 2005). This requires the cultural competence of individual forensic mental health nurses in how they relate and work humanely with people with learning disability. They need to develop a strong knowledge base and an understanding of the range of diversity issues that impact on this client group, and be able to challenge stereotypes, stigma, racism and inequalities that people with learning disability are confronted with (Fern, 1994b; Addo, 2001; Byrt et al, 2007). Cultural awareness is needed in order to understand and incorporate the practical demands and opportunities that the individual's diversity produces (Tasman, 2000; Addo, 2006; Byrt et al, 2007). This requires effective communication where mutual understanding is reached based on consideration of the range of perspectives that all stakeholders bring to the fore (see *Box 4.9*).

Forensic nurses' failure to embrace and work with equality and diversity in the context of health and social care delivery in a multi-diverse nation such as the UK can lead to increasing perceptions of inequalities, with people with learning disability feeling marginalised in their experience of care received. We must not forget that society and the laws of the land recognise that vulnerable people are part of society and need to be protected, to which end the law makes us aware of our professional roles, responsibilities and accountabilities in interacting and working with those defined as vulnerable (Gallop, 1998; Human Rights Act, 1998; Austin, 2001; Department of Health, 2001; Nursing and Midwifery Council, 2008; Disability Discriminatory Act, 2005; Scottish Executive 2001, 2006a).

Conclusion

In this chapter we have suggested that embracing equality and diversity is paramount for the well-being of people with learning disability and the advancement of society and forensic nursing practice. The key to making these two concepts a reality in service provision and for forensic mental health nurses working with learning disability clients, is by shared learning and partnership so that the issues that are important to clients can be listened to and acted upon. This in turn helps to raise our awareness of the diverse contributions that people with learning disability make to society. They face a challenging task in equity of access and involvement on different levels and areas. It is therefore essential that nurses and forensic mental health nurses in particular, learn from people with learning disabilities in order to understand better their needs, wishes and aspirations and be placed at the centre of the care equation. This requires channels of effective communication between all stakeholders.

As forensic nurses, we need to think creatively about issues of difference. It must be accepted that clients with a learning disability in a forensic setting are no less deserving of living a positive and enriching life. The social participation of people with learning disability in society needs to be encouraged through our work with them. Without this acceptance, then perceptions of inequalities by marginalised groups in society will continue to breed discontent and social ills.

A visionary role is important for forensic mental health nurses in explicating about how socio-political structures and cultural issues contribute to the plight of people living with learning disability and related issues. Forensic mental health nursing's vision for people with learning disability will be developed as we each speak out about the inequalities that people with learning disability in secure care environments experience, and about how it is best responded to and relieved, and about a future in forensic nursing work where no one is treated less favourably because of difference.Forensic mental health nurses have what it takes to lead the way in championing the equality and diversity agenda for all through the nature of our work.

References

Addo M (2000) The role of the forensic nurse in clinical supervision. In: Robinson D, Kettles A (ed) *Forensic Nursing and Multidisciplinary Care of the Mentally Disordered Offender* (Chapter 11) Jessica Kingsley: London

Addo M (2001) I am Mental Illness. *Contact: Disabling Society, Enabling Love*, **136**, 3–4

Addo M (2006) Cultural, spirituality and ethical issues in caring for clients with personality disorder. In: National Forensic Nurses' Research and Development Group: Woods P, Kettles AM, Byrt R, Addo M, Aiyegbusi A, Coffey M, Collins M, Doyle M, Garman G, Watson C (eds) *Forensic Mental Health Nursing: Interventions with People with Personality Disorder*. Quay Books: London

Aldridge J (2004) Learning disability nursing: A model for practice. In: Turnbull J (ed) *Learning Disability Nursing*. Blackwell Publishing: Oxford

Arnold E, Boggs KU (2003) *Interpersonal Relations: Professional Communication Skills for Nurses* (4th edn). Saunders: Philadelphia

Austin W (2001) Relational ethics in forensic psychiatric settings. *J Psychosoc Nurs* **39**(9) 12–17

Baillie D, Strachan V (2006) *An Essential Guide to Legal Issues in Scotland for Health Professionals*. NHS Grampian: Aberdeen

Bartlett C, Bunning K (1997) The importance of communication partnerships: A study to investigate the communicative exchanges between staff and adults with learning disabilities. *Brit J Learning Disabilities* **26** 148–153

Basil C (1992) Social interaction and learned helplessness in severely disabled children. *Augmentative and Alternative Communication* **8**(3) 188–199

Boyd MA (1998) Communication and therapeutic relationship. In: Boyd MA, Nihart M (eds) *Psychiatric Nursing: Contemporary Practice*. pp 247–248. Lippincott: Philadelphia

Brown M (2001) The equalizer. *Nursing Standard* **15**(16) 17

Brown M, Paterson D (2003) Addressing inequalities. In: Brown M (ed) *Learning Disability: A Handbook for Integrated Care*. APS Publishing: Wiltshire

Brown M, Rennie J (2003) From policy to practice. In: Brown M (ed) *Learning Disability: A Handbook for Integrated Care*. APS Publishing: Wiltshire

Burrow S (1993a) The treatment and security needs of special hospital patients: A nursing perspective. *J Adv Nurs* **18** 1267–1278

Burrow S (1993b) An outline of the forensic nurse's role. *Brit J Nurs* **2**(18) 899–904

Byrt R, Hardie T, Aigebusi A, Addo M (2007) Cultural and diversity issues. In: National Forensic Nurses' Research and Development Group: Kettles AM, Woods P, Byrt R, Addo M, Coffey M, Doyle M (eds) *Forensic Mental Health: Forensic Aspects of Acute Care*. Quay Books: London

Cox M (1994) A supervisor's view. In: Cordess C, Cox M (eds) *Forensic Psychotherapy: Crime Psychodynamics and the Offender Patient*. Jessica Kingsley: London

Curtice L (2003) Listening and including people with learning disabilities. In: Brown M (ed) *Learning Disability: A Handbook for Integrated Care*. APS Publishing: Wiltshire

Department of Health (1999) *National Service Framework for Mental Health*. HMSO: London

Department of Health (2001) *Valuing People: A New Strategy for Learning Disability for the*

21st Century. HMSO: London

Department of Health (2004) *Agenda for Change.* HMSO: London

Department of Health (2005) *Disability Discrimination Act.* HMSO: London

Department of Health (2006) *Equality Act.* HMSO: London

Fern P (1994a) Individual planning. In: Brown H, Benson S (ed) *A Practical Guide to Working with People with Learning Disabilities* (Chapter 4). Hawkers Publication: London

Fern P (1994b) Meeting the needs of Black people. In: Brown H, and Benson S (ed) *A Practical Guide to Working with People with Learning Disabilities* (Chapter 14). Hawkers Publication: London

Ferris-Taylor R (2003) Communication. In: Gates B (ed) *Learning Disabilities – Towards Inclusion.* Elsevier Science: Churchill Livingstone

Fitzsimmons J, Barr O (1997) A review of the reported attitudes of health and social care professionals towards people with learning disabilities. Implications for education and further research. *J Learning Disabilities for Nursing Health and Social Care* **1**(2) 57–64

Gallop R (1998) Abuse of power in the nurse client relationship. *Nursing Standard* **12**(37) 43–47

Grant G, Goward P, Richardson M, Ramcharan P (2005) *Learning Disability: A Life Cycle Approach to Valuing People.* Oxford University Press: London

Hammer R (2000) Caring in Forensic Nursing. *J Psychosoc Nursing* **38**(11) 18–24

Kettles A, Woods P, Collins M (2002) *Therapeutic Interventions for Forensic Mental Health Nurses.* Jessica Kingsley: London

Markova J, Jahoda A, Cattermole M, Woodward D (1992) Living in hospital and hostel: The pattern of interactions of people with learning disabilities. *J Intellectual Disability Research* 36 115–127

McCarthy J (1996) Choice dilemma: Who decides? *Practice Nursing* **7**(5) 17–18

McConkey R, Morris I, Purcell M (1999b) Communication between staff and adults with intellectual disabilities in naturally occurring settings. *J Intellectual Disability Research* **43** 194–205

McConkey R, Purcell M, Morris I (1999a) Staff perceptions of communication with a partner who is intellectually disabled. *J Applied Research in Intellectual Disabilities* **12** 204–210

Millan B (2001) *Report on the Review of the Mental Health (Scotland) Act 1984.* Scottish Executive: Edinburgh

Narayanasamy A, White E (2005) A review of transcultural nursing. *Nurse Education Today* **15** 102–111

National Health Service Quality Improvement Scotland (2006) *Promoting Access to Healthcare for People With a Learning Disability – A Guide for Frontline NHS Staff. Best Practice Statement.* NHS QIS: Edinburgh

Nursing and Midwifery Council (2001) *Supporting Nurses and Midwives Through Lifelong Learning.* NMC: London

Nursing and Midwifery Council (2008) *The Code: Standards of Conduct, Performance and Ethics for Nurses and Midwives.* NMC: London

Oxford University Press (1998) *The Oxford Popular Dictionary/Thesaurus.* Oxford University Press: Oxford

Papadopoulos I (2001) Anti-racism, multiculturalism and the third way. In: Baxter E (ed) *Managing Diversity and Inequality in Health Care.* Baiilliere Tindall, Royal College of Nursing: Edinburgh

Papadopoulos I, Tilki M, Lees S (2001) Culturally appropriate care should be at the heart of mental health services. *Openmind* **110** 20–21

Perske R (1987) The legacy of Marc Gold. In: McLoughlin C, Garner J, Callahan M (eds) *Getting Employed, Staying Employed: Job Development and Training for Persons With Severe Handicaps.* Paul H. Brookes: Baltimore

Randle A (2006) Communication and Adults with Learning Disabilities. In: Peate I, Fearns D (ed) *Caring for People with Learning Disabilities.* John Wiley: Chichester

Registered Nurses' Association of Ontario (2007) *Professionalism in Nursing.* Registered Nurses' Association of Ontario: Ontario Canada

Rogers C (1957) The necessary and sufficient conditions of therapeutic personality change. *Consulting Psychology* **5** 2–10

Royal College of Nursing (2006) *Meeting the Health Needs of People with a Learning Disability: Guidance for Nursing Staff.* Royal College of Nursing: London

Scottish Executive (2000) *The Same As You: A Review of Services For People With Learning Disability.* Scottish Executive: Edinburgh

Scottish Executive (2001) *Report on the Review of the Mental Health (Scotland) Act 1984.* Scottish Executive: Edinburgh

Scottish Executive (2002) *Promoting Health, Supporting Inclusion: The National Review of the Contribution of All Nurses and Midwives to the Care and Support of People With Learning Disabilities.* Scottish Executive: Edinburgh

Scottish Executive (2006a) *Rights, Relationship and Recovery. The National Review of Mental Health Nursing in Scotland.* Scottish Executive: Edinburgh

Scottish Executive (2006b) *The 10 Essential Shared Capabilities for Mental Health Practice.* National Health Service Education for Scotland: Edinburgh

Swinton J, Boyd J (2000) Autonomy and personhood: The forensic nurse as a moral agent. In: Robinson D, Kettles A (eds) *Forensic Nursing and Multidisciplinary Care of the Mentally Disordered Offender.* Jessica Kingsley: London

Tasman A (2000) Culture, spirituality and psychiatry. *Curr Opin Psychiatry* **13**(6) 533–534

Thompson N (2003) *Promoting Equality: Challenging Discrimination and Oppression* (2nd edn). Palgrave: Basingstoke

Tingle J (2002) An introduction to clinical negligence: Nurses and the law. *Brit J Nurs* **11**(15) 1033–1035

Tschudin V (1987) *Counselling Skills for Nurses* (2nd edn). Bailliere Tindall: London

Turnbull J (2004) *Learning Disability Nursing.* Blackwell Publishing: Oxford

United Kingdom Central Council (1999) *Fitness for Practice.* UKCC: London

United Nations (1975) *The Declaration on the Rights of Disabled Persons. General Assembly Resolution 3447 (XXX) of December 9.* UN: New York

Wolfensberger W (1975) *The Origin and Nature of Our Institutional Models.* Human Policy Press: New York

Wolfensberger W (1983) Social role valorisation: A proposed new term for the principle of normalization. *Mental Retardation* **21**(6) 234–239

CHAPTER 5

Power and participation in forensic services: An introduction

Richard Byrt

Introduction

Are empowerment and participation possible in secure hospitals and prisons? To what extent can forensic mental health nurses enable meaningful empowerment and participation? The next three chapters explore these questions. To avoid repetition, 'secure hospitals' will be used to include high secure hospitals, medium secure units and low secure units; and 'forensic services' to refer to both secure hospitals and prison health services.

The term 'patient' has been criticised because of its connotations with passivity, and with individuals following the advice of professional 'experts', instead of taking an active part in their care and treatment (Byrt and Dooher, 2003). Despite these negative connotations, the term 'forensic patient' will be used in the next three chapters to describe individuals who are (willing or unwilling) recipients of assessment, treatment, rehabilitation and recovery services in secure hospitals and prison health services. This is partly because, in the author's experience, most individuals, in secure hospitals at least, are referred to as 'patients'. In some ways, this may be a more honest term than 'client' or 'resident', which suggest that the individual is able to choose a service (Byrt and Dooher, 2003). However, some individuals understandably object to being placed, against their will, in a 'patient' role (Mason and Chandley, 1990; Mason and Mercer, 1998).

Power, empowerment and participation are complex, multi-dimensional concepts that are explored in the next three chapters, starting with a general overview.

Power

There is a vast literature on power, spanning at least three millennia, and encompassing ideas from philosophy, religion, sociology, politics and psychology (Westwood, 2002). Spiritual and other beliefs are often a source of empowerment to the individual (Narayanasamy, 2001). Interpersonal relationships and interactions in social groups and organisations are said to invariably involve power issues (Hinshelwood, 2001; Robb et al, 2004); and have inspired many literary works, films, television and other dramas (Foakes, 2003). For example, much of the plot of *One Flew Over the Cuckoo's Nest* involves the power struggles between Randle McMurphy (who is described as 'psychopathic' in the novel) and Nurse Ratched (Kesey, 1962).

In relation to health, most definitions of power refer to the following:

- The individual's belief that he/she has control over his/her life and health and other goals (Taylor, 2003; Tones and Green, 2004).
- The achievement of outcomes desired by the individual (Morgan, 1999; Westwood, 2002).
- 'The ability to make other people do what you want them to do' (Masterton and Maslin-Prothero, 1999: 212), often in relation to specific goals (Laverack, 2005). In the literature, *authority* refers to legitimate means to achieve this, e.g. through a formal role in an organisation. *Coercion* refers to the illegitimate use of power, e.g. through violence (Westwood, 2002; World Health Organisation, 2000).
- Having the means to influence others economically, politically and ideologically. Ideological power includes the successful imposition of beliefs, values and ways of seeing everyday reality. It also involves possessing what others see as 'expert' knowledge and language (Westwood, 2002).
- Having status or social position in relation to social class, gender, ethnic group, sexual orientation, age, health and abilities that are valued in society (Westwood, 2002).

Each of these aspects of power is relevant to forensic patients and other stakeholders (i.e. people with a stake or interest in forensic services, Byrt and James, 2007). It can be argued that forensic patients have limited power in relation to the areas considered above. For example, most of these individuals appear to have limited control over their lives or health, particularly on admission to secure hospitals or prisons (Byrt with James, 2007). Almost all have been compulsorily admitted, and have lost considerable freedoms. Many have different goals to those seen as desirable by staff (Mason and Chandley, 1990) and are likely to experience difficulties in influencing the decisions of people in positions of power, for example, the Home Office and Mental Health Review Tribunals (Kenny, 2005; Stern, 2006). The versions of reality of those in power appear to be given more credence than those of patients (Foucault, 1991; Fox, 1999). An example of ideological power, in relation to this, would be a professional group in a secure hospital who see themselves as the only people holding the sole 'correct' version of the truth related to patients' illness, treatment and risk – with patients, other professionals, the public and politicians all believing this version of the 'truth', without question. Some critics have argued that forensic psychiatrists have occupied this position of ideological power, and that the views of patients and others have been marginalised and seen as unimportant (Foucault, 1991; Szasz, 2000).

In addition, forensic patients experience a lack of power because of social exclusion. This is related to their often disadvantaged backgrounds, their role as 'mental health patient' and 'offender' and membership of other discriminated groups (Bartlett, 2004; Byrt et al, 2007).

Empowerment

Empowerment can be defined as increases in the amount of power possessed by an individual or group of people, usually with the intention that this will result in benefits to themselves and/or other people. In some instances, empowerment involves transferring power from other individuals or groups (Byrt and Dooher, 2002; Dooher and Byrt, 2005). Following a detailed review of the literature, Byrt and Dooher (2002: 19) concluded that 'empowerment involves increases or transfers of power involving four dimensions':

- 'Individual: the individual service user's/carer's feelings of power.' Individual empowerment relates to a wide range of needs. Empowerment at an individual level is related to the diversity and uniqueness of each individual.
- 'Service-initiated.' In this dimension of empowerment, 'professionals and managers enable service users and carers to gain and/or share power'.
- 'Service change. The successful bringing about of change desired by service users and carers.'
- The 'social inclusion and social change' dimension goes beyond professional interventions and services, and involves:
    'Access to the quality of life and life opportunities of most people.
    'Elimination of discrimination, stigmatisation and social exclusion.
    'The gaining of political power.'
        (Byrt and Dooher, 2002:19; Dooher and Byrt, 2005:115)

Individual needs and empowerment

Individual empowerment (or its lack) can involve a wide range of individuals' needs (see *Figure 5.1*). For example, an individual who is a patient in a secure hospital, although experiencing disempowerment in relation to loss of freedom and other factors, could be empowered in relation to the needs listed below. Arguably, the meeting of these needs may lead to increased empowerment (Kettles et al, 2007). However, conflict theorists would question this, given that patients cannot usually choose whether they are admitted to secure hospitals (Szasz, 2000).

- *Safety needs.* Care in an environment to ensure the individual's physical and psychological safety, including preventing him/her from harming others or being bullied by other patients (Bowers et al, 1999).
- *Physical needs.* Access to fresh air, exercise and primary and other health care services to ensure optimum physical health (Birmingham et al, 2005).
- *Psychological needs.* Meeting of essential psychological needs: e.g. for respect, self-esteem, achievement (Kettles et al, 2007).
- *Relationship and psychosexual needs.* This includes enabling the individual to maintain relationships important to him/her, where possible; express his/her identity as a man or a woman; and maintain as much privacy as possible (Aiyegbusi and Byrt, 2006).
- *Spiritual needs.* Enabling the individual to have or maintain hope, meaning and purpose – and to practise any religious or other beliefs important to him/her, e.g. provision of space for quiet, meditation or prayer (Addo, 2006).
- *Cultural needs.* Meeting the individual's needs related to his/her culture (Byrt et al, 2007).
- *Diversity needs.* Meeting the individual's needs related to his/her ethnic group, gender, age, disability, sexual orientation and gender identity (Byrt and Hardie, 2007).
- *Social needs.* Opportunities to socialise with others and enjoy social and recreational events (Barker and Buchanan-Barker, 2005).
- *Vocational needs.* Opportunities for fulfilling, meaningful activities and eventual vocational training (Barker and Buchanan-Barker, 2005).
- *Economic needs.* Ensuring that the individual is enabled to access monies to which he/she is entitled (Barker and Buchanan-Barker, 2005).
- *Legal and advocacy needs.* Access to legal and other advocates independent of the system, who can enable the individual to exercise his/her rights (Kenny, 2005).

Components of psychological empowerment

For some individuals, important aspects of empowerment include increases in self-esteem and *self-efficacy*. The latter term 'refers to an individual's belief that he/she is able to achieve specific goals' (Byrt and Dooher, 2003: 9, citing Tones and Green, 2002). For some forensic patients, violent

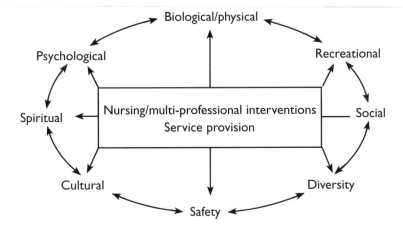

Figure 5.1: Aspects of health need relevant to individual empowerment of clients.

offending has been a source of self-esteem and self-efficacy and the aim of nursing interventions and treatment may be to enable the individual to find other sources of these aspects of empowerment.

Increased internal locus of control can also be seen as a component of psychological empowerment. Individuals with an internal locus of control see themselves as feeling relatively in control and responsible for achieving their health goals or reduction in offending behaviours. External locus of control involves beliefs that, for example, professional 'experts' are mostly responsible for the individual's health; or that other people have some responsibility for the individual's offending behaviours (McGuire, 2002). Examples of the latter include: 'There's no reason why I shouldn't steal from supermarkets. They can afford it with the excessive profits they make.'

For some individuals, important components of psychological empowerment include increased pride in aspects of identity. This may be achieved by 'coming out': declaring one's membership of a minority group (e.g. 'forensic patient'), and challenging stigmatisation in wider society (Barnes and Bowl, 2001). Pride in identity, often shared with other members of the group, involves raised consciousness and awareness of oppression and, for some people, determination to challenge discrimination and social exclusion (Byrt and Dooher, 2002).

Components of 'service-initiated' and 'service change' dimensions of empowerment

Components of 'service-initiated' (Byrt and Dooher, 2002:24) empowerment are concerned specifically with managers and professionals increasing patients' power by effecting improvements in their care and treatment and the service that they receive. These components include opportunities to put forward ideas and concerns and being given information and opportunities for consultation. Professional attitudes, 'communication and relationships', organisational culture and therapeutic models and frameworks are also included as components of the service-initiated component of Byrt and Dooher's (2002) model, although these items might more appropriately be viewed as facilitators of empowerment (Finfgeld, 2004).

'Service change' (Byrt and Dooher, 2002:24) components include those related to the achievement of improvements that patients and carers perceive to be of benefit to them, and include 'choice, availability and accessibility of services, autonomy…complaints and other systems, rights/advocacy' (Dooher and Byrt, 2005: 115). The service-initiated and service change dimensions of empowerment will be considered further in *Chapter 7*, in relation to patient satisfaction surveys in forensic services.

The 'social inclusion and social change' dimension of empowerment

This dimension of empowerment is concerned with the achievement of changes in society related to decreases in negative attitudes, discrimination and social exclusion, so that all members of stigmatised groups (including people who are, or have been, 'forensic patients') have the same life opportunities as others – in relation, for example, to accommodation, education, employment, and financial benefit (Repper and Perkins, 2003; Tew, 2005). This dimension of empowerment is also relevant to notions of *recovery*, with an emphasis on individuals making decisions about their lives and the goals that are important to them (Repper and Perkins, 2003; Tew, 2005).

The relationship of individual power with the collective power of communities to bring about social change has been described (Laverack, 2004; Tones and Green, 2004). For example, Thompson (2003: 17) outlines the links between 'personal', 'cultural' and 'structural' power, the latter involving 'social, economic and political aspects'.

Some 'opposites' of empowerment

The term *powerlessness* often refers to individuals' feelings and experience that they have little or no power. This concept is allied to *learned helplessness*, a concept in psychology (Smith et al, 2003), in which individuals have discovered, from personal experience, that their actions have no influence on others who have more power (Seligman, 1975). An example would be a patient ('Mr Roy Red': a pseudonym) who feels unable to trust nurses because of feelings of helplessness related to people whom he sees as having power over him. Roy experienced helplessness as a child in relation to parents and other adults who abused him, and later, abuse from other prisoners. Whether Roy's feelings of helplessness and distrust are compounded or alleviated following his admission to a forensic service, may depend largely on the extent that nurses are aware, through thorough assessment, of his helplessness and enable Roy to feel more empowered. Kirby and Cross (2002) suggest that this could be achieved partly through demonstrating respect, establishing trust and a therapeutic alliance; and being prepared to listen to, and empathise with the individual patient's perspectives and experiences. These goals might be achieved 'through mutual exploration of the patient's understanding and experience' (Kirby and Cross, 2002: 96).

The term *disempowerment* also refers to an absence of power, but is used in the literature to describe not only individuals' feelings but also powerlessness in relation to having no control or influence over what happens to them (Dooher and Byrt, 2005), for example, in relation to nursing interventions, treatment and restrictions related to safety.

Participation

The achievement or gaining of power sometimes involves participation. Within health services, participation has been defined as:

> *The involvement of service users or carers in responsibility and/or decision making, which has an intended [and positive] impact on services and/or policies which affect the individual participant and/or other service users/carers.*
>
> (Byrt and Dooher, 2002:29).

From an analysis of the concept, based on various research methods, including a literature review, Byrt (1994) concluded that the concept consists of a number of dimensions, including *degree* and *level* (see *Figure 5.2*). For example, the participation of patients in a secure hospital could, in relation to degree, start with involvement in decision making concerning their care, and progress to consultation with professionals, and representation of patients from each ward in a patients' forum in which participants discuss concerns with managers. On leaving the secure hospital, these individuals might play an 'equal participation' role in a voluntary organisation, such as Women in Secure Hospitals (WISH) (2008) or the Matthew Trust (2008) concerned with secure hospital rights, or have 'total control' in its running. In addition, their participation in the voluntary organisation could be at a number of levels: from individual rights to central Government or global levels (Byrt, 2001).

	A Explanation	B Consultation	C Direct representation	D Equal participation	E Total control
6. Global (e.g. membership of a worlwide organisation)					
5. Central Government					
4. Region or health district					
3. Trust					
2. Small group or organisation					
1. Individual					

←——————— Degree of client participation or empowerment ——————→

Figure 5.2: Degrees and levels of participation. Reproduced from Byrt (2001) with kind permission of Quay Books, Mark Allen Publishing Ltd.

Examples of participation in forensic services

Examples of participation in forensic services include the following:

- The individual's active involvement in his/her assessment, care and treatment (Byrt et al, 2005).
- In some settings (e.g. those using cognitive-behavioural therapy and therapeutic community principles) contributing to other patients' care, e.g. through the sharing of experiences (Byrt, 2006; Byrt et al, 2005).
- Independent advocacy services concerned with patients' rights, for example, as detained patients (Kenny, 2005).
- Participation in patients' forums and patients' councils to influence the service provided, e.g. by voicing views, concerns and complaints to advocates and/or managers, sometimes on behalf of other patients. Garman et al (2003) outline such a service in a medium secure unit.
- Participation in decisions about the management of the service, as in the Van der Hoeven Clinic, a secure hospital in Utrecht (Van Marle, 2002).
- Other forums to enable the expression of views, e.g. patient satisfaction surveys (see *Chapter 7*) and ward community meetings (Byrt, 2006).
- Any or all stages of research projects, including projects run solely by present or former patients (Spiers et al, 2005; Halsall, 2006).
- Education of professionals and students. For example, patients on Cannock ward at Arnold Lodge medium secure unit (see *Chapters 11* and *12*), provide professionals and student nurses with valuable teaching on problem solving techniques, including anger management.

Stages of participation

Participation can occur at various stages of a project. For example, several authors have outlined the participation of patients in secure hospitals in all stages of research projects: from formulation of initial research topics to data analysis and writing and presentation of findings (Faulkner and Morris, 2003; Spiers et al, 2005; Halsall, 2006).

However, the success of many projects to increase empowerment and participation in secure hospitals and prisons appears to depend on the initial sanction of people in positions of power before patients are involved. For example, despite what some critics have seen as an increasingly draconian penal policy (Stern, 2006), Grendon Prison has continued as a prison with modified therapeutic community wings, with relatively democratic principles. Prisoners participate in some areas of decision making, with free expression of problems and feelings and opportunities to try out more rewarding roles, relationships and behaviours (Rawlings, 1998). The literature on Grendon

Prison suggests that the therapeutic community wings have survived, as examples of inmate participation, partly because staff have been able to compromise and conform with some aspects of organisational power as manifested, for example, in expectations of conformity with aspects of prison regime. However, this wider power is said to interfere with optimum therapeutic functioning of the therapeutic communities (Rawlings, 1998). Another possible reason for the latter's continued survival is that it has been shown to work, with reductions of violent offending and institutional disturbances, such as riots (Lees et al, 2004). Finally, and perhaps most importantly, Grendon Prison has met with the publicly stated approval of at least one Home Secretary (BBC News, 1999).

Solanki and Byrt (2003) considered the gains in empowerment (e.g. from self-expression) in a creative writing project at Arnold Lodge medium secure unit. The authors outlined the need to ensure the success of the project before it commenced. This appeared to necessitate initial consultation with the unit's managers and senior staff; and to ensure that funding for the project was acquired before patients were consulted or otherwise enabled to participate if they wished. Critics could argue that meaningful and complete participation of patients necessitated their involvement from the outset. However, Solanki and Byrt (2003) argue that any level of patient participation would have been impossible if, for example, consultant psychiatrists and senior managers had not agreed with the scope and aims of the creative writing.

Problems with the concepts of empowerment and participation

One problem with the concepts of both empowerment and participation is that they have often uncritically been seen as a 'good thing', but with insufficient consideration of *practical ways that ideas can be implemented*, in order, for example, to benefit forensic patients and their informal carers. This relates to the lack of clarity about the meaning of the concepts; and a lack of awareness of their complexity, including their various dimensions. Successful implementation appears to depend partly on awareness of specific goals and the benefits and problems related to empowerment and participation (Dooher and Byrt, 2003; Dooher and Byrt, 2005).

The NHS Act, 2006, based on previous policy initiatives, legislates specific ways that health service bodies are required to facilitate participation in forensic and other health services. This includes the setting up of local Patients' Forums; a Commission for Patient and Public Involvement, partly to oversee patient and public participation at local level; and a Patient Information Advisory Group to advise on proposed future health service legislation (HM Government, 2006). Policy initiatives include Patient

Advice and Liaison Forums in each NHS Trust (Department of Health, 2000) and Healthcare Commission (2008) requirements for national patient satisfaction surveys in community mental health and other services.

Cultural and other perspectives

Writing on empowerment has been criticised for being excessively influenced by beliefs from Western societies concerning both the salience to individuals of being empowered and assumptions that certain components are necessarily experienced as 'empowering' by people of non-Western cultures (Mok, 2001). Laverack (2004) comments that some writers on empowerment insufficiently consider the extent that some individuals wish to subsume their own wishes for power to that of their families or communities.

Cultural and other perspectives need to be borne in mind when considering the empowerment and participation of each patient. Also important are research findings that individuals vary considerably in their wish to participate or gain power (Collins et al, 2007). There is also variation in the extent that 'patients' in secure hospitals perceive themselves as being in a 'sick role' or wish to receive, let alone participate in, nursing interventions and treatment, which may be seen as imposed and unwanted (Mason and Chandley, 1990). Empowerment which is imposed by the nurse is likely to be seen as disempowering (Byrt and Dooher, 2003).

Rhetoric about empowerment and participation has been criticised for not actually resulting in increases in power, including changes being made or action taken, in relation to consequences desired by patients and/or their informal carers. This situation has been described as 'pseudo-empowerment' or 'pseudo-participation' (Arnstein, 1969): 'The patient, and less obviously, family...rarely has any power base, despite all the urging to "empowerment"' (Barker, 2000: 4–5). Several authors have commented that people in positions of power will only allow 'empowerment' or 'participation' if patients or carers agree with, and do not oppose them (Coleman, 2000; Anonymous, 2003). The former author points out that nothing has changed in response to patients' views since the late 17th century, when individuals incarcerated in Bethlem Hospital 'complained about physical restraints and treatments...their environment and poor food' (Coleman, 2000: 60), just as many patients do today.

Stakeholders in secure hospitals and prison health services

Who should be empowered and have the opportunity to participate in relation to secure hospitals and prison health services? Much of the relevant literature on health services in general includes (often unquestioning) assumptions that clients and their carers at home should be the main stakeholders who are empowered or have opportunities to participate (Byrt and Dooher, 2003; Laverack, 2005; Tones and Green, 2004). However, all health services have a wide range of stakeholders, including taxpayers and other members of the public, politicians, professionals and other employees, managers, researchers, investors in private services and individuals making profits from pharmaceutical and other health-related companies (Hogg, 1999). Health services in general attract considerable political and media interest (Phillips, 2003). However, secure hospital and prison health services have additional stakeholders (Byrt with James, 2007: 38). These include, importantly, the victims of offences; the partners, relatives and friends of both victims and perpetrators; and voluntary organisations, some of whom act as pressure groups representing their interests (Treatment Advocacy Center, 2008; Zito Trust, 2008). The Home Office, Ministry of Justice and other Government departments concerned with crime are important stakeholders, as are groups representing patients' rights and interests. The latter include the Matthew Trust (2008) and Women in Secure Hospitals (WISH) (2008). The gaze of the media is particularly focused on secure hospitals, especially if something goes wrong (Phillips, 2003). Other stakeholders include the judiciary, politicians, the police, taxpayers and other members of the public. There is a wide and often contradictory range of views about what should happen to people who have offended, with disagreement over the roles of punishment, revenge, retribution, risk reduction, remorse, reparation, treatment, rehabilitation, forgiveness and upholding the rights of prisoners/patients (Prins, 2005).

The various stakeholders in secure hospitals and prison health services may wish to have power in influencing these organisations' specific goals. Even if managers and professionals perceive patients' needs, rights and empowerment as paramount, the literature (and the author's experience) suggest that it is difficult (some would say impossible) to ignore the power of other stakeholders. In some instances, the latter's needs and rights coincide with, and complement, those of patients. In other instances, they conflict (Treatment Advocacy Center, 2007).

'Victims' and 'offenders'

Much forensic nursing (using this term in a generic sense) is concerned with victims of offending: for example, the work of Sexual Assault Nurse Examiners, particularly in the USA (Burgess, 2002; Ledray, 2005). It is suggested that forensic mental health nurses and forensic nurses working with victims can learn a great deal from each other. Overlapping roles of 'victim' and 'perpetrator' are reflected in research findings that many people who offend have, themselves, been victims of crime (Prins, 2005). This is contrary to images conveyed in some of the media, which suggest a sharp polarisation between 'innocent' victims and 'bad' (and/or 'mad') perpetrators (Morris, 2006). Factors involved in the causation of crime are complex and multifactorial, but studies have found that some violent offenders have, themselves, been victims, from childhood, of violent physical, sexual and emotional abuse within their families (Adshead, 1997; Gilligan, 2001; Barker, 2005):

> *Helplessness and victim status [involve]...a real power imbalance... Aggressors select victims who are vulnerable, against whom they can win... The hurt self must not be allowed to die or be repressed; there must be pity for one's own distress, or there will be no pity for the distress of others*
> (Adshead, 1997: 121. Present author's emphasis)

Shared trauma from homicides

Various accounts suggest that serious trauma results from the commission of homicide by an individual diagnosed with mental illness or personality disorder. This trauma is often experienced both by people close to the victim and significant others of the perpetrator. In one UK study, relatives constituted 64% of people killed by individuals with mental health problems (MacInnes, 2000, cited in Lester and Glasby, 2006).

Partners, relatives and friends of both victims and perpetrators can be seen as significant stakeholders in forensic services in view of their experiences. Accounts by these people can enable us to reflect on the roles of forensic mental health nurses in relation to empowerment. For example, a number of issues concerning power are especially relevant in the extract from Delfin, 2003 in *Box 5.1*. These include:

Box 5.1: 'Parents of murdered boy, 11, still struggling with their grief'

'Sometimes, it seems like it just happened yesterday...I don't see how it can ever get better, and I'm not sure that it should. Our son is not here with us any more...'

...A mentally ill man whom family members say refused treatment, is awaiting trial...If convicted of the boy's murder, he could be sentenced to death.

Cathy Katsnelson said overwhelming community support has kept her going. However, she said, everyday things...hit her hard.

'I see the school bus...and it's obvious he's missing', she said. '...A huge part of our family is missing.'

'Sometimes it's hard to open your eyes in the morning', her husband said.

(From Delfin, 2003)

- The powerless of the boy who was killed, and of his parents, both in being able to prevent his death and, perhaps, in relation to their grief.
- Possible powerlessness of the man with mental illness. Was his action constrained by symptoms of mental illness, over which his control was limited? To what extent should he be seen as responsible for his behaviour (Prins, 2005)?
- Possible empowerment to Mr and Ms Katsnelson from the 'community support', and to members of the community from providing this (Laverack, 2005; Tones and Green, 2004).
- The powerlessness of the man who killed the boy, in the face of a death sentence. (However, the extent of his powerlessness would probably be related to spiritual and cultural factors: Addo, 2006).
- Finally, does having the death penalty empower or disempower citizens of the State in which it is enacted? (Gilligan, 2001)

Some family members have felt powerless because they have not been able to get help at times of crisis, including violent offending (Fisher, 2003; McKeown and McCann, 2000; Treatment Advocacy Center, 2007). Adshead (1997) refers to the 'power imbalance', often against the family member/partner in such situations:

Some relatives and partners have felt powerless in the face of their loved one's admission to secure and other hospitals; and have not been given information to alleviate powerlessness. An example is given in *Box 5.2*.

Box 5.2: Afraid to visit

When the author started work as a Charge Nurse in a 'rehabilitation ward', earlier in his career, he found that many clients had few or no visitors. Like many present-day patients in secure hospitals and prisons, some of the clients had been inpatients for many years, and had lost contact with family, former partners and friends. A few clients, on being asked, said they would like help with writing to people they had been close to in the past.

A day or two after they had received a letter from 'Mark' (a pseudonym), his family arrived on the ward to see him. They had last visited Mark several years ago, soon after he was admitted to the hospital. Members of Mark's family had felt very disempowered. They said they had lost contact with Mark because they had been afraid of his frightening, and apparently inexplicable behaviour.

'No one explained to us what was wrong', they said. 'We had no information, and the staff just didn't welcome us on the ward.' Over cups of tea, both Mark, and (with Mark's agreement) the author, explained that they were very welcome to visit, and to receive information about Mark's illness, his gradual recovery and progress, and to be involved in his rehabilitation.

However, the literature includes examples of forensic mental health professionals empowering patients' relatives and partners by, for example, considering their perspectives and enabling them effectively to reduce stress related to the individual's offending and symptoms of mental illness (McKeown and McCann, 2000; Cross and Kirby, 2002). At the Van der Hoeven Clinic, Utrecht, family meetings are held from an early stage following the patient's admission, with all the significant individuals in his or her life being invited to attend; and a recognition that these people play an important role in the patient's recovery and subsequent life (Van Marle, 2002). The provision of support to families in both community and inpatient forensic settings in the UK has also been documented, as has the recognition of the expertise of relatives and partners (Edment, 2002; McKeown and McCann, 2000). This work with families is relevant to some components of empowerment which have been identified in the literature, including 'voice': having a say in areas of importance to the individual; being consulted; seeing carers as partners with at least equal expertise; and enabling them to develop coping strategies which increase self-efficacy (Dooher and Byrt, 2005).

Working with the media and the public

Phillips (2003) suggests that working with the media can be a source of empowerment to forensic patients and nurses. This may include nurses' acceptance of the right of the media to criticise forensic mental health services and nursing; and where possible, see the media as a 'critical friend' whose views may sometimes inform their work. Forensic nurses may also be able to use the media for public education and information and to explain to the public, as stakeholders, the goals of nursing and services (MacDonald and Cank, 2000; Phillips, 2003). A pioneer of this approach was Dr John Connolly who invited Charles Dickens and another journalist to *Twelfth Night* celebrations at Hanwell Asylum, thus bringing the work of this organisation to a wide audience (Dickens and Wills, 1969 cited in Phillips, 2003).

More recently, one medium secure unit received a very bad press following an official local inquiry which reported various problems. Following this, a newly appointed manager initiated work that recognised the importance of the participation of not only patients, but also local residents and the local media as stakeholders. Managers met regularly with local residents, listened to their views and concerns and invited them to visit the unit. Improved liaison was developed with the local MP and county constabulary. Young people living nearby were invited to use the unit's sporting facilities when these were not in use by patients. A local newspaper and radio station were used to convey non-confidential information about the medium secure unit, partly in an attempt to reduce the mystique surrounding the service (MacDonald and Cank, 2000). These efforts are reminiscent of Citizens' Advisory Panels: bodies of local people throughout Canada, who participate in decisions about the running of prisons in their neighbourhoods (Correctional Services Canada: Citizens' Advisory Committees, 2007).

Conclusion

This chapter has reviewed theories of power and the nature and components of empowerment and participation in relation to forensic settings. Some examples of participation in secure hospitals and prisons were given, followed by a consideration of various stakeholders: people and organisations who have an interest in forensic services. These include not only patients but also victims of offences, the significant others of both victims and patients, the media and members of the public, including those living near forensic services.

The next chapter reviews specific aspects of power and participation in secure hospitals and prison health services.

References

Addo M (2006) Cultural, spirituality and ethical issues in caring for clients with personality disorder. In: National Forensic Nurses' Research and Development Group: Woods, P, Kettles AM, Byrt R, Addo M, Aiyegbusi A, Coffey M, Collins M, Doyle M, Garman G, Watson C (eds) *Forensic Mental Health Nursing: Interventions with People with Personality Disorder*. Quay Books: London

Adshead A (1997) The challenge of the victim. In: Van Marle H (ed) *Challenges in Forensic Psychotherapy*. Jessica Kingsley: London

Aiyegbusi A, Byrt R (2006) Gender and sexuality issues. In: National Forensic Nurses' Research and Development Group: Woods P, Kettles AM, Byrt R, Addo M, Aiyegbusi A, Coffey M, Collins M, Doyle M, Garman G, Watson C (eds) *Forensic Mental Health Nursing: Interventions with People with Personality Disorder*. Quay Books: London

Anonymous (2003) Drumming on the sidelines: A user experience of involvement in local strategic planning. In: Dooher J, Byrt R (eds) *Empowerment and the Health Service User*. Quay Books: Dinton, Salisbury

Arnstein SR (1969) A ladder of citizen participation. *J Amer Institute of Planners* **35**(4) 216–224

Barker GT (2005) *Dying to be Men: Masculinity and Social Exclusion*. Routledge, Taylor and Francis Group: London

Barker P (2000) The construction of mind and madness: From Leonardo to the Hearing Voices Network. In: Barker P, Stevenson C (eds) *The Construction of Power and Authority in Psychiatry*. Butterworth Heinemann: Oxford

Barker P, Buchanan-Barker P (2005) *The Tidal Model: A Guide for Mental Health Professionals*. Brunner-Routledge/Taylor and Francis Group: Hove

Barnes M, Bowl R (2001) *Taking Over the Asylum: Empowerment and Mental Health*. Palgrave: Basingstoke

Bartlett A (2004) Fashions in Psychiatric Care: Implications for Sense of Self. In: Crisp A. H (ed) *Every Family in the Land: Understanding Prejudice and Discrimination Against People with Mental Illness* (Chapter 49) Royal Society of Medicine Press: London

BBC (1999) *Health. A Therapeutic Approach to Crime.* Available from: http://news.bbc. co.uk/1/hi/health/279972.stm [Accessed 4 September, 2007]

Birmingham L, Peckham C, Baxter V (2005) Specific Joint Working II: The Ideal and Reality of Multidisciplinary Working in Prisons. In: Wix S, Humphreys M (eds) *Multidisciplinary Working in Forensic Mental Health Care.* Elsevier: Edinburgh

Bowers L, Jarrett M, Clark N (1999) Absconding. Part 1. Why patients leave. *J Psychiatr Ment Health Nurs* **6**(3): 199–205

Burgess A (2002) *Violence Through a Forensic Lens* (2nd edn) King of Prussia, PA: Nursing Spectrum

Byrt R (1994) *Consumer Participation in a Voluntary Organisation for Mental Health.* Unpublished PhD Thesis. Loughborough University, Loughborough

Byrt R (2001) Power, influence and control in practice development. In: Clark A, Dooher J, Fowler J (ed) *The Handbook of Practice Development.* Quay Books: Dinton, Salisbury

Byrt R (2006) Nursing Interventions in Therapeutic Communities. In: National Forensic Nurses' Research and Development Group: Woods P, Kettles AM, Byrt R, Addo M, Aiyegbusi A, Coffey M, Collins M, Doyle M, Garman G, Watson C (eds) *Forensic Mental Health Nursing: Interventions with People with Personality Disorder.* Quay Books: London

Byrt R, Aigebusi A, Hardie T, Addo M (2007) Cultural and diversity issues. In: National Forensic Nurses' Research and Development Group: Kettles AM, Woods P, Byrt R, Addo M, Coffey M, Doyle M (eds) *Forensic Mental Health: Forensic Aspects of Acute Care.* Quay Books: London

Byrt R, Dooher J (2002) Empowerment and Participation: Definitions, Meanings and Models. In: Dooher J, Byrt R (eds) *Empowerment and Participation: Power, Influence and Control in Contemporary Healthcare* (Chapter 2) Quay Books: Dinton, Salisbury

Byrt R, Dooher J (2003) Service users and carers and their desire for empowerment and participation. In: Dooher J, Byrt R (eds) *Empowerment and the Health Service User* Quay Books: Dinton, Salisbury

Byrt R, Hardie T (2007) Cultural sensitivity and cultural competence. In: National Forensic Nurses' Research and Development Group: Kettles AM, Woods P, Byrt R, Addo M, Coffey M, Doyle M (eds) *Forensic Mental Health: Forensic Aspects of Acute Care.* Quay Books: London

Byrt R, James L (2007) Towards therapeutic environments: Challenges and problems. In: National Forensic Nurses' Research and Development Group: Kettles AM, Woods P, Byrt R, Addo M, Coffey M, Doyle M (eds) *Forensic Mental Health: Forensic Aspects of Acute Care.* Quay Books: London

Byrt R, Wray C, 'Tom' (2005) Towards hope and inclusion: Nursing interventions in a medium secure service for men with 'personality disorders'. *Ment Health Pract* **8**(8) 38–43

Coleman R (2000) The politics of the illness. In: Barker P, Stevenson C (eds) T*he Construction of Power and Authority in Psychiatry.* Butterworth Heinemann: Oxford

Collins S, Britten N, Ruusuvuori J, Thompson A (eds) (2007) *Patient Participation in Health Care Consultations. Qualitative Perspectives.* McGraw Hill, Open University

Press: Maidenhead

Correctional Service of Canada: Citizens' Advisory Committeees (2007) *Mission of the Citizens' Advisory Committees.* Available from: www.abcgta.ca/docs/csc-citizens.doc [Accessed 5 November 2007]

Cross D, Kirby SD (2002) Using psychosocial interventions within an integrated psychological approach in forensic mental health and social care. In: Kettles AM, Woods P, Collins M (eds) *Therapeutic Interventions for Mental Health Nurses.* Jessica Kingsley: London

Delfin D (2003) *Parents of murdered boy, 11, still struggling with their grief. Burlington County Times.* Available from: http://www.psychlaws.org/GeneralResources/article166. htm [Accessed 17 July 2007]

Department of Health (2000) *The NHS Plan: A Time for Investment, A Plan for Reform.* Department of Health: London

Dickens C, Wills WH (1969) A curious dance round a curious tree. In: Stone H (ed) *The Uncollected Writings of Charles Dickens. Household Words, 1850–1859*, Volume 2. Allen Lane/Penguin Books: London

Dooher J, Byrt R (2003) Conclusions. In: Dooher J, Byrt R (eds) *Empowerment and the Health Service User.* Quay Books: Dinton, Salisbury

Dooher J, Byrt R (2005) A Critical Examination of the Concept of Empowerment. In: Cutcliffe JR, McKenna H (eds) T*he Essential Concepts of Nursing. Building Blocks for Practice.* Elsevier, Churchill Livingstone: Edinburgh

Edment H (2002) Nursing interventions and future directions in community care for mentally disordered offenders. In: Kettles AM, Woods, P, Collins M (eds) *Therapeutic Interventions for Mental Health Nurses.* Jessica Kingsley: London

Faulkner A, Morris B (2003) *Expert Paper: User Involvement in Forensic Mental Health Research and Development.* National Forensic Mental Health Research and Development Programme: Liverpool

Finfgeld DL (2004) Empowerment of individuals with enduring mental health problems. Results from concept analyses and qualitative investigations. *Adv Nursing Sci* **27**(1) 44–52

Fisher J (2003) Participation and empowerment of users and carers in mental health services. In: Dooher J, Byrt R (eds) *Empowerment and the Health Service User.* Quay Books: Dinton, Salisbury

Foakes RA (2003) Shakespeare and Violence. Cambridge University Press: Cambridge

Foucault M (1991) *Discipline and Punish. The Birth of the Prison.* Translated from the French by Alan Sheridan. Penguin Books: Harmondsworth

Fox KJ (1999) Changing violent minds: Discursive correction and resistance in the cognitive treatment of violent offenders in prison. *Social Problems* **46**(1) 88–103

Garman G, Kelly R, Waldron S (2003) Setting up a successful patients' council. *Ment Health Pract* **6**(7) 20–22

Gilligan J (2001) *Preventing Violence.* Thames and Hudson: London

Halsall K (2006) *Forensic Users Research Project.* Booklet: London

Healthcare Commission (2008) From: www.healthcarecommission.org.uk/ [Accessed 30 August 2008]

Hinshelwood RD (2001) *Thinking about Institutions. Milieux and Madness.* Jessica

Kingsley: London

HM Government (2006) *The NHS Act, 2006*. The Stationery Office: London

Hogg C (1999) *Patients, Power and Politics. From Patients to Citizens*. Sage Publications: London

Kenny PJ (2005) The place of a legal representative or advocate working for their client. In: Wix S, Humphreys M (eds) *Multidisciplinary Working in Forensic Mental Health Care*. Elsevier: Edinburgh.

Kesey K (1962) *One Flew Over the Cuckoo's Nest*. Methuen: London

Kettles AM, Byrt R, Woods P (2007) Introduction. In: National Forensic Nurses' Research and Development Group: Kettles AM, Woods P, Byrt R, Addo M, Coffey M, Doyle M (eds) *Forensic Mental Health: Forensic Aspects of Acute Care*. Quay Books: London.

Kirby SD, Cross D (2002) Socially constructed narrative interventions. A foundation for therapeutic alliances. In: Kettles AM, Woods P, Collins M (eds) *Therapeutic Interventions for Mental Health Nurses*. Jessica Kingsley: London

Laverack G (2004) *Health Promotion Practice. Power and Empowerment*. Sage Publications: London

Laverack G (2005) *Public Health. Power, Empowerment and Professional Practice*. Palgrave Macmillan: Basingstoke

Ledray LE (2005) Sexual assault. In: Lynch VA, Duval JB (eds) *Forensic Nursing*. Elsevier. Mosby: St. Louis

Lees J, Manning N, Rawlings B (2004) Therapeutic community research: An overview and meta-analysis. In: Lees J, Manning N, Menzies D, Morant N (eds) *A Culture of Enquiry: Research Evidence and the Therapeutic Community* (Chapter 2) Jessica Kingsley: London

Lester H, Glasby J (2006) *Mental Health Policy and Practice*. Palgrave Macmillan: Basingstoke

MacDonald J, Cank D (2000) *Conference paper*. Delivered at: New York University and University of Central Lancashire Forensic Mental Health Conference, New York. June, 2000

McGuire J (2002) Motivation for what? Effective programmes for motivated offenders. In: McMurran M (ed) *Motivating Offenders to Change. A Guide to Enhancing Engagement in Therapy*. John Wiley and Sons: Chichester

MacInnes D (2000) Relatives and informal carers. In: Chaloner C, Coffey M (eds) *Forensic Mental Health Nursing: Current Approaches*. Blackwell Science: Oxford

McKeown M, McCann G (2000) Psychosocial interventions. In: Chaloner C, Coffey M (eds) *Forensic Mental Health Nursing: Current Approaches*. Blackwell Science: Oxford

Mason T, Chandley M (1990) Nursing models in a special hospital: A critical analysis of efficacy. *J Adv Nurs* **15** 667–673

Mason T, Mercer D (1998) *Critical Perspectives in Forensic Care: Inside Out*. Macmillan: Basingstoke

Masterson A, Maslin-Prothero S (1999) Power, politics and nursing. In: Masterson A, Maslin-Prothero S (eds) *Nursing and Politics. Power Through Practice*. Churchill Livingstone: Edinburgh

Matthew Trust. (2008) From: www.matthewtrust.org/ [Accessed 30 August 2008]

Mok E (2001) Empowerment of cancer patients: From a Chinese perspective. *Nursing Ethics* **8** 69–75

Morgan I (1999) *Power and Politics.* Hodder and Stoughton: London

Morris G (2006) *Mental Health Issues and the Media: An Introduction for Mental Health Professionals.* Routledge, Taylor and Francis Group: London

Narayanasamy A (2001) *Spiritual Care: A Practical Guide for Nurses and Health Care Practitioners* (2nd edn). Quay Books: Dinton, Salisbury

Phillips R (2003) The good, the bad and the ugly: The role of local radio as a medium for overcoming prejudice. In: Dooher J, Byrt R (eds) *Empowerment and the Health Service User.* Quay Books: Dinton, Salisbury

Prins H (2005) *Offenders, Deviants or Patients?* (3rd edn). Routledge, Taylor and Francis Group: London

Rawlings B (1998) The therapeutic community in the prison: Problems in mainitaining therapeutic integrity. *Therapeutic Communities* 19(4): 281–94

Repper J, Perkins R (2003) *Social Inclusion and Recovery: A Model for Mental Health Practice.* Bailliere Tindall: Edinburgh

Robb M, Barrett S, Komaromy C, Rogers A (eds) (2004) *Communication, Relationships and Care: A Reader.* Routledge, Taylor and Francis Group/The Open University: London

Seligman MEP (1975) *Helplessness.* Freeman: San Fransisco

Smith EE, Nolen-Hoeksema S, Frederickson B, Loftus GR (eds) (2003) *Hilgard's Introduction to Psychology* (14th edn). Harcourt College Publishers: Fort Worth

Solanki M, Byrt R (2003) Finding a voice. Writing and empowerment. In: Dooher J, Byrt R (eds) *Empowerment and the Health Service User.* Quay Books: Dinton, Salisbury

Spiers S, Harney K, Chilvers C (2005) Service user involvement in forensic mental health: Can it work? *J Forensic Psychiatry Psychol* **16**(2) 211–220

Stern V (2006) *Creating Criminals. Prisons and People in a Market Society.* Fernwood Publishing: Halifax, Nova Scotia

Szasz T (2000) The case against psychiatric power. In: Barker P, Stevenson C (eds) *The Construction of Power and Authority in Psychiatry.* Butterworth Heinemann: Oxford

Taylor SE (2003) *Health Psychology* (5th edn) McGraw–Hill: New York

Tew J (ed) (2005) *Social Perspectives in Mental Health: Developing Social Models to Understand and Work with Mental Distress.* Jessica Kingsley: London

Thompson N (2003) *Promoting Equality: Challenging Discrimination and Oppression* (2nd edn) Palgrave, Macmillan: Basingstoke

Tones K, Green J (2002) The empowerment imperative in health promotion. In: Dooher J, Byrt R (eds) *Empowerment and Participation: Power, Influence and Control in Contemporary Health Care.* Quay Books: Dinton, Salisbury

Tones K, Green J (2004) *Health Promotion. Planning and Strategies.* Sage Publications: London

Treatment Advocacy Center (2007) Website. www.treatmentandadvocacycenter.org [Accessed 17 July 2007]

Van Marle HJC (2002) The Dutch Entrustment Act (TBS): Its principles and innovations. *Int J Forensic Ment Health* **1**(1) 83–92

Westwood S (2002) *Power and the Social.* Routledge: London

Women in Secure Hospitals (WISH) (2008) From: www.womenatwish.com [Accessed 30 August 2008]

World Health Organization (2002) *World Report on Violence and Health.* World Health Organization: Geneva

Zito Trust (2008) From: www.zitotrust.co.uk/ [Accessed 30 August 2008]

CHAPTER 6

Negative control or life saving? Perspectives on power

Richard Byrt

Introduction

The last chapter considered a variety of stakeholders, who may vary considerably in the extent that they view particular goals of forensic services as salient. Whether empowerment and participation are seen as important in secure hospitals and prisons depends, in part, on the officially stated goals of these organisations and those that are important to its stakeholders (Handy, 1993). For example, 'punishment' and 'therapy' have been seen by some authorities as opposed, with clear views expressed that it is unethical for mental health professionals to be involved in 'punishment' (Mason and Mercer, 1998; Wiertsema and Derks, 1997):

> ...*One must not try to treat and punish simultaneously...The goal of punishment is retaliation; the goal of treatment is resocialisation.*
> *This must be expressed in separate organisational structures, regimes, personnel and facilities*
>
> (Wiertsema and Derks, 1997: 76)

A frequent ethical dilemma in forensic mental health nursing is that increasing the power or the rights of a patient may adversely affect those of the public. Thus, if patients have more leave, this may increase their empowerment, in that it is what they want and results in increased self-efficacy and autonomy. However, patients' leave may be perceived by some members of the public as being at their expense, which, arguably, would certainly be the case if inadequate risk assessments had been conducted (Burrow, 1998).

Conflicting or complementary goals?

To facilitate empowerment and participation successfully, it is suggested that the following questions need to be considered (Byrt and Dooher 2002):

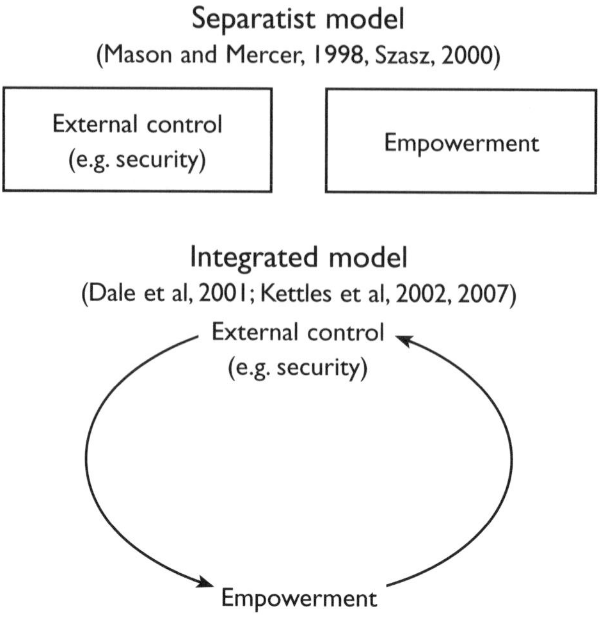

Separatist model
(Mason and Mercer, 1998, Szasz, 2000)

External control (e.g. security)	Empowerment

Integrated model
(Dale et al, 2001; Kettles et al, 2002, 2007)

Figure 6.1: External control (e.g. security) versus empowerment.

To what extent do the empowerment and participation of forensic patients *complement or conflict with*:

- The empowerment and participation of other stakeholders?
- The other goals of the secure hospital, prison or community service?

If empowerment and participation are goals of the service, is this:

- Intrinsic to *all* its other goals?
- Separate to its other goals?

In a 'separatist model', the facilitation of empowerment and participation is seen as separate from other goals; while in an 'integrated model', it is seen as inter-connected with them (see *Figure 6.1*). For example, managers who implemented measures to ensure the goal of security would consider not only safety, as a first priority, but also the short-term and long-term effects on empowerment. A policy on observation with engagement which integrated empowerment and participation with other organisational goals, would emphasise not only safety issues, but also consideration of patients' perspectives and experiences, giving them information and, as far as possible, participation in decisions related to the observation, awareness of the individual's needs for privacy and dignity; within safety parameters, engagement, and provision of intensive nursing care related to the unique needs of the individual (Cutcliffe, 2003; Kettles and Byrt, 2007).

However, critical analysis suggests that there are problems with enabling empowerment and participation in relation to observation. Whether giving information, involving the patient in decision making and so on count as 'empowerment' or 'participation' depends on one's viewpoint. It can be argued that none of the items listed are 'empowering' or 'participatory' if the patient does not wish to be observed (which will often be the case: Kettles and Byrt, 2007). Whether or not 'empowerment' or 'participation' can be seen as occurring, depends largely on individuals' perspectives, particularly the patient's; and in part, on whether this is understood from a consensus theory or conflict theory perspective.

Consensus and conflict theories

It can be argued that an understanding of a variety of perspectives related to both consensus theory and conflict theory can enable forensic mental health nurses to reflect on some of the ethical and clinical dilemmas with which we are faced (*Box 6.1*).

Within sociology, *consensus theory* is concerned with members of social groups or societies dealing with issues of power by sharing an 'agreed position, conclusion or set of values' (Marshall, 1994: 84); and is associated with much of the writing of Emile Durkheim and Talcott Parsons. Consensus theorists tend to see the exercise of some forms of power as conducive to the smooth and effective running of society. *Conflict theory*, developed as a critique of consensus theory, stresses 'coercion, rather than consensus, as the cause of social order' (Marshall, 1994: 82), and is concerned with unequal distributions of power among individuals, and with differences in their perspectives. Conflict theorists include Max Weber, who studied bureaucracies, with managers in formal roles with legitimate authority to exert power (Gerth and Mills, 1948), as occurs in secure hospitals and prisons. Karl Marx, and social scientists influenced by Marxist thought, have studied power related to social class, unequal distributions of wealth in capitalist societies, and the relationship between economic power, political power and ideological power. The latter term refers to the control of people in positions of power over what is seen as 'knowledge' and accepted, 'taken for granted' ways of perceiving everyday 'reality' (Westwood, 2002). Foucault (1971, 1991) argued that power pervades virtually all aspects of everyday life. An example of ideological power is given in *Chapter 5*.

Other conflict theorists include authors who consider power in relation to sources of discrimination and social exclusion (Thompson, 2003) and

---

Box 6.1: Consensus versus conflict models applied to forensic nursing

Consensus model

- It is possible to combine therapeutic interventions with security.
- Therapeutic interventions have beneficial consequences for both patients and wider society.

- The nurse has a *duty of care* to ensure safety of the patient and others. Security is for the good of the patient and the good of the public.
- It is always possible for nurses to enable forensic patients' empowerment and participation – even if this is only to a limited extent.

Conflict model

- Therapeutic and security aims conflict and cannot co-exist.
- 'Interventions' are solely to keep individuals under control when they are judged to be 'deviant' by people in positions of power; and for the benefit of the latter.
- Nursing should be concerned only with what the patients perceive to be in their interests, not with public safety.

- 'Forensic patient' is a disempowering term. It is nonsensical to talk of individuals' empowerment and participation when they have no choice but to be in a secure hospital or prison.

(National Forensic Nurses' Research and Development Group, 2006, 2007; Foucault, 1991; Szasz, 2000; and many other references)

---

groups of theorists referred to as antipsychiatrists, critical psychiatrists and critical sociologists, who question conventional ideas about 'mental illness' and 'treatment'. These critics have argued that the problem lies, not with the individual diagnosed 'mentally ill', but with coercive families (Laing and Esterson, 1967), institutions (Goffman, 1968), or society, particularly psychiatrists and others in positions of power (Szasz, 1961, 1963, 1971, 2000). *Box 6.1* illustrates some differences between consensus and conflict theories in relation to forensic nursing.

Negative social control and/or life saving?

Some conflict theorists stress the negative social control functions of secure hospitals and prisons (Mason and Mercer, 1998; Szasz, 2000; Pilgrim and Rogers, 2005). In contrast, consensus theorists are likely to emphasise these organisations' essential functions to ensure the well-being of the patient and the safety of the public. The latter is emphasised (together with some consideration of social control issues) in texts on forensic mental health nursing (Dale et al. 2001; Kettles et al, 2002; National Forensic Nurses' Research and Development Group, 2007), forensic multidisciplinary care (Wix and Humphreys, 2005), and forensic psychiatry (Stone et al, 2000). Opposing views are illustrated in the following quotes:

...So long as conventional wisdom decrees that...society must be protected from the mental patient, and that [this task] rightfully belongs to...psychiatry...psychiatric power will remain unreformable.

(Szasz 2000: 52)

versus:

Freeing the mentally ill to defecate, urinate, sleep, starve, freeze, murder and be murdered in the streets of our larger cities. All in the name of autonomy.

(Gaylin and Jennings, 1996, quoted in Charen, 1998)

The institution of psychiatry rests on civil commitment and the insanity defence, and...each is a perversion of power.

(Szasz 2000:52)

versus:

Without State power, all manner of worse abuses of personal power [might occur].

(Parsons and Armstrong, 2000: 219)

Thomas Szasz: Views of an 'antipsychiatrist'

For Szasz (1963, 2000), forensic mental health nurses, and in particular forensic psychiatrists, abuse power. Professionals, and the services in which they work, are tools of the State, and psychiatry and related disciplines are used mainly to ensure that 'patients' conform. According to Szasz (1961), mental illness is a 'myth': a socially constructed idea, particularly of people in positions of power, rather than having an objective 'reality'. People who are seen by society as being 'deviant' are labelled 'mentally ill'. Just as certain people were scapegoated and labelled as 'witches' in Europe at the time of the Spanish Inquisition, in the same way, other people are hunted out and confined by psychiatrists, who are the new inquisitors (Szasz, 1971).

Szasz (1971, 2000) is opposed to State-provided 'mental health services' and to compulsory admission and treatment. He also criticises the tendency to 'psychiatrise' offending behaviours. Szasz (1963, 2000) has argued that diagnosing mental disorder in people who offend is taking away their responsibility. He stated that:

...liberty was an inalienable right, and that the mental health movement, by providing excuses for abnormal behaviour, was eroding moral standards and extending the power of the State...

(Jones, 1993: 177).

Szasz enables us to be aware of the current dangers of labelling individuals as 'mentally disordered', particularly if they fail to conform, e.g. through offending behaviours. Szasz (1961, 1971, 2000) produces evidence for such labelling in the past and present. Historical examples include the diagnosis of 'drapetomania...a disease that made slaves run away' (Pilgrim and Rogers, 2005). In the last century, women who were single mothers, or who disagreed with their husbands were compulsorily detained (Byrt et al, 2001), and gay men were given 'electric shock' aversion therapy (Smith et al, 2004). In addition, there is considerable very recent evidence that people have been compulsorily admitted or treated because they fail to conform, and not because of evidence of a mental health problem. Examples include individuals from minority ethnic groups, whose cultural beliefs have been incorrectly thought to be delusional (Littlewood and Lipsedge, 1997; Fernando, 2002), and the detention for treatment of 'dangerous people with severe personality disorders' solely because they are deemed to be at risk of harming others (Byrt and Dooher, 2006), despite the questionable accuracy of risk assessments (Jones and Plowman, 2005).

Szasz's contention that psychiatrists, in particular, and other mental health professionals are 'tools of the State' is contradicted by their recent (in some cases, considerable) opposition, both to the 'dangerous and severe personality disorder' initiative (Byrt with Dooher, 2006), and to the mental health Bills preceding the Mental Health Act (for England and Wales) 2007. Many mental health professionals have criticised recent proposals to curtail freedoms of clients, including some people receiving care in the community. In some cases, professionals have united with service users in opposition to such proposals, e.g. through the Mental Health Alliance (2008).

Also against Szasz's views is evidence that some people develop mental health problems, and associated offending, in the absence of labelling or apparent efforts to exert social control over them (Pilgrim and Rogers, 2005). In addition, research suggests that some individuals resist and challenge labels, rather than passively accepting them (Camp et al, 2002). However, some individuals appear to desire psychiatric labels (even forensic ones), e.g. through diagnosis and/or hospital admission, even though professionals may be reluctant to provide this. Labelling theorists sometimes pay insufficient attention to the possibility that individuals' offending behaviours may be related to particular features or symptoms of mental illness or personality disorder, rather than because they are labelled by other people (Pilgrim and Rogers, 2005).

Individual power from violent offending

For some individuals, violent offending is an important source of power and positive self-identity (Gilligan, 2001; Barker, 2005). While there are many factors related to violent offending in teenagers and adults (Gilligan, 2001; Prins, 2005), research indicates that sometimes this is associated with multiple sources of disempowerment from early childhood. Relevant factors include lack of attachment, abuse and neglect with inconsistent love, security and discipline; relative poverty and material deprivation; educational and occupational underachievement; and unemployment. In addition, some individuals who have offended violently have experienced discrimination related to social class, ethnicity and other factors, with considerable social exclusion, including an absence of life opportunities available to most people (Barker, 2005; Duggan et al, 2007; Gilligan 2001). For some individuals, violent offending provides a source of self-efficacy, achievement, self-respect and respect from, and solidarity with, others – in the absence of other means to achieve these important aspects of empowerment:

> In…my psychotherapeutic work with violent criminals…references to the desire for respect as the motive for violence kept recurring, with remarks like: 'I never got so much respect before in my life as I did when I first pointed a gun at some dude's face.
> (Gilligan, 2001: 29).

From a consensus viewpoint, a crucial part of forensic mental health work is to understand the reasons for violent behaviours and patients' past experiences of disempowerment, and to offer alternative sources of empowerment which benefit both patients and public. This includes opportunities for further education. Several studies have found statistically significant correlations between increasing prisoners' educational levels and reducing rates of violent reoffending (Gilligan, 2001).

Another reason why empowerment and participation are important in forensic mental health nursing relates to the variety of ways that individuals' empowerment may be affected by their mental health problems (*Box 6.2*), and using psychosocial interventions and other means to alleviate patients' difficulties. However, seeing an individual's mental health problems as only resulting in disempowerment can itself be disempowering. For example,

---

Box 6.2: Mental health problems, violence and power

An individual's mental illness may affect his/her power to:
* Reduce stress.
* Manage distressing symptoms:, e.g. delusions, hallucinations.
* Make rational judgements.
* Exert controls over behaviours.
* Distinguish external and internal 'realities'.
* Have hope, self-esteem, self-efficacy, internal locus of control.

An individual's antisocial personality disorder may affect his/her power to:
* Empathise with others.
* Plan for the future.
* Learn from consequences of behaviour.
* Experience remorse.
* Express anger creatively and assertively.

(Prins, 2005)

---

individuals' use of their mental health problems to inspire their writing, including great works of literature, has been described (McArdle and Byrt, 2001; Post, 1994). Writers on recovery have argued for greater emphasis on the strengths, aptitudes and aspirations of mental health service users, rather than concentrating solely on issues of psychopathology and an over-emphasis on 'problems', 'deficits' and 'symptoms' (Repper and Perkins, 2003, Tew, 2005a). Members of mental health survivor movements have defined their shared experiences as sources of creativity, consciousness raising and challenging social exclusion (Sayce, 2000; Tew, 2005a).

Diagnosis and empowerment

Whether a psychiatric diagnosis is empowering or disempowering depends, in part, on the extent that it labels or stigmatises the patient ('Oh no, not another personality disorder for admission') – or has implications for understanding different individuals and their experiences, and for their care and treatment (Wing, 1978). A review of the experiences of people with a personality disorder suggests that while some have found the diagnosis helpful, especially if this has been explained, others have noted negative changes in professionals' attitudes towards them (Byrt et al, 2006; Castillo, 2003). Whether a psychiatric diagnosis is empowering or disempowering depends, also, on professionals' willingness to collaborate with the patient (within safety parameters) in relation to treatment and care (Charland, 2004), and take the patient's values and perspectives seriously (Fulford, 2004). Tew (2005b: 26) argues that:

Medical diagnosis may...deliver a 'life sentence' of dependence on services...Users have argued for more holistic definitions in terms of the ability to 'get on with life' in a way that seems...meaningful for them... [This includes] living with parts of...their experience that had previously appeared frightening or shameful...challenging structures or relationships which have been oppressive, discriminatory and abusive...establishing new social networks of support and mutuality...[and] reclaiming aspects of ordinary life, such as decent housing and employment opportunities.

Empowerment, autonomy and responsibility

One aspect of individual empowerment concerns the extent that the person has *autonomy*. This term refers to the individual's ability to make informed decisions and choices, and take informed actions, unconstrained by both internal and external factors (Thompson et al, 2006). Internal factors include constraints caused by mental health problems, e.g. effects on abilities to make what others perceive to be rational judgements. External factors include, for example, professionals' imposition of levels of security, compulsory admission and treatment and the rules and routines of the institution (Dunn, 1998).

There appears to be general agreement among writers on nursing ethics that limits on patients' autonomy are justified only to meet superordinate ethical imperatives, such as beneficence ('the principle that we should do good to others': Thompson et al, 2006: 381). Beneficence includes the nurse's duty of care to prevent the patient from harming (perhaps killing) himself/herself and others (Thompson et al, 2006). Arguably, from a consensus perspective, beneficence also involves a consideration of the autonomy and empowerment of the individual patient versus those of others, including wider society (Dunn, 1998; Chadwick and Aindow, 2004). This includes recognition that the autonomy of an individual may vary over time: 'Whose wishes should we follow and respect? The person at the time of the treatment, or the person at the start of the mental illness?' (Parsons and Armstrong, 2000: 216). Chan (1998) has argued that it is more appropriate to view mental health clients as having varying amounts of autonomy, rather than seeing them as having complete autonomy or none at all.

Within the ethics literature, there has been debate about the extent that the individual's actions are *determined* by various factors, including those that are biological, psychological and psychiatric; or mediated through the exercise of *free will* (Dickenson et al, 2000; Thompson et al, 2006). Consideration has been given to the effect of mental illness and personality disorder on individuals' responsibility for their actions, including offending behaviours (Charland, 2004; Prins, 2005), with some authors arguing that to deny individuals' responsibility for their offending behaviour can be disempowering, and, in the case of women, sexist (Allen, 1987). The NHS Security Management Service has set up a Legal Protection Unit, which has enabled an increasing number of nurses to successfully prosecute patients for assaulting them (NHS Business Services Authority: Counter-Fraud and Security Management Service, 2006).

Can temporary disempowerment result in future increases in empowerment?

Can temporary disempowerment result in future increases in empowerment at a later date? This question appears to have received little consideration in the literature. The answer depends partly on the sociological perspective employed. Consensus theorists might argue that admitting and treating 'Barry Blue' (a pseudonym) may increase his power because, as a result, his offending behaviours are no longer 'controlled' by symptoms of mental illness. In addition, Mr Blue's admission may be seen as increasing public power by contributing to others' safety. However, from a conflict perspective, Mr Blue becomes permanently disempowered, as his admission and discharge depend on conformity to dominant values of those in power. In addition, it might be argued, from this perspective, that it is difficult to demonstrate that Mr Blue's admission and 'treatment' will significantly contribute to public safety. *Figure 6.2* illustrates better outcomes, in relation to longer-term empowerment, for Mr Blue ('patient B' in the graph), compared with an individual who does not receive treatment. More research is needed to measure whether or not admission to a secure hospital or prison health service has positive outcomes, not only according to measures such as decreased recidivism and symptomatology (McMurran, 2002), but also in relation to gains in empowerment, e.g increased social inclusion and the extent that individuals are able to achieve their own goals (Repper and Perkins, 2003; Tew, 2005a).

From a 'consensus' perspective, forensic mental health nursing attempts to integrate efforts to ensure safety, relieve the individual's distress and provide holistic care which meets the needs of the individual, including those related to diversity (Kettles et al, 2007). According to this view, the imposition of controls (e.g. physical security) by people in power is intended to enable individuals to regain their own inner controls over their behaviours, with increasing freedoms being granted as this is achieved with gains to both patient and public (see *Figure 6.3*).

However, this consensus view of external controls to benefit both the individual and society contrasts with the work of many conflict theorists who have described the all-pervasive power of institutions and their harmful effects

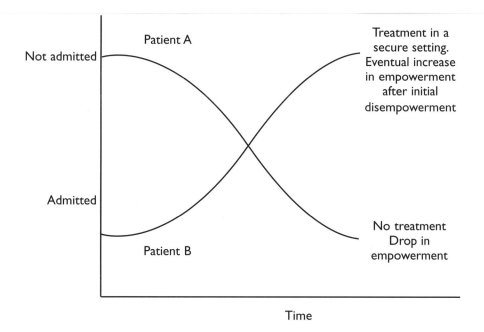

Figure 6.2: *Is it possible for temporary decreases in empowerment to result in increased power later?*

on individuals (Goffman, 1968; Foucault. 1971, 1991). For Foucault (1991), the prison and the psychiatric hospital and their managers and staff exert an all-seeing, all-knowing power. Foucault (1991) refers to the Panoptican, a type of prison designed by Jeremy Bentham in the late 18th century, which allowed

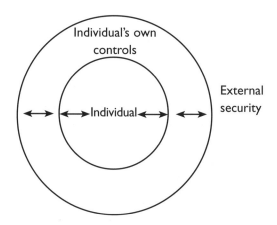

Figure 6.3: *Inner mastery or outer control?*

staff to see, at any one time, all the inmates, who are aware of being under surveillance, but not precisely when they are being observed.

> *Power should be visible and unverifiable...The inmate must never know whether he is being looked at at any moment'*
>
> (Foucault 1991: 201).

For both Goffman (1968) and Foucault (1991), the all-pervasiveness of the institution affects every area of the person's life, with little opportunity for choice or individuality. The inmate is expected to conform and to accept the 'truth' of professionals and others in positions of power: for example, the 'correct version' that one is mentally ill and has 'criminal styles of thinking'. Fox's (1999) research is in the tradition of a Foucauldian 'conflict' view of institutions. She described how, in a programme using cognitive-behavioural therapy, psychologists acted as 'agents of social control', using 'language as coercion...reflecting dominant ideas that conceal the disciplinary function of State agencies' (Fox 1999: 88–9). These 'dominant ideas' included those concerning 'criminal thinking styles', with prisoners being expected to change ways of thinking and behaving in order to leave prison (Fox, 1999).

In contrast to the views of conflict theorists, other authors, while acknowledging institutional constraints and power-related issues, describe ways that individuals are, nevertheless, enabled to participate and gain power: for example, in developing aptitudes and managing anger in therapeutic communities (Liderth, 2003; Rawlings, 1998) and in units using cognitive-behavioural, dialectical-behavioural and schema-focused therapies (Perseius et al, 2003; Byrt et al 2005; Doyle et al, 2006). Rogers and Vidgin (2006: 277–8) comment on:

'
> *...working* **with**, *as opposed to working* **against** *people who are angry. In doing so, we will hopefully challenge some of the existing professional rhetoric and traditional practices used...against people who are angry...*
>
> *The negative effects of being a 'patient' in the psychiatric system are well recognised, with...disempowerment, lack of autonomy and loss of control all regular features...*
>
> *Strategies of control...seclusion, restraint, enforced medication...can... [adversely] affect clients' anger considerably*

Nevertheless, in support of conflict theory, research on forensic and acute admission wards has found an over-emphasis on reactive measures, e.g. control, restraint and seclusion, sometimes used in the absence of communication and therapeutic and preventative interventions. This is despite patients emphasising the importance of communication to them (Secker et al, 2004; Duxbury and Whittington, 2005; Meehan et al, 2006). A leading member of the UK mental health survivors' movement wrote:

> *Go into the smoke room…and smash the window…That's the only power we've got because you've denied us any real power.*
>
> (Coleman, 2000: 61)

Values and empowerment

This brings us on to values in forensic mental health nursing in relation to power and participation. Fulford's (2004) comments on the importance of psychiatry being value-based, as well as evidence-based, are of relevance to values in forensic mental health nursing. Fulford's (2004) list of values include the following:

- Skilful listening to individuals and taking careful account of their values and perspectives.
- Noting and recording any differences in patient and staff perspectives (Neuman, 1995).
- Finding 'common ground' with the patient (Fulford, 2004)

Fulford (2004) reminds us that it is easy for us to have:

- Value blindness: a failure to question values, to take them for granted without critical reflection (e.g. not questioning rules and regimes which unnecessarily restrict patients).
- Value myopia: 'our tendency to…assume that other people's values are the same as our own' (Fulford, 2004:216–7) (e.g. assuming that patients see a need to reduce problems leading to offending behaviours when they see no reason to change).

Different perspectives of patient and nurse

Value blindness and value myopia are relevant to power and participation because it may be easy for us, as forensic nurses, to forget that patients may have different perspectives, or to understand the reasons for this, as part of culturally sensitive and culturally competent care (Byrt et al, 2007). Differences of perspective can be explored using certain models of nursing, such as the Betty Neuman systems model (Neuman, 1995) and Barker's tidal model (Barker and Buchanan-Barker, 2005). However, Mason and Chandley (1990) described problems of implementing nursing models in a high secure hospital because some patients saw themselves as 'prisoners serving time'. This role appeared to be an important part of their identity. Patients did not wish to be seen as 'mentally ill' or want nurses to have a therapeutic, as opposed to a custodial role. In such situations, the literature suggests that therapeutic progress or attempts to enable empowerment or participation, even in a limited way, depends on 'negotiation', finding 'common ground'; appreciating 'the individual's perspectives', including those 'related to his or her cultural background...establishment of trust and a therapeutic alliance' and 'eventual shared agreement, e.g. related to care planned goals' (Byrt et al, 2007: 225). Of particular importance in preventing and reducing violence and aggression is avoiding patients 'losing face', with respect for individuals and their perception of self. This involves producing an outcome where, as far as possible, there is a 'win–win' situation, with individuals managing to express anger creatively and safely, and without feeling that they have lost the respect of their peers (Lowe, 1992; McDougall, 2000).

Power in discourse and 'knowledge'

Various theorists have proposed that discourse and 'knowledge' are important aspects of power (Foucault, 1991; Miers, 1999). Discourse has been defined as 'commonly accepted assumptions that claim to explain reality' (Wilkinson, 1999: 21); 'reality' in this sense meaning ways of seeing and describing the world which are taken for granted, accepted as 'normal' or 'usual'. An example would be a nurse being completely used to institutionalised, unnecessary and excessively secure regimes, without reflecting on their disempowering effects on patients.

The term 'discourse' includes language, ideology and what counts as 'knowledge'. Foucault (1991) proposes that part of 'ideological power' is patients and prisoners coming to accept without question the beliefs of professionals and other powerful people concerning their offending behaviours. This includes the 'hold' that psychiatrists and other 'experts' have 'on individuals; not only on what they do, but on what they are, will be, may be' (Foucault 1991: 18).

A criticism of Foucault's position is that he appears to consider to a limited extent individuals' abilities to resist sources of ideological and organisational power, including professionals' attempts to assess, diagnose, treat and ameliorate mental health problems associated with offending behaviours. Notable examples of individuals who have successfully resisted considerable coercive power are Mahatma Gandhi (Fischer, 1982),

Tsunesaburo Makiguchi and Josei Toda (Ikeda, 1994), Nelson Mandela (Mandela, 1965), and Martin Luther-King, Rosie Parkes and other civil rights activists (Davis, 2001). These individuals, and many others, have resisted imprisonment, torture and other means used by people in positions of power to effect individual change, including changes in their spiritual and other beliefs.

Furthermore, it can be argued that, within at least some societies, aspects of conflict, such as resistance to ideological and other forms of power, have become institutionalised and accepted (Kriesberg, 1996). To some extent, this resistance has included campaigns by people who have faced discrimination, including individuals with mental health problems (Bishop, 2002). In addition, the development of science as a series of challenges to, and overthrow of, dominant paradigms has been described (Okasha, 2002). Of relevance to forensic nursing are the regular challenges to nursing from often unwilling patients which, it has been argued, should be incorporated into our practice (Warner, 1992). Goffman (1968) referred both to some patients who 'worked the system' (i.e. found ways of getting round the rules) and others who conformed to institutionalised regimes and professionals' expectations. Goffman's (1968) observations and the author's experience suggest that, while we should not ignore very real and sometimes undesirable power differentials, it is not just a question of all-pervasive institutions over which patients have limited power, as Foucault (1991) and Fox (1999) appear to suggest. Rather, variations in personality, culture and other factors result in some individuals conforming or over-conforming to professional and organisational expectations, and others refusing to accept these and resisting 'expert' explanations for their behaviours. Perhaps the majority of forensic patients adopt a position somewhere in the middle of these two positions.

Practical applications in forensic mental health nursing

There are various ways that discourse and 'knowledge' have practical applications in forensic mental health nursing. These include the following:

- Acknowledgement that the patient and nurse will probably have some similarities, but also, certain differences in their cultural backgrounds, including their beliefs and their ways of perceiving and describing the world (O'Brien and Morrison-Ngatai, 2003).
- Having respect for individuals and their culture and unique experiences and perspectives (Freeth, 2007).
- Preparedness to listen actively to the patient (Freeth, 2007).
- Endeavouring to apply person-centred principles of congruence,

empathy and unconditional positive regard (Freeth, 2007; Rogers, 1978) in circumstances where this may be difficult (Bowers, 2002).

- Acceptance of individuals, without necessarily agreeing with their behaviour (Adshead, 1997; Rogers, 1978). (Schafer and Peternelj-Taylor, 2003, found that individuals with personality disorder in one secure hospital preferred nurses to question certain behaviours and found this helpful.)

- Awareness of potentially stigmatising, but taken-for-granted language. (An example is professionals' use of the term 'mentally disordered offender' in an unthinking way: the author has not heard patients use this term to describe themselves.)

- However, whether professionals who use this term are necessarily stigmatising in their attitudes is debatable. The question can be asked: Does talking about patients in a negative way in clinical supervision or over coffee with a colleague provide a valuable release which enables the nurse to work professionally and effectively with patients? (Bowers, 2002; Walsh, 2007). Or does this reinforce negative attitudes in practice?

- Instead of using professional jargon which is intimidating to patients, it may be more empowering to use at least some of the patient's own language (Coulter et al, 1998). For example, one individual found it much more helpful in care planning to use her own term of 'browned off' to describe her disenchantment with life, rather than the author's term, 'depressed'.

- At the same time, in relation to client-centred principles, authenticity is important, with, in the author's view, a balance being struck between avoiding jargon and speaking in one's own voice, and avoiding patronising patients in the manner of Nurse Ratched in *One Flew Over the Cuckoo's Nest* (Kesey, 1962). In both the book and the film, patients' concerns are ignored.

Boyle (2000: 70), citing Foucault (1991), describes 'disciplinary power', including professional power, which 'disbars alternative versions' and 'operates…through the creation of privileged ways of talking and writing'. However, mental health patients have their own source of power from their unique experiences and knowledge of their specific mental health problems. In addition, they exercise power through deciding what thoughts and feelings to disclose and may resist nurses' efforts at communication (Chambers, 2005). Breeze and Repper (1998) discovered, in their research of mental health clients described as 'difficult', that both clients and nurses struggled for control. These authors distinguish between unhelpful 'power over' and 'power to' clients. They found that, when nurses listened to and respected clients and enabled them to participate in their care, clients' anger was reduced. This was the case even if nurses made decisions with which the clients did not agree:

> *Some [nurses] are prepared to listen and act upon what I say, or might even refuse and say 'no', but they do listen, and they give me their opinion on why, and give me reasons why not.*
>
> (Breeze and Repper, 1998: 1301–2)

Importance to patients of therapeutic communication and relationships

From his review of several studies of forensic patients' views, Coffey (2006: 79) concluded that these individuals saw relationships with staff as crucial to their satisfaction or dissatisfaction. The importance to patients of communication with staff and therapeutic relationships has been emphasised in several studies of forensic patients' views (Byrt and Reece, 1999; Coffey, 2006; Halsall, 2006), as in the following comments during a patient satisfaction survey at Arnold Lodge medium secure unit:

> *[I'd like] to be listened to more [and for] staff to take on board what we, as patients say.*
>
> *In X mental health unit...they were too busy to talk to me...Here, they talk to you'*
>
> *...[Staff] agree to see me. I could...chat [to them] about problems. They give me good advice*
>
> (Arnold Lodge, 2006)

Self-awareness

Several authors point out that self-awareness is a crucial precursor of working effectively with forensic mental health patients, including (by implication), their empowerment (Adshead, 1997; Schafer and Peternelj-Taylor, 2003). At the beginning of practice placements at Arnold Lodge medium secure unit, student nurses are invited to consider the following questions:

Is it OK for you to:

- Feel angry or frustrated with a patient?
- Feel appalled at a patient's index offence?
- Maintain your own values and beliefs about offending behaviour and how it should be responded to?

At Arnold Lodge, a message is conveyed to student nurses that they are, of course, entitled to their feelings and views about patients' offences, but that it is essential to ensure that these do not interfere with professional and effective work with patients; and to discuss any negative feelings with practice mentors. Adshead (1997) argues that, while forensic mental health professionals should endeavour to appreciate the reasons for offending behaviours, this does not mean that they should view the latter as 'acceptable'. Several authors indicate the importance of professionals' honest recognition of disgust and other feelings, so that their expression does not (perhaps unconsciously) result in negative attitudes that disempower patients, with adverse consequences for their assessment and care (Welldon and Van Velson, 1997; Bowers, 2002; Prins, 2005). Research suggests that nursing interventions are adversely affected when forensic nurses do not progress beyond perceptions that patients are 'evil' (Mercer et al, 1999; Bowers, 2002). Equally, Bowers (2002) found that when nurses in high secure hospitals were self-aware, with positive attitudes, this enhanced their respect and understanding for patients and appeared to have positive effects on nursing interventions.

Empowerment in security?

From a Foucauldian perspective, aspects of security cannot be other than disempowering to patients. For Foucault (1991), security comprises not only locked doors and high walls, but surveillance: 'a microscope of conduct' (1991: 173) and 'conscious and permanent visibility that assures the automatic functioning of power' (1991: 201). Within the context of increasing surveillance in society generally (Westwood, 2002), it is the constant surveillance of forensic patients that poses specific ethical issues related to their assessment and care. Foucault (1991) and other writers on institutions can help us reflect on whether, as nurses, we too readily take for granted the adverse effects of surveillance and other aspects of security. The author has known patients to express their concern that every word and action may be scrutinised, and possibly used as evidence of risk.

Goffman (1968) refers to the tendency of mental health professionals to see 'normal' assertive expressions of anger as pathological and evidence of mental illness or 'risk'. Hopton (1995) stresses the importance of nurses' recognition of the justifiable anger that some patients may feel and express, for example, in response to racism and other forms of discrimination in wider society. Where assertive anger is 'pathologised' (Goffman, 1968), this is disempowering to patients, and indeed, to the general public, since in order to accurately assess risk, it is essential to distinguish between assertive and aggressive expressions of anger (Morgan and Wetherell, 2004). Warner (1992) comments, in relation to patients in a high secure hospital:

Nurses must accept that successful programmes are likely to lead patients to question nursing interventions...

Staff...may wrongly attribute patients' assertiveness to 'non-compliance', rather than seeing it as a reflection of growing independence...
(Warner, 1992:46, quoted in Byrt and Doyle, 2007:74)

Kilshaw (1999) produced a useful checklist related to whether or not a secure ward has features of Goffman's (1968) concept of total institution. These include the extent that staff structure patients' time, insist on patients sharing activities only because this is the routine of the organisation, strip patients of their identity on admission, and limit patients' freedoms unless they submit to psychological and physical treatments.

The disempowering nature of aspects of security which are unnecessary to ensure patient, staff or public safety has been described by several former patients of secure hospitals (Laing and McQuarrie, 1989; George, 1998; Anonymous, 2000); and in Government enquiries (Department of Health and Social Security, 1980; HM Government, 1992; Ramsbotham, 2005). Given this, besides frequent risk assessments and reviews of security, *regular audits of organisational culture* appear to be essential, with assessments of the extent that an institution's 'rules, regimes and routines' (Byrt and James 2007: 36) are essential to maintain safety, or unnecessary. There is evidence that, in addition to infringing patients' rights, excessive security is disempowering, and results in increased propensities to self-harm and suicide (Towl et al, 2000) and riots and other institutional disturbances. Conversely, the latter have been found to be less frequent in prison wings run as modified therapeutic communities, with more democratic regimes (Lees et al, 2004).

The degree of structure of organisational programmes in secure hospitals and prisons has also been found to be related to factors concerning patient participation and empowerment. Too little structure, with insufficient meaningful activities, has been found to result in dissatisfaction with services, boredom, frustration and increased violence and aggression. Conversely, excessive, over-stimulating activity is associated with increased distress and violence and aggression in some individuals (Byrt, 2007).

When the structure is too loose, there is insufficient control, but when it is too rigid, we do not stimulate the patient to develop his capacities.
(Wiertsema and Derks, 1997).

Several authors refer to the importance of secure environments providing 'holding', with (from a psychodynamic perspective) the provision of safety, stability and nurturing for people who may not have experienced this in parent–child relationships (Zachary, 1997; Hartmann and Smith, 2002). Also emphasised, in the literature on therapeutic communities, is the role of staff in a secure environment in involving residents in ensuring their own and others' safety, although staff always maintain ultimate responsibility for this. For example, at the Van der Hoeven Clinic, a secure therapeutic community in Utrecht, patient participation is a very clear goal of the organisation, explicitly stated in its philosophy and in various literature. Patients have been involved in decisions about security (Wiertsema and Derks, 1997), something which is hard to imagine in a UK context:

> *After treatment, the patient will be held responsible for his own behaviour in less controlled conditions...This is why, at the Van der Hoeven Clinic, he is given as much responsibility for his treatment as possible.*
> (Wiertsema and Derks, 1997: 72)

Conclusion

This chapter has considered aspects of empowerment and participation in relation to the goals of forensic services, as perceived by various stakeholders. Patient power and participation can be considered from the perspectives of both consensus and conflict sociological theories. The former stress benefits to both patient and public from professional interventions. Conflict theorists, including Foucault, Goffman and Szasz, are concerned with the social control functions of institutions; and the conflicts between patients' interests and those of the public and of people in positions of power.

The chapter then reviewed empowerment in relation to individuals' self-identity from violent offending, their specific mental health problems, and autonomy. Empowerment has also been viewed *vis-a-vis* values and perspectives, therapeutic communication and relationships, and aspects of security.

The next chapter is concerned with barriers to patient empowerment and participation in forensic services, and ways to overcome these.

References

Adshead A (1997) The challenge of the victim. In: Van Marle H (ed) *Challenges in Forensic Psychotherapy.* Jessica Kingsley: London

Allen H (1987) *Justice Unbalanced: Gender, Policy and Judicial Decisions.* Open

University Press: Milton Keynes

Anonymous (2000) The experience of being a black patient. In: Kaye C, Lingiah T (eds) *Race, Culture and Ethnicity in Secure Psychiatric Practice: Working with Difference.* Jessica Kingsley: London

Arnold Lodge Medium Secure Unit with 'Together' Independent Advocacy Service (2006) *2005 Patient Satisfaction Survey Report of Findings.* Unpublished, internal report by R Byrt Arnold Lodge, Nottinghamshire Healthcare NHS Trust, Leicester

Barker GT (2005) *Dying to be Men: Masculinity and Social Exclusion.* Routledge, Taylor and Francis Group: London

Barker P, Buchanan-Barker P (2005) *The Tidal Model: A Guide for Mental Health Professionals.* Brunner-Routledge/Taylor and Francis Group: Hove

Bishop A (2002) *Becoming an Ally: Breaking the Cycle of Oppression in People* (2nd edn) Zed Books: Halifax, Nova Scotia

Bowers L (2002) *Dangerous and Severe Personality Disorder: Response and Role of the Psychiatric Team.* Routledge: London

Boyle M (2000) Diagnosis, science and power. In: Barker P, Stevenson C (eds) *The Construction of Power and Authority in Psychiatry.* Butterworth Heinemann: Oxford

Breeze L, Repper J (1998) Struggling for control: The care experiences of 'difficult' patients in mental health services. *J Adv Nursing* **28**(6) 1301–1311

Burrow S (1998) Therapy versus security: Reconciling healing and damnation. In: Mason T, Mercer D (eds) *Critical Perspectives in Forensic Care: Inside Out.* Macmillan: Basingstoke

Byrt R (2007) Towards therapeutic environments: Alternatives and solutions. In: National Forensic Nurses' Research and Development Group: Kettles AM, Woods P, Byrt R, Addo A, Coffey M, Doyle M (eds) *Forensic Mental Health Nursing: Forensic Aspects of Acute Care.* Quay Books: London

Byrt R, Dooher J (2002) Empowerment and participation: Definitions, meanings and models. In: Dooher J, Byrt R (eds) *Empowerment and Participation: Power, Influence and Control in Contemporary Healthcare* (Chapter 2) Quay Books: London

Byrt R, Dooher J (2006) The social consequences of a 'personality disorder' diagnosis. In: National Forensic Nurses' Research and Development Group: Woods P, Kettles AM, Byrt R, Addo M, Aiyegbusi A, Coffey M, Collins M, Doyle M, Garman G, Watson C (eds) *Forensic Mental Health Nursing: Interventions with People with 'Personality Disorder.* Quay Books: London

Byrt R, Graley-Wetherell R, Studley R, D'Silva K, James L, Pocock T (2006) Service user experiences and professional attitudes. In: National Forensic Nurses' Research and Development Group: Woods P, Kettles AM, Byrt R, Addo M, Aiyegbusi A, Coffey M, Collins M, Doyle M, Garman G, Watson C (eds) *Forensic Mental Health Nursing: Interventions with People with Personality Disorder.* Quay Books: London

Byrt R, Hardie T, Aigebusi A, Addo M (2007) Cultural and diversity issues. In: National Forensic Nurses' Research and Development Group: Kettles AM, Woods P, Byrt R, Addo M, Coffey M, Doyle M (eds) *Forensic Mental Health: Forensic Aspects of Acute Care* Quay Books: London.

Byrt R, James L (2007) Towards therapeutic environments: Challenges and problems. In: National Forensic Nurses' Research and Development Group: Kettles AM, Woods P,

Byrt R, Addo M, Coffey M, Doyle M (eds) *Forensic Mental Health: Forensic Aspects of Acute Care* Quay Books: London

Byrt R, Lomas C, Gardiner J, Lewis D (2001) Working with women in secure environments. *J Psychosoc Nurs Ment Health Services* **39**(9) 42–50

Byrt R, Reece J (1999) Patients' perspectives of self harm in a medium secure unit. *Ment Health Pract* **3**(3) 30–36

Byrt R, Wray C, 'Tom' (2005) Towards hope and inclusion: Nursing interventions in a medium secure service for men with 'personality disorders'. *Ment Health Pract* **8**(8): 38–43

Camp DL, Finlay WML, Lyons E (2002) Is low self-esteem an inevitable consequence of stigma? An example from women with chronic mental health problems. *Soc Sci Med* **55**(5) 823–834

Castillo H (2003) Personality Disorder: Temperament or Trauma? Jessica Kingsley: London

Chadwick R, Aindow G (2004) Treatment and research ethics. In: Radden J (ed) *The Philosophy of Psychiatry: A Companion*. Oxford University Press: Oxford

Chambers R (2005) *Involving Patients and the Public: How to Do It Better*. Radcliffe Publishing: Abingdon

Chan P (1998) Re-evaluating paternalism: How may parenting models assist in the care of the mentally ill? *Psychiatric Care* **5**(1) 22–25

Charen M (1998) Lock up those who need psychiatric care. Jewish World Review, 29 July, 1998, quoting: Gaylin W, Jennings B (1996) *The Perversion of Action: The Proper Uses of Coercion and Constraint in a Liberal Society*. Free Press, New York City. [Online]. Available from: http://www.jewishworldreview.com/cols/charen072998.html [Accessed 12 October, 2007]

Charland LC (2004) Character. Moral treatment and the personality disorders. In: Radden J (ed) *The Philosophy of Psychiatry: A Companion*. Oxford University Press: Oxford

Coffey M (2006) Researching service user views in forensic mental health: A literature review. *J Forensic Psychiat Psychol* **17**(1) 73–107

Coleman R (2000) The politics of the illness. In: Barker P, Stevenson C (eds) *The Construction of Power and Authority in Psychiatry*. Butterworth Heinemann: Oxford

Coulter A, Entwhistle V, Gilbert D (1998) *Informing Patients*. King's Fund: London

Cutcliffe J (2003) Engagement and observation of people at risk. In: Barker P (ed) *Psychiatric and Mental Health Nursing: The Craft of Caring*. Arnold: London

Dale C, Thompson T, Woods P (eds) (2001) *Forensic Mental Health: Issues in Practice*. Bailliere Tindall/Royal College of Nursing: Edinburgh

Davis JE (ed) (2001) *The Civil Rights Movement*. Blackwell Publications: Malden, Mass

Department of Health and Social Security (1980) *Report of the Review of Rampton Hospital (Boynton Report) Cmnd 8073*. HMSO: London

Dickenson D, Fulford B (KWM) with Birley JLT (eds.) (2000) *In Two Minds: A Casebook of Psychiatric Ethics*. Oxford University Press: Oxford

Doyle M, Aiyegbusi A, Burbery P (2006) Personality disorder: Specialist psychological approaches. In: National Forensic Nurses' Research and Development Group: Woods P, Kettles AM, Byrt R, Addo M, Aiyegbusi A, Coffey M, Collins M, Doyle M, Garman G, Watson C (eds) *Forensic Mental Health Nursing: Interventions with People with Personality Disorder*. Quay Books: London.

Duggan C, Mason L, Banerjee P, Milton J (2007) Value of standard personality assessments in informing clinical decision-making in a medium secure unit. *Brit J Psychiatry Suppl* **190** s15–s19

Dunn CJ (1998) *Ethical Issues in Mental Illness*. Ashgate Publishing: Aldershot

Duxbury J, Whittington R (2005) Causes and management of patient aggression and violence: Staff and patient perspectives. *J Adv Nurs* **50**(5) 469–478

Fernando S (2002) *Mental Health, Race and Culture* (2nd edn) Palgrave: Basingstoke

Fischer L (1982) *The Life of Mahatma Gandhi*. Grafton Books: London

Foucault M (1971) *Madness and Civilisation: A History of Insanity in the Age of Reason*. Tavistock Social Science Paperback: London

Foucault M (1991) *Discipline and Punish. The Birth of the Prison*. Translated from the French by Alan Sheridan. Penguin Books: Harmondsworth

Fox KJ (1999) Changing violent minds: Discursive correction and resistance in the cognitive treatment of violent offenders in prison. *Social Problems* **46**(1) 88–103

Freeth R (2007) *Humanising Psychiatry and Mental Health Care: The Challenge of the Person-Centred Approach*. Radcliffe Publishing: Oxford

Fulford KWM (2004) Facts/values: Ten principles of values-based medicine. In: Radden J (ed) *The Philosophy of Psychiatry: A Companion*. Oxford University Press: Oxford

Gaylin W, Jennings B (1996) *The Perversion of Action: The Proper Uses of Coercion and Constraint in a Liberal Society*. Free Press, New York City, quoted in: Charen, M Lock up those who need psychiatric care. *Jewish World Review* (1998) 29 July 1998. Available from: http://www.jewishworldreview.com/cols/charen072998.html [Accessed 12 October, 2007]

George S (1998) More than a pound of flesh: A patient's perspective'. In: Mason T, Mercer D (eds) *Critical Perspectives in Forensic Care: Inside Out*. Macmillan: Basingstoke

Gerth HH, Mills CW (eds) (1948) *From Max Weber: Essays in Sociology*. Routledge and Kegan Paul: London

Gilligan J (2001) *Preventing Violence*. Thames and Hudson: London

Goffman E (1968) *Asylums*. Penguin Books: Harmondsworth

Halsall K (2006) *Forensic Users Research Project*. Booklet: London

Handy C (1993) *Understanding Organisations* (4th edn) Penguin Books: Harmondsworth

Hartman D, Smith L (2002) Developing community groupwork on a locked psychiatric intensive care unit. *Therapeutic Communities* **23**(1) 5–16

HM Government (1992) *Report of the Committee of Inquiry into Complaints at Ashworth Hospital (Chair Sir Louis Blom-Cooper)*. HMSO: London

Hopton J (1995) The application of the ideas of Frantz Fanon to the practice of mental health nursing. *J Adv Nursing* **21** 723–728

Ikeda D (1994) *The Human Revolution, Vol.1*. Soka Gakki International, UK. Taplow: Maidenhead

Jones J, Plowman C (2005) Risk assessment: A multidisciplinary approach to estimating harmful behaviour in mentally disordered offenders. In: Wix S, Humphreys M (eds) *Multidisciplinary Working in Forensic Mental Health Care*. Elsevier, Churchill Livingstone: Edinburgh

Jones K (1993) *Asylums and After: A Revised History of the Mental Health Services: From the Early Eighteenth Century to the Nineteen Nineties.* The Athlone Press: London

Kesey K (1962) *One Flew Over the Cuckoo's Nest.* Methuen: London

Kettles AM, Byrt R (2007) Observation with engagement in acute areas. In: National Forensic Nurses' Research and Development Group: Kettles AM, Woods P, Byrt R, Addo M, Coffey M, Doyle M (eds) *Forensic Mental Health: Forensic Aspects of Acute Care* Quay Books: London

Kettles AM, Byrt R, Woods P (2007) Introduction. In: National Forensic Nurses' Research and Development Group: Kettles AM, Woods P, Byrt R, Addo M, Coffey M, Doyle M (eds) *Forensic Mental Health: Forensic Aspects of Acute Care* Quay Books: London

Kettles AM, Woods P, Collins M (eds) (2002) *Therapeutic Interventions for Forensic Mental Health Nurses.* Jessica Kingsley: London

Kilshaw J (1999) Can medium secure units avoid becoming total institutions? In: Tarbuck P, Topping-Morris B, Burnard P (eds) *Forensic Mental Health Nursing: Strategy and Implementation.* Whurr Publishers: London

Kriesberg L (1996) Conflict, social. In: Kuper A, Kuper J (eds) *The Social Science Encyclopaedia* (2nd edn) Routledge, Taylor and Francis Group: London

Laing J, McQuarrie D (1989) *Fifty Years in the System.* Mainstream, Edinburgh

Laing RD (1961) *Self and Others.* Tavistock: London

Laing RD, Esterson D (1967) *Sanity, Madness and the Family.* Penguin Books: Harmondsworth

Lees J, Manning N, Rawlings B (2004) Therapeutic community research: An overview and meta-analysis. In: Lees J, Manning N, Menzies D, Morant N (eds) *A Culture of Enquiry: Research Evidence and the Therapeutic Community* (Chapter 2) Jessica Kingsley: London

Liderth S (2003) Untitled section. In: Dooher J, Byrt R (eds) *Empowerment and the Health Service User.* Quay Books: Dinton, Salisbury

Littlewood R, Lipsege M (1997) *Aliens and Alienists* (3rd edn) Penguin Books: Harmondsworth

Lowe T (1992) Characteristics of effective nursing interventions in the management of challenging behaviour. *J Adv Nursing* **17** 1226–1232

McArdle S, Byrt R (2001) Fiction, poetry and mental health. Expressive and creative uses of literature. *J Psych Ment Health Nurs* **8**(6) 517–525

McDougall T (2000) Violent incidents in a forensic adolescent unit: A functional analysis. *NT Research* **5**(5) 346–362

McMurran M (ed) (2002) *Motivating Offenders to Change: A Guide to enhancing Engagement in Therapy.* John Wiley and Sons: Chichester

Mandela N (1965) *No Easy Walk to Freedom: Articles, Speeches and Trial Addresses.* Heinemann: London

Marshall G (ed) (1994) *The Concise Oxford Dictionary of Sociology.* Oxford University Press: Oxford

Mason T, Chandley M (1990) Nursing models in a special hospital: A critical analysis of efficacy. *J Adv Nurs* 15 667–673

Mason T, Mercer D (1998) *Critical Perspectives in Forensic Care: Inside Out.* Macmillan: Basingstoke

Meehan T, McIntosh W, Bergen H (2006) Aggressive behaviour in high-secure settings:

The perceptions of patients. *J Psych Ment Health Nurs* **13**(1) 19–25

Mental Health Alliance (2008) From: http://www.mentalhealthalliance.org.uk/ [Accessed 15 September 2008]

Mercer D, Mason T, Richman J (1999) Good and evil in the crusade of care. *J Psychosoc Nurs Ment Health Services* **37**(9) 13–17

Miers M (1999) Health teams in the community. In: Wilkinson G, Miers M (eds) *Power and Nursing Practice*. Macmillan: Basingstoke

Miller P, Rose N (eds) (1986) *The Power of Psychiatry*. Polity Press, Cambridge with Basil Blackwell: Oxford

Morgan S, Wetherell A (2004) Assessing and Managing Risk. In: Norman I, Ryrie I (eds) *The Art and Science of Mental Health Nursing: A Textbook of Principles and Practice*. Open University Press: Maidenhead

National Forensic Nurses' Research and Development Group: Woods P, Kettles AM, Byrt R, Addo M, Aiyegbusi A, Coffey M, Collins M, Doyle M, Garman G, Watson C (eds) (2006) *Forensic Mental Health Nursing: Interventions with People with Personality Disorder*. Quay Books: London

National Forensic Nurses' Research and Development Group: Kettles AM, Woods P, Byrt R, Addo M, Coffey M, Doyle M (eds) (2007) *Forensic Mental Health: Forensic Aspects of Acute Care* Quay Books: London

Neuman B (1995) *The Neuman Systens Model* (3rd edn) Appleton and Lange: Norwalk, CT

NHS Business Management Service. Counter-Fraud and Security Management Service (2006) *Areas of Work. Legal Protection Unit*. Available from: http://www.cfsmsnhs.uk/sms/lpu.html

O'Brien AJ, Morrison-Ngati E (2003) Providing culturally safe care. In: Barker P (ed) *Psychiatric and Mental Health Nursing: The Craft of Caring*. Arnold: London

Okasha S (2002) *Philosophy of Science: A Very Short Introduction*. Oxford University Press: Oxford

Parsons S, Armstrong A (2000) Psychiatric power and authority: A scientific and moral defence. In: Barker P, Stevenson C (eds) *The Construction of Power and Authority in Psychiatry*. Butterworth Heinemann: Oxford

Perseius K-I, Ojehagen A, Ekdahl S, Asberg M, Samuelsson M (2003) Treatment of suicidal and deliberate self-harming patients with borderline personality disorder using dialectical behavior therapy: The patients' and the therapists' perceptions. *Arch Psych Nurs* **17**(5) 218–227

Pilgrim R, Rogers A (2005) *The Sociology of Mental Health and Illness* (3rd edn) Open University Press: Maidenhead

Post F (1994) Creativity and psychopathology: A study of 291 world-famous men. *Brit J Psychiatry* **164** 22–34

Prins H (2005) *Offenders, Deviants or Patients?* (3rd edn) Routledge and Francis Group: London

Ramsbotham D (2005) *Prisongate: The Shocking State of Britain's Prisons and the Need for Visionary Change*. Free Press: London

Rawlings B (1998) The therapeutic community in the prison: Problems in maintaining therapeutic integrity. *Therapeutic Communities* **19**(4) 281–294

Repper J, Perkins R (2003) *Social Inclusion and Recovery: A Model for Mental Health*

Practice. Bailliere Tindall: Edinburgh

Rogers C (1978) *Carl Rogers on Personal Power: Inner Strength and Its Revolutionary Impact*. Constable: London

Rogers P, Vidgen A (2006) Working with people with severe mental illness who are angry. In: Gamble C, Brennan W (eds) *Working with Serious Mental Illness: A Manual for Clinical Practice*. Elsevier: Edinburgh

Sayce L (2000) *From Psychiatric Patient to Citizen: Overcoming Discrimination and Social Exclusion*. Macmillan: Basingstoke

Schafer P, Peternelj-Taylor C (2003) Therapeutic relationships and boundary maintenance: The perspective of forensic patients enrolled in a treatment program for violent offenders. *Issues in Ment Health Nurs* **24** 605–625

Secker J, Benson A, Balfe E, Lipsedge M, Robinson S, Walker J (2004) Understanding the social context of violent and aggressive incidents on an inpatient unit. *J Psych Ment Health Nurs* **11**(2) 172–178

Smith G, Bartlett A, King M (2004) Treatments of homosexuality in Britain since the nineteen fifties: An oral history: The experience of patients. *Brit Med J* **328**(7437) 427–429

Stone JH, Roberts M, O'Grady J, Taylor AV, O'Shea, K (2000) *Faulk's Basic Forensic Psychiatry* (3rd edn) Blackwell Publishing: Oxford.

Szasz T (1961) *The Myth of Mental Illness*. Dell: New York

Szasz T (1963) *Law Liberty and Psychiatry*. Macmillan: New York

Szasz T (1971) *The Manufacture of Madness*. Routledge and Kegan Paul: London

Szasz T (2000) The case against psychiatric power. In: Barker P, Stevenson C (eds) *The Construction of Power and Authority in Psychiatry*. Butterworth Heinemann: Oxford

Tew J (ed) (2005a) *Social Perspectives in Mental Health: Developing Social Models to Understand and Work with Mental Distress*. Jessica Kingsley: London

Tew J (2005b) Power Relations, Social Order and Mental Distress. In: Tew J (ed) *Social Perspectives in Mental Health: Developing Social Models to Understand and Work with Mental Distress*. Jessica Kingsley: London

Thompson IE, Melia KM, Boyd KM, Horsburgh D (2006) *Nursing Ethics* (5th edn) Churchill Livingstone, Elsevier: Edinburgh

Thompson N (2003) *Promoting Equality: Challenging Discrimination and Oppression* (2nd edn) Palgrave, Macmillan: Basingstoke

Towl G, Snow L, McHugh M (2000) *Suicide in Prisons*. BPS Books: Leicester

Van Marle HJC (2002) The Dutch Entrustment Act (TBS): Its principles and innovations. *Int J Forensic Ment Health* **1**(1) 83–92

Walsh E (2007) *The Emotional Labour of Prison Nurses in England and Wales*. Presentation, based on PhD thesis at International Custody and Caring Conference, September, 2007 (hosted by the College of Nursing, University of Sakatchewan in collaboration with the Regional Psychiatric Centre (Prairies), Correctional Service, Canada. Saskatoon, Canada)

Warner C (1992) Responding to aggression. *Nursing Times* **88**(30) 46–47

Welldon EV, Van Velsen C (1997) Introduction. In: Welldon EV, Van Velsen C (eds) *Forensic Psychotherapy*. Jessica Kingsley: London

Westwood S (2002) *Power and the Social.* Routledge: London

Wiertsema, H, Derks F (1997) Residential forensic treatment: The interplay between case management and institutional management. In: van Marle H (ed) *Challenges in Forensic Psychotherapy.* Jessica Kingsley: London

Wilkinson G (1999) Theories of power. In: Wilkinson G, Miers M (eds) *Power and Nursing Practice.* Macmillan: Basingstoke

Wing J (1978) *Reasoning About Madness.* Oxford University Press: Oxford

Wix S, Humphreys M (eds) (2005) *Multidisciplinary Working in Forensic Mental Health Care.* Elsevier, Churchill Livingstone: Edinburgh

Zachary A (1997) Murderousness. In: Van Marle H (ed) *Challenges in Forensic Psychotherapy.* Jessica Kingsley: London

CHAPTER 7

Patient empowerment and participation: Barriers and the way forward

Richard Byrt, Linda Hart and Linnette James-Sow

Introduction

This chapter considers barriers to patient empowerment and participation in secure hospitals and prison health services and considers some possible ways forward. Patients' perspectives are of crucial importance (Laing with McQuarrie, 1989; Anonymous, 2000; 'George', 1998; Hart, 2007) and the chapter starts with two poems related to this. The chapter also considers patient satisfaction surveys, cultural and diversity issues and economic, political and other factors.

Poems on disempowerment

Skewered
by Linda Hart

You dream of fishing,
trout, salmon, bream,
whatever the weather
in the highlands of Scotland.

I, like the Laird's lug,
hear you dreaming.

But now, in the lowlands,
a doctor of minds,
you pay your tithes to the Knights of Dishonour,
the trawler of nuts,
and fish, their way.

Throw back into the raging waters, minnows;
cast aside red herrings;
pass electric eels through heads of the depressed;
seclude troublesome pike in whirlpools of privation;
harpoon the helpless and hopeless in eddies of empathy;
net psychotics in thread so fine
they don't even realise they've been, caught –
mended into knotted robots.

So now you are a fisher of men,
like Jesus Christ.
But, as Jesus Christ was a man-made, wish-fulfilment,
your wish is unfulfilled
in obliterating our souls by feeding us
a diet of worms.

Someday, you will return to be a fisher of fish,
trout, salmon, bream,
and leave us to the waters we breathe,
and dream like you once did,
whatever the weather.

Mad or bad
by Linnette James-Sow

As I walked through the doors, the setting looks so familiar.
It reminded me of my time spent incarcerated
However, instead of being welcomed by men and women dressed in
  uniforms, which was a clear distinction between staff and inmates
I was greeted by two plain clothes men and one woman.
I was relieved....gone are the days when I would be stripped
  searched! dictated to about when I should retire to bed and when
  I should get up in the mornings...help has finally arrived... I have
  been sent to a place where I will finally be understood and cared
  for...well so I thought.

I was led down a steep corridor which was the entrance to my new
  home.
There, I met three women and four other men
They seemed welcoming, however, I couldn't help but notice the
  manner in which I was being scrutinised by the nurses.

One looked at me with utter disgust, as if to say you have been wrongly
  placed.
As the days went by, I began to realised that my dreams were short
  lived
My dream home was not what it initially appeared to be.

Freedom was still limited, I was made to feel on several occasions that
  I was a time waster
I was made to feel that I wasn't unwell and should and could take
  responsibility for my actions.

How am I ever going to be able to get the care that I so need and
  craved if no one can understand my plight.
I was rejected at birth, rejected in childhood
Got thrown from one prison to the next because society didn't know
  what to do with my kind and...and now that I have been put in what is
  called a Forensic Unit, it's happening all over again.

The problem is, nurses seemed to be more tolerant of the textbook
  presentation of what constitutes being mentally unwell

the delusional beliefs
  the flight of ideas
    the ideas of referencing

They seem to find it difficult to accept that through these periods of one
  being unwell that they can resort to an act, as callous as what I have
  committed.

An act that is out of character for myself when well.

Not everyone expresses grandiose delusional beliefs
Some of us experience persecutory beliefs and through these beliefs
  react as an act of defence.

I am the violent thug who's hiding behind the security of a mental
  institute, they believe.
But they are so wrong, I am just a man who was given a diagnosis that
  I was and still am ill-equipped to deal with.

I don't understand much about my illness and the manner in which it
  presents itself

But I do know that I am a horrible being or so I am led to believe.
Horrible enough to be rejected over and over again
Judged and ostracised by those I come in contact with

Even my own carers... the very professionals.

Consumerism

Written accounts by service users and carers, and reflective narratives by staff can enable us to consider the perspectives of recipients of forensic mental health services (McArdle and Byrt, 2001). Patient satisfaction surveys, related to consumerist participation, are another way of achieving this.

Some components of empowerment appear to overlap with the concept of consumerist participation (Lupton et al, 1998; Braye, 2000; Thompson, 2007). The latter is based on consumerism: the introduction of free market ideas, such as choice and 'customer' satisfaction, to public services. Consumerism in forensic health and other public services has developed since the first Thatcher Government in 1979 (Hogg, 1999). Consumerist participation is concerned with patients' needs and how these can be met by a service, and with issues of 'accessibility, information, choice, redress and representation' (Braye, 2000: 18). It can be argued that patient satisfaction surveys enable participation of forensic patients because they provide opportunities to give views about services, and at best, influence change. However, it has been argued that a democratic model of participation gives opportunities for more meaningful involvement, as the aim is to give service users the power to affect the formulation of policies, decide how resources will be used and be involved in how a service is managed (Braye, 2000). In addition, the democratic model of participation is concerned with enabling people to have greater control and social inclusion in their lives in general (Thompson, 2007).

Patient satisfaction surveys

Patient satisfaction surveys are an example of consumerist participation. A conflict theorist might well respond: 'Why ask patients in secure hospitals and prisons their views when they have no choice but to be patients?' (Byrt, 2001). This is a question that has been considered at Arnold Lodge medium secure unit, where the rationale for the surveys relates to the Unit's aim 'to provide patients with assessment, care, treatment and rehabilitation of a high standard' (Byrt, 2001), as well ensuring public safety. In addition, the conduct of patient satisfaction surveys is in line with NHS Trust and central Government requirements (Department of Health, 2002 cited in Carlin et al, 2005; Healthcare Commission, 2007).

It is crucial that the problems and contradictions identified by conflict theorists (e.g. Foucault, 1991; Mason and Mercer, 1998; Szasz, 2000) are recognised. Nevertheless, many, if not all the Arnold Lodge stakeholders involved in planning surveys, consider that, while a secure service is necessary for the safety of others, it should still be possible to enable patients to express views to identify areas of both satisfaction and dissatisfaction, so that 'good practice' and areas for change and improvement can be identified (Byrt, 2001). The majority of 'patient participation in Arnold Lodge is consumerist and concerned with attempts to introduce changes [in aspects of the service] based on patients' views. In Arnold Lodge, consumerist participation is easier to introduce, partly because of possible safety issues and the expectations of other stakeholders' (Byrt, 2001). Within the Unit, besides several patient satisfaction surveys on a wide range of topics, there have been studies of the views of women (Byrt et al, 2001) and patients of minority ethnic groups. Other projects have been concerned with patients' perspectives of the care programme approach, occupational therapy, therapeutic groups, length of treatment, ward atmosphere, drug use, and self-harm (Byrt and Reece, 1999).

Service user participation in patient satisfaction and other research

Many patient satisfaction surveys in secure hospitals have been facilitated by staff members (Coffey, 2006). However, individuals with experience as service users in forensic and other mental health services have been increasingly involved in planning, conducting and reporting on their own research projects (Spiers et al, 2005; Halsall, 2006). Much of this work has been facilitated by the former UK National Forensic Mental Health Research and Development Programme, which enabled the participation of forensic patients and clients in commissioning and conducting research (Spiers et al, 2005). One project, sponsored by the National Forensic Mental Health Research and Development Programme, was of a survey of patients' views at Bracton Medium Secure Unit. All stages of the research were carried out by two people who had been forensic patients and one individual with other mental health service user experience. The research report includes summaries of the views of both women and men and recommendations based on patients' views (Halsall, 2006).

A similar model of solely patient-owned research would have advantages for other secure hospitals (Spiers et al, 2005). Since 1998, surveys at Arnold Lodge have been facilitated by one or more staff members, with, in most surveys, the participation of a variety of stakeholders, who have been:

...involved in working groups to plan surveys and contribute to the design of questionnaires/interview schedules. Most importantly, working groups have included patients, whose views have possibly ensured that issues of salience to them are included, and that questions are clearly worded. Participants from independent organisations have been involved, in both planning and conducting the survey, and in making recommendations for change. As individuals who are both concerned about patients' needs and rights, and who are not part of 'the system', they are able to perceive, in a fresh way, both good practice and areas needing change and development.

(Byrt, 2001).

These stakeholders have included participants in the 'Together' independent advocacy service, which provides patient advocacy to Arnold Lodge and other secure hospitals in Nottinghamshire Healthcare NHS Trust; and the Unit's Commissioning Advisory Panel (comprising people with experience as mental health service users) who advise the commissioners of the service on quality issues, and who meet regularly with Arnold Lodge patients. Managers within Nottinghamshire Healthcare NHS Trust and its Forensic Directorate have been involved in planning one recent survey, which was conducted in other forensic services besides Arnold Lodge. Other stakeholders have included representatives of Remit, service commissioners from a local Primary Care Trust and the former Leicestershire Community Health Council. At the time of writing, it is hoped, in future, to involve other stakeholders, including a local organisation representing the rights of local people with mental health problems from minority ethnic groups.

There are opportunities for every Arnold Lodge patient, manager and staff member to be involved. People who wish to do so, but cannot attend working group meetings, or who dislike this forum, are seen individually or in a ward meeting or invited to submit ideas by email.

The 'audit cycle'

Work involving patient satisfaction surveys involves an 'audit cycle' (Taylor and Jones, 2006), with planning for a survey taking into account the questions asked in the previous study; and making modifications in the light of any problems encountered, e.g. in the wording of questions. Planning includes informing all patients, managers and staff of the survey a few months before it is due to take part. Following the carrying out of the survey, data are collated and analysed by staff members and a summary and/or full, illustrated report is sent to every patient, manager and directly involved stakeholder; and made available to staff. An action plan is devised. This includes informing staff

---

Box 7.1: Example of an action plan

Item	Information about accessing health records
Progress achieved by (date)	'Ward noticeboards are being checked quarterly' Patients assessed as 'generally happy with the clarity of information' 'Notice boards clearly advertise where to obtain further information'
Lead manager/staff	AS, Clinical Governance Manager
Further action/comments	Further quarterly audits

---

of examples of good practice, which is assumed to be equated with high ratings of satisfaction for specific items. The action plan also includes the items receiving the lowest ratings, with specified action to be taken, person responsible for implementation, and deadline for achievement. (*Box 7.1* shows an example of an action plan.) The following survey (conducted one to two years later) measures whether or not high patient satisfaction has been maintained; and the extent of improvements in satisfaction in response to areas of prior dissatisfaction. Importantly, where it is not possible to effect improvements (e.g. because of lack of resources) patients are informed of this, e.g. in their copy of the report on the survey findings. For example, although patients, understandably, have wanted increased access to the Unit's sports field, this has been delayed because of extensive building works at a time when new wards were being constructed.

The questionnaire/interview schedule at Arnold Lodge

Questions are agreed by Working Group members and administered 'as a self-completed questionnaire or an interview schedule' (Byrt, 2001). Surveys are concerned with 'treatment, information and communication; environment and living conditions; and...food' (Byrt, 2001). Most questions are scored on a Likert rating scale (Murphy-Black, 2006), for example, 'very good', 'good', 'satisfactory', 'bad' and 'very bad'. At least one open-ended question asks respondents to list particular likes and suggested changes and improvements. Patients have also been asked to give their ethnic group and ward, so that comparisons can be made.

Conducting the survey

Originally, the NHS Trust that managed Arnold Lodge saw the surveys as research projects, so research ethics committee approval was sought and granted.

The surveys are well supported by managers and staff, as well as by patients, with response rates ranging from 63% to 85%.

Before a survey takes place, each individual is seen by a working group member, and given information about the survey and the ensuing action plan, with an opportunity for discussion. A brief illustrated leaflet with a phone number for queries, is distributed. Some patients have expressed preferences for 'user-friendly' leaflets, with a dislike of more formal information.

Surveys occur on the wards at times that suit patients and staff, fitting round important activities for patients, including, one year, a crucial televised football tournament. Of especial importance is ensuring that the survey is 'as relaxed, informal and enjoyable as possible' (Byrt, 2001). This is facilitated by purchasing food for a buffet to accompany the survey. People are informed of confidentiality and anonymity, with the proviso that if the individual voiced intentions to harm self or others, this would be passed on to a nurse (Byrt and Reece, 1999). (Such intentions have never been mentioned in the patient satisfaction surveys.) It is also explained that anonymised data may be presented at meetings or conferences or in publications.

Choice of researcher and questionnaire or interview

Each individual is given the choice of a self-completed questionnaire, with help available if required, or a relaxed interview with working group members who are independent advocates or other voluntary organisation participants; or with a staff member on the respondent's ward. This choice may well influence survey findings, particularly in relation to the number and detail of patients' comments. However, it is felt that offering choice in this area needs to be the prime consideration. Advantages include achievement of a relatively high response rate and results that enable identification of themes and the highest and lowest areas of overall satisfaction and dissatisfaction.

Results of surveys and subsequent action plans

In general, patients have expressed relatively high satisfaction in relation to staff, activities related to education, occupational therapy, sports and recreation, privacy and 'access to tea and coffee on the wards' (Byrt, 2001). The latter item has had the highest rating among over 50 items in several surveys. In general, there are lower ratings for aspects of information, with two items related to this and 'privacy when using the telephone' showing little or no improvement following action plans and low levels of patient satisfaction in at least two surveys (Arnold Lodge, 2006: See *Box 7.2*).

There is little point in conducting patient satisfaction surveys unless they result in positive changes reflecting patients' views, with a manager

---

Box 7.2: Results of surveys and subsequent actions plans

Areas with consistently high ratings over several surveys
- Access to tea and coffee on the wards
- Help/quality of care from nursing staff
- Patient education
- Occupational therapy/therapeutic activities, including exercise/sport
- Social and recreational activities
- Opportunities for fresh air
- Privacy in the bathroom/shower

Areas with little or no improvement following action plans
- Privacy when using the telephone
- Information on how to access your health records.
- Information on side effects/risks of medication

Areas of greatest improvement following action plans
- Social and recreational activities
- Aspects of the physical environment
- Access to books
- Laundry facilities
- Dental services
- Cost and variety of items in the patients' shop

(Arnold Lodge, 2006)

---

with responsibility for formulating and implementing an action plan. Halsall (2006: 4) reports that, in the Bracton Unit survey, patients asked if the 'user-led research would be listened to'. At times, some Arnold Lodge patients have expressed dissatisfaction with delays in effecting change in general, or in specific areas. Patients' ideas are carefully considered, with honest explanations given if they are difficult to implement, e.g. for safety reasons.

At Arnold Lodge, for some areas, patient satisfaction has increased following intensive improvements as a result of implementing action plans. When wards were redecorated and new furniture and more space provided, there was a statistically significant increase in overall satisfaction with 'several aspects of the physical environment' (Byrt, 2001). Following funding for books for a patients' library, a librarian and a social and recreational officer, satisfaction with access to books and leisure activities increased markedly. Over the last few years, the opening of the Unit's dental suite and the appointment of dental staff has resulted in increased satisfaction with dental services, but with this area still being rated lowly in comparison with most aspects of care, treatment and service.

A critique of patient satisfaction surveys

Do patient satisfaction studies actually measure 'patient satisfaction'? This question is related to considerations of validity (Coffey, 2006; Gerrish and Lacey, 2006). A number of researchers have concluded that ticking set responses (e.g. such as in a Likert rating scale) does not give an accurate picture of patients' views (Dougall et al, 2000; Jenkinson et al, 2002). In most research using Likert scales, few respondents choose the lowest rated answers (e.g. 'poor' or 'very poor') (Edelmann, 2000). There is also the problem of interpreting results. (If 70% of patients rate access to their solicitors as 'good', should this be seen as a favourable result? Or does the fact that 30% rated it as less than 'good' give cause for concern?)

Some researchers have found that qualitative research gives a much more detailed and accurate picture of individuals' satisfaction, and therefore, provides more useful and accurate material to inform improvements in care. Some qualitative research has included opportunities for patients to give detailed responses to open-ended questions and state what they consider to be important. In two studies, while patients gave high scores in patient satisfaction surveys in answer to rated questions, they identified many sources of dissatisfaction in qualitative research (Dougall et al, 2000; Jenkinson et al, 2002).

Coffey (2006: 78–9) identifies many methodological and ethical problems in his review of research on patient satisfaction. These include particular methods and methodologies chosen; and 'consistency in [their] application; failure to clearly outline the approach...used to analyse responses' and a tendency to take findings at their 'face value', without cognisance of 'the situated and context-bound nature of the production of accounts'. Importantly, Coffey (2006) concludes that, 'forensic mental health researchers have not yet accessed views of services in a sustained, systematic and critical fashion or in a way that represents the multiple perspectives of service users' (Coffey 2006: 82).

At best, patient satisfaction surveys may influence changes in care, treatment and services within secure hospitals and prison health services, particularly if patients are involved in the research process and action is taken to implement changes in response to their views (Spiers et al, 2005; Halsall, 2006). However, it can also be argued, particularly by conflict theorists, that such surveys do not consider inequalities in power or the fact that patients have no choice but to be in the institution. It is doubtful whether patient satisfaction surveys result in patients' 'democratic participation' (Braye, 2000) in policy formulation and decision making at higher levels.

Issues of culture, equality and diversity

Patient empowerment and participation is related, in part, to the extent that care is culturally sensitive and competent, that it relates to principles of equality and diversity and avoids discrimination (Byrt et al, 2007). These issues are particularly relevant to the empowerment and participation of forensic patients, partly because so many of them face 'double prejudice, negative discrimination [and] social exclusion' (Byrt et al, 2007: 221, citing Bartlett, 2004). This relates to their roles as both mental health patients and people with histories of offending, with many patients 'facing further social exclusion because of ethnic group, culture, religion, sexual orientation, gender identity, age, disability' (Byrt et al, 2007: 221). Some conflict theorists have considered power and its lack in relation to being a woman (Showalter, 1987; Prior, 1999), having minority ethnic group status (Fernando, 2002), being gay or lesbian (Godfrey, 2003), and having a disability (Barnes and Mercer, 2003) or mental health problem (Repper and Perkins, 2003; Tew, 2005).

Research has found that individuals subject to discrimination in wider society also sometimes experience this within forensic and other mental health services (Pilgrim and Rogers, 2005). In the UK, black people of African, Caribbean and African Caribbean origin are over-represented in prison populations. In addition, they are more likely to be compulsorily admitted, transferred to secure hospitals, diagnosed with schizophrenia, and prescribed antipsychotics (Byrt et al, 2007). Three Government inquiries into secure hospitals found evidence of racism (HM Government, 1992; Prins et al, 1993; Blofeld, 2003), with, in one instance, assumptions that black men were more 'dangerous' than other patients (Prins et al, 1993). The inquiry into the death of David Bennett in a medium secure unit found that, shortly before Mr Bennett's death while being restrained, his complaints about another patient's racist comments had been ignored, and that during Mr Bennett's stay in various services, his cultural and spiritual needs were not adequately assessed or met (Blofield, 2003).

In addition, research findings suggest that individuals of minority ethnic groups often experience disempowerment because they find mental health services frightening and inaccessible, and at times overtly or institutionally racist, with some staff lacking cultural sensitivity and cultural competence (Fernando, 2002; Secker and Harding, 2002). In relation to this, the Department of Health (2005a, b) has set out targets for forensic and other mental health services to achieve. These include reduction of the number of black patients who are admitted compulsorily; ensuring that mental health services are more accessible and more effectively meet the needs of people of minority ethnic groups, with greater cultural sensitivity and cultural competence; and providing relevant training to staff. Community workers have been appointed to liaise between local community, religious and voluntary organisations and mental health services (Department of Health, 2005a, b, 2006).

The Equality Act (HM Government, 2006) requires forensic and other public services to avoid discrimination, with several requirements related to individuals' religious and other beliefs, ethnic group, disability, and gender. Further relevant targets are given in the Department of Health's (2006) Single Equality Scheme, 2006–2009. These include revision of the Mental Health Act Code of Practice to reflect equality and diversity issues, further research on compulsory admissions of 'young black men', and steps to lessen stigmatisation. NHS Trusts are required to work towards implementing the action outlined in the Single Equality Scheme at a local level. This included the following outcomes for forensic mental health services in Oxleas NHS Foundation Trust:

- Need for staff to attend equality and diversity training.
- Monitor access to culturally appropriate food.
- Monitor incidents/complaints involving racial abuse/violence.
- Monitor use of interpreting services.
- Need for culturally appropriate advocacy.
- Continue to provide advocacy for women service users.
- Monitor admissions and length of stay by ethnicity.
                                    (Oxleas NHS Foundation Trust 2006: 40)

Byrt and Hardie (2007: 235) outline various 'cultural competencies' in relation to 'communication and the nurse–patient relationship…information and interpreting services…empathy, validation and affirmative counselling'. This list of competencies also includes recognition of cultural factors in relation to risk assessments; and the individual's needs related to spirituality, physical health, gender, disability, sexuality and relationships. 'Organisational aspects', including 'policies…recruitment…and clinical supervision' are also listed.

Table 7.1 indicates sources of disempowerment for individuals who are lesbian, gay, bisexual or transgendered clients and ways to increase empowerment.

Social inclusion

An important dimension of empowerment relates to social inclusion (Byrt and Dooher, 2002; Dooher and Byrt, 2005). Besides the factors considered earlier in this chapter, many forensic patients have experienced social

Table 7.1: Lesbian and gay patients' sources of disempowerment and empowerment (Aiyegbusi and Byrt, 2006)

Source of disempowerment	*Source of empowerment in nursing/ multidisciplinary interventions*
Experience of homophobia in both wider society and within health services	Recognition of the individual's experience of homophobia Avoidance of homophobia in care, service and treatment provided
Many health assessments reflect staff assumptions that all individuals are heterosexual or have a fixed gender identity	Assessments that avoid such assumptions
Partner or friend of the same gender: • Often not recognised by staff as being the most significant person in the patient's life • May be refused information or visiting opportunities, despite the patient's/client's requests	Asking the patient whom he/she would like recorded as his/her significant person for visits, given information and contacted in emergencies
Limited treatment is available for transsexual individuals	Explaining to the patient the assessment process and opportunities for treatment
Lack of gay, lesbian, bisexual or transsexual affirmative approaches	Providing counselling and other approaches that affirm and validate the individual's sexual orientation and gender identity

exclusion because of their reduced opportunities and life chances, both as children and adults, prior to admission to a forensic service (Gilligan, 2001). The latter adds to social exclusion, partly because of the stigma and because of separation from partner/spouse, children, other relatives and friends; and loss of freedom and valued roles and activities (Hufft, 1999; Harner, 2004; Byrt and James, 2007).

An important aspect of social inclusion is an emphasis, not only on important issues related to individuals' symptoms and problems and associated risk, but also on opportunities for them to discover and develop a wide range of aptitudes, abilities and interests; and fulfil goals that enable each individual to find hope, purpose and meaning, in accordance with recovery principles (Repper and Perkins, 2003). At Arnold Lodge, for example, all patients have chances to further their education, participate in individualised health and fitness programmes and learn a musical instrument (Byrt et al, 2005). Other stakeholders (e.g. some members of the public and politicians) might argue that providing further education is a waste of taxpayers' money; or that patients are being educated to conform to the expectations and dominant 'knowledge' of those in power (Foucault, 1991). However, research findings suggest that increasing individuals' education levels reduces recidivism (Gilligan, 2001).

Aspects of social exclusion, and action to increase social inclusion are shown in *Table 7.3* (Morris, 2006; National Forensic Nurses' Research and Development Group, 2006, 2007; Repper and Perkins, 2003; Tew, 2005).

Economic and political power and patient empowerment

Notions of patient empowerment can appear nonsensical, or, at best, limited, when services fail to meet forensic patients' basic needs and rights (Lester and Glasby, 2006). It can be argued that ideas of empowerment and participation of forensic patients (and nurses) are constrained because of their lack of political, economic and ideological power (Foucault, 1991). In particular, some aspects of power are largely dependent on global, political and economic factors (Westwood, 2002), which appear to influence, in part, the quality and availability of services. For example, there are appalling conditions in some prisons (Ramsbotham, 2003; Stern,

Table 7.3: Aspects of social exclusion and action to increase inclusion in secure hospitals and prison health services

Aspect of social exclusion	Action to increase social inclusion (within safety parameters)
Stigma from patient and offender status and other sources	Enable the individual to gain self-esteem and develop aptitudes Public education and information
Not being respected or valued by staff	Ensure both patients and staff are valued and respected
Loss of freedom and autonomy	Avoid levels of security and restrictions greater than warranted by the individual's assessed level of risk

Loss of contact with partner, spouse, children, other family, friends Unnecessary restrictions on visiting	Visiting areas (and staff) that are welcoming and child, teenager and adult friendly
Loss of close emotional and sexual relationships Limited opportunities for sexual expression.	Enable continuation of close relationships as far as possible Enable expression of gender identity Respect need for privacy
Losses in family, work and other important roles, identities and activities	Fulfilling, meaningful activities. Enable development of abilities, aptitudes and skills
Impoverished physical environments	Physically therapeutic environments
Loss of contact with local community, including cultural and spiritual networks	Public open days Invite local groups into the service Enable patients to maintain contacts
Exclusive focus on narrow perceptions of risk, symptoms and problems	Use of a recovery model, concerned also with areas important to the individual
Focusing on a narrow range of needs	Attempt to assess and meet a wide range of needs
Limited recognition and meeting of diversity needs	Assessment and implementation of care and treatment sensitive to the individual's diversity needs
Failure to recognise the importance of the individual's experiences of discrimination and social exclusion	Recognition of the importance to the individual of his/her experiences of discrimination and social exclusion
Failure to recognise the adverse effects of being a patient in a secure hospital or prison	Recognition of, and attempts to ameliorate, these adverse effects
Limited recognition of needs for legal and independent voluntary advocates Limited provision of the latter	Provision of accessible information on legal and independent voluntary advocates Provision of the latter
Limited opportunities for empowerment and participation	Considerable opportunities for empowerment and participation

2006), with many prisoners with mental health problems failing to receive the care, treatment and services that they need (Coid et al, 2003; Rollin, 2006). Some individuals' rights are infringed because they receive care in levels of security higher than is warranted by their assessed level of risk. There are moves to reduce this in the UK (Collins et al, 2005). However, there is a lack of facilities for recovery and rehabilitation (Lester and Glasby, 2006). Public safety, security and other goals take precedence over participation and empowerment, therapy and rehabilitation (Lester and Glasby, 2006), including measures that do not necessarily increase public safety, even though, arguably, they infringe patients' rights. Examples include increased security measures in high secure hospitals, following the Tilt Review (Department of Health, 2000) and policy and services for people described by the Government as having 'dangerous and severe personality disorders' (Byrt and Dooher, 2006). In addition, political power also appears to influence whether some people who commit serious offences associated with mental illness or personality disorder are sentenced by courts to prison or a secure hospital (Eastman, 1997).

Lukes' (1974) three 'dimensions of power' are of relevance to these aspects of political power. *'Success in the decision-making process'* (Morgan 1999: 17) refers to a number of individuals achieving clear political or other aims. *'Setting the decision-making agenda'* is the way that groups in positions of political power are able to ensure that policies with which they disagree are ignored (Morgan, 1999). This means that certain issues become politically invisible (Godfrey, 2003). An example is a shortage of services that means that some patients, ready to move to less secure facilities, are detained in conditions of security greater than is warranted by their assessed level of risk. This does not appear to be have attracted the level of political concern or visibility that some would argue is required, given the infringement of individual patients' rights (Collins et al, 2005; Lester and Glasby. 2006). Luke's third dimension of power is *'shaping the preferences of others'*. This involves the success of a group in controlling the mass media to present certain things as 'facts', while ignoring others (Morgan, 1999). Thus, powerful interests appear to be successful in presenting, in newspapers, violent and other negative images of patients in secure hospitals, rather than focusing on the achievements of patients or staff (Phillips, 2003). In this way, there is a 'shaping' of readers' images of forensic patients and nurses.

Power and action by forensic mental health nurses

Despite the difficulties highlighted earlier in this chapter, it has been argued that forensic mental health nurses could usefully take a political role, especially in situations where there are Government proposals for legislation and policy that both infringe patients' rights and fail to contribute to public safety (Kettles et al, 2006). However, Welchman and Griener (2005) argue that, in practice, it is difficult for forensic nurses to advocate successfully, in North America, at least, because such a role is not entirely supported by their registration bodies. Notwithstanding these and other problems, the following are ways that forensic nurses can exercise power and otherwise facilitate patient empowerment and participation:

- Working with individuals with experience as forensic patients and with groups representing their interests (The Matthew Trust, 2008; Women in Secure Hospitals, 2008).
- Bringing to managers' attention (and where no action is taken, to the attention of the Nursing and Midwifery Council) any infringements of patients' rights and adverse effects on their care and treatment (e.g. shortage of resources) (Dimond, 2005).
- Joining professional allies/associations and trade unions to contribute to positive changes and to influence central and local Government policy (Mental Health Alliance, 2008).
- Developing roles in public education (Morris, 2006).
- Skilful use of the media (Phillips, 2003).
- Overcoming individual and organisational inertia that prevents questioning of the status quo, and taking action in response to forensic patients'/carers' views (Henriksen and Drayton, 2006)

Other means to increase patient empowerment and participation

In addition, it is suggested that the following factors facilitate empowerment and participation of forensic patients and their carers. This list is based on the literature (Dooher and Byrt, 2003; Tones and Green, 2004; Laverack, 2005; Collins et al, 2007) and the author's experience:

- Have a clear idea of the type, level and degree of empowerment and participation to be achieved.
- Have clear 'aims, goals and strategies' (Dooher and Byrt, 2003:278).
- Start small, with easily achievable results that make a positive difference to patients and/or their carers.
- Be honest about limits to participation/empowerment.
- Enable the empowerment and participation of grassroots staff, as well as patients.
- Consider the empowerment and participation of other stakeholders.
- Identify someone to take a lead to facilitate.

- Identify and provide resources.
- Devise and implement action plans in response to patients' views.
- Share good practice with colleagues.
- Measure the extent that participation/empowerment has led to positive changes.
- Include empowerment and participation as part of a service philosophy, agreed by patients, managers and staff.
- Promote an organisational culture conducive to the empowerment and participation of patients, carers and other stakeholders – including staff.
- Promote a shared commitment to empowerment and participation.
- Apply therapeutic frameworks/models which empower patients and carers and enable their participation.

Disempowering practices in historical perspective

Finally, the following quote illustrates the importance of practice based on critical thought and the ability to think ahead to the future:

> *The wisdom of hindsight allows us to smile…at some of the 'knowledge'… once passed off as psychiatric wisdom…*
> *Shall we look back in another 100 years with a similar incredulity at today's [forensic nursing practice]?*

(Barker, 2000: 3)

Conclusion

To what extent is patient empowerment and participation possible in forensic services? This chapter has attempted to answer this question, with a consideration of poems, patient satisfaction surveys, service user participation in research, issues of culture, equality and diversity, and social inclusion. It is concluded that economic and political factors are paramount in determining the extent of empowerment and participation of forensic nurses, as well as patients. The chapter concludes by considering ways to exert political influence and other means to increase patient empowerment and participation in forensic services.

Acknowledgements

Richard Byrt would like to thank IBC Conferences for agreement to quote and cite material from Byrt R (2001) Involving Service Users to Improve Quality in Arnold Lodge Medium Secure Unit. In: *Improving Mental Health Services Conference Pack*. Used as a basis for an IBC Ltd conference presentation, by C Lomas, P Sturman and R Byrt in March, 2001; and the Organising Committee for the College of Nursing, University of Saskatachewan and Regional Psychiatric Centre, Saskatoon Caring and Custody Conference, 2007, for the opportunity to present some of the material in *Chapters 5 to 7* at this conference.

References

Aiyegbusi A, Byrt R (2006) Gender and sexuality issues. In: National Forensic Nurses' Research and Development Group: Woods P, Kettles AM, Byrt R, Addo M, Aiyegbusi A, Coffey M, Collins M, Doyle M, Garman G, Watson C (eds) *Forensic Mental Health Nursing: Interventions with People with 'Personality Disorder'*. Quay Books, MA Healthcare Ltd, London

Anonymous (2000) The experience of being a black patient. In: Kaye C, Lingiah T (eds) *Race, Culture and Ethnicity in Secure Psychiatric Practice: Working with Difference*. Jessica Kingsley, London

Arnold Lodge Medium Secure Unit with 'Together' Independent Advocacy Service (2006) *2005 Patient Satisfaction Survey Report of Findings*. Unpublished, internal report by R Byrt. Arnold Lodge, Nottinghamshire Healthcare NHS Trust, Leicester

Barker P (2000) The construction of mind and madness: from Leonardo to the Hearing Voices Network In: Barker P, Stevenson C (eds) *The Construction of Power and Authority in Psychiatry*. Butterworth Heinemann, Oxford

Barnes C, Mercer G (2003) *Disability*. Polity Press, Cambridge

Blofield J (2003) *Independent Inquiry into the Death of David Bennett. An Independent Inquiry Set Up Under HSG (94) 27*. Department of Health, London

Braye S (2000) Participation and involvement in social care: an overview. In: Kemshall H, Littlechild R (eds) *User Involvement and Participation in Social Care: Research Informing Practice*. Jessica Kingsley, London

Byrt R (2001) Involving service users to improve quality in Arnold Lodge medium secure unit. In: *Improving Mental Health Services Conference Pack* (IBC Global Conferences, Ltd). March 2001. IBC Global Conferences, Ltd, London

Byrt R, Dooher J (2002) Empowerment and participation: Definitions, meanings and models. In: Dooher J, Byrt R (eds) *Empowerment and Participation: Power, Influence and Control in Contemporary Healthcare* (Ch 2). Quay Books, Mark Allen Publishing, Ltd, Dinton, Salisbury

Byrt R, Dooher J (2003) Service users and carers and their desire for empowerment and participation. In: Dooher J, Byrt R (eds) *Empowerment and the Health Service User*. Quay Books, Mark Allen Publishing, Dinton, Salisbury

Byrt R, Dooher, J (2006) The social consequences of a 'personality disorder' diagnosis. In: National Forensic Nurses' Research and Development Group: Woods P Kettles, AM Byrt R, Addo M, Aiyegbusi A, Coffey M, Collins M, Doyle M, Garman G, Watson C (eds) *Forensic Mental Health Nursing: Interventions with People with 'Personality Disorder'*. Quay Books, MA Healthcare Ltd, London

Byrt R, Hardie T (2007) Cultural sensitivity and cultural competence. In: National Forensic Nurses' Research and Development Group: Kettles AM, Woods P, Byrt R, Addo M, Coffey M, Doyle M (eds) *Forensic Mental Health: Forensic Aspects of Acute Care*.

Quay Books, MA Healthcare, London

Byrt R, Hardie T, Aigebusi A, Addo M (2007) Cultural and diversity issues. In: National Forensic Nurses' Research and Development Group: Kettles AM, Woods P, Byrt R, Addo M, Coffey M, Doyle M (eds) *Forensic Mental Health: Forensic Aspects of Acute Care*. Quay Books, MA Healthcare, London

Byrt R, James L (2007) Towards therapeutic environments: challenges and problems. In: National Forensic Nurses' Research and Development Group: Kettles AM, Woods P, Byrt R, Addo M, Coffey M, Doyle M (eds) Forensic Mental Health: Forensic Aspects of Acute Care. Quay Books, MA Healthcare, London

Byrt R, Lomas C, Gardiner J, Lewis D (2001) Working with women in secure environments. J Psychosoc Nurs Ment Health Services 39(9): 42–50

Byrt R, Reece J (1999) Patients' perspectives of self harm in a medium secure unit. Mental Health Practice 3(3): 30–6

Byrt R, Wray C, 'Tom' (2005) Towards hope and inclusion: nursing interventions in a medium secure service for men with 'personality disorders'. Ment Health Pract 8(8): 38–43

Carlin P, Gudjonsson G, Yates M (2005) Patient satisfaction with services in medium secure units. J Forensic Psychiatry Psychol 16(94): 714–28

Coffey M (2006) Researching service user views in forensic mental health: a literature review. Journal Forensic Psychiatry Psychol 17(1): 73–107

Coid J, Petruckevitch A, Bebbington P, Jenkins R, Brugha T, Lewis G, Farrell M, Singleton N (2003) Psychiatric morbidity in prisoners and solitary cellular confinement, II: special ('strip') cells. J Forensic Psychiatry Psychol 14(2): 320–40

Collins M, Davies S, Ashwell C (2005) The security needs assessment profile: a multidimensional approach to measuring security needs. Int J Forensic Ment Health 4(1): 39–52

Collins S, Britten N, Ruusuvuori J, Thompson A (eds) (2007) Patient Participation in Health Care Consultations. Qualitative Perspectives. McGraw Hill, Open University Press, Maidenhead

Department of Health (2000) Report of the Review of Security at the High Security Hospitals. (Chairman: Sir John Tilt). Department of Health, London

Department of Health (2002) Modernising Mental Health Services: Inspecting Mental Health Services. The Stationery Office: London. Cited in: Carlin P, Gudjonsson G, Yates M (eds) Patient satisfaction with services in medium secure units. J Forensic Psychiatry Psychol 16(94): 714–28

Department of Health (2005a) Delivering Race Equality and the Government's Response to the Inquiry into the Death of David Bennett. Department of Health, London

Department of Health (2005b) New Blueprint to Tackle and Eradicate Discrimination in Mental Health Services Over the Next Five Years. Department of Health, London

Department of Health (2006). Single Equality Scheme 2006–2009. The Stationery Office, London

Dimond B (2005) Legal Aspects of Nursing. Pearson Longman, Harlow

Dooher J, Byrt R (2003) Conclusions. In: Dooher J, Byrt R (eds) Empowerment and the Health Service User. Quay Books. Mark Allen Publishing, Dinton, Salisbury

Dooher J, Byrt R (2005) A critical examination of the concept of empowerment. In:

Cutcliffe JR, McKenna H (eds) The Essential Concepts of Nursing. Building Blocks for Practice Elsevier, Churchill Livingstone, Edinburgh

Dougall A, Russell A, Rubin G, Ling J (2000) Rethinking patient satisfaction: patient experiences of an open access flexible sigmoidoscopy service. Soc Sci Med **5**(1): 53–62

Eastman N (1997) Psychopathic disorder and therapeutic jurispudence. In: Van Marle H (ed) *Challenges in Forensic Psychotherapy*. Jessica Kingsley, London

Edelman RJ (2000) Attitude measurement. In: Cormack DFS (ed) *The Research Process in Nursing* (4th edn). Blackwell Science, Oxford

Fernando S (2002) *Mental Health, Race and Culture* (2nd edn). Palgrave, Basingstoke

Foucault M (1991) *Discipline and Punish. The Birth of the Prison*. Translated from the French by Alan Sheridan. Penguin Books: Harmondsworth

Gerrish K, Lacey A (eds) (2006) *The Research Process in Nursing* (5th edn). Blackwell Publishing, Oxford

Gilligan J (2001) *Preventing Violence*. Thames and Hudson, London

George S (1998) More than a pound of flesh: a patient's perspective'. In: Mason T, Mercer D (eds) *Critical Perspectives in Forensic Care: Inside Out*. Macmillan: Basingstoke

Godfrey J (2003) The lesbian gay man and transgendered experience as users of healthcare services. In: Dooher J, Byrt R (eds) *Empowerment and the Health Service User*. Quay Books, Mark Allen Publishing, Dinton, Salisbury

Halsall K (2006) *Forensic Users Research Project*. Booklet, London

Harner HM (2004) Relationships between incarcerated women: moving beyond stereotypes. J *Psychosoc Nursing Ment Health Serv* **42**(1): 38–46

Hart L (2007) The pharmacaust and its relevance to nursing forensic mental health clients. In: National Forensic Nurses' Research and Development Group: Kettles AM, Woods P, Byrt R, Addo M, Coffey M, Doyle M (eds) *Forensic Mental Health: Forensic Aspects of Acute Care. Quay Books*, MA Healthcare, London

Healthcare Commission (2008) From: www.healthcarecommission.org.uk/ [Accessed 30 August 2008]

Henriksen K, Drayton E (2006) Organisational silence and hidden threats to patient safety. *Health Services Research* **41**(4): 1539–54

HM Government (1992) *Report of the Committee of Inquiry into Complaints at Ashworth Hospital*. (Chair Sir Louis Blom-Cooper) HMSO, London

HM Government (2006) *Equality Act 2006*. The Stationery Office, London

Hogg C (1999) *Patients, Power and Politics: From Patients to Citizens*. Sage, London

Hufft A (1999) Girl scouts beyond bars: a unique opportunity for forensic psychiatric nursing. *J Psychosoc Nurs Ment Health Services* **37**(9): 45–51

Jenkinson C, Coulter A, Bruster S, Richards N, Chandala T (2002) Patients' experiences and satisfaction with health care: results of a questionnaire study of specific aspects of care. *Quality and Safety in Health Care* **11**(4): 335–9

Kettles AM, Woods P, Byrt R (2006) Conclusions. In: National Forensic Nurses' Research and Development Group: Woods P, Kettles AM, Byrt R, Addo M, Aiyegbusi A, Coffey M, Collins M, Doyle M, Garman G, Watson C (eds) *Forensic Mental Health Nursing: Interventions with People with 'Personality Disorder'*. Quay Books, MA Healthcare Ltd, London

Laing J, McQuarrie D (1989) *Fifty Years in the System.* Mainstream, Edinburgh

Laverack G (2005) *Public Health. Power, Empowerment and Professional Practice.* Palgrave Macmillan, Basingstoke

Lester H, Glasby J (2006) *Mental Health Policy and Practice.* Palgrave Macmillan: Basingstoke

Lukes S (1974) Power: A Radical View. Cited in: Morgan I (1999) *Power and Politics.* Hodder and Stoughton: London

Lupton C, Peckham S, Taylor P (1998) *Managing Public Involvement in Healthcare Purchasing.* Open University Press, Buckingham

McArdle S, Byrt R (2001) Fiction poetry and mental health. Expressive and creative uses of literature. *J Psychiatr Ment Health Nurs* **8**(6): 517–25

Mason T, Mercer D (1998) *Critical Perspectives in Forensic Care: Inside Out.* Macmillan, Basingstoke

Matthew Trust (2008) From: www.matthewtrust.org/ [Accessed 30 August 2008]

Mental Health Alliance (2007) Website: http://www.mentalhealthalliance.org.uk/

Morgan I (1999) *Power and Politics.* Hodder and Stoughton, London

Morris G (2006) *Mental Health Issues and the Media: An Introduction for Mental Health Professionals.* Routledge, Taylor and Francis Group, London

Murphy-Black T (2006) Using questionnaires. In: Gerrish K, Lacey A (eds) *The Research Process in Nursing* (5th edn). Blackwell Publishing, Oxford

National Forensic Nurses' Research and Development Group: Woods P, Kettles AM, Byrt R, Addo M, Aiyegbusi A, Coffey M, Collins M, Doyle M, Garman G, Watson C (eds) (2006) *Forensic Mental Health Nursing: Interventions with People with 'Personality Disorder'.* Quay Books, MA Healthcare Ltd, London

National Forensic Nurses' Research and Development Group: Kettles AM, Woods P, Byrt R, Addo M, Coffey M, Doyle M (eds) (2007) *Forensic Mental Health: Forensic Aspects of Acute Care.* Quay Books, MA Healthcare: London.

Oxleas NHS Foundation Trust (2006) *Single Equality Scheme and Action Plan 2005–2008.* (Author: A Burnal). Oxleas NHS Foundation Trust, London

Phillips R (2003) The good, the bad and the ugly: the role of local radio as a medium for overcoming prejudice. In: Dooher J, Byrt R (eds) *Empowerment and the Health Service User.* Quay Books, Mark Allen Publishing, Dinton, Salisbury

Pilgrim R, Rogers A (2005) *The Sociology of Mental Health and Illness* (3rd edn). Open University Press, Maidenhead

Prins H, Backer-Holst T, Francis E, Keitch I (1993) *Big, Black and Dangerous: Report of the Committee of Inquiry into the Death in Broadmoor Hospital of Orville Blackwood and a Review of the Death of Two Other Afro-Caribbean Patients.* Special Hospitals Service Authority (SHSA): London

Prior PM (1999) *Gender and Mental Health.* Macmillan, Basingstoke

Ramsbotham D (2003) *Prisongate: The Shocking State of Britain's Prisons and the Need for Visionary Change.* Free Press, London

Repper J, Perkins R (2003) *Social Inclusion and Recovery: A Model for Mental Health Practice.* Bailliere Tindall, Edinburgh

Rollin HR (2006) The mentally ill should be in hospital, not in jail. *J Forensic Psychiatry Psychol* 17(2): 326–9

Secker J, Harding C (2002) African and African Caribbean users' perceptions of inpatient services. *J Psychiatr Ment Health Nurs* **9**: 161–7

Showalter E (1987) *The Female Malady: Women, Madness and English Culture, 1820–1930*. Virago, London

Spiers S, Harney K, Chilvers C (2005) Service user involvement in forensic mental health: can it work? *J Forensic Psychiatry Psychol* **16**(2): 211–20

Szasz T (2000) The case against psychiatric power. In: Barker P, Stevenson C (eds) *The Construction of Power and Authority in Psychiatry*. Butterworth Heinemann, Oxford

Taylor L, Jones S (2006) Clinical governance in practice: closing the loop with integrated audit systems. *J Psychiatr Ment Health Nurs* **13**(2): 228–33

Tew J (ed) (2005) *Social Perspectives in Mental Health: Developing Social Models to Understand and Work with Mental Distress*. Jessica Kingsley, London

Thompson A (2007) The meaning of patient involvement and participation in health care consultations: a taxonomy. In: Collins S, Britten N, Ruusuvuori J, Thompson A (eds) *Patient Participation in Health Care Consultations: Qualitative Perspectives*. McGraw Hill, Open University Press, Maidenhead

Tones K, Green J (2004) *Health Promotion. Planning and Strategies*. Sage Publications: London

Welchman J, Griener GC (2005) Patient advocacy and professional associations: individual and collective responsibilities. *Nurs Ethics* **12**(3): 296–304

Westwood S (2002) *Power and the Social*. Routledge, London

Women in Secure Hospitals (2008) From: www.womenatwish.com [Accessed 30 August 2008]

CHAPTER 8

Role of the forensic mental health nurse in nutrition: Towards recovery

Gillian Archibald

Introduction

This chapter aims to help forensic nurses in their role as screeners of nutritional risk, providers of good nutrition and supporters of nutritional status improvement. Mental health, and particularly food-related behaviour, has a direct effect on nutritional status and poor nutritional intake has a direct effect on mental health and may be the cause of some mental illnesses (Mentality, 2003a).

Forensic mental health nurses will be acutely aware of the poor nutritional status of patients and the difficulties they face in decision making around food choice (Mentality, 2003a). However, there is a lack of research in the area of diet and mental illness, and particularly in the speciality of forensic mental health care. Throughout the chapter, research at all levels to discover and explore new areas to enable improvement in mental health with nutritional treatments and diet therapy is encouraged. Forensic patients, in particular, prove difficult subjects when studying diet and mental health, owing in part to the huge effort required mentally, physically and financially to support any changes advised (Pendlebury et al, 2007). Here the role of the nurse is essential as a 24-hour resource for the patient and as patient advocate for members of the multidisciplinary team (NHS Education for Scotland and Scottish Recovery Network, 2007). Mental illness can develop at any age, but this chapter focuses on adults aged 18–65 years, with a forensic diagnosis, based in either an acute or community setting.

This chapter will discuss the areas and role of nutrition, health and food through:

- Assessment of nutritional risk.
- Provision of a balanced diet.
- Support of food choice.
- Recovery to good mental and physical health.

It touches on current standards nursing staff should be aware of, as well as practical advice to support these standards. Specific nutrient roles and current thinking on nutritional treatment options will be discussed to focus nurses on their role as recovery supporters, including the provision of the life skills of food provision, budgeting, food preparation and food safety.

The role of other professions when the patient is recovering should also be considered, as a multidisciplinary approach provides the best recovery option (NHS Education for Scotland and Scottish Recovery Network, 2007). Due to limitations of space, specific areas are not adequately covered in this chapter. These include:

- Maternal and foetal nutrition.
- Smoking cessation.
- Pica (the eating of non-food substances, e.g. soap, cigarettes, etc.)
- Eating disorders.
- Nutrition and behaviour.
- Learning disabilities.

Further reading in these areas is encouraged.

Role support

Forensic units within the hospital setting, and forensic mental health nurses in the community, should have access to a nutrition and dietetic service to enable the key skills of dietetic assessment, training and their resources to be available to all mental health professionals (State Hospital Carstairs Department of Dietetics and Therapeutic Activity, 2005; British Dietetic Association Special Interest Group in Mental Health, 2007). This access to support should either be through the community mental health team, GP or psychiatrist, although access to all allied health professions (AHPs) is moving towards patient and nurse self-referral to AHPs as a whole, or through the AHP services based within the hospital setting. Access to other areas of dietetic speciality, e.g. diabetes, renal, gastroenterology, etc., would be through the local community or acute hospital-based specialist services. It is certainly, in the author's experience, common to rely on these key areas of speciality to support recovery of the mental health patient, who often presents with other physical illnesses such as renal impairment, diabetes and irritable bowel syndrome.

- Dietitians translate the science of nutrition into practical eating advice, and are uniquely skilled to assess a patient's nutritional status.
- Forensic nurses play a key role in the recovery of psychiatric patients

to an achievable occupational, physical and behavioural level, and are uniquely placed to screen a patient's nutritional risk.
• Good nutritional status relies on the timely provision, accurate advice, appropriate support and availability of food within the institutions of prison and hospital and at the patient's residence in the community.

The role of the catering, portering, nursing, dietetics, occupational therapy, speech and language therapy, physiotherapy, medical and support services are essential to guarantee a health promoting environment for forensic patients (NHS Quality Improvement Scotland, 2003). Food choice, exercise availability and good nursing care allow patients to make an informed decision about their own mental and physical health improvement. Although this appears a very obvious statement, it requires a great deal of co-operation, policy writing, team support and some financial support provided on a daily basis (Expert Consensus Meeting, Dublin, 14-15 April, Consensus Summary 2005).

Role development

Often forensic mental health nurses are occupied with risk assessment and de-escalation of situations harmful to the patient, before they are able to turn their attention to health improvement issues on the ward. A new admission to a forensic unit can easily 'tip the balance' of time available to concentrate on these nutrition-related issues. With the development of the recovery model, values based nursing assessment and care planning has to be focused around health improvement, alongside diagnosis, treatment and assessment of mental health (Brown et al, 1999; Mental Welfare Commission for Scotland, 2005).

This should include a nursing care plan for screening and if necessary improvement of nutritional status (NHS Quality Improvement Scotland, 2003), and requires a good ward routine or community care plan to ensure that, where possible, the patient's nutritional status is supported as optimum. Poor nutritional status will hinder recovery and maintenance of good mental health (Council of Europe Resolution Food and Nutritional Care in Hospitals, 2003; Scottish Executive, 2006a).

The role of the dietitian is developing here too, to work both as part of the mental health team, and as a combined service provided by AHPs, ensuring that life and occupational skills, exercise options and nutritional knowledge are provided together and in a cooperative way, accessible both from the acute hospital setting and the community. Development of this co-operative model is presently progressing within NHS Grampian Mental Health, and should provide an example of how all AHPs could offer a joint approach to recovery and support.

Assessment

Dietitians based in hospital focus on good nutrition support to treat and manage illness, including physical illnesses as well as mental illnesses. However, they also play a key role in nutrition education of staff, including the study of the influence of food intake on health and wellbeing.

(State Hospital Carstairs Department of Dietetics and Therapeutic Activity, 2005)

Scotland's clinical effectiveness organisation, NHS Quality Improvement Scotland (NHS QIS), alongside the British Association of Parenteral and Enteral Nutrition (BAPEN), has produced a very useful and supportive document including a nutritional screening tool called the Malnutrition Universal Screening Tool (MUST), see *Appendix 1* and *2* (NHS Quality Improvement Scotland, 2003) to aid the screening, by nurses, of the nutritional risk of their patients on admission to and while in an acute setting, as well as their progress once returned to the community, including the forensic units throughout Scotland and the UK.

It is the role of forensic nurses to screen the nutritional risk of their patients on admission, to document this risk and formulate a nursing care plan to promote recovery. Alongside this, QIS recommends that a screening tool is used in the acute setting. Here the role of the dietitian is to support nutritional screening and train nurses in this skill.

Dietitians within Grampian now recommend that all nursing staff use the MUST, for all admitted adult patients. The patient's body mass index (BMI = weight in kilograms divided by height in metres squared, see *Box 8.1*) is also an important assessment of both obesity and nutritional status, and a goal for weight reduction through health improvement. A loss of 10% of body weight for an obese patient should offer some health improvement, and offers a goal to work towards in the nursing care plan (NICE, 2006). BMI alone is not a full nutritional assessment but is a useful tool for nurses to use. When screening a patient on admission the following are good indicators of previous long-term poor dietary intake:

- Dry skin, poor nails, dull hair.
- Sores around the mouth, bleeding gums.
- Excessive bruising.
- Pale skin, shortness of breath.
- Poor wound healing.
- Constant infections, post-viral fatigue.
- Body mass index of less than 18.

Box 8.1: BMI Categories

Body mass index = weight (kg)/height (metres) squared

<16	Severely underweight
16–19	Underweight
20–25	Normal
26–30	Overweight
31–34	Grade 1 obesity
35–40	Grade 2 obesity
40+	Morbid obesity

(From Thomas and Bishop, 2007)

It is unusual to see these symptoms in isolation, and most patients present with more than one symptom. Most nutrition texts will guide you to clear deficiency symptoms, but patients may be on a spectrum of deficiency. For example, the deficiency symptom of vitamin C is scurvy, a condition that is sometimes seen on mental health wards when patients have been neglecting their physical health and dietary intake or abusing alcohol for some time before admission. However, certain cancers have been associated with a poor intake of antioxidants, such as vitamin C, but the patient may not have the clinical signs of scurvy.

Alongside nutritional screening, based on weight, height, body mass index and previous weight history, *Box 8.2* suggests questions to help assess nutritional status, and to help discuss any eating difficulties the patient may have.

A total food and fluid intake chart is a useful tool when assessing the patient's food intake (see Appendix 1). The dietitian working as part of the multidisciplinary team can support nurses' nutrition screening, and should be integral to the training of all forensic mental health nurses. In the author's experience there are two distinct types of nutritional problem referred to the dietetic department from the forensic services. These are shown in *Box 8.3*.

The two fictitious patients in *Box 8.3* require a complex nutritional nursing care plan to support both their mental health recovery and physical health improvement. In the author's experience the majority of forensic patients gain weight in hospital due in part to medication regimens, high intake of sugary drinks, boredom-related snacking and comfort eating. Exercise may become difficult because of the sedative effects of medication, poor balance, and poor motivation for self-help after an acute illness episode. Patients may be dysmorphic, delusional and at risk of self-harm so are unable to attend exercise opportunities. Patients with schizophrenia have an increased risk of diabetes and dyslipidaemia (Gothelf et al, 2002), and are more likely to exhibit metabolic syndrome (glucose intolerance, raised cholesterol, central obesity). Obesity has a direct effect on mental health with low self-esteem

---

Box 8.2: Questions to assess nutritional status

- Does the patient's drug therapy have any effect on his or her nutritional status? (Medication can affect personality, reduce initiative, motivation, have gastrointestinal effects, etc.)
- Is the patient able to feed him/herself and report likes/dislikes?
- Does the patient have the correct, well-fitting dentures or have good oral health in order to chew and swallow well?
- Is the patient's taste perception affected by mental health, physical health or drug therapy?
- Does the patient have any beliefs. religious or otherwise, or express any psychotic or anxiety-driven ideas or fears around food, affecting his food choice?
- Is the patient requesting specific religious dietary requirements?
- Is the patient able to make a good food choice in view of his or her physical and mental health?
- Are there any behaviours that may affect food choice, oral intake or nutrient requirements, e.g. smoking, consumption of carbonated, caffeinated drinks, pica of substances/items affecting appetite and digestion, mouth or teeth scrubbing?
- Has the patient any self-harm/purgative beliefs which may affect food choice or nutritional status?

---

and low mood (McReadie, 1998) and significant impairment of functioning (social/cognitive/occupational/interpersonal/financial) (Dietitians in Obesity Management UK, 2007) to support health improvement (Henderson et al, 2000). In the author's experience, medication compliance also improves with better physical and mental health.

Provision (what the client wants versus what the professional advises)

Forensic patients' physical health has historically been neglected with high rates of mortality from coronary heart disease and a high incidence of nutrition-related problems such as constipation, raised cholesterol, glucose intolerance, dental caries, obesity and raised blood pressure (Thomas and Bishop, 2007). Recently, many documents have been produced to highlight this issue and support nurses in their screening and provision of a health promoting environment (Wellbeing Support Programme, Business to Business Solutions, 2007). Government key objectives include the improvement of the physical health of patients with mental illness (National Institute for Health and Clinical Excellence, 2002). The new pre-registration

---

Box 8.3: Two types of nutrition problem

Patient 1

The patient is in a manic phase of illness and has lost approximately two stone in weight, is unable to contemplate meal preparation and planning and is missing meals due to fears, anxieties or beliefs associated with his mania.

Patients in this situation may have acted out self-harm or swallowed non-food items or overdosed on medications or alcohol and may be disabled in their digestive function. On admission to the forensic unit they may have poor nutritional status, be underweight and unable to keep a meal down. They may suffer from chronic irritable bowel symptoms and constipation, and have an intense fear of staff trying to poison or otherwise 'interfere' with food offered.

Patient 2

The patient has spent six months on a forensic long-stay unit, focused on behaviour improvement, appropriate medication and mental health improvement.

Patients in this situation are often chronically obese, have low exercise threshold, and are institutionalised in their meal provision. They suffer from indigestion and rely heavily on high fat, high sugar snacks which reduce appetite at meal times.

---

consultation document in Scotland (NHS Education for Scotland, 2007) for nurses also has a much greater emphasis on the physical health of patients.

Support

In order that the nursing care plan, dietetic advice and hospital health care can be provided in a way that supports the patient recovery journey, a comprehensive care and treatment plan is required with the support of all members of the multidisciplinary team. All staff that patients come into contact with during their stay must have a united approach when advising health improvement. This is applicable to both patient scenarios discussed earlier, and is illustrated in *Box 8.4*.

Recovery (good mental health and good physical health – a joint approach)

There is very little evidence of effective health promotion targeted at people with mental health problems (Mentality, 2003b). A shift in thought has to be made in order to address these complex issues of health improvement, and patients are requesting that this issue is dealt with (Mental Welfare Commission for Scotland, 2005). The report of the National Review of Mental Health Nursing in Scotland (Scottish Executive, 2006b) discusses

---

Box 8.4: Singing from the same songsheet

Patient 1

The nursing care plan should include nutritional supplements as prescribed by the dietitian and a suitable ward routine to support frequent nutritious meals and snacks throughout the day. Meal times should be protected, i.e. nurses should be 'freed' to allow help with food choice advice, feeding, accurate monitoring of food intake, and peer support. Catering departments should have a suitable menu to support healthy choices and be nutritionally complete for the forensic patient, who is often reliant on all meals being provided. Often the dietetic department will have a list of nutritious snacks recommended for when a patient is malnourished (first-line nutritional support) and a list of healthy snacks available for obese patients wishing to lose weight.

Patient 2

Here the care plan and nurse support should be around good portion size control, with guidance from the dietitian. There should be easily available low sugar snacks and drinks and the provision of an exercise regimen, with advice from the physiotherapist, designed to support either weight maintenance or weight loss. The hospital shop, patient café, relatives and bank staff all require to be supportive and informed about the patient's wish to lose weight, and support the provision of appropriate foods (Dietitians in Obesity Management UK, 2007).

---

the role of patient choice and the role of the nurse in supporting recovery of both mental and physical illness, and should be the cornerstone of the progression of forensic patients from the acute setting into the community. Everyday healthy eating messages require the support of the forensic nurse as both advisor and advocate, and are even more of a priority than on a general nursing ward. A rationale for healthy eating messages in mental health is shown in *Box 8.5*.

Some common difficulties reported when talking to forensic patients about what issues have influence on their food choice and energy intake are shown in *Box 8.6*.

In the author's experience, a change in taste perception and food choice often results in a high intake of fizzy, high sugar, high energy, low nutrient dense drinks, including alcohol, which add greatly to total energy intake and therefore weight gain. A simple ward-based policy of provision of chilled low energy drinks including iced water, may assist in thirst quenching without weight gain. Regular cola, milk, fruit juice and milk shakes should be limited where possible and viewed as foods rather than thirst quenchers. These foods/drinks have a role as nutrient providers in the diet, but in limited amounts to prevent excessive intake and weight gain. Other foods such as

---

Box 8.5: Rationale for healthy eating messages in mental health

- Good mental health is central to all health and well-being because how we think and feel has a strong impact on physical health.
- Depression increases the risk of heart disease fourfold even when other factors like smoking are controlled for.
- People who use mental health services, in particular those with a diagnosis of schizophrenia and bipolar disorder, are at an increased risk of a range of physical illnesses including coronary heart disease, cancer, diabetes, infections and respiratory disease. They are twice as likely to die from coronary heart disease than the general population.
- Some medications used to treat mental illness have side effects, including weight gain, raised blood pressure, raised lipid profile and gastrointestinal problems.
- Patients given dietary advice before starting atypical antipsychotics are more likely to control any weight increase.
- Early intervention is recommended because of the association between non-compliance and weight gain.
- Causes of weight gain are multi-factorial, often weight stabilises one year after treatment has commenced. Weight gain is not inevitable but it is common.
- A ward-based policy with nursing, physiotherapy, catering and dietetic support helps prevent excessive weight gain for the patient
- Weight control must be integral to the overall monitoring of the medication, the illness and the individual.
- Best practice states that any patient wishing to lose weight should be given an exercise plan alongside weight reducing advice.

    (From Expert Consensus Meeting, Dublin, 14-15 April, Consensus Summary, 2005)

Box 8. 6: Some common difficulties affecting food choice

- Loss of or exaggerated thirst sensation
- Poor taste perception
- Poor oral health
- Dry mouth and swallow
- Drinks have to be sweet and fizzy to quench thirst
- Milk 'helps my food go down'
- Morning after effect of medication affects breakfast appetite
- Mouth too dry to enjoy toast
- Milk tastes 'off' at breakfast time
- Constipation and acid reflux
- Sugar and caffeine are heavily relied on to promote attention and concentration

---

Box 8.7: Five key messages

Try to eat
- Plenty of fruit and vegetables
- Plenty of bread, rice, potatoes, pasta and other starchy foods – choose wholegrain varieties when you can
- Some milk and dairy foods
- Some meat, fish, eggs, beans and other non-dairy sources of protein
- Just a small amount of foods and drinks high in fat and/or sugar

(From Food Standards Agency, 2007)

---

chocolate bars, crisps and other snacks often become 'meal replacers' as the patient may have a poor appetite for large meals and may often miss hospital meals due to poor sleep pattern, treatments, or anxiety. Here the nurse plays a role in offering smaller portions of regular, balanced meals, and in being in attendance at meal times. This is more difficult to support as a community-based nurse, but may include helping the patient attend cooking classes and helping with budgeting and shopping and store cupboard planning to prevent reliance on high fat, high sugar snacks. One particular tool to help with meal planning is the newly revised *Eat Well Plate* (Food Standards Agency, 2007). This enables the patient to choose a balanced meal, and includes advice on five key health messages, which are given in *Box 8.7.*

In the author's experience, patients' nutritional status deteriorates on discharge, as less support is available around food provision. It is now that the patient's mental health may suffer due to low nutrient intake, e.g. of vitamins, minerals and essential fatty acids (Peet and Horrobin, 2002). A high level of trust and initial supervision is required from the nurse in order that a balanced supportive relationship can be fostered towards health promotion, with non-judgemental, practical, easily attained goals and changes. Sometimes it may be necessary to wait until the patient is in the community before an individual care plan can be discussed for weight control. Group-based peer support is successful for most patients wishing to lose or control weight. (NICE, 2006). The feeling of 'being back in control of my life' is essential, and weight control advice can falter for any of the following reasons.

- Poor body image, poor self-confidence, lack of exercise opportunities, finance.
- Presence of over-enthusiastic, helpful relatives.
- Fear of attending groups for weight control or exercise.
- Poor posture and balance during exercise.

- Profuse sweating, thirst, poor stamina, muscle weakness and exhaustion.

It is important to note here that sometimes patients may over-exercise due to self-harm, purgative reasons, poor body image, fear of loss of control over body, etc. and this should be borne in mind when exercise regimens are discussed. Here the physiotherapist is a great resource to the forensic team.

Good nutrient intake and mental health

Nutrition is not an alternative or complementary therapy to mental illness treatment, but is the basis of brain metabolism and function. The author's observations of forensic patients' food intakes suggest that patients have low vitamin C, folate and fibre, high sugar, saturated fat and omega 6 trans fat intake, and have a high incidence of smoking tobacco. Low antioxidant/ vitamin/iron intakes are common.

During screening of the patient either on admission to hospital or during rehabilitation back into the community, it is good practice to be aware of the common reasons for nutrient deficiencies.

- Weight change.
- Eating disorder.
- Smoking.
- Binge/starve/purge cycle.
- Poor bowel health.
- Cravings.
- Poor nutrition budgeting and cooking knowledge/skills.

Most nutrient deficiencies require an expert in nutrition to diagnose, and access to such experts can be difficult. Blood results are not always available or indeed accurate or relevant when assessing nutritional status. Often the special blood results required are not routinely offered by the biochemistry department, although they can be requested if appropriate.

A clear diet history and complex assessment would highlight possible deficiencies, and it is here the author recommends a referral of the patient to the nutrition and dietetic service, where such skills are available.

The brain comprises approximately 80% fat and is reliant upon glucose as a fuel. It is very sensitive to dehydration, and requires approximately 20% of the total daily calorie intake. The fat composition of the brain is affected by a good diet at birth, genetics, and starvation. Certain food additives such as caffeine cross from the blood stream to the brain and affect brain function. In the author's experience, patients with a mental illness often rely heavily on caffeine intake for alertness. Regular complex carbohydrates and a simple sugar intake throughout the day may improve memory, and again in the author's experience, patients rely on sugary snacks and drinks for 'energy boosts'. Regular meal provision including a slow-release carbohydrate-based food (wholemeal rice, pasta, bread, potato, cereal) may help control glucose sensitivity, intolerance and appetite.

A varied protein source, including high tryptophan foods (Shaw et al, 2002) and a regular source of omega 3 fat three times weekly, e.g. oily fish, seeds or nuts (Peet and Horrobin, 2002) may also support good mental health and recovery. Omega 3 fats found in oily fish, nuts and flax seeds, have been known to improve some behaviours and symptoms of some mental illnesses (Ruxton et al, 2007), but more research is required into the role and function of specific nutrients in mental health and illness.

There is a lack of good randomised controlled trials into brain function, mental health and diet. Therefore the current key themes of a healthy dietary intake for forensic patients are exactly the same as the current healthy eating messages aimed at all adults (see *Box 8.7*). The author would recommend further reading here to support nutrition and brain function knowledge and support further research, particularly in forensic mental health care.

Conclusion

In conclusion, it remains to emphasise the importance of the nursing and dietetic services working jointly to provide expert nutrition screening and assessment, risk monitoring and risk reduction, and healthy living opportunities for this vulnerable patient group (NHS Health Scotland, 2005). This patient group experiences chronic lifestyle issues which require an ongoing, regular, supportive, knowledgeable, adaptive service to encourage optimum mental and physical health. The road to mental health recovery is directed by many forces, with nutrition being a fundamental requirement for healthy brain function and disease prevention. Further research into nutrition and brain function, behaviour and mental health symptoms is required alongside the development of multidisciplinary/multiagency approaches to recovery support and in forensic mental health care in particular.

References

British Dietetic Association Special Interest Group in Mental Health. (2007). The Role of the Dietician. Members website. [Online]. Available from: http://www.bda.uk.com/ (Accessed 22nd November 2007).

Brown S, Birtwistle J, Roe L, Thompson C (1999) The unhealthy lifestyle of people with schizophrenia. Psychol Med 29(3): 697–701

Business to Business Healthcare Solutions (2007) Well-being support programme.

Sponsored by Lilly and Royal College of Nursing. Accredited BB443, March 2007

Council of Europe Resolution Food and Nutritional Care in Hospitals (2003) 10 Key Characteristics of Good Nutritional Care in Hospitals. Available from: http://www. bapen.org.uk/pdfs/coe_leaflet.pdf [Accessed 9 November 2007]

Dietitians in Obesity Management (DOM UK) (2007) The Dietetic Weight Management Intervention for Adults in the One to One Setting. British Dietetic Association: Quorn, Loughborough

Expert Consensus Meeting, Dublin, 14–15 April, Consensus Summary (2005) Metabolic and lifestyle issues and severe mental illness – new connections to well-being? J Psychopharmacol 19(6 Suppl) 118–22

Food Standards Agency (2007) The Eat Well Plate. Available from: http://www.food.gov. uk/multimedia/pdfs/eatwellplatelarge.pdf [Accessed 9 November 2007]

Gothelf D, Falk B, Singer P, Kairi M, Phillip M, Zigel L, Poraz I, Frishman S, Constantini N, Zalsman G, Weizman A, Apter A (2002) Weight gain associated with increased food intake and low habitual activity levels in male adolescent schizophrenic inpatients treated with Olanzapine. Amer J Psychiatry 159: 1055–7

Henderson DC, Cagliero E, Gray C, Nasrallah RA, Hayden DL, Schoenfeld DA, Goff DC (2000) Clozapine, diabetes, weight gain and lipid abnormalities: a five-year naturalistic study. Amer J Psychiatry 157(6): 975–81

McReadie RG (1998) Dietary intake of schizophrenic patients in Nithsdale, Scotland: case-control study. Brit Med J 317: 784–5

Mentality (2003a) Making it effective: A guide to evidence based mental health promotion. Radical mentalities – Briefing paper 1. Mentality: London. Available from: http://www. scmh.org.uk/80256FBD004F3555/vWeb/flKHAL6UEKYU/$file/makingiteffective.pdf [Accessed 5 November 2007]

Mentality (2003b) Not all in the mind: the physical health of mental health service users. Radical mentalities – Briefing paper 2. Mentality: London. Available from: http://www. scmh.org.uk/80256FBD004F3555/vWeb/flKHAL6PQLA9/$file/not+all+in+the+mind. pdf [Accessed 5 November 2007]

Mental Welfare Commission for Scotland (2005) Unannounced visit report 2005: our impression of mental health acute admission wards in Scotland. Mental Welfare Commission for Scotland: Edinburgh. [Online]. Available from: http://www.mwcscot. org.uk

National Institute for Health and Clinical Excellence (NICE) (2002). Schizophrenia: Core Interventions in the Treatment and Management of Schizophrenia in Primary and Secondary Care. NICE: London. [Available from: http://www.nice.org.uk/nicemedia/ pdf/cg001fullguideline.pdf [Accessed 9 November 2007]

National Institute for Health and Clinical Excellence (NICE) (2006) Obesity: Guidance on the prevention, identification, assessment and management of overweight and obesity in adults and children. NICE: London. Available from: http://www.nice.org. uk/nicemedia/pdf/CG43NICEGuideline.pdf [Accessed 5 November 2007]

NHS Health Scotland (2005) Health Promoting Health Service. NHS Health Scotland: Edinburgh. Available from: http://healthscotland.com/uploads/documents/4576-hphs%20intro.pdf [Accessed 9 November 2007]

NHS Quality Improvement Scotland (2003) Clinical Standards: Food, Fluid and Nutritional care in Hospitals. NHS Quality Improvement Scotland, Edinburgh.

NHS Education for Scotland, Scottish Recovery Network (2007) Realising Recovery: A National Framework for Learning and Training in Recovery Focused Practice. NHS Education for Scotland: Edinburgh

NHS Education for Scotland (2007) Educational actions arising from 'Rights, Relationships and Recovery' the Report of the National Review of Mental Health Nursing in Scotland. Available from: http://www.nes.scot.nhs.uk/mentalhealth/work/#values [Accessed 26 November 2007]

Peet M, Horrobin D (2002) A dose-ranging study of the effects of ethyl-eicosapentaenoate in patients with ongoing depression despite apparently adequate treatment with standard drugs. Arch Gen Psychiatry 59: 913–19

Pendlebury J, Bushe CJ, Wildgust HJ, Holt RIG (2007) Long term maintenance of weight loss in patients with severe mental illness through a behavioural programme in UK. Acta Psychiatr Scand 115(4): 286–94

Ruxton CHS, Reed SC, Simpson MJA, Millington KJ (2007) The health benefits of omega-3 polyunsaturated fatty acids: a review of the evidence. J Human Nutrition and Dietetics 20(3): 275–85

Scottish Executive (2006a) Delivering for Mental Health. Scottish Executive: Edinburgh. Available from: http://www.scotland.gov.uk/Resource/Doc/157157/0042281.pdf [Accessed 9 November 2007]

Scottish Executive (2006b) Rights, Relationships and Recovery: The Report of the National Review of Mental Health Nursing in Scotland. Scottish Executive: Edinburgh. Available from: http://www.scotland.gov.uk/Resource/Doc/112046/0027278.pdf [Accessed 9 November 2007]

Shaw K, Turner J, Del Mar C (2002)Tryptophan and 5-Hydroxytryptophan for depression. Cochrane Database of Systematic Reviews, Issue 1

Thomas B, Bishop J (2007) Manual of Dietetic Practice (4th edn). Blackwell Publishing, Oxford

State Hospital Carstairs Department of Dietetics and Therapeutic Activity (2005) Guide for patients and Staff. The State Hospitals Board for Scotland: Lanark. Available from: http://www.tsh.scot.nhs.uk/.../docs/Public%20Health/Diabetic%20Dept%20Leaflet%20 -%2021%20Sep%2005.pdf [Accessed 9 November 2007]

Appendix 1: MUST Total Intake Chart

Reproduced by kind permission of Aberdeen Royal Infirmary, Nutrition and Dietetic Department (2007)

Total intake chart Please record all food and drink taken by the patient. Fluids may also need to be recorded on a fluid balance chart					
Name:		Ward:		Date:	
Meal	Food/drink offered Please give detailed description	Amount offered Please record actual amount offered	Amount taken Please circle amount	Dietitian's use Energy (kcals)	Protein (g)
Night duty					
Drink			None – all		
Biscuit			None – all		
Supplement			None – all		
Other			None – all		
Breakfast					
Cereal			None – all		
Milk			None – all		
Bread/toast/roll			None – all		
Drink, eg tea/coffee			None – all		
Supplement			None – all		
Other			None – all		
Mid-morning					
Drink			None – all		
Biscuit			None – all		
Supplement			None – all		
Other			None – all		
Lunch					
Soup			None – all		
Fruit juice			None – all		
Potato/rice/pasta			None – all		
Vegetable			None – all		
Main course			None – all		
Pudding\Drink			None – all		
Supplement			None – all		
Bread/other			None – all		
Mid-afternoon					
Drink			None – all		
Biscuit			None – all		
Supplement			None – all		
Other			None – all		
					Continued

Total intake chart (continued)					
Meal	Food/drink offered Please give detailed description	Amount offered Please record actual amount offered	Amount taken Please circle amount	Dietitian's use Energy (kcals)	Protein (g)
Evening meal					
Soup			*None* – *all*		
Potato/rice/pasta			*None* – *all*		
Vegetable			*None* – *all*		
Main course			*None* – *all*		
Sandwich			*None* – *all*		
Pudding/cake			*None* – *all*		
Fruit			*None* – *all*		
Drink			*None* – *all*		
Supplement			*None* – *all*		
Bread/other			*None* – *all*		
Bedtime					
Drink			*None* – *all*		
Biscuit			*None* – *all*		
Supplement			*None* – *all*		
Other			*None* – *all*		
Total fluid intake (ml)					

Appendix 2: Malnutrition Universal Screening Tool

Reproduced by kind permission of BAPEN (2007)

 'Malnutrition Universal Screening Tool'

BAPEN
Advancing Clinical Nutrition

BAPEN is registered charity number 1023927   www.bapen.org.uk

'MUST'

'MUST' is a five-step screening tool to identify **adults,** who are malnourished, at risk of malnutrition (undernutrition), or obese. It also includes management guidelines which can be used to develop a care plan.

It is for use in hospitals, community and other care settings and can be used by all care workers.

This guide contains:

- A flow chart showing the 5 steps to use for screening and management
- BMI chart
- Weight loss tables
- Alternative measurements when BMI cannot be obtained by measuring weight and height.

The 5 'MUST' Steps

Step 1
Measure height and weight to get a BMI score using chart provided. *If unable to obtain height and weight, use the alternative procedures shown in this guide.*

Step 2
Note percentage unplanned weight loss and score using tables provided.

Step 3
Establish acute disease effect and score.

Step 4
Add scores from steps 1, 2 and 3 together to obtain overall risk of malnutrition.

Step 5
Use management guidelines and/or local policy to develop care plan.

Please refer to *The 'MUST' Explanatory Booklet* for more information when weight and height cannot be measured, and when screening patient groups in which extra care in interpretation is needed (e.g. those with fluid disturbances, plaster casts, amputations, critical illness and pregnant or lactating women). The booklet can also be used for training. See *The 'MUST' Report* for supporting evidence. Please note that 'MUST' has not been designed to detect deficiencies or excessive intakes of vitamins and minerals and is of **use only in adults.**

Step 1 – BMI score (& BMI)

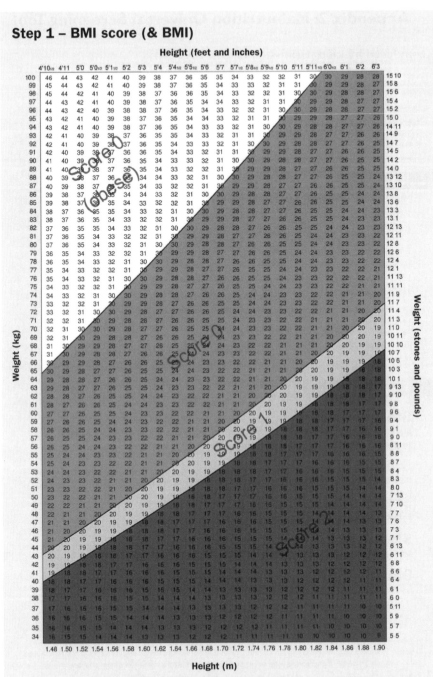

Height (feet and inches)

Weight (kg)

Weight (stones and pounds)

Height (m)

Note : The black lines denote the exact cut off points (30,20 and 18.5 kg/m²), figures on the chart have been rounded to the nearest whole number.

Step 1
BMI score

+

Step 2
Weight loss score

+

Step 3
Acute disease effect score

BMI kg/m²	Score
>20(>30 Obese)	= 0
18.5-20	= 1
<18.5	= 2

Unplanned weight loss in past 3-6 months

%	Score
<5	= 0
5-10	= 1
>10	= 2

If patient is acutely ill **and** there has been or is likely to be no nutritional intake for >5 days
Score 2

If unable to obtain height and weight, see reverse for alternative measurements and use of subjective criteria

Step 4
Overall risk of malnutrition

Add Scores together to calculate overall risk of malnutrition
Score 0 Low Risk   Score 1 Medium Risk   Score 2 or more High Risk

Step 5
Management guidelines

0
Low Risk
Routine clinical care

- Repeat screening
  Hospital – weekly
  Care Homes – monthly
  Community – annually
  for special groups
  e.g. those >75 yrs

1
Medium Risk
Observe

- Document dietary intake for 3 days if subject in hospital or care home

- If improved or adequate intake – little clinical concern; if no improvement – clinical concern - follow local policy

- Repeat screening
  Hospital – weekly
  Care Home – at least monthly
  Community – at least every 2-3 months

2 or more
High Risk
Treat*

- Refer to dietitian, Nutritional Support Team or implement local policy
- Improve and increase overall nutritional intake
- Monitor and review care plan
  Hospital – weekly
  Care Home – monthly
  Community – monthly

* Unless detrimental or no benefit is expected from nutritional support e.g. imminent death.

All risk categories:
- Treat underlying condition and provide help and advice on food choices, eating and drinking when necessary.
- Record malnutrition risk category.
- Record need for special diets and follow local policy.

Obesity:
- Record presence of obesity. For those with underlying conditions, these are generally controlled before the treatment of obesity.

Re-assess subjects identified at risk as they move through care settings
See *The 'MUST' Explanatory Booklet* for further details and *The 'MUST' Report* for supporting evidence.

Step 2 – Weight loss score

Weight before weight loss (kg)	SCORE 0 Wt Loss < 5%	SCORE 1 Wt Loss 5-10%	SCORE 2 Wt Loss > 10%
34 kg	<1.70	1.70 – 3.40	>3.40
36 kg	<1.80	1.80 – 3.60	>3.60
38 kg	<1.90	1.90 – 3.80	>3.80
40 kg	<2.00	2.00 – 4.00	>4.00
42 kg	<2.10	2.10 – 4.20	>4.20
44 kg	<2.20	2.20 – 4.40	>4.40
46 kg	<2.30	2.30 – 4.60	>4.60
48 kg	<2.40	2.40 – 4.80	>4.80
50 kg	<2.50	2.50 – 5.00	>5.00
52 kg	<2.60	2.60 – 5.20	>5.20
54 kg	<2.70	2.70 – 5.40	>5.40
56 kg	<2.80	2.80 – 5.60	>5.60
58 kg	<2.90	2.90 – 5.80	>5.80
60 kg	<3.00	3.00 – 6.00	>6.00
62 kg	<3.10	3.10 – 6.20	>6.20
64 kg	<3.20	3.20 – 6.40	>6.40
66 kg	<3.30	3.30 – 6.60	>6.60
68 kg	<3.40	3.40 – 6.80	>6.80
70 kg	<3.50	3.50 – 7.00	>7.00
72 kg	<3.60	3.60 – 7.20	>7.20
74 kg	<3.70	3.70 – 7.40	>7.40
76 kg	<3.80	3.80 – 7.60	>7.60
78 kg	<3.90	3.90 – 7.80	>7.80
80 kg	<4.00	4.00 – 8.00	>8.00
82 kg	<4.10	4.10 – 8.20	>8.20
84 kg	<4.20	4.20 – 8.40	>8.40
86 kg	<4.30	4.30 – 8.60	>8.60
88 kg	<4.40	4.40 – 8.80	>8.80
90 kg	<4.50	4.50 – 9.00	>9.00
92 kg	<4.60	4.60 – 9.20	>9.20
94 kg	<4.70	4.70 – 9.40	>9.40
96 kg	<4.80	4.80 – 9.60	>9.60
98 kg	<4.90	4.90 – 9.80	>9.80
100 kg	<5.00	5.00 – 10.00	>10.00
102 kg	<5.10	5.10 – 10.20	>10.20
104 kg	<5.20	5.20 – 10.40	>10.40
106 kg	<5.30	5.30 – 10.60	>10.60
108 kg	<5.40	5.40 – 10.80	>10.80
110 kg	<5.50	5.50 – 11.00	>11.00
112 kg	<5.60	5.60 – 11.20	>11.20
114 kg	<5.70	5.70 – 11.40	>11.40
116 kg	<5.80	5.80 – 11.60	>11.60
118 kg	<5.90	5.90 – 11.80	>11.80
120 kg	<6.00	6.00 – 12.00	>12.00
122 kg	<6.10	6.10 – 12.20	>12.20
124 kg	<6.20	6.20 – 12.40	>12.40
126 kg	<6.30	6.30 – 12.60	>12.60

Weight before weight loss (st lb)	SCORE 0 Wt Loss < 5%	SCORE 1 Wt Loss 5-10%	SCORE 2 Wt Loss > 10%
5st 4lb	<4lb	4lb – 7lb	>7lb
5st 7lb	<4lb	4lb – 8lb	>8lb
5st 11lb	<4lb	4lb – 8lb	>8lb
6st	<4lb	4lb – 8lb	>8lb
6st 4lb	<4lb	4lb – 9lb	>9lb
6st 7lb	<5lb	5lb – 9lb	>9lb
6st 11lb	<5lb	5lb – 10lb	>10lb
7st	<5lb	5lb – 10lb	>10lb
7st 4lb	<5lb	5lb – 10lb	>10lb
7st 7lb	<5lb	5lb – 11lb	>11lb
7st 11lb	<5lb	5lb – 11lb	>11lb
8st	<6lb	6lb – 11lb	>11lb
8st 4lb	<6lb	6lb – 12lb	>12lb
8st 7lb	<6lb	6lb – 12lb	>12lb
8st 11lb	<6lb	6lb – 12lb	>12lb
9st	<6lb	6lb – 13lb	>13lb
9st 4lb	<7lb	7lb – 13lb	>13lb
9st 7lb	<7lb	7lb – 13lb	>13lb
9st 11lb	<7lb	7lb – 1st 0lb	>1st 0lb
10st	<7lb	7lb – 1st 0lb	>1st 0lb
10st 4lb	<7lb	7lb – 1st 0lb	>1st 0lb
10st 7lb	<7lb	7lb – 1st 1lb	>1st 1lb
10st 11lb	<8lb	8lb – 1st 1lb	>1st 1lb
11st	<8lb	8lb – 1st 1lb	>1st 1lb
11st 4lb	<8lb	8lb – 1st 2lb	>1st 2lb
11st 7lb	<8lb	8lb – 1st 2lb	>1st 2lb
11st 11lb	<8lb	8lb – 1st 3lb	>1st 3lb
12st	<8lb	8lb – 1st 3lb	>1st 3lb
12st 4lb	<9lb	9lb – 1st 3lb	>1st 3lb
12st 7lb	<9lb	9lb – 1st 4lb	>1st 4lb
12st 11lb	<9lb	9lb – 1st 4lb	>1st 4lb
13st	<9lb	9lb – 1st 4lb	>1st 4lb
13st 4lb	<9lb	9lb – 1st 5lb	>1st 5lb
13st 7lb	<9lb	9lb – 1st 5lb	>1st 5lb
13st 11lb	<10lb	10lb – 1st 5lb	>1st 5lb
14st	<10lb	10lb – 1st 6lb	>1st 6lb
14st 4lb	<10lb	10lb – 1st 6lb	>1st 6lb
14st 7lb	<10lb	10lb – 1st 6lb	>1st 6lb
14st 11lb	<10lb	10lb – 1st 7lb	>1st 7lb
15st	<11lb	11lb – 1st 7lb	>1st 7lb
15st 4lb	<11lb	11lb – 1st 7lb	>1st 7lb
15st 7lb	<11lb	11lb – 1st 8lb	>1st 8lb
15st 11lb	<11lb	11lb – 1st 8lb	>1st 8lb
16st	<11lb	11lb – 1st 8lb	>1st 8lb
16st 4lb	<11lb	11lb – 1st 9lb	>1st 9lb
16st 7lb	<12lb	12lb – 1st 9lb	>1st 9lb

Alternative measurements and considerations

Step 1: BMI (body mass index)

If height cannot be measured
- Use recently documented or self-reported height (if reliable and realistic).
- If the subject does not know or is unable to report their height, use one of the alternative measurements to estimate height (ulna, knee height or demispan).

If height & weight cannot be obtained
- Use mid upper arm circumference (MUAC) measurement to estimate BMI category.

Step 2: Recent unplanned weight loss

If recent weight loss cannot be calculated, use self-reported weight loss (if reliable and realistic).

Subjective criteria

If height, weight or BMI cannot be obtained, the following criteria which relate to them can assist your professional judgement of the subject's nutritional risk category. Please note, use of these criteria is not designed to assign a score.

1. BMI
- Clinical impression – thin, acceptable weight, overweight. Obvious wasting (very thin) and obesity (very overweight) can also be noted.

2. Unplanned weight loss
- Clothes and/or jewellery have become loose fitting (weight loss).
- History of decreased food intake, reduced appetite or swallowing problems over 3-6 months and underlying disease or psycho-social/physical disabilities likely to cause weight loss.

3. Acute disease effect
- No nutritional intake or likelihood of no intake for more than 5 days.

Further details on taking alternative measurements, special circumstances and subjective criteria can be found in *The 'MUST' Explanatory Booklet*. A copy can be downloaded at www.bapen.org.uk or purchased from the BAPEN office. The full evidence-base for 'MUST' is contained in *The 'MUST' Report* and is also available for purchase from the BAPEN office.

BAPEN Office, Secure Hold Business Centre, Studley Road, Redditch, Worcs, B98 7LG. Tel: 01527 457 850. Fax: 01527 458 718. bapen@sovereignconference.co.uk   BAPEN is registered charity number 1023927.   www.bapen.org.uk

© BAPEN 2003   ISBN 1 899467 90 4   Price £2.00

© BAPEN. First published May 2004 by MAG the Malnutrition Advisory Group, a Standing Committee of BAPEN. *Reviewed and reprinted with minor changes March 2008* 'MUST' is supported by the British Dietetic Association, the Royal College of Nursing and the Registered Nursing Home Association.

Alternative measurements: instructions and tables

If height cannot be obtained, use length of forearm (ulna) to calculate height using tables below. *(See The 'MUST' Explanatory Booklet for details of other alternative measurements (knee height and demispan) that can also be used to estimate height).*

Estimating height from ulna length

Measure between the point of the elbow (olecranon process) and the midpoint of the prominent bone of the wrist (styloid process) (left side if possible).

HEIGHT (m) Men(<65years)	1.94	1.93	1.91	1.89	1.87	1.85	1.84	1.82	1.80	1.78	1.76	1.75	1.73	1.71
Men(>65years)	1.87	1.86	1.84	1.82	1.81	1.79	1.78	1.76	1.75	1.73	1.71	1.70	1.68	1.67
Ulna length(cm)	32.0	31.5	31.0	30.5	30.0	29.5	29.0	28.5	28.0	27.5	27.0	26.5	26.0	25.5
HEIGHT (m) Women(<65years)	1.84	1.83	1.81	1.80	1.79	1.77	1.76	1.75	1.73	1.72	1.70	1.69	1.68	1.66
Women(>65years)	1.84	1.83	1.81	1.79	1.78	1.76	1.75	1.73	1.71	1.70	1.68	1.66	1.65	1.63

HEIGHT (m) Men(<65years)	1.69	1.67	1.66	1.64	1.62	1.60	1.58	1.57	1.55	1.53	1.51	1.49	1.48	1.46
Men(>65years)	1.65	1.63	1.62	1.60	1.59	1.57	1.56	1.54	1.52	1.51	1.49	1.48	1.46	1.45
Ulna length(cm)	25.0	24.5	24.0	23.5	23.0	22.5	22.0	21.5	21.0	20.5	20.0	19.5	19.0	18.5
HEIGHT (m) Women(<65years)	1.65	1.63	1.62	1.61	1.59	1.58	1.56	1.55	1.54	1.52	1.51	1.50	1.48	1.47
Women(>65years)	1.61	1.60	1.58	1.56	1.55	1.53	1.52	1.50	1.48	1.47	1.45	1.44	1.42	1.40

Estimating BMI category from mid upper arm circumference (MUAC)

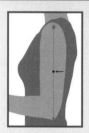

The subject's left arm should be bent at the elbow at a 90 degree angle, with the upper arm held parallel to the side of the body. Measure the distance between the bony protrusion on the shoulder (acromion) and the point of the elbow (olecranon process). Mark the mid-point.

Ask the subject to let arm hang loose and measure around the upper arm at the mid-point, making sure that the tape measure is snug but not tight.

If MUAC is < 23.5 cm, BMI is likely to be <20 kg/m^2.
If MUAC is > 32.0 cm, BMI is likely to be >30 kg/m^2.

The use of MUAC provides a general indication of BMI and is not designed to generate an actual score for use with 'MUST'. For further information on use of MUAC please refer to *The 'MUST' Explanatory Booklet*.

CHAPTER 9

Assessment, management and treatment of sex offenders

Paul Burbery and Mohammed Khoshdel

Introduction

Sex offenders and their management is a subject that seems to create a lot of anxiety and public discussion but is seldom debated in a productive and thoughtful way (Matravers, 2003). One of the most important factors to understand is that we do not know who most sex offenders are (Lotke, 1996). Home Office estimates from 1993 indicate that at that time at least 260 000 men over 19 years of age had been convicted of a sexual offence, 110 000 of whom had offended against children (Marshall, 1997).

What is clear is that forensic mental health nurses will come into contact with sex offenders and therefore be involved in their care, if not their treatment. A survey by Hughes and Webb (2005) found that 41% of patients in a medium secure hospital had a history of sexually abusive behaviours ranging from convictions for sexual assault through to current episodes of sexual harassment. In a similar setting, Doyle (2006) found (in a medium secure hospital in the north west of England) that in a population of 110 male patients, 16 had convictions for sexual offences prior to admission.

This chapter defines and describes sexual offending and sex offenders. It examines some of the theories that attempt to explain this type of behaviour and, through the use of a case study and care plans, it describes how nurses can play an active role in the assessment, management and treatment of sex offenders.

This chapter refers only to male sex offenders as we have limited experience of female offenders. However, a short characterisation of female offenders based on the work of Nathan and Ward (2001, 2002) is also included.

What is sexual offending?

From a legal perspective, sexual offences are defined with respect to non-consensual behaviours such as penetrative sex, touching or voyeurism and victim types such as adult or child (NOTA, 2005). Although this

Table 9.1: Types of contact vs. non-contact offences (From Carich and Calder, 2003)

Non-contact offences	Contact offences
Obscene telephone calling	Physical sexual harassment
Stalking	Fondling (frottage)
Peeping (voyeurism)	Paedophilia (sex with children)
Flashing (exhibitionism)	Attempted rape
Verbal sexual harassment	Date rape
Unwarranted computer sex	Sadistic rape
Photography	Stranger rape
Pornography	Marital rape
Mail/computer sex	Bestiality (sex with animals)
	Sexual attempted murder
	Sexual murder
	Serial sexual murder
	Necrophilia (sex with the dead)

may be practical for law enforcement purposes, it often masks a much more complicated motivation that is not explicitly defined in the legal definition. Gordon and Grubin (2004) note that some crimes may be committed in such a manner that they do not appear sexually explicit but may be sexually motivated, such as burglary (where the woman's clothing is stolen) or murder.

A sexual offender in the legal sense is a person who has been convicted of a sexual offence. In the UK the Sexual Offences Act 2003 and the Children and Young Persons Act 1933 cover sexual offences. The Sexual Offences Act 2003 identifies nearly 50 separate sexual offences. *Table 9.1* identifies types of contact and non-contact sex offences.

Sexual deviancy

Sexual deviancy, also known medically as paraphilia, is a relatively stable pattern of deviant sexual arousal (e.g. age-inappropriate, non-consenting people, animals or inanimate objects) that causes distress or social dysfunction (American Psychiatric Association, 1994). The arousal does not have to be accepted or enjoyed (Boer et al, 1997). There is an almost infinite variety of sexual paraphilias that have been labelled within the ICD-10 (World Health Organisation, 1992) (see *Table 9.2*). Although psychiatry has offered a useful labelling system, it offers little by way of understanding or explanation for these behaviours.

Table 9.2: ICD-10 Disorders of sexual preference (From World Health Organisation, 1992)

Disorder	Description
F65.0 Fetishism	Reliance on some non-living object as a stimulus for sexual arousal and gratification, often an extension of the human body (e.g. footwear or clothing) or characterised by a particular texture (e.g. rubber, plastic). Such fantasies are common, they do not amount to a disorder unless they lead to rituals that are so compelling and unacceptable as to interfere with sexual intercourse and cause the individual distress
F65.1 Fetishistic transvestism	Wearing opposite sex clothes to obtain sexual excitement
F65.2 Exhibitionism	A recurrent or persistent tendency to expose genitalia (usually to the opposite sex). Often followed by masturbation
F65.3 Voyeurism	A recurrent or persistent tendency to look at people engaging in sexual behaviour. Usually leads to sexual excitement, and masturbation is carried out without the observed people being aware
F.65.4 Paedophilia	A sexual preference for children
F65.5 Sadomasochism	A preference for sexual activity that involves bondage or the infliction of pain or humiliation. Recipients – masochists, providers – sadists
F65.6 Multiple disorders of sexual preference	Sometimes more than one disorder present with none having clear precedent. Most common combination is fetishism, transvestism and sadomasochism
F65.8 Other disorders of sexual preference	This includes less common disorders such as making obscene phone calls, frotteurism, and necrophilia

Not all sexual deviancies are illegal and, in fact, what might be seen as sexually deviant in some cultures may be normal in others. Also, beliefs about what is deviant may change in particular cultures over time. It was not that long ago that homosexuality was considered deviant and illegal in the UK. However, all sexual offending is deviant as it is an unacceptable behaviour.

Prevalence of sexual offending

Sexual offending is relatively uncommon when compared to other crimes. Between 1997 and 2003 sexual offences accounted for approximately 1% of all recorded crime and 5% of all recorded violent offences (National Criminal Records Service, 2003). The National Criminal Records Service also reported that within the total of 52070 sexual offences, 26709 were indecent assaults against adult females and 1942 were for gross indecency against children. A total of 13247 rapes were recorded, 93% of which were against females.

Estimating the exact number of sexual offences and sex offenders is however much more difficult. A great deal of sexual abuse occurs within the home or in institutions and is not reported and therefore remains undetected as an offence. The statistics mentioned above do not recognise if offenders committed more than one offence and do not mention demographics such as age, which is an important risk indicator (Thornton, 2002).

Identifying the extent of sexual offenders who have never been convicted is problematic. Many victims of sexual assault, both adults and children, have never reported their experiences to the authorities (Marshall et al, 1999). The majority of alleged sexual offenders investigated by social services child protection teams are never convicted (Craisatti, 2004). A study by McClurg and Craisatti (1999) found that only between 0% and 8% of alleged child abusers in two London boroughs were convicted as a result of allegations of sexual abuse made to social services.

Although sexual offending accounts for approximately 1% of all recorded crime, the actual prevalence could be as much as 10 times higher (NOTA, 2005). About 1% of convicted perpetrators are female (Home Office, 2003) and between 30% and 40% of male abusers are juveniles (Lovell, 2002).

Types of offenders

Sex offenders are a heterogeneous group and cannot be categorised by any single aetiological or motivational factor (Carich and Calder, 2003). Many sex offenders present as 'ordinary normal men': as heterosexual, gay or bisexual members of society who cannot be typified in terms of class, profession, wealth or family status (Calder and Skinner, 2000).

However, sex offenders are often grouped according to victim age or sex, or by the nature of the act (NOTA, 2005). Sex offenders are therefore often described as child molesters or adult rapists, or they are described in terms of having committed offences such as indecent assault, rape or indecent exposure. NOTA (2005) argue that although these distinctions may be practically useful, they often disguise a more complex picture where offenders may offend against a wide range of victims in more than one way.

Typologies have been identified for all major types of sexual aggressor (NOTA, 2005); in this section we will identify the main characteristics of adult rapists and child abusers and provide brief descriptions of adult female sex offenders.

Child abusers

The majority of child abuse is perpetrated by someone who knows the victim. Elliot et al (1995) found that 46% of adult child abusers felt that a 'special relationship' with the child was vital and that 66% knew their victims. Most child abusers can be separated into three categories based on their relationship with the victim: family members, friends or acquaintances, and strangers (Carich and Calder, 2003). Family members and friends or acquaintances were similar in numbers, and strangers less common (Elliot et al, 1995). However, Elliot et al's (1995) study was based on a sample of convicted sex offenders, therefore, given that much sexual abuse goes unreported, some studies suggest this may be as high as 90% (Calder, 1999; Carich and Calder, 2003) and therefore these figures should be viewed with some caution.

Erooga (2002a) citing a study by Fisher (1994) reports that with regard to basic demographic variables, there is no significant difference between men who abuse children and men who do not. However, Erooga (2002b) did identify the following characteristics among many men who sexually abuse children:

- They were more likely to experience relationship problems.
- Men in treatment tended to lack self-confidence, were underassertive, had difficulties in understanding the perspective of others, were poor at dealing with emotional distress and typically emotionally isolated (Beckett et al, 1998).
- They were more likely to have been abused as children when compared to non-offending populations (Abel et al, 1984).

It is important to remember though, that the majority of men who are abused as children do not go on to become abusers (Erooga, 2002b). Also, caution needs to be taken when considering these factors, as many people who have relationship problems, lack self-confidence or who are emotionally isolated are not child abusers (NOTA, 2005).

Groth (1982) identified two types of child abusers, regressed and fixated offenders. Regressed offenders do not have a lengthy history of offending, they offend later in life and have conventional lifestyles and age-appropriate relationships prior to offending. Later in life they sexually focus on children,

Table 9.3: An integrative model of child abusers (From Carich and Calder, 2003)

Type 1: Regressed offender	Low risk to re-offend by actuarial measure • Primarily incest offender • Short offending history (time span and frequency) • Few (1–2) victims • Preference for appropriate consenting sex
Type 2: Situational/ opportunity to offend	Low to moderate risk to re-offend by actuarial measure • Sporadic/occasional (2–4) victims • No serious Axis 1 and 2 problems • Takes advantage of situation to offend • Preference towards opposite sex victim • Moderate offending history
Type 3: Chronic offender	High risk to re-offend by actuarial measure • Strong deviant arousal patterns • Negative lifestyle • Personality disorder • Preference towards same sex
Type 4: Extreme hard core	Extreme high risk to re-offend by actuarial measure • Low motivation for change • High psychopathy index • Long history of offending • Diverse victim pattern • Large number of victims
Type 5: Mentally disordered offender	• Serious Axis 1 diagnosis • Organic brain damage • Mental impairment

often triggered by stress, or an inability to cope with life and/or interpersonal conflicts and tension. They are now viewed as situational offenders (Freeman-Longo and Blanchard, 1998; Carich and Calder, 2003).

Fixated offenders (Groth, 1982) or preferential offenders (Freeman-Longo and Blanchard, 1998) are long-term, chronic offenders. Their sexual preference is for children and they often develop lifestyles centred on offending. Groth (1982) describes those attracted to prepubescent children as paedophiles and those attracted to young teenagers or adolescents as hebophiles.

A more elaborate taxonomy has been developed by Knight and Prentky (1990). This involves two axes: Axis 1 involves sexual deviance, while Axis 2 involves social competence. They have developed models for both child molesters and adult rapists; for more details see Carich and Calder (2003).

Campbell et al (2000) have developed a five-factor typology to summarise the typologies discussed above (see *Table 9.3*).

Adult rapists

Groth et al (1977) developed one of the first typologies to identify critical aspects of adult rapists' behaviour. They proposed that rape was a pseudosexual way of expressing anger and demonstrating power. Four sub-types were identified based on the functions of power and anger within rape. 'Power dominance' and 'power reassurance' are seen as motivations for some groups of rapists, in contrast to the more aggressive 'anger retaliation' and 'anger excitation' sub-types – these use sexual aggression as a means of expressing hostility towards women, or because it excites them (NOTA, 2005). Groth (1982) describes three typical types of rape (see *Table 9.4*).

Rapists have also been classified as situational, i.e. taking advantage of an opportunity with little planning or by carefully planned stalking behaviours (Carich and Calder, 2003). There are no stereotypical rapists; they are as diverse as any group that is defined by a particular behaviour and should be viewed as a heterogeneous cross-section of any society, who offend in a range of contexts and driven by differing motivations (NOTA, 2005).

Table 9.4: Types of rape (From Carich and Calder, 2003 quoting Groth, 1982)

Anger rape	• Intended to hurt, debase and express contempt for victim • Marked by gratuitous violence • The act is not sexually satisfying for rapist • Sexuality often seen as offensive and therefore an appropriate weapon
Power rape	• Serves as a means of exercising dominance, mastery, strength, authority and control over victim • Little need for excessive physical force
Sadistic rape	• Represents the most severe pathologies and the most dangerous type of assault • The ritual of torturing the victim and the perception of degradation becomes eroticised • As the assailant's arousal increases so may the violence of his acts • Can progress to murder

Female offenders

Although accounting for only approximately 1% of convicted sex offenders (Home Office, 2003) it is becoming clearer that women commit sexual offences against children and that they are a varied group with distinct motives and needs (Nathan and Ward, 2001). It is also likely that the extent is underestimated (Finkelhor and Russell, 1984). This underestimation is encouraged by socio-cultural resistance to accepting the concept of female sexual aggression (Beckett, 2005).

Although the literature is limited it appears that the majority of female offenders are aged 20–30 years, come from a dysfunctional family of origin and experience high levels of (often severe) physical, emotional and/or sexual abuse as a child (Nathan and Ward, 2002).

Grayston and De Luca (1999) found that mental health problems were common, including personality disorders, chemical dependency, depression, suicidal ideation and cognitive impairment, and that their experiences of being abused as children themselves, left many with post-traumatic stress symptoms. The most common personality disorders diagnosed among female sex offenders are borderline, dependent and histrionic, while male offenders are most likely to be diagnosed with antisocial personality disorder (Grayston and De Luca, 1999; Mayer, 1983). However, Nathan and Ward (2002) found marked antisocial and persecutory personality traits.

The majority of victims are girls and, typically, the abuser will either be the child's mother, close relative or primary carer. Victims fall within pre-school and school age range and the abusive behaviour can range in duration from one episode of less than one hour to multiple offences over a number of years (Nathan and Ward, 2002). The impact upon victims is particularly under-researched, as is the professional response to this problem (Denov, 2003).

The most regular observation about female abusers is that the majority of offences occur with a male accomplice, however Nathan and Ward (2002) state that it is important to remember that not all women are coerced and that in fact some women, even when convicted with male co-offenders, played an active and forceful role in the offending and appeared to enjoy the experience.

Some explanations and potential treatments

As mentioned previously, sex offenders are a heterogeneous group, therefore there is no single cause as there are no typical sex offenders. NOTA (2005) also argue that it may be inaccurate to think of factors that contribute to offending as causal, as it gives the impression that sex offenders have no choice over how they choose to behave or that they are driven by some uncontrollable internal or external force

A number of theories to explain sexual aggression have been developed over the years. We will discuss some of these below and the ways they can be linked to treatment.

Biological explanations

Biological explanations link sexual behaviour and dysfunctions to hormonal (Hucker and Baines, 1990) and nervous system processes (Kafka, 1997). Testosterone has been linked to both sex and aggression and early medical explanations suggest that because of this link, sexual aggression could be treated with castration. Studies did show a reduction in sexual recidivism (Ortmanm, 1980) although by the 1970s this practice was largely abandoned due to development of hormonal treatments and because of ethical issues (Gordon and Grubin, 2004).

In the UK the most frequently used medication is cyproterone acetate (Craissati, 2004). It acts by blocking testosterone receptors and reduces serum levels of testosterone, luteinising hormone and follicle-stimulating hormone but increases serum prolactin levels (Gordon and Grubin, 2004). The sexual drive is reduced or inhibited; potency, sperm production and orgasm are all affected. Men also report reduced sexual thoughts and fantasies, frequency and pleasure of masturbation and lowered sexual frustration (Craissati, 2004).

Unfortunately, there are a number of potentially serious side effects such as gynaecomastia (which may not be reversible), breathlessness, fatigue and lassitude, weight gain, changes in hair pattern and, rarely, osteoporosis (British National Formulary, 2007). Care must also be taken to monitor mood as depression has been noted (Gordon and Grubin, 2004).

Withdrawal rates are high and therefore cyproterone should only be prescribed alongside group or individual psychological treatment (Gordon and Grubin, 2004). An examination of studies that assessed the efficacy of anti-libidinal medication by the American Psychiatric Association (1999) found that sexual recidivism rates were greatly reduced where compliance with treatment was properly established.

Selective serotonin reuptake inhibitors (SSRIs) have been found to be effective in the treatment of sex offenders (Greenberg and Bradford, 1997). Kafka (1997) found that monoaminergic dysregulation influenced some forms of paraphilia. Obsessional-compulsive and impulse control disorders have similarities to a number of paraphilias in terms of their presentation (Craissati, 2004). SSRIs reduce obsessive-compulsive behaviour, which is associated with sexual offending behaviour in the form of sexual ruminations, intrusive fantasies and sexual urges (Gordon and Grubin, 2004).

SSRIs appear to be particularly effective where paraphilia is co-morbid with anxiety and depression and have been found to decrease deviant sexual interest without impairing non-deviant sexual interest (Craissati, 2004). Advantages of SSRIs over hormonal treatments are that they are better tolerated and that mental health professionals are much more familiar with them (Gordon and Grubin, 2004). Side effects include nausea, vomiting, dry mouth, weight loss or gain, diarrhoea and sexual dysfunction (British National Formulary, 2007). Craissati (2004) highlights this paradox as they may cause delayed ejaculation or lack of orgasm, which could then increase feelings of sexual frustration. As with cyproterone, they should not be relied upon alone; their use should be combined with psychotherapy (Gordon and Grubin, 2004).

Antipsychotic medication has long been known to have an antilibidinal effect and interfere with sexual functioning (Craissati, 2004).

Evolutionary explanations

Thornhill and Palmer (2000) argued that rape might serve an evolutionary function because it is primarily driven by sexual desire and because rapists offend against younger women. They argue that rape may be a mating strategy similar to the non-consensual mating strategy seen in various primates.

However, this is contrary to much of the evidence we know about sex offenders. Rape is multi-determined, driven by sexual desire, power and a range of negative emotional states (Prentky and Knight, 1991) and men, whether rapists or not, are more attracted to youth (Buss, 1994). This theory does not account for the fact that men rape women of all ages, other men and children and disregards the actions of female offenders. Also, Tang-Martinez and Mechanic (2000) argue that rape or 'forced copulation' is not at all successful with regard to reproduction.

This evolutionary confusion regarding rape has come from animal studies, including ducks where the animals' mating behaviour is seen as forceful (NOTA, 2005). Gould (1997) describes it as 'truly insidious...', as '...falsely describing an inherited behaviour of birds with an old name for a deviant human action...'

Social and psychological explanations

Three broad strands can be identified which contribute to the question of sex offence causality; these are societal and cultural norms, developmental and early life experiences, and psychological functioning.

Sexual violence, especially rape, has been found to be most common in societies characterised by a predominance of male authority and power, and where violence is regarded as a legitimate form of problem solving (Sanday, 1981). Feminist theory views rape as a form of social control and that 'myths' such as men have 'uncontrollable sex drives' and women 'ask for it' or 'want to be raped' are perpetuated by social processes (Burt, 1980).

Early attachment history has been found to be an important determinant of sexual aggression (Stripe, 2003). Marshall (1994, 1996) established that early problems in a child's relationship with its parents could result in disrupted attachment experiences, which can, in conjunction with other experiences, contribute to the development of sexual offending behaviour (NOTA, 2005).

A study of sexual murders by Burgess et al (1986) described how an inadequate social environment (e.g. little parental control or support, excessive demands on the child) when the child is growing up, alongside early traumatic experiences (e.g. bullying or abuse) can provide the circumstances for the development of violent fantasies and distorted attitudes as a means of coping. In some cases, these violent attitudes and fantasies can become sexualised as the individual reaches puberty and are reinforced through masturbation. MacCulloch et al (1983) describe how elaborate fantasies were present in the histories of sadistic sexual offenders who felt compelled to act them out.

Sex offender treatment often targets deviant sexual fantasies either through aversion therapy, covert sensitisation or masturbatory reconditioning (Marshall et al, 1999). However, sex offenders rarely self-report deviant sexual fantasies (O'Donohue et al, 1997) especially prior to their first offence, although more admit deviant fantasies prior to subsequent offences (Marshall et al, 1999)

From a psychological perspective, individuals are seen as a complex system of related facets based in cognition, affect and behaviour that interact in a social context. Psychological explanations of sex offending and interventions have therefore developed around these features of functioning and personality. The main factors in understanding sex offenders are also the main factors involved in the treatment and assessment of sex offenders.

Treatment targets include self-esteem, intimacy deficits, social skills deficits, empathy deficits, cognitive distortions and deviant sexual arousal. Also, at the individual level there are other factors that contribute, such as anxiety or depression in response to situations or life events. We will discuss these in more detail when we look at treatment programmes and describe, through the case study and care plans, how nursing interventions can assist and support the offender through the treatment process.

Sexual offending and individuals with mental illness

Although sexual offending is widely researched in both forensic psychiatry and psychology, mentally disordered sexual offenders have received less attention (Hughes and Webb, 2005). Sohata and Chesterman (1998) report that sex offenders with a mental illness account for approximately 8% of all men charged with a sexual offence. Given that many people cannot comprehend sexual offending behaviour (England et al, 1999) it might make it seem more plausible to label sex offenders as mentally disordered. However, what research is available tends to support the idea that mentally disordered sex offenders are not significantly different from sex offenders without a mental disorder (Sohota and Chesterman, 1998).

Sex offenders may fall into a number of psychiatric diagnostic categories (Craissati, 2004). Most do not have a major mental illness, although people with psychosis may commit sexual offences or display abnormal sexual behaviour (Gordon and Grubin, 2004). Hughes and Webb (2005) report that there is no evidence to suppose that sex offenders with any form of mental disorder are a homogeneous group or that their offending is necessarily linked to their illness.

The research regarding sex offenders with schizophrenic who have committed sexual offences is inconclusive and a careful appraisal of the role of symptoms should be evaluated against more specific factors associated with sexual offending (Sahota and Chesterman, 1998). Craissati (2004) identifies four main themes with regard to the role schizophrenia may play in the sexual offender. First, the sexual assault may occur as a direct result of hallucinations or delusional beliefs. Second, the assault may be influenced by less explicit features of the illness, for example, heightened feelings of arousal and irritability or confused thought processes. Third, the sexual assault may be related to negative symptoms such as blunting of affect, lowered social performance and social isolation. In some ways these are similar to the social competency dynamic risk factors, such as low self-esteem, and social skills, empathy and intimacy deficits. Finally, the sexual assault may have no relation to schizophrenia but be driven by fixed deviant sexual interests and/or personality problems (Craissati, 2004).

Individuals with personality disorders

Craisatti (2004) identifies two particular personality disorders that are particularly relevant to sex offenders, these are dissocial/antisocial and borderline. Dissocial or antisocial personality disorder is relevant due to the extreme disparity between the individual's behaviour and what is seen as the prevailing social and cultural norms.

The presence of antisocial personality disorder has important risk implications due to acting out and hence re-offending (Langevin and Watson, 1996). This is largely due to weak impulse control, a willingness to engage in inappropriate behaviour in exchange for the most fleeting gratification and without consideration of the consequences (Calder and Skinner, 2000).

This, added to a callous unconcern for the feelings of others (World Health Organisation, 1992) would increase the likelihood of someone behaving in a sexually aggressive manner. Another feature of this personality disorder is frequent lying and deceptive behaviour; this could have a negative effect upon treatment and also invalidate any self-report questionnaires (Calder and Skinner, 2000).

Although there is a tendency to diagnose repeat offenders with dissocial or antisocial personality disorder, the diagnosis cannot be made on the basis that a sex offender has committed a large number of offences (Craissati, 2004). Psychopathy, also described as both antisocial and dissocial personality disorders (Boer et al, 1997), has been found to be a very strong indicator for sexual violence and for sexual sadism (Hart and Hare, 1997).

Craissati (2004) also identifies borderline personality disorder as having particular relevance for sexual offending behaviour. Borderline personality disorder, with its pervasive pattern of unstable interpersonal relationships, impulsivity without consideration for others' feelings, unstable self-image and affects can impact upon how a person decides to offend or not. Craissati and Beech (2001) also found that these features could have a chaotic effect on how someone presents at treatment, characterised by intense distress and a raised risk of self-harm. When such an individual engages in a standard cognitive-behavioural sex offender group work programme, Craissati (2004) regards it important to consider appropriate medication – for high levels of emotional lability – as well as psychological treatments for non-offenders with personality disorders.

Individuals with mental impairment

Holland et al (2002) report that people with learning disabilities are significantly over represented in various parts of the criminal justice system and in particular, this applies to sexual offending (O'Conner, 1997). Thompson and Brown (1997) identified that between 25% and 50% of men with learning disabilities admitted to specialist treatment facilities had committed a sexual offence. However, Thompson and Brown also caution against assuming people with learning difficulties are more likely to commit sexual offences as there is an increased likelihood that their offending is more observable because of their impulsivity and the lack of privacy when living in institutions (Courtney and Rose, 2004).

The relationship between the learning disability and the offence may be difficult to determine (Craissati, 2004), the offender may not be able to fully understand the concept of consent, and, in the case of child victims, may have difficulties in establishing age-appropriate relationships or the child may reflect the offender's emotional immaturity. Craissati (2004) also highlights the fact that people diagnosed with mental impairment are three to four times more likely to have a diagnosis of another form of mental disorder and therefore the offending may be more related to a personality disorder or a fixed deviant sexual interest.

Case study: John

John (a pseudonym) is a 45-year-old Caucasian man who has been known to the psychiatric services since he was 27. He is currently detained in a medium secure unit (MSU) under Sections 37/41 and has a primary diagnosis of schizophrenia. He was convicted of one count of rape of a female under the age of 16 and two indecent assaults on two girls aged under 14. These offences took place in 2003 at John's place of residence. He met his victims (three girls aged 15, 13 and 12) at 11.30pm in a bus station after he had been out drinking all day. They had run away from a care home, were hungry and had nowhere to stay. He played the role of a good Samaritan, telling then he was a social worker, that they could stay at his place for the night and he would help them find accommodation in the morning. He took the girls to his flat, where he raped one of them and indecently assaulted the other two.

John denied all the offences, he was adamant that the girls had approached him and that he had taken them home as they had nowhere to go. He claims that when they got to his flat, they told him that they were prostitutes and that he could have sex with all of them for £50. He described them as streetwise and cunning and claimed that he had been set up. He did admit to having sex with the older girl but insisted that she appeared to be at least 18 years old and that she had initiated sex. He was subsequently charged and convicted of the above offences in 2004. His presentation while in custody was such that he was transferred to an MSU. Upon admission, John was found to be restless, chaotic and elevated in mood. He was also thought disordered with flight of ideas but there was no aggression or threatening behaviour. It was regularly reported that John, while in the company of self, would be gesticulating and talking as if in discussion with several people.

Nursing staff also reported that shortly after admission, grandiosity was noted to be a prominent feature and John would frequently talk about grand, multinational business ventures that he had pioneered. He also often referred to famous people as close personal friends. During this period, persecutory and delusional ideas were also noted. For example, in relation to the index offence, John maintained that he was 'framed' by certain business partners. He also believed that the same people were plotting to kill him by various methods, for example, by poisoning his food. With reference to his index offence, John accepted that he had had sex with his victims, but would refute any suggestions that he had forced them to have sex with him, thus rejecting any notion that 'rape' had taken place. Furthermore, for quite some time he remained adamant that his victims' appearances led him to believe that they were not under age. Also notable within the nursing reports was John's behaviour towards female staff. For example, he would politely shake hands with female staff particularly those who were not regular ward staff. In the course of doing so, John would attempt to kiss their hands while bowing and at the same time discretely glancing at their breasts. Or he would make remarks with a sexual undertone as well as attempting to make body contact by various tactics such as brushing his body against the female staff in the course of an activity.

John would not accept that he was suffering from any form of mental illness, becoming intolerant of suggestions of psychiatric treatment. While in the community he was maintained on depot injection. However, he began refusing his treatment, thus becoming increasingly unsettled. Following the index offence and while in custody he continued to refuse medication. This situation seemed to improve following John's admission to the MSU, where he was commenced on olanzapine Velotabs. John has had two other admissions to an MSU in the past and indeed his forensic history dates back to the late 1970s when there was a series of offences of burglary and theft. In early 2000 he was convicted of actual bodily harm and false imprisonment of his then girlfriend. His records again indicate that he was not complying with his depot medication around the time of the offence. Also, while an inpatient on a psychiatric ward, John assaulted a female nurse resulting in severe bruising to her body. He has a history of excessive alcohol use, especially when he has withdrawn from local mental health services.

At a young age, John's parents separated and he was cared for by his mother although he maintained contact with his father. John is the eldest of three children born to his parents and there is no report of any mental illness in his family. Both parents developed separate relationships subsequently which resulted in four half-siblings from his mother and several from his father's relationship. His early development appears unremarkable, achieving all his milestones but he left school without any formal qualifications.

As the new medication took hold, the symptoms of John's illness began to alleviate, however, despite an expectation that inappropriate sexual behaviour would also recede, there was only a moderate reduction in this area. John might not make overt references to female staff or women in general any more but innuendoes and certain remarks continued to persist. For example he would frequently ignore requests of female staff on the ward but fully comply if a male staff asked the same. More significantly, John continued to minimise the impact of his index offence upon his victims.

With regard to John's case, there is no evidence to indicate that his offending occurred as a direct result of hallucinations or delusions. What appears clear is that at the time he committed his offence he was expressing grandiose and delusional ideas and displayed a heightened sense of arousal. It is likely that these secondary symptoms contributed to his offences. This was also evident from his over familiarity and sexual intrusiveness towards female nursing staff. Underlying this, and it became increasingly evident as his mental state improved, was a sense of sexual entitlement, misogynistic attitudes, a lack of victim empathy and an unwillingness to accept that his offending behaviour had been anything more than a spur of the moment decision or that he presented as a considerable risk of re-offending.

Care Plan 1: Short-term management of sexually aggressive and/or inappropriate behaviour

Rationale

John has presented with evidence of sexually inappropriate behaviour. He has made inappropriate comments to female staff as well as making physical contacts. Some examples include touching, inappropriately shaking hands, brushing self against the body of female staff and invading their personal space.

John has a history of aggressive and recently sexually assaultative behaviour. He has in the past physically attacked his girlfriend and held her hostage. He has also been charged with rape of a female under the age of 16 as well as sexual assault of two females under the age of 14.

John has also assaulted a female member of nursing staff while an inpatient in a psychiatric ward. He punched her several times causing severe bruising to her body.

This care plan seeks to minimise any actual or potential risk John may pose, given the above. (Other care plans address other aspects of John's needs and cares.)

Objective

The objective of the care plan is to ensure the safety of others on the ward.

- All staff to be aware of potential risks. Female professionals are not to isolate themselves with John or put themselves at risk. Should professional female visitors attend the ward, they are to be advised that they need to be accompanied by another (ward-based) member of staff.
- Under no circumstance should any female member of staff enter John's bedroom unaccompanied. She can only enter in the presence of at least one other member of ward-based staff who is aware of potential risks.
- If John invades the personal space of others, he should be advised of more appropriate behaviour. Nurse-in-charge or primary nurse (key worker) to explore with John how this makes other people feel.

- A notice to be placed on the ward entrance door requesting visiting female staff to ring the ward office prior to entering the ward. Recipient of phone call to ensure that visitors enter the ward safely and visit the ward office immediately as a first port of call.
- If John makes any inappropriate sexualised comments or contacts with female or male staff, the victim should immediately inform John that this is inappropriate and unacceptable and report the incident to the nurse in charge. If necessary, pinpoint alarm should be activated and in all cases the incident should be recorded.
- If John does not respond positively to nursing staff's prompts then he should be escorted from the ward area to a quiet place (e.g. intensive nursing suite) with two members of staff and the opportunity should be given to John to ventilate his feelings and explore any precipitating factors for these behaviours.
- If John makes any threats towards others, these should be explored and an appropriate risk management plan put in place. This plan will reduce the risk that John presents towards that individual.
- Should John become involved in any verbal altercations, it must be recognised that these can and have led to physical confrontation. Staff to intervene and request calmly but assertively that John accompany them to the intensive nursing suite. Staff to be aware of their non-verbal interactions and ensure these do not appear confrontational as this may exacerbate the situation.

Evaluation method
Evaluation will involve use of an integrated computer information system, hand-overs, clinical team meetings, primary nurse sessions, and liaison between primary nurse and Sex Offender Treatment Programme (SOTP) specialist nurse.

This care plan describes nursing interventions to safely manage John's sexually aggressive and inappropriate behaviour following his admission, its main objective being to ensure the safety of staff, fellow patients and visitors by preventing any further incidents.

There is limited research regarding the relationship between depression and sexual offending, most likely because the prevalence is so low (Craissati, 2004). However, as mentioned above, Gordon and Grubin (2004) report on the potential value of SSRIs in the treatment of paraphilias. Individuals sometimes present to services with anxieties regarding recurring sexual thoughts or impulses to sexually offend or have sexually deviant preoccupations, which mask an underlying depressive illness (Craissati, 2004). It is also important to establish if the offender's depression contributed to or was a result of the sexual abuse; did it precipitate the abuse or is it a result of the abusive act(s) or their discovery (Calder and Skinner, 2000)?

Risk assessment

Risk assessment is the process of identifying and studying hazards to reduce the probability of their occurrence (Boer et al, 1997). With regard to sex offenders this refers to the likelihood of recidivism (NOTA, 2005). The assessment of sex offenders, is aimed at risk management and therefore the goal of risk assessment is to identify the factors related to the risk for sexual offending (Carich and Calder, 2003).

A meta analysis of studies by Hanson and Brussiere (1998) examined a database of 28 972 cases of convicted sex offenders. It found that the following were the strongest predictors of recidivism:

- Phallometrically assessed deviant interest in children – this was the strongest predictor.
- The number and type of prior sexual convictions – the more previous convictions, the higher the risk and offences against boys or strangers outside the family.
- Men who failed to complete treatment presented as an increased risk of both sexual and non-sexual offending.
- The younger the offender, the more likely to re-offend.
- A diagnosis of dissocial or antisocial disorder increased the likelihood of recidivism.

Risk variables pertinent to sexual recidivism are divided into static risk factors and dynamic risk factors. Static risk factors are variables that have been shown to have an empirical relationship with the risk of re-offending but which are not amenable to clinical intervention. Examples include age and the number and nature of previous convictions. These variables affect the likelihood of a person re-offending; they do not change over time and cannot be affected by sex offender treatment (Hanson and Bussiere, 1998). Dynamic risk factors are variables that have also been shown to have a relationship with the risk of re-offending but can change as a result of treatment. Examples include drug or alcohol use, deviant sexual interest, deviant sexual fantasy, and negative attitudes to women. Hanson and Harris (1998, 2000) further divide dynamic risk variables into stable dynamic factors and acute dynamic factors.

Stable dynamic factors can change over time but are relatively enduring, they include the offender not seeing himself as a risk or having a lack of insight into his potential to re-offend, and attitudes that condone and support sexual entitlement. They may hold rape myths about women or have distorted views about children and sexuality. Sexual preoccupation, deviant thoughts and fantasies, along with poor emotional and general self-regulation and negative social influences, are also important stable dynamic variables and should be considered when assessing risk (Hanson and Harris, 1998, 2000).

Acute dynamic risk factors can change over a short period of time. These include the opportunity for victim access, intoxication with drugs or alcohol, deterioration in mental health, changes in mood, loss of remorse, and victim blaming (Hanson and Harris, 1998, 2000).

There is a wide variety of risk assessment tools that have been developed to assess a sex offender's risk of recidivism. See Calder (1999, 2000), NOTA (2005) and Craig et al (2005) for comprehensive descriptions.

Actuarial assessment tools are based on static risk variables. The Risk Matrix 2000 (RM2000) by Hanson and Thornton (2000) is an example of one and is utilised by both the Police and Probation Service in England and Wales. See *Box 9.1* for description and scoring classification.

For John (described earlier in this chapter) the pertinent variables within the RM2000 are the number of his previous criminal convictions (he had more than five previous convictions for violent and non-violent offences) and stranger victims (he had met his victims on the night of the assaults). The scoring system indicates a score of 2 and therefore a category of medium risk.

One of the difficulties with actuarial risk assessment tools is that they are based on historical variables only. They therefore do not assess individuals' ability to learn from their mistakes nor their views about their past conduct, neither do they assess individuals' understanding of the harm that is caused by their behaviour. They do not take note of any of the dynamic risk variables (mentioned above) that are empirically researched to be associated with recidivism.

The Sex Offender Need Assessment Rating (SONAR) developed by Hanson and Harris (2000) measures stable dynamic factors (over the last year) and acute dynamic risk factors (over the past month). With regard to John, pertinent dynamic risk variables included: poor sexual self-regulation; his misogynistic beliefs and attitudes; poor general self-regulation due to the deterioration in his mental health and associated disinhibtion and impulsivity; a lack of insight into the harm his behaviour has caused and a general unwillingness to accept responsibility for his offending behaviour.

Boer et al's (1997) Sexual Violence Risk–20 (SVR-20) is a 20-item risk assessment process that considers both actuarial and dynamic risk factors and can be used with a wide range of sexual offences. Rather than providing a score, it allows for the consideration of items that are most pertinent to the particular individual's risk, it also provides a comprehensive formulation of risk including the nature, likelihood, severity and imminence as well

---

Box 9.1: RM2000/S: Risk of sexual offending (From Thornton, 2007)

Step 1

Age at commencement of risk	Points
<18 years	0
18–24 years	2
25–34 years	1
>35 years	0

Sexual appearances	Points
1	0
2	1
3, 4	2
>5	3

Criminal appearances	Points
<5	0
>5	1

Total: 0 = Low risk, 1–2 = Medium risk, 3–4 = High risk, 5–6 = Very high risk

Step 2: Aggravating factors

Any conviction for a contact offence against a male?	Yes/No
Any conviction for a contact offence against a stranger? (Count as stranger if victim did not know offender 24 hours before offence)	Yes/No
'Single' (Count as single if absence of cohabiting intimate relationship in excess of two years	Yes/No
Any conviction for a non-contact sex offence?	Yes/No

Increase risk category if two or more aggravating risk factors are present
Low risk/Medium risk/High risk/Very high risk

---

as identifying any risk enhancing or risk reducing factors. The following provides an example of the SVR-20 risk formulation for John.

Sexual Violence Risk–20: Formulation of risk for John

The following questions (pp. 192–194) are all from Boer et al (1997).

Nature

- What kinds of sexual violence might this person commit?
- What are the triggers/antecedents of past sexual violence?
- What is the likely motivation?
- Who are the likely victims?

John appears most likely to commit acts of sexual violence in situations where he misconstrues his potential victim's behaviour. Triggers to his previous episode appear to be deterioration in his mental health following non-compliance with medication and disinhibition through alcohol. The likely motivation is for his own sexual gratification. Victims are most likely to be vulnerable young girls.

Severity

- What would be the physical/psychological harm to victims?
- Is there a chance that the sexual violence might escalate to life-threatening levels?

John's victims do not appear to have suffered any serious physical harm; this is based on a police surgeon's report who examined the victims after they reported John to the police. However the psychological harm will be profound.

There is no evidence to indicate that John's sexual violence might escalate to life-threatening levels.

Frequency

- In general, how frequent or common is this type of sexual violence?

In general terms, this is not a frequent or common occurrence. John has made only one court appearance for sexual violence.

Likelihood

- What is the probability that this person will commit this type of sexual violence?

The probability that John might commit future acts of sexual violence is not high. (Risk Matrix 2000 – Medium Risk is based primarily on number of previous court appearances for non-sexual violence – although this was against females.)

Imminence

- How soon might the sexual violence occur?
- Are there any warning signs that might signal that sexual violence risk is increasing or imminent?

Warning signs that John's risk might increase would include excessive alcohol consumption, a withdrawal from mental health aftercare, and refusal of medication and consequent deterioration in mental health.

Other considerations

- Is there anything else that should be taken into consideration?
  - Gaps in information?
  - Co-operation of the service user?

John has co-operated with the assessment although he has vastly different views of his risk of committing future acts of sexual violence. He does not believe that he has in fact committed an act of sexual violence.

Risk-enhancing factors

- What events, occurrences, or circumstances might increase this person's sexual violence risk?
- What factors might lead this person to consider or choose to act violently?

Risk enhancing factors include alcohol consumption (John claimed that alcohol impaired his judgement when he decided to offer the girls somewhere to stay) and deterioration in mental health.

Risk-reducing factors

- What events, occurrences, or circumstances might decrease this person's sexual violence risk?
- What factors might prevent this person from considering or choosing to act violently?

Risk reducing factors would include John fully complying with the care and treatment package that will be put together for him prior to discharge. John has also agreed to participate in a group work sex offender treatment programme here at Edenfield MSU. This will start on 1 November, 2007 and last approximately 18 months. Hopefully, this will help John to gain more understanding of his behaviour that night, gain insight into his deviant motivation, an understanding of victim issues in general and the harm that his behaviour has caused in particular and develop a robust relapse prevention plan.

Care Plan 2: To assess risk of and attitude to sexual offending

Rationale

John has a history of sexually inappropriate behaviour which has resulted in a number of serious offences against females. He has in the past taken a woman, reported to have been his girlfriend, hostage and physically assaulted her. John's recent index offence included rape of a female under the age of 16 and two sexual assaults on girls under the age of 14. In a previous admission to a psychiatric ward John also assaulted a female nurse resulting in severe bruising to her body.

This care plan seeks to assess John's suitability to undergo Sex Offenders Treatment Programme (SOTP) treatment.

Goals

To assess

- The level of deviant sexual arousal.
- John's understanding of his behaviour.
- The need for SOTP engagement.
- John's motivation to address his offending behaviour.

In the absence of psychosis, regular individual sessions to be arranged focusing on such areas as:

- John's attitude to his offences.
- Does John consider his behaviour as a problem?
- How similar or different is John's account of his offences to those of his victims/any witnesses?
- In John's view, how he can reduce the risk of re-offending?

Whether or not John will engage with SOTP it is important for all nursing staff (and indeed all those who have contact with John) to reinforce certain key qualities. These include:

- Acting as role models – staff to be extra vigilant that interactions among themselves when John is in the vicinity are equally as important as when directly engaging with John. Therefore there should be no derogatory comments aimed at demeaning women and no innuendoes or sexually motivated comments
- Encourage pro-social attitude, reinforce self-worth and improve self-

esteem, challenge inappropriate behaviour, challenge misogynistic attitude, improve problem solving ability, and encourage resistance to lifestyle impulsiveness. These are some of the factors embraced by most societies as the accepted norms. Research indicates that some or all of these dynamic factors have been disabled to varying degrees in sex offenders.

These sessions are to be held under the supervision of an identified member of the SOTP team and areas covered should be revisited periodically to reinforce change

In addition to general ward level observations, nursing staff to be extra vigilant to note and chart John's activities and behaviour. These include:

- John's daily habits, for example, does he get up in the mornings or need several prompts, does he utilise access to fresh air, cooperate with the nursing/clinical team, and is he able to function independently, etc?
- What John watches on TV, for example, does he watch a fair range of programmes (documentaries, soaps, movies, news, etc.) or mainly watch children programmes or movies with violent scenes and/or sex scenes and if so does he display overt emotions (become elated)?
- What kind of material John reads, for example, fiction or non-fiction, does he display a preference to read articles on sex/violence, age appropriate materials?
- John's ability to form friendships and whether or not his conduct in the relationship is appropriate, in particular is there evidence of any exploitation?
- Content of John's speech in all his social interactions, particularly with reference to women and children, whether in direct contact or when members of these two groups are the subject of conversation.
- John's motivation to self-care, his appearance, dress code etc., also, are there any specific times, for example, when there are more female staff on shift, that John is noted to pay particular attention to self-care; does he dress appropriately?
- Hobbies, interests and activities.
- Self-image and self-appraisal, for example, does John hold a negative view of self or is presence of grandiosity evident, etc.

The above is not an exhaustive list and ward staff are reminded to note any observation they feel might be of relevance. These should be logged in the provided assessment logbook.

Evaluation

Evaluation will involve logbook evaluation; integrated computer information system and discussion with SOTP.

Care Plan 2 identifies how nursing staff can assist in the risk assessment processes and what particular behaviours to observe and monitor. It also provides guidance on how staff can act as positive role models and challenge John's negative attitudes.

Sex offender treatment

When we talk about sex offender treatment, it is important to remember that sex offending is not an illness and therefore there can be no cure. However, through group treatment, sex offenders can learn new ways to control their behaviour and so reduce their risk of re-offending.

The prime modality for sex offender treatment is through cognitive-behavioural group work. By far the largest provider of this type of treatment in the United Kingdom is the Prison Service. The Prison Service has developed the Sex Offender Treatment Core Programme (HM Prison Service, 2000), an accredited version of which has been running in prisons since 1992. The programme consists of 75–95 two-hour sessions.

A study by Friendship, Mann and Beech (2003) examining the effectiveness of the Core Programme, suggests that the programme had a significant impact on reducing risk in medium and low risk offenders. It also found positive results in reducing non-sexual violent offending even though this was not specifically targeted. However, additional treatment needs to be developed and provided for high-risk offenders. The Core Programme is also provided by the probation service throughout England and Wales and at a number of high and medium secure hospitals. In conjunction with this, a number of both private and public mental health services have developed programmes adapted to meet the needs of individuals with a mental disorder or mental impairment who are sex offenders. The Prison Service has also developed an adapted Sex Offender Treatment Programme for men with mild learning disabilities. To date, no specific group work programme has been developed for female offenders.

The major treatment targets of the Core Programme are group cohesion, increased awareness of risk factors and personal attributes related to offending, re-evaluation of pro-offending attitudes, increased understanding of victim harm and skills practice for more effective interpersonal functioning. Core 2000 is a recent revision of the programme and in particular, more emphasis is placed on developing group cohesion, identifying patterns of offending, identifying motivations for offending rather than just accounts of offending, teaching coping strategies, generalising from the programme to everyday functioning and role-playing new skills and strategies.

HM Prison Service (2002) identifies three particular treatment methods that are used throughout the group work programme (see *Table 9.5*).

Other treatment methods such as social restructuring (generating changes in the offender's interpersonal relationships), arousal control (managing deviant arousal), and cycle intervention (centering treatment on assault cycles) are key processes of contemporary treatment (Carich and Calder, 2003).

A number of factors have been identified that are believed to contribute to group work being more effective with sex offenders than individual work (see *Box 9.2*).

Care plan 3 – Nursing support and engagement during SOTP

Rationale

John has agreed to engage in a Sex Offenders Treatment Programme (SOTP). The programme aims to minimise John's offending behaviour by promoting a change in his attitude, core beliefs, victim empathy, etc. It also calls for recognition of the role of cognitive distortions and risky behaviour among other factors. In doing so certain emotions will surface that John may find difficult to deal with.

Research indicates some offenders have ineffective or little capacity

---

Box 9.2: Positive factors contributing to group effectiveness

- Sex offenders publicly acknowledge their need to change
- Socially acceptable norms and interactions are conveyed
- Other offenders can challenge an offender's distorted pattern of thinking and behaviour
- A supportive environment is provided to rehearse new attitudes and behaviours
- Less chance to maintain lies
- More feedback – often from fellow offenders
- Chances for worker collusion reduced
- Effective change occurs as a result of the integration of emotions, cognitions and behaviours – group experience can offer the context to achieve this
- Offenders help each other access/resolve issues, they learn how to develop and maintain coping skills
- A group intensifies the change experience

(From Carich and Calder, 2003)

Table 9.5: SOTP Core 2000 treatment methods (From HM Prison Service, 2002)

Treatment method	Description	Examples
Cognitive restructuring (Sex offenders often justify or excuse offences, they commonly minimise the harm they have caused)	The therapeutic process of changing the offenders' cognitions. To help sex offenders reassess their beliefs through appropriately framed questions. Socratic questions, i.e. thought provoking non-hostile questions that assist recipients in working things out for themselves	What links can you make between each of your offences in terms of what was going on in your mind beforehand? What other reasons might there have been for that happening? When you hear other people saying that something just happened, what do you think about why they might be saying that?
Modelling	The demonstration of anti-criminal attitudes and behaviours by the therapist. For it to be meaningful, it must be clear and both verbal and non-verbal	Take responsibility for what you do Treat and talk about others with respect at all times Demonstrate effective problem solving Keep every promise you make Do not put yourself down Do not put others down Do not complain, emphasise that you and not outside forces are in control of your life Always talk about women and children in a respectful way
Positive reinforcement	Refers to the giving of some sort of reward (verbal or non-verbal) in response to the expression of anti-criminal attitudes and/or behaviour	An immediate statement of approval to what the offender has just said. This can be verbal or non-verbal. An elaboration of the reason why approval is being offered. The expression of approval should be sufficiently intense to distinguish it from the baseline level of support and interest that should usually be offered by therapists

to deal with emotions and have inadequate coping strategies (Serran and Marshall, 2006). Therefore, it is not unknown that some group members during treatment become withdrawn, display signs of depression, or present as anxious and/or agitated and irritable. To maximise the potential for a successful outcome it is essential that treatment goals are acknowledged and support within a therapeutic milieu is provided (Norton, 2004).

This care plan can act as a reference point for both John and ward-based staff.

Goal

The goal is to provide a safe environment for John so he can successfully achieve the expected outcome of the SOTP.

All nursing staff need to:

- Acknowledge the level of support John will require as he experiences difficult emotions and to encourage continued participation within the group.
- Encourage pro-social attitudes and behaviours by acting as role models. These include being honest, taking responsibility for one's actions, respecting the rights of others, demonstrating positive coping techniques and encouraging skills for resolving conflicts, while challenging inappropriate behaviour or misogynistic attitudes.
- Display a positive attitude, which would help instil and promote higher self-worth and confidence in John, hence help create an environment where his self-esteem can flourish. Nursing staff should therefore positively reinforce (verbally and/or non-verbally) any expression of pro-social attitudes and behaviours. This should be immediate and include the reason for approval. It should also be of sufficient intensity to be distinguished from the usual support and interests offered by the nursing staff.
- Positively acknowledge and support change.
- Remain non-judgemental but acknowledge deviant sexual behaviour is unacceptable.
- Ensure, throughout the treatment and as long as John is an inpatient, that their work is collaborative and that close supervision with SOTP facilitators is sought out.

The primary nurse (key worker) needs to:

- Continue work on improving problem solving ability and encourage resistance to lifestyle impulsiveness.
- Provide support with John's diary and log book entries.

- Note that as John begins to realise victim empathy and accepts responsibility for his deviant behaviour, he may develop deep feelings of shame which can be 'toxic' by way of leading to a sense of low self-worth, promoting depression and contributing to maladaptive and impaired coping strategies. In the process of this chain reaction, risk of re-offending may be increased. It is of key importance that signs and symptoms are recognised early and effective strategies developed and deployed.
- Liaise with SOTP facilitators.

This can be a challenging and rewarding work. All nursing staff involved should seek clinical supervision and must recognise limits of their therapeutic effectiveness and in particular, note potential negative outcome of transference/counter-transference (Murphy, 2003). In supporting John through the treatment programme, nursing staff are advised to familiarise themselves with the support manual developed by Naylor (2006)

Evaluation

Evaluation will involve logbook and diary evaluation, integrated computer information system, supervision sessions, and discussion with SOTP facilitators.

Care plan 3 identifies how nursing staff can support John through the treatment programme and reinforce the lessons that John learns from the group.

Supervision and support

It is important to consider the personal feelings and experiences of nurses working with sex offenders (Coffey, 2000). Many nurses might experience strong emotions such as fear, anger, dread and disgust (Hilton and Mezey, 1996). It might therefore be difficult for forensic mental health nurses to display the level of empathetic understanding and respect that plays such a large role in nurses' professional functioning (Coffey, 2000). It is therefore vital that nurses utilise what support structures are in place, such as expert clinical supervision, managerial supervision and/or reflective practice groups. At Ashworth Hospital, nurses who facilitate on the hospital's SOTP receive regular clinical supervision and also have access to an independent counselling service to discuss any negative thoughts or feelings that this type of work might raise. It is suggested that all mental health services that provide care and treatment for sex offenders should consider such services as a minimum.

Conclusion

Although working with sexual offenders can be emotionally demanding, it can also be rewarding (Scheela, 2001). When one considers that the primary aim of all sex offender treatment is to reduce re-offending then it can be easier to accept the task in hand. As nurses a 'duty to care' is incumbent upon all of us to provide this care for all. Nevertheless working with sex offenders can present a number of difficulties not least because of the abhorrence of the offending act itself. Nurses involved in working with sex offenders must consider their own beliefs, feelings and attitudes towards these offenders. Additionally, as Coffey (2000) emphasises, it is imperative to receive regular expert supervision. Equally important is the exploration of new theories and their potential application in practice, since basic nurse training does not include this type of specialised work.

In this chapter we have attempted to present from an introductory point, the work of the Sex Offender Therapy Programme (SOTP) and the important contribution forensic mental health nurses can make in assisting an individual on the programme. The case study in this chapter was based on a number of our previous and current group members. With the majority, there have been positive outcomes. This is, at least in part, the result of close collaboration between the ward-based nurses and SOTP therapists.

References

Abel GG, Becker JV, Cunningham-Ranthner J, Kaplan M, Reich J (1984) The Treatment of Sex Offenders. SBC-TM: New York. Cited in: Carich MS, Calder MC (2003) *Contemporary Treatment of Adult Male Sex Offenders*. Russell House Publishing: Lyme Regis

American Psychiatric Association (1994) *Dangerous Sex Offenders: A Task Force Report*. Washington, DC: APA

American Psychiatric Association (1999) *Diagnostic and Statistical Manual of Mental Disorders*, 4th Edn. Washington,DC: APA

Beckett R (2005) What are the characteristics of female sex offenders? *NOTA News* **51** 6–7

Beckett R, Beech A, Fisher D, Scott-Fordham (1998) *Community Based Treatment for Sex Offenders: An Evaluation of Seven Treatment Programmes*. Home Office Publications Unit: London

Boer DP, Hart SD, Kropp PR, Webster CD (1997) *Manual for the Sexual Violence Risk – 20: Professional Guidelines for Assessing Risk of Sexual Violence*. British Columbia Institute Against Family Violence and The Mental Health, Law and Policy Institute: Vancouver

British National Formulary (2007) *BNF – 54* September 2007. [Online]. Available from: http://bnf.org.bnf/current128089.htm [Accessed 10 November 2007]

Burgess AW, Hartman CR, Ressler RK, Douglas JE, MacCormack A (1986) Sexual homicide: A motivational model. J Interpersonal Violence **1** 251–272 Cited in: Calder

MC (1999) *Assessing Risk in Adult Males who Sexually Abuse Children*. Russell House Publishing: Lyme Regis

Burt MR (1980) Cultural myths and supports of rape. *J Personality and Soc Psychol* **38** 217–30

Buss DM (1994) *The Evolution of Desire*. Basic Books: London

Calder MC (1999) *Assessing Risk in Adult Males who Sexually Abuse Children*. Russell House Publishing: Lyme Regis

Calder MC (2000) T*he Complete Guide to Sexual Abuse Assessments*. Russell House Publishing: Lyme Regis

Calder MC, Skinner J (2000) The comprehensive assessment of adult males who sexually abuse. In: Calder MC (ed) *The Complete Guide to Sexual Abuse Assessments*. Russell House Publishing: Lyme Regis

Campbell T, Carich M S, Burgener J (2000) 5-Factor Typology of Sex Offenders. Unpublished Handout. Cited in: Carich MS, Calder MC (2003) *Contemporary Treatment of Adult Male Sex Offenders*. Russell House Publishing: Lyme Regis

Carich MS, Calder MC (2003) *Contemporary Treatment of Adult Male Sex Offenders*. Russell House Publishing: Lyme Regis

Coffey M (2000) Working with sex offenders. In: Chaloner C, Coffey M, (eds) *Forensic Mental Health Nursing Current Approaches*. Blackwell Science: Oxford

Courtney J, Rose J (2004) The effectiveness of treatment for sexual offenders with learning disabilities: A review of the literature. *J Sexual Aggression* 10(2): 215–36

Craig AC, Browne KD, Stringer I, Beech A (2005). Sexual recidivism: A review of static, dynamic and actuarial predictors. *J Sexual Aggression* **11**(1): 65–84

Craissati J (2004) *Managing High-Risk Sex Offenders in the community: A psychological approach*. Brunner-Routledge: Hove

Craissati J, Beech A (2001) Attrition in a community treatment programme for child sexual abusers. *J Interpersonal Violence* **16**: 205–21

Denov MS (2003) To a safer place? Victims of sexual abuse by females and their disclosures to professionals. *Child Abuse and Neglect* **27**(1): 47–61

Doyle M (2006) *Edenfield Centre Patient Needs Assessment*. Unpublished: Adult Forensic Mental health Services Directorate: Bolton Salford and Trafford Mental Health NHS Trust

Elliot M, Browne K, Kilkoyne J (1995) Child sexual abuse prevention: What offenders tell us. *Child Abuse and Neglect* **19**(5): 579–594

England P, Murphy M, Duckworth P (1999) Crisis interventions and risk management of sex offenders. In: Ryan T (ed) *Managing Crisis and Risks in Mental Health Nursing*. Stanley Thorns Ltd: Cheltenham

Erooga M (2002a) citing: Fisher D (1994) Adult sex offenders: Who are they? Why and how do they do it? In Morrison T, Erooga M, Becket RC (eds) *Sex Offending Against Children: Assessment and Treatment of Male Abusers*. Routledge: London

Erooga M (2002b) *Adult sex offenders, Characteristics of adult sex offenders*. NSPCC: London. [Online]. Available from: http://www.nspcc.org.uk/Inform/research/Briefings/adultsexoffenders_wda48227.html [Accessed 15 October 2007]

Finkelhor D, Russell D (1984) Women as perpetrators. In: Finkelhor D (eds) *Child Sex Abuse: New theory and research*. The Free Press: New York

Freeman-Longo RE, Blanchard GT (1998) *Sexual Abuse in America: Epidemic of 21st Century*. Safer Society Press: Brandon, VT

Friendship C, Mann R, Beech A (2003) *The Prison-Based Sex Offender Treatment Programme – An Evaluation*. Home Office research Findings No205. Home Office Research Development and Statistics Directorate: London

Gordon H, Grubin D (2004) Psychiatric aspects of the assessment and treatment of sex offenders. *Adv Psychiatric Treatment* **10**: 73–80

Gould SJ (1997) *Dinosaur in a Haystack*. Penguin: London

Grayston AD, De Luca RV (1999) Female perpetrators of child sexual abuse: A review of the clinical and empirical literature. *Aggression and Violent Behaviour* **4**: 93–106

Greenberg DM, Bradford JMW (1997) Treatment of paraphilic disorders: A review of the role of the selective serotonin reuptake inhibitors. *Sexual Abuse: A Journal of Research and Treatment* **8**: 349–60

Groth N (1982) The incest offender. In: Sgroi SM (ed) *Handbook of Clinical Intervention in Child Sexual Abuse*. Lexington Books: Lexington MA

Groth N, Burgess W, Holstrom LL (1977) Rape: power, anger and sexuality. *Am J Psychiatry* **134**(11): 1239–43

Hanson RK, Brussiere MT (1998) Predicting relapse: A meta-analysis of sexual offender recidivism. *J Consult Clin Psychol* **66**(2): 348–62

Hanson RK, Harris A (1998) *Dynamic Predictors of Sexual Recidivism*. Department of the Solicitor General of Canada: Ottawa. [Online]. Available from: http://ww2.ps-sp.gc.ca/publications/Corrections/199801b_e.pdf [Accessed 11 November 2007]

Hanson RK, Harris A (2000) T*he Sex Offender Needs Assessment Rating (SONAR): A Method for Measuring Change in Risk Levels*. Department of the Solicitor General of Canada: Ottawa

Hanson RK, Thornton D (2000) Improving risk assessments for sex offenders: A comparison of three actuarial scales. *Law and Human Behaviour* **24**: 119–36

Hart SD, Hare RD (1997) Psychopathy: Assessment and association with criminal conduct. In: Stoff DM, Brieling J, Maser J (eds) *Handbook of Antisocial Behaviour*. John Wiley: Ney York

Hilton MR, Mezey GG (1996) Victims and perpetrators of child sexual abuse. *Brit J Psych* **169**: 408–515

HM Prison Service (2000) *SOTP Core 2000: Theory Manual*. Offending Behaviour Programmes Unit, Home Office: London

HM Prison Service (2002) *SOTP Core 2000: Treatment Manual, Version 2*. Offending Behaviour Programmes Unit, Home Office: London

Holland T, Claire ICH, Muckhopadhyay T (2002) Prevalence of "criminal offending" by men and women with intellectual disability and the characteristics of "offenders": Implications for research and service development. *J Intellectual Disability and Research* **46**(Sup 1): 6–20

Home Office (2003) *Home Offices Criminal Statistics for England and Wales*. [Online]. Available from: http://www.homeoffice.gov.uk.rds/pdfs04/cs2003vol2pt1.xls [Accessed 15 May 2007]

Hucker SJ, Baines J (1990) Androgenic hormones and sexual assault. In: Marshall WL, Barbaree HE (eds) *Handbook of Sexual Assault: Issues, Theories and Treatment of the*

Offenders. Plenum: New York

Hughes GV, Webb J (2005) Problematic sexual behaviour in a secure psychiatric setting: Challenges and developing solutions. *J Sexual Aggression* **11**(1): 95–102

Kafka MP (1997) The monoamine hypothesis for the pathophysiology of paraphilic disorders: an update. *Arch Sexual Behaviour* **26**(4): 343–58

Knight RA, Prentky RB (1990) Classifying sexual offenders: The development and corroboration of taxonomic models. In: Marshall WL, Laws DR, Barbaree H (eds) *Handbook of Sexual Assault*. Plenum Press: New York

Langevin R, Watson RJ (1996) Major factors in the assessment of paraphiliacs and sex offenders. *J Offender Rehabil* **23**: 33–70

Lotke E (1996) Issues and Answers – Sex Offenders: Does Treatment Work? (Internet source: www.ncianet.org.ncia/sexo.html) [Accessed 15 October 1997]. Cited from: England P, Murphy M, Duckworth P (1999) Crisis interventions and risk management of sex offenders. In Ryan T (ed) *Managing Crisis and Risks in Mental Health Nursing*. Stanley Thorns Ltd. Cheltenham

Lovell E (2002) *I Think I Might Need Some More Help With This Problem: Responding to children and young people who display sexually harmful behaviour*. NSPCC: London

Marshall WL (1994) Treatment effects on denial and minimisation in incarcerated sex offenders. *Behav Res Therapy* **32**: 559–64

Marshall WL (1996) The sexual offender: Monster, victim or everyman. *Sexual Abuse: A Journal of Research and Treatment* **8**: 317–35

Marshall P (1997)*The Prevalence of Convictions for Sexual Offences. Home Office Research Finding No. 55*. Home Office Research and Statistics Directorate: London

Marshall WL, Anderson D, Fernandez Y (1999) *Cognitive Behavioural Treatment of Sex Offenders*. John Wiley & Sons, Ltd: Chichester

Matravers A (2003) *Sex Offenders in the Community: Managing and Reducing the Risks*. William Publishing: Cullompton

Mayer A (1983) *Incest: A Treatment Manual for Therapy With Victims, Spouses and Offenders*. Learning Publications: Florida

McClurg G, Craisatti J (1999) A descriptive study of alleged sexual abusers known to social services *J Sexual Aggression* **4**(1): 22–30

MacCulloch MJ, Snowdon PR, Wood PJ, Mills HE (1983) Sadistic fantasy, sadistic behaviour and offending behaviour. *Brit J Psych* **143**: 20–9

Murphy B (2003) *Psychodynamic approaches with individuals. In: Barker P (ed) Psychiatric and Mental Health Nursing. The Craft of Caring*. London: Arnold

Nathan P, Ward T (2001) Females who sexually abuse children: Assessment and treatment issues. *Psych, Psychol Law* **8**(1): 44–56

Nathan P, Ward T (2002) Female sex offenders: Clinical and demographic features. *J Sexual Aggression* **8**(1): 5–21

National Criminal Records Service (2003) *Recorded Crime Statistics*. [Online]. Available from: http://www.homeoffice.gov.uk.rds.recordedcrime/htm/ [Accessed 21 September 2007]

Naylor K (2006) *Manual For Support Sessions For Sex Offender Treatment Programme*. Unpublished work Ashworth Special Hospital. Mersey Care NHS Trust

Norton K (2004) The therapeutic milieu In: Norman I, Ryrie I (eds) *The Art and Science of*

Mental Health Nursing. A Textbook of Principles and Practice. Open University Press: Maidenhead

NOTA (National Organisation for the Treatment of Abusers) (2005) *Frequently Asked Questions.* [Online]. Available from: http://www.nota.co.uk/indexphp?id=fqs [Accessed 19th May 2007]

O'Conner W (1997) Towards an environmental perspective on intervention for problem sexual behaviour in people with an intellectual disability. *J Appl Res Intellectual Disabilities* **10**: 159–75

O'Donohue W, Letourneau E, Dowling H (1997) The measurement of sexual fantasy. *Sexual Abuse: Journal of Research and Treatment* **9**: 167–1=78

Ortmanm J (1980) The treatment of sexual offenders: Castration and anti-hormone therapy. *Int J Law Psych* **3**: 443–51

Prentky RA, Knight RA (1991) Identifying critical dimensions for discriminating among rapists. J Consult Clin Psychol **59**(5): 643–61

Sanday PR (1981) The socio-cultural context of rape: A cross cultural study. *J Soc Issues* **37**(4): 2–27

Scheela RA (2001) Sex offender treatment: Therapists' experiences and perceptions. *Issues in Ment Health Nursing* **22**(7): 49–67

Serran GA, Marshall LE (2006) Coping and mood in sexual offending In: Marshall WL, Fernandez YM, Marshall LE, Serran GA (eds) *Sexual Offender Treatment. Controversial Issues.* John Wiley and Sons: Chichester

Sohota K, Chesterman P (1998) Sexual offending in the context of mental illness. *J Forensic Psych* **9**: 267–80

Stripe T (2003) *An Investigation of Adult Male Sexual Offenders' State-of-Mind Regarding Childhood Attachment and its Relationship to Victim Choice.* Ontario Institute for Studies in Education: Toronto

Tang-Martinez Z, Mechanic MB (2000) *Response to Thornhill and Palmer on Rape.* The Sciences: NY Academy of Sciences

Thompson D, Brown H (1997) Men with intellectual disabilities who sexually abuse: A review of the literature. *J Appl Research in Intellectual Disabilities* 10: 140–58

Thornhill R, Palmer CT (2000) *A Natural History of Rape: Biological Bases of Sexual Coercion.* MIT Press: Cambridge, MA

Thornton D (2002) Constructing and testing a framework for dynamic risk assessment. *Sexual Abuse: A Journal of Research and Treatment* **14**(2): 139–52

Thornton. D (2007) *2007 Scoring Guide for Risk Matrix 2000.a/SVC.* Avaliable from http://psg.bham.ac.uk/forensic_centre [Accessed 22 September 2008]

World Health Organisation (1994) *The ICD-10 Classification of Mental and Behavioural Disorders: Clinical descriptions and diagnostic guidelines.* WHO: Geneva

CHAPTER 10

Risk assessment, measurement and management

Phil Woods

Introduction

This chapter explores the role of forensic mental health nurses in risk assessment and management. Furthermore, it examines some of the growing literature looking critically at notions of risk and placing these in a social, political and historical context. There is little doubt that risk assessment and its related management is the guiding force for clinicians working in forensic care; and that this is the central component in the assessment process (Woods, 1996; Doyle and Coffey, 2007). By their very nature, patients who find themselves in forensic mental health services have done so through the risk they have posed and it will undoubtedly be the reduction in this risk that helps them move on from these services back into the community. Throughout this chapter we will see that forensic mental health nurses must take an active role in this process. Moreover, they have an important insight to share as they spend more time with patients than other professionals.

What is risk assessment?

Risk may, generally, be defined as the probability of a bad consequence; or as the likelihood that a harmful event will recur (Prins, 1996). It involves such issues as outcome and probability. Therefore it can be simply defined as 'determining the probability of harm to self or others or a serious unwanted event such as suicide or homicide'. The author has previously argued that within forensic mental health care risk assessment is mainly concerned with three highly interrelated components: the risk posed in the past, now, and in the future. Moreover, the most important points at issue are (1) will re-offending occur, and (2) what is the potential for change (Woods, 2001)?

Kettles (2004: 487) states:

> *Forensic risk is a specific type of risk related to the behaviour of those patients who have committed a crime or who exhibit challenging behaviour*

and are committed by law or are diverted from custody to forensic psychiatric settings... Forensic risk assessment aims to assess whether or not a patient is a risk to themselves or to others in terms of serious violence, sexual violence, dangerousness, absconding and recidivism in the past, now or in the future....Forensic risk assessment is different to those risk assessments conducted elsewhere in mental health.

So is risk assessment an easy process? Well it appears it should be. However, it is not a magical process (Scott, 1977) but rather a complex issue determined to a large degree by who defines the risk and how it is defined (McClelland, 1995). Indeed, Kettles (2004) in her concept analysis of forensic risk, clearly indicates that health professionals often tend to understand risk in many different ways. Forensic mental health professionals are expected to be able to assess risk adequately (Bingley, 1997), and this is probably owing to their patient group. However, risk assessment is a key skill, and a skill which has to rely heavily on clinical judgement (Chiswick, 1995).

Pollock and Webster (1990) and Monahan and Steadman (1994) give some insight, highlighting that assessments need to be systematic and based on the population undergoing assessment; with identified risk factors required to be broken down into more manageable components, further assessed through effective treatment planning and outcomes evaluated through recovery status. Furthermore, Borum (1996) makes three recommendations to improve clinical practice in risk assessment: (1) improve assessment technology, (2) develop clinical practice guidelines, and (3) develop training programmes and curricula.

Approaches to risk assessment

There are a number of main approaches that can be found in the literature to assist in risk assessment. First there is the clinical approach. This is probably the most widely used approach in most practice. It is based upon professional opinion concerning a patient's self-presentation, and clinical or situational variables. Of course, this opinion is very much dependent on the clinician's skill, knowledge and experience (Anderson et al, 2004). This approach looks for explanations for specific violent behaviour and is concerned with how individuals behave, how they react in various situations, how they have been known to behave, how willingly they accept treatment, and how much insight they have into their condition. This clinical approach has been opposed by many researchers who prefer the second approach arguing that it may be contaminated by 'assessor bias', and that it is only as good as its theoretical base. Previous studies did support this scepticism finding that on occasion predictions from clinicians are no better than chance (Monahan, 1988). However, recent studies do indicate more reliable results from clinicians (Grove et al, 2000; Lewis and Webster, 2004, Norko and Baranoski, 2005).

The second approach has been termed the actuarial or statistical approach. Here assessment is done on predetermined, often historical, variables that have been shown to be predictive of risk. It is based on the assumption that an individual coming from a population within which a certain type of behaviour is common is more likely to display this form of behaviour (Doyle and Dolan, 2002). Sceptics have criticised this approach in relation to the lack of change that can occur and therefore not allowing for patient risk to reduce, i.e. once assessed as being high risk, always high risk.

More recently, and driving current research, is the strong consensus in the literature that there should be a balance between these two approaches, with actuarial factors serving as an anchor for more dynamic clinical risk assessment. This has been termed third generation research or structured clinical judgement (Doyle and Dolan, 2002). Therefore, these previously static actuarial risk markers only provide a guide for risk management planning, and any assessment is individualised to the particular person through individual clinical risk factors relating to current behaviour.

What is risk management?

Risk management is the process or intervention through which identified risks are reduced or alleviated. Put another way, it is vitally important that once a risk assessment has occurred that a risk management plan focuses on the likelihood of the probability or outcome occurring (Woods, 2001). Vinestock (1996) describes risk management as a method of balancing probable consequences of decisions which assists in formalising the decision-making process in relation to the risk of harm to self or others. The Department of Health (2007: 14) states:

> *The aim of risk management is first to assess the likelihood of risk events and then to work with the service user to identify ways of reducing the likelihood of them occurring. Risk management should be based on a plan to reduce the risk of harm occurring and increase the potential for a positive outcome.*

Nurses' role in assessing and managing risk

As was previously highlighted, forensic mental health nurses have a key role in the assessment and management of risk in their patients, be this in relation to risk to others, risk to self, risk of relapse or risk of re-offending. Lewis and Webster (2004) indicate that, historically, risk assessment has been regarded as a task for psychologists and psychiatrists, however, they go on to discuss that nowadays, nurses are expressing more interest. Lewis and Webster report that some doubt exists if nurses have the skills to undertake such assessments, but point out that studies are beginning to emerge suggesting this is not the case (for example, Watt et al, 2003). Indeed, more and more research is appearing in the literature in relation to nurses' interest in developing a role in risk assessment and management. Some of this is reported in this chapter.

Measurement

It is obvious that in order to assess and then effectively manage risk, you first have to measure it in some way. However, as many have pointed out this is an inexact science and clinical judgement will play a vital role in risk decisions of the multi-disciplinary team. Forensic mental health nurses should have a clear structured approach to risk assessment and this should involve utilising the array of rating scales that are available to help in this decision making process, as well as behavioural observation during the 24-hour period. Some of the scales that may be of particular relevance for forensic mental health nurses would be: Historical, Clinical, Risk – 20 (HCR-20; Webster et al, 1997); Short-Term Assessment of Risk and Treatability (START; Webster et al, 2004); Behavioural Status Index (BEST-Index; Reed and Woods, 2000; Woods et al, 2005); Broset Violence Checklist (BVC; Almvik et al, 2000); Violence Risk Scale (VRS; Wong and Gordon, 2000); Staff Observation and Aggression Scale – Revised (SOAS-R; Nijman et al, 1999) to name but a few. In essence, this is the utilisation of structured clinical judgement, informed by clear awareness of the different types of risk factors. The Department of Health (2007: 13) indicates that risk factors can be defined in a number of ways:

- Static factors – those that cannot be changed. For instance, history of violence, offending behaviour.
- Dynamic factors – those that can change over time making them more amenable to management. For instance, individual or environmental aspects such as substance misuse and social networks.
- 'Stable or chronic factors' – those 'dynamic factors that are quite stable and change...slowly over time' (Department of Health, 2207:13). These could also possibly include the examples given for dynamic factors but of course are specific to the individual.

Many have offered suggestions in estimating the level of risk and among others Doyle (1999: 49) indicates seven key questions:

- What is the likelihood of harm occurring?
- How often is this likely to occur?
- What possible outcomes could there be?
- Who is at risk?
- What is the immediacy of the risk?
- What is the timescale for assessment?
- What are the circumstances that are likely to increase or decrease the risk?

Understanding key risk variables

There are many variables that have been identified within the literature that have been either found to be associated with certain risk or may contribute to risk to self or others. For violence to others; unit-related variables (time of day, incident location, staffing, census, patient mix); interactional variables (staff–patient interactions, staff–patient rapport, coercive interactional style); and patient-related variables (Johnson, 2004). Anderson et al (2004) reviewed these patient-related variables in some detail and, considering the multiple, patient-related risk factors that exist for inpatient violence, concluded that assessment of risk of aggression cannot be made on clinical diagnosis alone. Accordingly, they organised patient-related risk factors into four areas: dispositional (demographic, cognitive, personality), contextual (stress perception, social support, means for violence), clinical (diagnosis and symptom patterns, functioning, substance abuse), and historical (prior hospitalisation and outcome, prior violence, social factors). Risk to self will include mental health state, current circumstances and feelings around this, future circumstances, social issues and maybe threats from others, to name but a few.

It is important that forensic mental health nurses are aware and understand what these key risk variables are and how much they may or may not contribute to individual patient risk. While some of the more actuarial scales and simple rating scales may list many of these, it is still important that nurses have awareness of the total contribution in relation to a patient's individual clinical variables.

Substance abuse

Within the literature, substance abuse is a reliable factor that has been found to contribute both to risk to others (Swanson et al, 1990; Phillips, 2000; Steadman et al, 2000; D'Silva and Ferriter, 2003; Norko and Baranoski,

2005) and risk to self (Cassells et al, 2005). Ford and Woods (2006:163) suggest that successful risk assessment must give an integrated account of the patient's mental health difficulties, their past and current use of psychoactive substances and their criminal behaviour. These authors are of the opinion that the bi-directional interactions between these domains require a complex and dynamic understanding of patients and their environment if risk management is be successful. They further suggest assessment for substance abuse should include:

- The type of drugs used – the doses, frequency, duration and route of use.
- In relation to alcohol abuse – the number of units per week, daily unit frequency, early morning drinking, and how prolonged the abuse has been.
- Family and social relationships, including social isolation.
- Mental state, noting any changes that covary with periods of intoxication.
- Behaviour.
- Insight into both primary psychiatric diagnoses and substance use disorder.
- Motivation to change substance use.

Use of the nurse–patient relationship

The use of the nurse–patient relationship is an important part of any risk assessment and related management plan for the forensic mental health nurse. As we see later in this chapter (*Box 10.3*) Kettles (2004) highlights much of this in her work on defining the concept of forensic risk. Such key skills as active listening and developing rapport, as well as observation of non-verbal cues, are all important when interviewing during risk assessment and intervening through risk management plans.

Risk management

According to the Royal College of Nursing (1997) the assessment of risk is undertaken to decide which risk management measures are required to minimise harm and increase likelihood of benefits for the person assessed. Essentially, it is the next stage from risk assessment and a vitally important part of the forensic mental health nurses' practice. Doyle (1999: 41) has defined risk management as 'the systematic, organised effort to eliminate or reduce the likelihood of misfortune, harm, damage or loss'. Perhaps in the area of forensic mental health practice, this should also include offending and relapse.

There are a number of key issues that need to be considered in the risk management measures that are utilised in forensic mental health practice. To effectively operationalise this risk management plan, forensic mental health nurses need to state precisely and specifically the nature or level of the risk, placing this in situational context, and outlining the relationships between the risky behaviours presented. Clear statements of anticipated risk and how these are, or can be avoided, need to be made, thus minimising the impact of any risk. In order to do this through the risk assessment, the forensic mental health nurse should have gained a detailed knowledge of the individual's personal circumstances, mental health, forensic histories, etc., then the early warning signs of any risk can be anticipated. In turn the risk management plan can focus specifically on the responses required to deal with these potential or anticipated risks and effectively and clearly monitor the effects of the risks and any progress which is made through the implementation of the plan. In essence, this is dynamic risk assessment.

From a good practice standpoint the risk management plan should dictate which responses are made when a crisis occurs (i.e. the risk is observed to occur). This could involve physical restraint or isolation from others on the unit to allow the individual to ventilate feelings on a one-to-one basis through to measures taken in the community setting. It is vitally important that the focus of the management plan (i.e. the person who has been assessed as risky) is informed of the risk(s) which have been identified; what will happen if they occur; and why. In practice, this may involve the individual being given the opportunity to select from a range of alternative management strategies. If this is to occur therapeutically to allow the individual to develop and hopefully learn from a risky situation, thereby reducing potential risk, creative thinking, which promotes positive risk taking would need to happen (Woods, 2001). In effect, this is what the Department of Health (2007) calls positive risk management.

Of course, for the plan to be evaluated effectively, it needs to be continuously reviewed, within identified time constraints, with results communicated to all relevant people involved in the care process. Thus the process of risk assessment, through management and re-assessment, bears resemblance to the nursing process. Doyle (1999:40–41) offers some practical advice in the form of a six-stage risk management cycle:

1. Identification.
2. Risk assessment.
3. Rating risk.
4. Implement risk management measures.
5. Monitoring of risk management measures.
6. Risk assessment review.

Box 10.1: Five-step structured professional approach to risk management

1. Case information – history, mental state, substance use
2. Presence of risk factors – historical, current, contextual
3. Presence of protective factors – historical, current, contextual
4. Risk formulation – nature, severity, imminence, likelihood, risk reducing/enhancing
5. Management plan – treatment, management, monitoring, supervision, victim safety planning

(From Doyle and Duffy, 2006)

Doyle further highlights how it is easily incorporated in the care programme approach. More recently, Doyle has reported a five-step structured professional approach to risk management (quoted in Doyle and Duffy, 2006:146). This offers useful framework for forensic mental health nurses (see *Box 10.1*).

The Department of Health (2007:5–6) has produced some advice on best practice in managing risk (see *Box 10.2*). It clearly indicates that the principles are applicable to all mental health settings from community through to high security forensic care.

Education

For forensic mental health nurses to effectively take on their role in relation to risk assessment and management, it is important for them to engage in post-registration education. More importantly, education that is part of life-long learning, as the evidence related to risk assessment and management is ever changing, so their skills and knowledge will need to be updated on a regular basis. Kettles (2004) quite rightly indicates that forensic risk is an educational term in its own right. She argues that skills, knowledge and attitude are needed to understand it and use it in clinical practice. Kettles clearly lays out these skills, attitudes and knowledge relationships to the domain of forensic risk (see *Box 10.3*). It is easy for individual forensic mental health nurses or even forensic organisations to incorporate Kettles' suggestions into an ongoing education plan in relation to assessing and managing risk.

The risk of risk assessment

Another important aspect that needs to be considered when undertaking risk assessments, not only by forensic mental health nurses, but also others in the clinical team, is what will be termed the risk of risk assessment. The

---

Box 10.2: Department of Health (2007: 5–6) best practice for risk management

1. Best practice involves making decisions based on knowledge of the research evidence, knowledge of the service user and their social context, knowledge of the service user's own experience, and clinical judgement.
2. Positive risk management as part of a carefully constructed plan is a required competence for all mental health practitioners.
3. Risk management should be conducted in a spirit of collaboration and based on a relationship between service users and their carers that is as trusting as possible.
4. Risk management must be built on a recognition of the service user's strengths and should emphasise recovery.
5. Risk management requires an organisational strategy as well as efforts by the individual practitioner.
6. Risk management involves developing flexible strategies aimed at preventing any negative event from occurring or, if this is not possible, minimising the harm caused.
7. Risk management should take into account that risk can be both general and specific, and that good management can reduce and prevent harm.
8. Knowledge and understanding of mental health legislation is an important component of risk management.
9. The risk management plan should include a summary of all risks identified, formulations of the situations in which identified risks may occur, and actions to be taken by practitioners and the service user in response to crisis.
10. Where suitable tools are available, risk management should be based on assessment using the structured clinical judgement approach.
11. Risk assessment is integral to deciding on the most appropriate level of risk management and the right kind of intervention for a service user.
12. All staff involved in risk management must be capable of demonstrating sensitivity and competence in relation to diversity in race, faith, age, gender, disability and sexual orientation.
13. Risk management must always be based on awareness of the capacity for the service user's risk level to change over time, and a recognition that each service user requires a consistent and individualised approach.
14. Risk management plans should be developed by multidisciplinary and multi-agency teams operating in an open, democratic and transparent culture that embraces reflective practice.
15. All staff involved in risk management should receive relevant training, which should be updated at least every three years.
16. A risk management plan is only as good as the time and effort put into communicating its findings to others.

Box 10.3: Domain of forensic risk and its relationship to knowledge, skills and attitudes (Kettles, 2004, after National Board for Nursing Midwifery and Health visiting for Scotland, 1999)

Models and approaches
Knowledge   Clinical judgement, actuarial, structured clinical judgement
Skills   Relationship building, listening, negotiating, analysing, making judgements, reflection
Attitude   Self-aware, confident, assertive, motivation to learn, willingness to take planned risks, objective

Medical risk assessment
Knowledge   Diagnosis and treatment for various disorders
Skills   Critical judgement, use of some standardised approaches
Attitude   Willingness to take responsibility, ethical attitude

Characteristics
Knowledge   Administrative decision-making, location on a continuum, continuous day-to-day management of the risky person
Skills   Balancing care and control, risk thinking, protecting others, advocacy of civil rights
Attitude   Caring, ability to challenge the logic that equates difference with danger

Professional attributes of forensic risk
Knowledge   Objectivity, evidence-based, multi-disciplinary functioning, prediction
Skills   Team participation, communication, observation and vigilance
Attitude   Willingness to participate robustly in team decision-making, recognition of own/others' limitations

Attributes of forensic risk
Knowledge   Dangerous behaviour, probability, responsibility
Skills   Risk management, organisational management, security
Attitude   Rigorous awareness, degree of objectivity, recognition of own/others' limitations

Security
Knowledge   Strategy, operational systems of control, relational security, physical security, procedural and operational security, ethics
Skills   Appropriate use of staff power/strategy, dynamic measures, passive measures

---

Box 10.3: (continued)

Attitude	Continuing education and training
Policy	
Knowledge	Government, legal, health service, prison service
Skills	Interpretation and implementation of policy and guidelines, standard setting, audit
Attitude	Openness

Homicide and suicide, violence

Knowledge	Prior violence and criminality, childhood experiences and violence, dual diagnosis with substance misuse, psychopathy, command hallucinations, anger, violent thoughts
Skills	Decision threshold for level of risk, prevention, interventions and their efficacy, treatment approaches, medication effects, interactions and adverse effects
Attitude	Awareness of consequences, willingness to act, prevention/reaction

Recording procedures

Knowledge	Care planning, incident reporting
Skills	Documentation, recoding and reporting
Attitude	Motivation to engage constructively in clinical supervision

Risk management

Knowledge	Substance misuse, dangerousness, hostage-taking, arson
Skills	Team working, collaboration, participation
Attitude	Sensitivity, motivation to engage constructively in continuing education

Instruments and tools

Knowledge	Assessment procedures, inter-rater reliability
Skills	Training in use of specific tools or instruments, collection of information by observation and interview
Attitude	Motivation to learn, understanding of subjective bias, being as objective as possible

(From: Kettles, 2004: 486 after National Board for Nursing, Midwifery and Health Visiting for Scotland, 1999)

---

results of risk assessment and related management plans can have a profound effect on those subject to these in forensic services, resulting in labelling and stigmatisation. Hepworth (1982) clearly explained that there is a risk of the dangerous individual becoming a 'non-person' in therapeutic terms; and his/her dangerousness becoming based solely on previous recorded violence.

Such an individual may well become static on the continuum of 'dangerous/ non-dangerous' or 'person/non-person'. Other examples include individuals being labelled as psychopaths or as having a personality disorder or being labelled with the new term dangerous and severe personality disorder. This can have consequences when trying to access services at a later date and the stigma they will receive. One does not have to look hard in the literature to find many examples of this. The important message for forensic mental health nurses to bear in mind, in relation to this risk of risk assessment, is that if your patient does not want to comply with your risk assessment is this the reason why?

Conclusion

This chapter has touched some of the edges of the complex world of risk assessment and management. Some of the fundamental aspects that are part of this complex world have been highlighted. It is clear that forensic mental health nurses have a vital and important part to play in all aspects of the risk assessment and management process. Indeed, their input offers an important 24 hour a day perspective. In order to offer an objective and informed role, they need to utilise structured clinical judgement using appropriate instruments and checklists alongside their clinical behavioural observation and assessment. They need to contribute their assessment alongside others in the multi-disciplinary team to develop true multi-professional risk management strategies and plans.

The whole process of risk assessment and management was summed up over two decades ago by Scott (1977):

> *It is patience, thoroughness and persistence in the process rather than any diagnostic brilliance that produces results. In this sense the telephone, the written requests for past records and the checking of information against other informants are the important diagnostic devices.*

References

Almvik R, Woods P, Rasmussen K (2000) The Brøset Violence Checklist (BVC): Sensitivity specificity and inter-rater reliability. *J Interpersonal Violence* **15**(12): 1284–96

Anderson TR, Bell CC, Powell TE, Williamson JL, Blount MA (2004) Assessing psychiatric patients for violence. *Community Ment Health J* **40**(4): 379–99

Bingley W (1997) Assessing dangerousness: Protecting the interests of patients. *Brit J Psychiatry* **170**(32): 28–9

Borum R (1996) Improving the clinical practice of violence risk assessment. *Amer Psychologist* **51**(9): 945–56

Cassells C, Paterson B, Dowding D, Morrison R (2005) Long- and short-term risk factors in the prediction of inpatient suicide: A review of the literature. *Crisis* **26**(2): 53–63

Chiswick D (1995) Dangerousness. In: Chiswick D, Cope R (Eds) *Seminars in Practical Forensic Psychiatry* (pp 210–42) Gaskell, London

Department of Health (2007) *Best Practice in Managing Risk: Principles and Evidence for Best Practice in the Assessment and Management of Risk to Self and Others in Mental Health Services*. Department of Health, London

Doyle M (1999) Organizational responses to crisis and risk: issues and implications for mental health nurses. In: Ryan T (Ed) *Managing Crisis and Risk in Mental Health Nursing* (Chapter 4, pp 40–56) Stanley Thornes, Cheltenham

Doyle M, Coffey M (2007) Forensic aspects of acute inpatient assessment. In: National Forensic Nurses' Research and Development Group – Kettles, A, Woods P, Byrt R, Addo M, Coffey M, Doyle M (Eds) *Forensic Mental Health Nursing: Aspects of Acute Care* (pp 101–20) London: Quay Books

Doyle M, Dolan M (2002) Violence risk assessment: combining actuarial and clinical information to structure clinical judgments for the formulation and management of risk. *J Psych Ment Health Nurs* **9**: 649–57

Doyle M, Duffy D (2006) Assessing and managing risk to self and others In: National Forensic Nurses' Research and Development Group – Woods P, Kettles A, Byrt R, Addo M, Aiyegbusi A, Coffey M, Collins M, Doyle M, Garman G, Watson C (Eds) *Forensic Mental Health Nursing: Interventions with People with 'Personality Disorder'* (pp 135–50) London: Quay Books

D'Silva K, Ferriter M (2003) Substance use by the mentally disordered committing serious offences – a high-security hospital study. *J Forensic Psychiatry Psychol* **14**(1): 178–93

Ford P, Woods P (2006) Dual diagnosis in a forensic setting. In: Rassool GH (Ed) *Dual Diagnosis Nursing* (pp 161–8) Blackwell Publishing, Oxford

Grove WM, Zald DH, Lebow BS, Snitz BE, Nelson C (2000) Clinical versus mechanical prediction: a meta-analysis. *Psychological Assessment* **12**: 19–30

Hepworth D (1982) Influence of the concept of "danger" on assessment of danger to self and others. *Medicine Science and the Law* **22**(4): 245–54

Johnson ME (2004) Violence on inpatient psychiatric units: state of the science. *J Amer Psychiatric Nurses Assoc* **10**: 113–21

Kettles AM (2004) A concept analysis of forensic risk. *J Psychiatric Ment Health Nurs* **11**: 484–93

Lewis AHO, Webster CD (2004) General instruments for risk assessment. *Curr Opin Psychiatry* **17**: 401–5

McClelland N (1995) The assessment of dangerousness: A procedure for predicting potentially dangerous behaviour. *Psychiatric Care* **2**: 17–19

Monahan J (1988) Risk assessment of violence among the mentally disordered: generating useful knowledge. *Int J Law Psychiatry* **11**: 249–57

Monahan J, Steadman HJ (eds) (1994) *Violence and Mental Disorder: Developments in Risk Assessment*. University of Chicago Press, Chicago

Nijman HLI, Muris P, Merckelbach HLGJ, Palmstierna T, Wistedt B, Vos AM, van Rixtel A, Allertz W (1999) The Staff Observation Aggression Scale–Revised SOAS-R. *Aggressive Behav* **25**(3): 197–209

Norko MA, Baranoski MV (2005) The state of contemporary risk assessment research. *Can J Psychiatry* **50**: 18–26

Phillips P (2000) Substance misuse, offending and mental illness: a review. *J Psychiatric Ment Health Nurs* **7**(6): 483–9

Pollock N, Webster C (1990) The clinical assessment of dangerousness. In: Bluglass R, Bowden P (Eds) *Principles and Practice of Forensic Psychiatry* (pp 489–97) Churchill Livingstone, Edinburgh

Prins H (1996) Risk assessment and management in criminal justice and psychiatry. *J Forensic Psychiatry* **7**(1): 42–62

Reed V, Woods P (2000) *The Behavioural Status Index: A Life Skills Assessment for Selecting and Monitoring Therapy in Mental Health Care.* Psychometric Press, UK

Royal College of Nursing (1997) *Risk Assessment: Guidance for Mental Health Nursing: Assessing and Managing the Risk of Harm to Others from People with Mental Health Problems.* RCN, London

Scott PD (1977) Assessing dangerousness in criminals. *Brit J Psychiatry* **131**: 127–42

Steadman HJ, Silver E, Monahan J, Appelbaum PS, Robbins PC, Mulvey EP, Grisso T, Roth LH, Banks S (2000) A classification tree approach to the development of actuarial violence risk assessment tools. *Law and Human Behavior* **24**(1): 83–100

Swanson J, Holzer C, Ganju V, Jono R (1990) Violence and psychiatric disorder in the community: Evidence from the epidemiological catchment area surveys. *Hosp Community Psychiatry* **41**: 762–70

Vinestock M (1996) Risk assessment: 'A word to the wise'? *Adv Psychiatric Treatment* **2**: 3–10

Watt A, Topping-Morris B, Rogers P, Doyle M, Mason T (2003) Pre-admission nursing assessment in a Welsh Medium Secure Unit (1991–2000): Part 2 – comparison of traditional nursing assessment with the HCR–20 risk assessment tool. *Int JNursing Studies* 40: 657–62

Webster CD, Douglas K, Eaves D, Hart S (1997) *HCR–20: Assessing Risk for Violence – Version 2.* Simon Fraser University: British Columbia, Canada

Webster CD, Martin ML, Brink J, Nicholls TL, Middleton C (2004) *Manual for the Short Term Assessment of Risk and Treatability (START). Version 1.0* (Consultation edn) St. Joseph's Healthcare Hamilton, Ontario, Canada, and Forensic Psychiatric Services Commission, Port Coquitlam, British Columbia, Canada

Wong S, Gordon A (2000) *Violence Reduction Programme: Phases of Treatment and Content Overview.* Regional Psychiatric Centre: Saskatoon, Saskatchewan, Canada

Woods P (1996) How nurses make assessments of patient dangerousness. *Ment Health Nurs* **16**(4): 20–2

Woods P (2001) Risk assessment and management. In: Dale C, Thompson T, Woods P (Eds) *Forensic Mental Health – Issues in Practice* (pp 85–97) Ballière Tindall, London

Woods P, Reed V, Collins M (2005) The Behavioural Status Index: Testing a social risk assessment model in a high security forensic setting. *J Forensic Nurs* **1**(1): 9–19

CHAPTER 11

Creative anger management: An overview

*Stuart Bowness, 'Algy', Richard Byrt, Romanus Ngeh,
Lauren Mason and Cathy Wray*

Introduction

The next two chapters are on anger management on Cannock ward at Arnold Lodge medium secure unit, Leicester. The ward was one of the first English medium secure facilities offering treatment specifically for men with personality disorders. Besides referrals from professionals in prisons, young offender institutions and high secure hospitals, people who are sentenced or remand prisoners are provided with information, and can refer themselves for initial pre-admission assessment to consider their specific problems, level of risk and motivation. If the individual is accepted for admission to Cannock, further thorough assessment continues. The ward offers a structured programme, including (mainly cognitive-behavioural) groups, with a particular emphasis on problem-solving techniques (McMurran et al, 2001b), and some modified therapeutic community principles within the parameters of safety and security. Patients have opportunities, not only to work intensively on problems, but also to develop strengths and abilities through a variety of educational, sporting, arts and other activities. The ward also enables the early stages of recovery and rehabilitation. Further information about Cannock is given in Byrt et al (2005) and Duggan et al (2007).

The nature of anger

Most patients on Cannock ward experience problems in managing anger. In the literature, there is a lack of agreement about the nature of anger, with many definitions (Rogers and Vidgen, 2006). The latter generally include the idea that anger is a subjectively felt emotion, accompanied by thoughts, and sometimes, behaviours, as well as by physiological changes. Anger 'varies in intensity from mild irritation to intense fury and rage' in response to 'both internal and external events' (American Psychological Association, 2007, quoting Spielberger). The emotion is often experienced as unpleasant (psychological arousal), with the individual thinking, or knowing, that other people or situations are responsible for being frustrating, wrong, unjust or unfair. Uncomfortable physiological changes (physiological arousal) occur because neurotransmitters travel 'from the hypothalamus…to the sympathetic nervous system, adrenal medulla, adrenal cortex [and] pituitary gland' (Smith et al, 2003, quoted in Byrt and Doyle, 2007:84–5). This results in more rapid breathing, raised heart beat, 'pulse rate and blood pressure', increased 'muscle tension, sweating, peristalsis in stomach and intestines' and an 'urgent desire to pass urine' (Byrt and Doyle, 2007:85). There is also decreased appetite and production of saliva, so that the individual's mouth becomes dry.

Usually, a trigger precipitates angry thoughts, feelings and behaviours. The trigger is often something which the individual experiences as particularly frustrating or negative (Paterson and Leadbetter, 1999). Anger is often associated with frustration in response to failure to achieve a desired goal, or being prevented from performing a desired action (Turnbull, 1999; Bjorkly, 2006). Research has found that some individuals who become angry more readily and more aggressively than average have a 'low tolerance of frustration, meaning…that they feel that they should not have to be subjected to frustration, inconvenience or annoyance' (American Psychological Association, 2007). However, some aggression is instrumental, with the individual behaving in this way in order to achieve a goal, rather than as a response to frustration or because he/she is angry (Turnbull, 1999). In addition, Williams (1993) argues that people have problems with managing anger if they have limited skills in communicating and relating to others. In relation to this, techniques may be used, for example, to enable individuals to reflect on (their sometimes inaccurate) perceptions fuelling anger, and avoid saying the first things that come to mind. Other techniques that have been suggested include the avoidance of triggers and the use of humour (American Psychological Association, 2007) (See *Box 11.1*).

Anger can become damaging to health when poorly managed. Just as any other human emotion, anger needs to be expressed to promote emotional well-being. However, this process needs to be safe and avoid hurting others (Richman, 2007).

Angry behaviours, such as thumping a faulty computer or shouting at another person, are accompanied by angry thoughts and feelings. For this reason, cognitive-behavioural therapies in anger management are concerned, not only with assessing and helping the individual to change the expression of anger through specific behaviours, but also the underlying thoughts and feelings (Doyle et al, 2006; Rogers and Vidgin, 2006). Further details of cognitive-behavioural therapy are given in *Box 11.2*.

Box 11.1: Ideas for the safe expression of anger

Pillow technique
This involves designing, on a pillow, a picture of an object or individual with whom the person feels angry; and hitting this image, without inhibition, in order to express, and eventually, get rid of the anger (Rhoades, 1995; Richman, 2007). This technique is more likely to be of help to people who are anxious about being assertive, and who express anger passively. However, studies indicate that some individuals' aggression is increased if the 'pillow technique' is used (Richman, 2007): a point needing careful consideration in relation to forensic patients.

The use of quiet space
A change of environment, such as going to a quiet room or space may help to reduce angry aggression and tension (American Psychological Association, 2007, Richman, 2007). Obviously, in forensic and other mental health settings, this would be used only if it is safe, and the individual would be accompanied by one or more staff members, with colleagues near at hand (Byrt and Doyle, 2007). With these provisos, the use of quiet space may reduce aggression in relation to the removal of the initial trigger (Richman, 2007) and the reduction of excessive noise and over-stimulation resulting in sensory overload (Byrt, 2007). Relaxation techniques may be helpful, including the use of music to induce calm and reduce tension (Richman, 2007). Byrt and Doyle (2007) describe the use of quiet space which appeared effectively to reduce the violent behaviours of an individual experiencing a hypomanic phase of a bipolar mental illness.

'Strive to forgive' (Richman, 2007)
Richman (2007) stresses the importance of the individual being able to forgive the person with whom he/she is angry. On Cannock ward, this is stressed in the Controlling Angry Aggression Group, in which patients are encouraged to find ways of 'letting go' of, and resolving, grudges and angry feelings, including those directed at other patients and staff.

The positive side of anger

Forensic and other mental health nurses tend to work with individuals who express anger in problematic ways (Rogers and Vidgin, 2006). Perhaps for this reason, some mental health nurses have been found to 'pathologise' anger: to assume that when patients express this emotion, that this is always undesirable and a 'symptom' of mental illness or personality disorder However, it has been argued that anger can be expressed creatively, with positive consequences for the individual and for others (Goffman, 1968;

Box 11.2: Cognitive-behavioural therapy

Cognitive-behavioural therapy (CBT) aims to:
- Assess and measure precisely:
    - the nature and frequency of a particular problem or symptom.
    - the distress associated with this problem or symptom.
    - any stressors (i.e. things that cause stress) and other triggers that seem to precipitate the problem or symptom.
- Use specific, clearly stated interventions to reduce or relieve symptoms, problems and associated distress and stress.
- Focus not only on individuals' problems and symptoms, but also on their strengths and positive coping strategies. In CBT, ideally, individuals should be enabled to recognise and develop these, and to use them to resolve or reduce symptoms and problems.
- Use precise measures to assess the extent that the interventions have been successful in reducing or alleviating symptoms or problems and/or associated stress and distress.

(Doyle et al, 2006; Rogers and Vidgin, 2006)

Cognitive restructuring is concerned with enabling individuals to question, and change the way that they think: for example, reminding themselves that becoming angry will not solve a particular problem

(American Psychological Association, 2007)

Hopton, 1995; Rogers and Vidgin, 2006). Burns (1980) describes 'mood therapy' to enable the creative and safe expression of anger.

A distinction has been made between three types of anger. In assertion, individuals express their anger in a way which takes account of the rights of others, and which avoids threatening or intimidating behaviour. According to some definitions, the presence of the latter is a feature of aggression, which may be accompanied by violence: the use of physical force or verbal hostility in order to harm others. Individuals who express anger passively 'bottle it up', they internalise the anger, often become depressed, and sometimes have sudden, explosive outbursts when they can no longer contain the anger (Duxbury 2000; Byrt and Doyle, 2007). However, definitions of 'assertive', 'aggressive' and 'passive' anger may depend, at least partly, on what individuals in particular cultural groups perceive to be 'appropriate' or 'inappropriate' behaviours (Fox, 1999; Byrt and Doyle, 2007). For example, some critics have argued that young men with diagnoses of antisocial personality disorder differ from clinicians in their values and understanding of 'masculine behaviour'; and the extent that they identify with, or feel alienated from, dominant social norms (Barker, 2005; Corbett and Westwood, 2005).

Individual methods of managing anger, related to assertion, aggression and passivity, include the following (American Psychological Association 2007):

- Suppression. This includes denying or 'bottling up' the anger. Individuals may ignore the reason they are angry and focus on other things instead.
- Expression. This includes channelling the anger: engaging in an activity which redirects and expresses anger constructively. An example would be a patient who dissipated his/her anger through a rigorous workout in the gym.
- Calming. This involves controlling angry behaviours and associated feelings and thinking, e.g. through relaxation techniques.

In summary, anger can be seen as a healthy emotion when expressed safely. However, certain individuals, including some people with antisocial and borderline personality disorders, find it hard to creatively manage anger (McMurran et al, 2001a). This may lead to adverse effects on personal and work relationships and on the individual's overall quality of life (McKay et al, 2003). Certainly, this has been the case, in the past, for most patients on Cannock ward.

Research on anger management using CBT

'A meta-analysis of 50 research studies' found that cognitive-behaviour therapy reduces aggressive anger (Rogers and Vidgin, 2006:274, citing Beck and Fernadez, 1998). A pilot study in a secure unit found that a 'social problem solving' approach with nine patients (six with mental illness and three with 'psychopathic disorder') resulted in improvements in effective solving of problems and lessened 'impulsivity/carelessness style (ICS)', as measured on the Social Problem-Solving Inventory (SSPI) (McMurran et al, 1999). These authors conclude that 'the positive change in ICS...suggests that problem-solving skills training corrects cognitive deficits, improves self-regulation, and hence reduces aggression and violence' (McMurran et al, 1999:321). In another pilot study, McMurran et al (2001a) found that, of four Cannock ward patients, three showed improvements following a 'Controlling Angry Aggression' (CAA) group. Mason (2005) found that various aspects of anger were reduced in eight Cannock ward patients (as measured by Spielberger's State-Trait Anger Expression Inventory), following their participation in a CAA group.

McMurran et al (2001b) describe the application of 'Stop and Think!' social problem skills to anger management on Cannock ward. The 'Stop and Think!' principles aim to enable patients to develop abilities in successfully identifying problems related to their anger; and to discover safe and creative solutions and ways to achieve these (McMurran et al, 2001b). Duggan et al (2007) report a high drop out rate from treatment on Cannock ward, but overall, improved problem solving skills 'at least to one year of follow up' with 'improvements in patients' behaviour' on Cannock ward (ibid:16–17), but only a slight reduction in recidivism, overall, following discharge from the ward. In addition, a randomised controlled trial of individuals with personality disorder living in the community has found 'significantly better problem solving skills, ...higher overall social functioning, ...and lower anger expression' in individuals receiving psychoeducation, followed by groups using an 'extension of...Stop and Think!' problem solving (Huband et al, 2007:307).

However, some problems may not have a ready solution. In such instances, it may be 'best...not to focus on finding the solution, but rather on how you handle and face the problem' (American Psychological Association, 2007).

CBT groups for managing anger on Cannock ward

The following groups are provided on Cannock ward to enable individuals to manage their anger effectively:

- Controlling Angry Aggression (CAA). This group uses Stop and Think! problem solving principles (McMurran et al, 2001b), and is described below. Emphasis is placed on the acquisition of skills in managing anger.
- Controlling Anger and Learning to Manage It (CALM: Winogron et al, 2004). On Cannock ward, patients sometimes participate in the CALM group after they have completed a CAA course. CALM enables individuals to acquire a more in-depth understanding of their anger and the reasons for it.
- Control of Violence for Angry Impulsive Drinkers (COVAID). This group helps participants to consider the links between their own previous violence and drinking alcohol. Each group member has a history of at least three episodes of violence associated with alcohol, and sometimes involving a partner. There is some evidence suggesting the effectiveness of COVAID with some individuals, although further studies are needed (McMurran and Cusens, 2003; McMurran, 2006).

Other groups on Cannock ward

The following is based on 'Algy's' experience as a patient.

Some of the other groups on Cannock ward include:

- Trust Self-Awareness Group. This group focuses on helping patients raise self-awareness and build up their trust in people, so that hopefully they can trust and get along with people once they are released
- Moral Reasoning Group. This group helps members develop confidence and enhanced self-awareness. The group consider things in general, with the generation of constructive debate and discussion. This enables members to reflect and develop better thinking skills, so that they do not always think negatively or in a one-sided way. Topics include relationships, politics or contemporary events.
- Psychological Inventory in Criminal Thinking Styles (PICTS). 'I found this group very beneficial. It made me think and change the way I've acted and looked at my behaviour, along with the negative consequences that came with it. I can now recognise that I have hurt a lot of people in the past (emotionally and physically). I can see what sort of an effect that I have had on the people around me. Also, I am now aware of different "criminal thinking styles" and which ones I had used during the time of my index offence.'

'During the PICTS Group, I looked at my "criminal thinking styles", and what I could have done differently without any negative behaviour being used. I began to understand why I committed my index offence, through answering some questions from the staff and other patients, questions like:
- Why did I commit my index offence?
- What thoughts crossed my mind?
- What thoughts did I try to block out or cut off?
- What did the person do to deserve what I did to them?
- Was I taking any drugs or alcohol or both at the time of my offence?'

This is a very intense group, but extremely beneficial to people who want to change their behaviour and want to make a go in life for themselves.
- Change Group. This group facilitates members' examination of their behaviours and areas that they need to change. There are four stages to this group: pre-contemplation/contemplation, preparation, action and maintenance (Prochaska and Di Clemente, 1984). These stages are related to group members' own experiences. If patients are totally honest and truthful, they will get the full benefits from the group. They need to remember that they will only get out of a group what effort they put in.

Patients look at the sort of obstacles they need to change, linked to their perceptions and thoughts and, eventually, attitudes and beliefs related to their past and present behaviours. Subsequently, patients will be able to understand and change the negative, and work towards future goals, in order to make a 'life' for themselves, and also be able to make the right kind of choices in life. The last part of the group work looks at relapse prevention, and most importantly, identifies 'high risk situations'. Patients are encouraged to find ways of overcoming these appropriately, without negative consequences.

- Relapse Prevention. The purpose of this group is to try to stop patients reverting back to negative, high risk situations and behaviours. Patients are enabled to identify and recognise high risk situations and find positive ways of dealing with these, without any negative behaviours and consequences. The group considers ways of dealing with day-to-day stress, failures and fear; and the learning of new skills to help build individuals' confidence and self-esteem.

The rest of this chapter considers the CAA group, starting with an account by 'Algy', describing his experience, as a patient on Cannock ward, of the use of Stop and Think! problem solving techniques.

Problem solving in CAA groups

There are six stages to problem solving in managing anger, described by McMurran et al (2001b), and which are used in problem solving on Cannock ward. (The six stages indicated below, are quoted from this source.) These enable patients to learn how to deal with problems in a positive way, without resorting to negative behaviours.

- 'What bad feelings do I have?' This might include feeling aggressive, or fed up.
- 'What's my problem?' For example, being told 'No'.
- 'What do I want?' For example, to be able to manage feelings when I've been told 'No'.
- 'What are my options?' (McMurran et al, 2001) These can be anything from smashing up my room (negative behaviour and consequences) to positive options, e.g. talking to other patients or using ward meetings to discuss feelings.

In the problem solving group, the positive and negative aspects of each option are considered (*Table 11.1*). Algy's experience is as follows.

Table 11.1: Positives and negatives for various options explored in problem-solving groups

Positives	Negatives
Getting anger out in the open	May not like what I hear
Makes me feel better	Wrong advice and no support
Get support from other patients	Make me feel worse
Builds my confidence and self-esteem	
Gets others' opinions and advice	

Table 11.2: Positives and negatives of the option: 'Smashing my room up'

Positives	Negatives
Makes me feel better (short term)	Doesn't solve the problem
Others are aware of what mood I'm in	Creates more problems
Makes others scared of me	Other patients will keep away from me
Makes me feel more powerful	May get further charges from the Police
	Extra days may be added to my sentence
	Lose friends and family members
	Seen as 'attention seeking'

Patient's experience: 'Algy'

'What's my plan?' (McMurran et al, 2001)

I have used the problem solving meetings, and have spoken to other patients to get their opinions about a variety of positive options. However, some options, such as smashing my room up (*Table 11.2*) have far too many negative consequences, so therefore, I shouldn't think about that option at all.

The final stage is to work out how my plan went after I have given it a few weeks. Hopefully, this gives enough time for the plan to work. If it doesn't, then I would rethink my plan and try to come up with another plan or change some of the options.

Review date

A review date is set to allow enough time for the plan to work.

How did I do?

At the time of the review date, I write whether my plan was a success or not. If it was not a success, the reasons for this are considered. I would then rethink my options and my plan to more effectively manage my anger.

Facilitator's perspective: Stuart Bowness

This group work programme was formulated by McMurran et al (2001a), who identified that 'controlling angry aggression is structured around a simple heuristic model that allows the integration of biological, psychological, and social theories of anger and aggression' (McMurran et al, 2001a:473–4). The purpose of the CAA course is to provide the opportunity for participants to learn and develop skills that will enable them to manage more positively their angry aggression in everyday life situations. The group is timetabled into the ward programme, once there are enough people identified who need access to this group. The optimum number of participants is six.

The group runs once a week for 2.5 hrs for 15 weeks. Each meeting has a 30 minute break half way through the session overall, including time spent on set homework. The course averages 50 hours in duration. Facilitators include a staff nurse or healthcare support worker, a clinical team leader and a psychologist, who are all based on the ward. To aid consistency and the climate of the group, it is closed, and will only be facilitated by two of the three identified ward staff. The group process uses role plays and presentations, with set homework. The course directly links into the participant's attitude and behaviour on the ward, and this is achieved through the use of anger diaries which are completed by participants whenever they are needed.

The participation and progress of two members of the group, 'Glen' and 'Hank', follows.

Glen and Hank were entered onto the course as they had a history of violence and aggression and a number of angry aggressive outbursts during their time on the ward. It was felt they would benefit from learning new strategies that would enable them to cope more positively with situations, initially while on the ward, where they could gain experience putting strategies into action. Ultimately, participants will become sufficiently familiar with strategies to be able to put them into practice when they return to their communities.

For participants to gain the most from this course, it is necessary to encourage them to be honest, open and genuine. As facilitators, we felt that in order for group members to feel safe enough to share previous experiences and become active participants, rather than passive recipients, we would initially place great emphasis on active listening, with a view to engaging in dialogue with the group's participants. These methods would be put into practice in unison with delivering the manualised course content. Hank presented as motivated and keen, not only to learn but also to explore concepts relating to 'controlling angry aggression' throughout the whole of the course. It was noticed that Hank's active participation inspired other group members to increase their level of involvement. In contrast, it took Glen a few sessions before we observed a level of participation that we knew he was capable of. This was partly due to Glen's belief that the anger course would be the same as the one that he had previously undertaken in prison. When Glen realised that it was different, his level of participation rose to the point where he felt motivated and comfortable to become more involved in role play scenarios and deliver presentations.

It became clear early on during this course that Hank was 'open' and motivated to learn. It also became apparent that he had understood and taken on board aspects of the course and put them into practice, as this was evidenced from the significant drop in recorded anger outbursts. Glen's fixed views about certain aspects of life made it difficult for him to challenge his personal beliefs and to take on board, and put into practice, new methods of responding to situations and acting more positively and pro-actively upon them. As the course progressed, Glen did appear more open to understanding and exploring new ways of managing situations.

One of the difficulties with facilitating this course was the danger of being drawn into extended discussions and debates if participants disagreed with a particular strategy as it related to specific scenarios. Facilitation skills were put to the test, as we had to present a particular strategy, explore it, then relate it to real-life situations. As facilitators, we had to remain focused upon delivering the course content and time management, while still creating the time and space for participants to connect with, and explore the issues.

Hank's attitude remained positive throughout the course and he would appropriately challenge aspects of the content that he felt unsure about. Rather than being dismissive, he would critically analyse the information with a view to developing a more informed opinion. Glen had developed long-standing fixed views about how he understands and deals with situations in everyday life, but this did not stop him from critically analysing aspects of the course content and discussing his opinions within the group setting. Initially, he presented as struggling to take certain methods and strategies on board, with a view to acting upon them. However, it was identified that outside of the group, these methods and strategies were, to varying extents, being put into practice.

Mid-way through the course, ward staff had to manage how other patients on the ward perceived their peers who were undergoing the CAA course. Some patients would criticise patients who were on the course if they expressed any degree of anger on the ward, as they felt they were not putting their learning into practice. On occasion, this made group members disheartened, instigating a feeling of failure. Ward staff and group facilitators had to encourage group members to maintain their learning; and, in addition, educate other patients about short and long-term learning expectations related to the group.

As facilitators, we felt that, as the course progressed, the participants became more open and honest and willing to share past experiences with us. This had the effect of testing us regarding our 'non-judgemental approach' and encouraged us to remain clearly focused on the specific treatment plan of each participant. It did become apparent, at times, when exploring participants' past experiences, that there were clear differences regarding personal values, related to why they became involved in some conflict situations and how they dealt with them. It was at these times that the content of the session was at risk of reaching an impasse because of this clash of values. As facilitators, it would sometimes take all our skills and energies to move through these scenarios, while still acknowledging past experiences.

Outcomes from the course

Hank's overt anger outbursts diminished significantly following the completion of the CAA course. When Hank did become irritated or angry, he presented himself as having increased self-control and did appear to utilise learned coping strategies to deal with situations. Also, it became apparent that he was able to manage potential conflict situations in a more positive manner. Glen's anger outbursts also diminished on the ward after the group sessions had finished, although it was not clear to what extent this was due to his putting newly learned strategies into practice. Observations by nursing staff did identify that avoidance and going to his room were the main strategies utilised in conflict situations. These strategies are useful basic first stage methods, but longer term and more proactive strategies were identified as needing to be put into practice. This issue was addressed through Glen's contact with his nursing team.

It has often been identified, from the evaluation of courses that are run on the ward, that participants value having trained staff who will see them through to their conclusion; and that this needs to be identified before the start of a course. Participants are always mindful of identified group ground-rules and place great emphasis on their being adhered to. As the course progressed, the participants felt safe and able to challenge each other appropriately in relation to a variety of issues. As with most group sessions and courses on Cannock ward, we often thought that more time would have been useful.

I have often been asked whether there is any value in working with individuals with personality disorder and histories of offending. I have always felt that we provide the opportunity for individuals to either enhance or gain knowledge, skills and abilities, in order to develop strategies and coping skills that will enable them to deal more positively with their angry aggression in 'conflict' situations in everyday life. Whether individuals put the skills they have learned into practice or not, is a choice they will make at the time.

Conclusion

This chapter has provided an overview of the nature of anger and its expression through assertion, aggression and passivity. The role of triggers, such as frustration, has been considered, although some aggression can be instrumental and calculated. There is evidence that cognitive-behavioural therapies are effective in helping some individuals manage their anger. This is also suggested by two pilot studies of patients on Cannock ward. Anger management and other groups on this ward are outlined, with particular reference to the managing angry aggression group from the perspectives of a patient and a staff member.

In the next chapter, Cannock patients give further experiences and views related to anger management.

References

American Psychological Association (2007) *APA Online: Controlling Anger – Before It Controls You.* Available from: http://www.apa.org/topics/controlanger.html [Accessed 7 October 2007]

Barker GT (2005) *Dying to be Men: Masculinity and Social Exclusion.* Routledge, Taylor and Francis Group, London

Beck R, Fernandez E (1998) Cognitive behavioral therapy in the treatment of anger: a meta-analysis. *Cognitive Ther Res* **22**: 63–74.

Bjorkly S (2006) Psychological theories of aggression: principles and application to practice In: Richter, D, Whittington R (eds) *Violence in Mental Health Settings: Causes, Consequences, Management.* Springer, New York

Burns DD (1980) *Feeling Good: The New Mood Therapy.* Signet, New York

Byrt R (2007) Towards therapeutic environments: Alternatives and solutions. In: National Forensic Nurses' Research and Development Group: Kettles AM, Woods P, Byrt R, Addo A, Coffey M, Doyle M (eds) *Forensic Mental Health Nursing: Forensic Aspects of Acute Care.* Quay Books, MA Healthcare, Ltd: London

Byrt R, Doyle M (2007) Prevention and reduction of violence and aggression. In: National Forensic Nurses' Research and Development Group: Kettles AM, Woods P, Byrt R, Addo M, Coffey M, Doyle M (Eds) *Forensic Mental Health: Forensic Aspects of Acute Care.* Quay Books, MA Healthcare, London

Byrt R, Wray C, 'Tom' (2005) Towards hope and inclusion: nursing interventions in a medium secure service for men with 'personality disorders'. *Ment Health Pract* **8**(8): 38–43

Corbett K, Westwood T (2005) Dangerous and severe personality disorder': a psychiatric manifestation of the risk society. *Crit Public Health* **15**(2): 121–33

Doyle M, Aiyegbusi A, Burbery P (2006) Personality disorder: specialist psychological approaches. In: National Forensic Nurses' Research and Development Group: Woods P, Kettles AM, Byrt R, Addo M, Aiyegbusi A, Coffey M, Collins M, Doyle M, Garman G, Watson C (Eds) *Forensic Mental Health Nursing: Interventions with People with 'Personality Disorder'*. Quay Books, MA Healthcare Ltd, London

Duggan C, Mason L, Banerjee P, Milton J (2007) Value of standard personality assessments in informing clinical decision-making in a secure unit. *Brit J Psychiatry* **190**(Suppl): s15–s19

Duxbury J (2000) *Difficult Patients*. Butterworth-Heinemann, Oxford

Fox KJ (1999) Changing violent minds: discursive correction and resistance in the cognitive treatment of violent offenders in prison. *Soc Problems* **46**(1): 88–103

Goffman E (1968) *Asylums: Essays on the Social Situation on Mental Patients and Other Inmates*. Penguin: Harmondsworth

Hopton J (1995) The application of the ideas of Frantz Fanon to the practice of mental health nursing. *J Adv Nurs* **21**: 723–8

Huband N, McMurran M, Evans C, Duggan C (2007) Social problem-solving plus psychoeducation for adults with personality disorder: Pragmatic randomised controlled trial. *Brit J Psychiatry* **190**: 307–13

Mason L (2005) *Unpublished Report*. Arnold Lodge Medium Secure Unit. Nottinghamshire Healthcare NHS Trust: Leicester

McKay M, Rogers PD, McKay J (2003) *When Anger Hurts: Quieting the Storm Within*. (2nd edn) New Harbinger Publications, Inc, Oakland, CA

McMurran M (Ed) (2002) *Motivating Offenders to Change: A Guide to enhancing Engagement in Therapy*. John Wiley and Sons, Chichester

McMurran M (2006) Controlled drinking goals for offenders. *Addiction Res Theory* **14**(1): 59–65

McMurran M, Charlesworth P, Duggan C, McCarthy L (2001) Controlling anger, aggression, and violence: A pilot group intervention with personality disordered offenders. *Behav Cognitive Psychother* **29**: 473–83

McMurran M, Cusens B (2003) Controlling alcohol-related violence: a treatment programme. *Criminal Behav Ment Health* **13**(1): 59–76

McMurran M, Egan V, Richardson C, Ahmadi S (1999) Social problem solving in mentally disordered offenders: a brief report. *Criminal Behav Ment Health* **9**(4): 315–22

McMurran M, Fyffe S, McCarthy L, Duggan C, Latham A (2001) Stop and think! Social problem-solving therapy with personality disordered offenders. *Criminal Behav Ment Health* **11**(4): 273–85

Paterson B, Leadbetter D (1999) De-escalation in the management of aggression and violence. In: Turnbull J, Paterson B (Eds) *Aggression and Violence: Approaches to Effective Management* (Ch 6) MacMillan, Basingstoke

Prochaska JD, DiClemente C (1984) *The Trans-theoretical Approach: Crossing Traditional*

Foundations of Change. William Morrow, New York

Rhoades GF Jr (1995) *Controlling the Volcano Within. General Manual: Anger Control Training (ACT) Manual*. L.L. Maxwell Publishing, Pearl City

Richman H (2007) *Improve Emotional and Physical Health! Five Free Tips Help Release Anger*. Sound Feeling Publishing, Tarzana, California. Available from: http://www. soundfeelings.com/free/anger.htm [Accessed 7 November 2007]

Rogers P, Vidgen A (2006) Working with people with severe mental illness who are angry. In: Gamble C, Brennan W (Eds) *Working with Serious Mental Illness: A Manual for Clinical Practice*. Elsevier, Edinburgh

Smith EE, Nolen-Hoeksema S, Frederickson B, Loftus G (Eds) (2003) *Atkinson's and Hilgard's Introduction to Psychology* (14th edn) Harcourt College Publishers, Fort Worth

Turnbull C (1999) Theoretical approaches to violence and aggression. In: Turnbull J, Paterson B (Eds) *Aggression and Violence: Approaches to Effective Management* (Ch 3) MacMillan, Basingstoke

Williams RB (1993) Hostility and the heart. In: Goleman D, Gurin J (Eds) *Mind/Body Medicine*. Consumers Union, New York

Winogron W, Van Dieten M, Gausas L, Grismi V (2004) *Controlling Anger and Learning to Manage It (CALM) Programme*. Multi-Health Systems Inc, Toronto

CHAPTER 12

Creative anger management: Patients' views and experiences

'Bede', 'Colm', 'Algy', 'Dirk', 'Ezra', 'Ferg' and Richard Byrt

Introduction

This chapter includes the perspectives of six individuals with experience as patients on Cannock ward. Mental health service users' views are considered by various authors to be important both in their own right (Barker et al, 1999), and in evaluating services, with a view to highlighting good practice and effecting improvements (Carlin et al, 2005; Spiers et al, 2005; Coffey, 2006). In addition, it has been argued that service user views can enable nurses to reflect on their practice (McArdle and Byrt, 2001). Until recently, there were few published personal accounts by service users with a personality disorder concerning the services they had received, and few research studies of their views. In the past few years, there has been a considerable increase in both personal accounts (Ashman, 2001; Pick, 2005; Byrt et al, 2006) and in research studies on the perspectives of people with a personality disorder diagnosis (Ryan et al, 2002; Castillo, 2003; Perseius et al, 2003; Horn et al, 2007).

The views given in this chapter are not, of course, necessarily representative of other people who are, or have been, Cannock patients.

Individuals' comments are given in relation to the following aspects of managing anger and related topics:

- Recognising anger-triggering situations.
- Clarification: Correcting misinterpretations of events.
- Withdrawing from a provoking situation and returning to it later.
- Feedback from other patients and staff.
- Cannock ward and its staff.
- Learning from living on Cannock ward.

Box 12.1: CALM (Controlling anger and learning to manage it)

CALM courses have been used in prisons with individuals 'whose offending is associated with poor emotional control. CALM aims to reduce the intensity, frequency and duration of negative emotions…associated with their offending. These emotions include anger, anxiety and jealousy' (HM Prison Service, 2007).

The programme has been criticised for enabling some prisoners to increase their violent offending skills, and there are plans to reduce its availability (Johnston, 2006, Travis, 2006; Gault, 2007). However, psychologists have pointed out that CALM is effective with people with impulsive behaviours who find it difficult to regulate their anger, but not effective with individuals whose aggression is instrumental and calculated (Gault, 2007, quoting Riley, and Winogron, 2006). One individual expressed scepticism about the efficacy of CALM courses, based on his/her experiences as a prisoner (Anon, 2006). However, Williams (2003), a journalist, describes various benefits from CALM reported by prisoners and psychologists at Pentonville.

Recognising anger-triggering situations

Dirk: It's helpful recognising the triggers, high risk situations, clarifying things, checking things out related to my paranoia, coping skills and doing role plays. It's about recognising triggers to a situation, the way you interpret things.

Ezra: In prison, I did a cognitive-behavioural programme – told to do it by the Parole Board. I did a CALM course in prison (see *Box 12.1*). I found it very useful. They teach you to be aware when you're angry – what to do when buttons are pushed, and stop you spilling over. But what they don't teach you, is what to do when things touch a raw nerve with you and you choose not to use the anger management skills.

Ferg: I've done the CALM course in prison. It helps reduce arousal, helps you realise what problems you have. As time goes on and you do more course work and one-to-one work, it gets better, I used to be really angry, but what I've discussed has helped me.

Clarification: Correcting misinterpretations of events

Ferg: Social skills groups have been helpful, mainly with interactions with others. This has been helpful with communication, and once you're able to clarify things, that's helpful: to ask what someone means.

Dirk: If you have an argument, you might interpret that someone is trying to mug you off. You're taught to clarify, thinking things through in your head. Sometimes, if you do this, you find they're not mugging you off, it's just your interpretation. You think 'that sounds insulting', but ask: 'Was it meant to be?'Role plays give you a chance to ask for clarification. We do it to each other in the group – and out of the group. An example is name-calling. I found that other patients only do it as a joke. I thought they were being serious.

Bede: I think problem solving and anger management go hand in hand because when you have an angry outburst, you can problem solve – go through the steps...Doing both together gives you a higher success rate.

Clarification is especially important. Self-talk is very important, for example, saying to yourself: 'Hang on to the anger'; 'Use the community for the support'. To reassure yourself, think positively, try not to always think negatively. Say to yourself: 'If I personalise anger, they may not hear it.' I try to think of the positive, rather than the negative. I use the ward community: being able to talk is tremendously helpful. Sometimes when I talk, anger disappears. There are opportunities to do this with patients and staff.

Withdrawing from a provoking situation and returning to it later

Dirk: One anger management technique is, if things get too heated, you can come back to the situation later. You give yourself a bit of space, rather than having a shouting match at each other.

Bede: I'm a beginner on the anger management, but I think it's taught me when I'm angry to go to my room, but before, I would have a face-to-face confrontation. What I want to do is process my thoughts there and then, but now I go to my room and relax and listen to music. For me it's helpful, it's a cut off point that works for me. I come out after 20 minutes and deal with the issue that made me angry, by going to the person, the situation that pissed me off, that particular thing that made me really frustrated. I clarify and find another alternative. You realise in clarifying, that you may be wrong. What made me angry may not be right. The person I'm angry with may explain. I might not agree, but the 20 minutes I had to chill out helps me to be calm, recharged, see things from a different angle.

The downfall is, it can make it worse by dwelling too much on it, you can lose the moment. But there's time to think things through, hopefully more clearly: an opportunity to look at both sides. Sometimes, I go back and apologise and say, 'I understand where you're coming from'. For me, it depends on what mood I'm in, what reaction I'm going to get.

Ferg: When I first came here, the main thing for me was problem solving. It helped reduce my anger – you go through the options, positive and negative. It gives you time to stop and think. It reduces arousal, so you've time to think things through. That's the group that's been helpful. For me, it was self-taught: things like telling yourself to take it easy and use breathing techniques so it helps you stay calmer. It's helpful because if you go through the bad feelings, it helps reduce them.

Ezra: In prison, they taught a range of techniques – to stop yourself getting aggressive. For me, it was taking a deep breath and counting to 10. I've used this since leaving prison.

If you're angry, other patients are very supportive and they give you space – that's the time out to calm yourself down and then deal with it when you're on the level. Plus you can get it off your chest with patients – and that lowers your anger and helps you calm down.

What's very important is the time out and the time in…Time in is when you have your say constructively. Time out is when you feel very angry. However, if you're only using time out, then you're not dealing with it.

Feedback from other patients and staff

Personal accounts and the findings of research studies suggest that people with a diagnosis of personality disorder see staff–patient communication and relationships as crucial (Ryan et al, 2002; Castillo, 2003; Byrt et al, 2006; Horn et al, 2007). This is reflected in the contributors' comments in the rest of this chapter. The importance of staff feedback (considered below) has also been emphasised by patients in a Canadian secure service for men with personality disorders (Schafer and Peternelj-Taylor, 2003).

Dirk: It's about how we come across. Staff help with giving feedback about how we come across. It can be brutal. I prefer staff to say directly. I'd rather someone said: 'You're acting a prat' and tell me, rather than wrap their words in cotton wool.

Staff give positive feedback, as well, you can use them as a test because certain things they do will wind you up, so they're helping you, without knowing it.

Role plays are a bit unnerving…We act out scenarios, so this gives us a chance to use skills, and show staff we can manage our anger. Staff make it easy. They role play first. You have a laugh at them, it helps break the ice.

Colm: I've had enormous support from patients. It's been massively beneficial, the group support. Not all plain sailing. There have been conflicts in relationships, but I've managed not to sock anyone. I've learnt to say what I have to say without offending people, and without being dominating. But it's frustrated me, the number of people who've gone back to prison.

I didn't get feedback from a senior member of nursing staff: hoped to impress her with the gardening, but no response. But you could say: 'What has that taught you? The significant people are not going to always react in the way you'd expect to.' But I thought: 'Where's the therapy?'

I've had superb support from my consultant psychiatrist. My relationship with them is central to everything...My psychiatrist is prepared to apologise for mistakes, and will apologise if you're correct and say 'You're right' – and that builds trust.

Bede: Sometimes other patients say, 'Calm down.' I tend to find out if someone is there to help me, rather than meddle, I'm likely to take [what they say] on board more. A lot of residents are helpful because we're all in it together.

Sometimes you could be right in a situation, but staff don't accept it because it goes against their grain...But it could be my opinion that staff stick together. I've come from a background of mistrust, abuse – to trust that anyone wants to help me is very hard to believe. Sometimes, when I think about it, I come to the conclusion they are helping me. It's about trusting them and giving them the benefit of the doubt.

They encourage me, e.g. 'Jake' [a staff nurse] says, 'How are you getting on with step-to-step guidance and dealing with arousal?' He'll say: 'Are you using it? Are you doing it right?' And I find it helpful. It's making sure I'm doing it – he says that helps, and if I've an angry outburst, he'll say, 'What should you have done?' And if there's anything I've done wrong, he'll say, 'This is where you should have cut off.' He's a very helpful tutor, and the fact that he's on my team, means I can trust him and I give him the freedom to say what he thinks. I say: 'If I'm out of order, do tell me, or I'm not going to learn.'

Positive things are fed back too. Certainly, I'm getting more from one-to-one situations than a group because it's time to yourself, but you can see the benefit from groups because you get different views from staff and residents. Because in the group are two or three facilitators plus patients, so you get something that hits you in the face, and you think, 'Wow, I never thought of that'. In one-to-one, you get full attention for an hour, but in a group, just 10 to 15 minutes.

One nurse says: 'Come, now think logically. Do you really think staff will have it in for you?' He says it simply and factually. Another nurse – I believe him, he saw me in gaol, so a bit of a bond, he was there at the beginning for my induction in the ward, and he asks me lots of questions. 'What work do you need to do about this?' 'How do you get it off your chest?' It's a big loss if he's not on the ward.

I like direction, straight as it is. If you know they don't go round the bushes, it's not bullshit. It's about someone being sincere, honest, people saying something to benefit you, believing in a relationship of trust. But I believe problem solving and anger management work together – but you need these extras (i.e. staff as support), as well, so that you have 110% success, rather than 90%.

Cannock ward and its staff

Bede: There are certain members of staff have that skill of what to say and how to say it. One of the nurses and my consultant psychiatrist are particularly good. I really believe my consultant psychiatrist wants to help me.

Ezra: I feel that the ward isn't run very well. Some staff say one thing, others say something else. There should be a rigid set of rules, and patients and staff should learn them. Because nothing's worse than staff saying different things. It causes problems.

If you think something could be better, you don't have a say. You can't negotiate. Everything is taken away and controlled. It's not as bad in prison.

Ferg: There's one-to-one work which is helpful, where you're able to talk through problems with your responsible medical officer, nurses and other patients. I think it can be helpful with managing anger because if you get heard, people help you to consider what you're doing.

Colm: My anger work on the ward (a few years ago) was a disaster. I didn't seem to fit the general anger pattern here. My anger would get stored up. When I had an outburst after a year, that lasted for over half an hour, things improved. After this time, people didn't wind me up, left me alone, listened to what I had to say. On Cannock, finally being allowed to show anger helped because they listened.

There was a lot of anger work to do. There were aggressive patients. There was one incident, where it was fed back that I had not handled the situation appropriately. I therefore asked to do anger management. One health care support worker was exceptionally helpful, but a nurse left me to do all the work, without much structure or intervention at all. A psychiatrist eventually became involved, doing two basic sessions before announcing that he didn't think I had a problem, anyway.

In the end, I got hold of an anger management course from another patient and worked through it myself. It was very helpful, as was a member of occupational therapy staff, who helped me with extra social skills work. I do think it would be helpful if a patient suggests something seriously, that the ward be flexible enough to adapt itself to his needs.

I'd say my relationship with my named nurse has been a disappointment. Quite honestly, I said I didn't want a named nurse who'd chase me. He said he wouldn't – but I don't think he put much effort in building a therapeutic relationship. I got very frustrated with his manner to me – and got angry. But my named nurse has done me a favour because I built up independence in me. I became much more self-sufficient. I do it all myself. I don't know if this was my named nurse as a person, or if it was a deliberate strategy. I took this to a problem solving group.

Learning from living on Cannock ward: Two concluding accounts

The following accounts are reminiscent of 'corrective emotional experiences' and 'living learning situations' (Jones, 1968): described in the literature as important features of therapeutic communities (Campling and Haigh, 1999; Kelly et al, 2004).

Algy: Learning to believe in myself.

I will give you some insight on how I turned my life around. One of the main things I have learnt in life is to believe in myself. (Remember, if you keep it realistic, then there is no reason why you cannot achieve it.) Also, remember anything is possible if you believe in yourself.

All this started for me when I arrived at Cannock ward as a way of building my confidence, also learning, coming to terms with my past and working through it in order to have a better chance in life.

From my childhood, I was told repeatedly that I was worthless and that I was no good at anything, so I started to believe it when I was growing up. Until the time when staff of a variety of professions on Cannock began to give me the courage and motivation to see better in myself. The staff encouraged me to slowly challenge myself by allowing me to complete various tasks, including computers, woodwork and painting on the ward. So I would like to take this opportunity in thanking everybody involved for believing in me, and for also letting me believe in myself again, as I couldn't have done it without your advice, support and words of encouragement, not just from the staff, but from each of my fellow patients, as well.

I found every single one of the groups was very beneficial to me because they made me see myself and the areas that I needed to change. Please don't get me wrong, the groups are very hard. At times, I didn't like what I heard about myself, and at times when it was getting hard, for me, I would say, 'I want to go back to prison', because it's a lot easier in there than looking at my past behaviours. However, I managed to stick it out and turn my life around for the better.

Colm: Disastrous events have been the most therapeutic.

Sometimes things that seem the most disastrous on Cannock ward have been the most therapeutic. I find different ways of coping I'd not thought of. It's made me stronger. It has developed strengths in me: new ways of coping.

If everything ran smoothly, what would that teach anybody? But because it's been a roller-coaster, things have stressed me, it's been beneficial.

I think the patients in general are encouraged to deal with difficulties, but they don't always take this on board. But I have. I found that you've got to do it – or you don't progress. The prize is life in the community and a more successful life. You've got to learn lessons. Like if a nurse is not talking to you, you learn a lesson. You realise: 'Well, he's like that!' You learn.

I landed up having a bust-up with a member of nursing staff. But I learnt from the way I reacted. He didn't prolong it, and I learnt I'd been able to say what I think and nothing terrible happened. I learn from Cannock ward and team situations.

Conclusion

This chapter, and the previous chapter have included the views of six people with experience as patients on Cannock ward, and a brief consideration of CALM (Controlling Anger and Learning to Manage It) courses. Contributors have considered a variety of areas that they consider to be important in managing anger creatively. These include: recognising triggers of anger, seeking clarification and avoiding misinterpretation of others. Some contributors mention various factors concerning the ward and its staff which were experienced as helpful or unhelpful. This includes feedback from other patients and staff. The chapter concluded with two individuals stating what they gained from the ward, with one contributor commenting that he had benefited from examining some of the difficulties that he had encountered.

References

Anonymous (2006) *Inside tracks.* The Guardian 24 April 2006 [Online] Available from: http://www.guardian.co.uk [Accessed 7 October, 2007]

Ashman D (2001) Desperately seeking understanding. *Ment Health Today* October 30–1

Barker P, Campbell P, Davidson B (eds) (1999) *From the Ashes of Experience: Reflections on Madness, Survival and Growth.* Whurr Publishers, London

Byrt R, Graley-Wetherell R, 'R', Studley R, D'Silva K, James L, Pocock T (2006) Service user experiences and professional attitudes. In: National Forensic Nurses' Research and Development Group: Woods P, Kettles AM, Byrt R, Addo M, Aiyegbusi A, Coffey M, Collins M, Doyle M, Garman G, Watson C (eds) *Forensic Nursing: Interventions with People with 'Personality Disorders'.* Quay Books, MA Healthcare, Ltd, London

Campling P, Haigh R (eds) (1999) *Therapeutic Communities: Past, Present and Future.* Jessica Kingsley, London

Carlin P, Gudjonsson G, Yates M (2005) Patient satisfaction with services in medium secure units. *J Forensic Psychiatry Psychol* **16**(94): 714–28

Castillo H (2003) *Personality Disorder: Temperament or Trauma?* Jessica Kingsley. London

Coffey M (2006) Researching service user views in forensic mental health: a literature review. *J Forensic Psychiatry Psychol* **17**(1): 73–107

Gault L (2007) Anger courses failing violent inmates: claim. Sunday Star Times 30 September [Online] Available from: http://www.dominion.co.nz [Accessed 7 October 2007]

HM Prison Service (2007) Offender behaviour programmes (OBPs) [Online] Available from: http:///www.hmprisonservice.gov.uk [Accessed 7 October 2007]

Horn N, Johnstone L, Brooke S (2007) Some service user perspectives on the diagnosis of borderline personality disorder. *J Ment Health* **16**(2): 255–69

Johnston P (2006) *Prisons drop anger control courses.* Daily Telegraph 25 April 2006 [Online] Available from: http://www.telegraph.co.uk [Accessed 7 October 2007]

Jones M (1968) *Social Psychiatry in Practice.* Penguin Books: Harmondsworth

Kelly S, Hill J, Boardman H, Overton I (2004) Therapeutic Communities. In: Campling P, Davies S, Farquharson G (eds) *From Toxic Institutions to Therapeutic Environments: Residential Settings in Mental Health Services.* Gaskell, London

McArdle S, Byrt R (2001) Fiction, poetry and mental health: expressive and creative uses of literature. *J Psychiatric Ment Health Nurs* **8**(6): 517–25

Perseius K-I, Ojehagen A, Ekdahl S, Asberg M, Samuelsson M (2003) Treatment of suicidal and deliberate self-harming patients with borderline personality disorder using dialectical behavior therapy: the patients' and the therapists' perceptions. *Arch Psychiatric Nurs* **17**(5): 218–27

Pick A (2005) Littleboylost. Desktop publishing production

Ryan S, Moore E, Taylor P, Wilkinson E, Lingiah T, Christmas M (2002) The voice of detainees in a high security setting on services for people with personality disorder. *Criminal Behav Ment Health* **12**: 254–68

Schafer P, Peternelj-Taylor C (2003) Therapeutic relationships and boundary maintenance: the perspective of forensic patients enrolled in a treatment program for violent offenders. I*ssues Ment Health Nurs* **24**: 605–25

Spiers S, Harney K, Chilvers C (2005) Service user involvement in forensic mental health: can it work? *J Forensic Psychiatry Psychol* **16**(2): 211–20

Travis A (2006) *Offenders' anger control classes make some more dangerous.* The Guardian 24 April. [Online] Available from: http://www.guardian.co.uk. [Accessed 7 October 2007]

Williams Z (2003) *Cool it.* The Guardian 15 November [Online] Available from: http://www.guardian.co.uk. [Accessed 7 October 2007]

Winogron W (2006) *Anger management has the power to rehabilitate offenders.* The Guardian 2 May [Online] Available from: http://www.guardian.co.uk. [Accessed 7 October 2007]

CHAPTER 13

Mental health and substance use: Problems within forensic practice

Mick Adams and Leah Evans

Introduction

The particular problems associated with co-morbid mental ill-health and substance misuse have been known for some time. In a study of people with psychotic illness in south London, Menezes et al (1996) found a 31.6% prevalence rate for alcohol problems and a 15.8% prevalence rate for drug problems. Young males were found to have a higher risk of substance misuse and those with such co-morbidity had spent almost twice the number of days in hospital over the previous two years when compared to individuals who did not misuse substances. More recently, Weaver et al (2003) conducted a cross sectional survey in four UK urban areas finding a 44% past year substance use prevalence (drug and/or alcohol), and higher prevalence rates of past year psychiatric problems among users of drug services (75%) and alcohol services (85%). Furthermore, most people with co-morbidity were found to be ineligible for cross referral between services, suggesting structural deficits in providing effective care for this group. It has been common for people with co-morbidity to receive parallel treatment from separate mental health and substance misuse agencies where these service providers did not communicate about shared care goals; or alternatively to 'fall between stools' and not receive care at all while agencies disputed case management responsibility (Welsh Assembly Government, 2004).

People with co-morbidity are often the most needy of clients with significantly poorer treatment outcomes, including worsening psychiatric symptoms, increased use of institutional services, poor medication adherence, homelessness, increased risk of HIV infection, poor social outcomes including impact on carers and family, and contact with the criminal justice system (Department of Health, 2002). Additionally, people with co-morbidity are described as a heterogeneous group with a spectrum of symptom severity. The nature of the relationship between substance misuse and mental health problems is considered to be complex, and is clearly affected by a multiplicity of variable individual factors.

It is apparent that the prevalence of co-morbidity within forensic mental health settings is higher than the generic mental health experience, with estimates from 'over half' (Dolan and Kirwan, 2001) to 75% (Barry et al, 2002). Yet it is not just increased prevalence that is the concern of forensic mental health practitioners, but also the potential catastrophic effects of substance misuse for service users and others which focuses attention. Possession and supply of illicit substances is a criminal offence punishable by the Misuse of Drugs Act 1971; additionally, individuals may have been involved in acquisitive crime such as theft, robbery and deception in order to procure funds for the purchase of substances. Snowden (2001) has discussed how substance misuse can be a risk factor in violent crime. Particular substances which have a positive association to violence include: cocaine and crack cocaine, amphetamines, anabolic steroids, alcohol, benzodiazepines and cannabis. This association of substance misuse with violent offending has also been found in a review by Soyka (2000), who commented that a large number of studies has shown links between substance misuse in schizophrenia with male gender, homelessness, greater psychotic symptoms, non-compliance, poor prognosis, and violence and aggression. Furthermore, the National Confidential Inquiry has reported a high incidence of substance misuse problems among people with mental illness who have been involved in suicides and homicides (University of Manchester, 2006).

Co-morbidity in foresic settings

A trend for more pessimistic perceptions of co-morbidity among staff who work in secure forensic settings has been noted (McKeown and Liebling, 1995; Dolan and Kirwan, 2001; Foster and Onyeukwu, 2003). Co-morbidity is seen as problematic, with staff articulating views that the course of mental health problems can be adversely affected and prolonged, ward environments can become more unsettled, non-substance using service users can be intimidated, with the general outcome being that staff have tended to advocate increased security type measures to manage the problem.

Foster and Onyeukwu (2003) utilised the Substance Abuse Attitude Survey (SAAS; Chappel et al, 1985) to ascertain that overall attitudes of a sample of forensic mental health practitioners to co-morbidity were suboptimal when contrasted with a similar study conducted with a group of mental health staff from a community setting (Richmond and Foster, 2003). The community group was found to have a tolerant and accepting attitude towards co-morbidity and was less inclined to adopt judgemental attitudes. Clearly, comparison of research findings between forensic and community care needs to be conducted with caution as care environments and contextual issues cannot be considered 'like for like', but it appears that this warrants further exploration.

In the UK, guidance has been published emphasising the need to take action to make inpatient settings drug and alcohol free (Department of Health, 2006). Suggested methods of managing substance misuse problems include increasing vigilance and security. Such interventions might include routine searching of individuals and their property, searching of visitors, random drug testing, and cancelling or restricting leave. Additionally, Nash (2005) has commented upon the increasing use of sniffer-dogs in mental health settings, as well as the structural and ethical problems that this practice poses.

Clearly, there is a need to maintain safe environments in forensic care, and it has been observed that many forensic mental health practitioners experience a security versus therapy conflict (Chaloner, 2000). Conversely, the application of security type interventions is likely to increase the potential for individuals to feel oppressed and may contribute to feelings of resentment between service users and staff. Young (2006) has observed how, in the UK, Government policy has traditionally been driven by top down anti-drug initiatives which have been characterised by strong language and little impact on the demand, supply and consumption of substances. Similarly, Governments have shied away from resolving the unsatisfactory conundrum between use of illegal substances, i.e. all illicit drugs are bad, and alcohol, which is possible to use within safe limits (Department for Culture, Media and Sport et al, 2005). Given this background, increased security measures on their own are unlikely to have a lasting impact on the problem of co-morbidity among forensic service users, and need to be considered in association with other therapeutic approaches.

Contemporary models of care

Within the substance misuse field, there exists a somewhat recalcitrant debate between the merits of abstinence and harm reduction philosophies, which has impacted on efforts to devise appropriate models to treat co-morbidity. Phillips and Labrow (2000) contend that the traditional treatment preference among mental health services has been the promotion of abstinence to the exclusion of more pragmatic harm reduction approaches. While abstinence may be considered preferable, it is acknowledged that the confrontational aspects sometimes employed are not always appropriate for people with co-morbidity. An example of this might be the research and guidance which has concentrated on negative connotations of harm and risks associated with co-morbidity and the lack of literature exploring reasons for use. Conversely, Saunders and Marsh (1999) contend that while some benefits of harm reduction, i.e. accepting continued but 'safer' use, may be superficially appealing, political and structural problems with this approach remain unresolved. Specifically, the utility of harm reduction may be open to question where the predictability of the effects of certain substances of misuse (e.g. solvents, MDMA) are difficult to ascertain, and even recreational use can in some cases have harmful life-threatening effects. Carey et al (2000) utilised focus group methodology to survey the views of expert practitioners in the US on the effectiveness of services and interventions; the survey participants recommended that existing treatment models needed systematic evaluation. Therefore, given the heterogeneous and complex presentation of co-morbidity and the lack of contextual consensus, forensic mental health practitioners might be best advised to develop critical awareness of the sometimes disparate advice, and apply models on an individual basis rather than adopt fealty to any particular approach.

Recent efforts in the UK to develop service structures to manage co-morbidity have concentrated on collaborative or integrated approaches (Department of Health 2002; Welsh Assembly Government, 2004), that is, developing shared care and effective co-working across agencies, with various expertise which can be brought to bear for the benefit of service users. In a review of treatment development for co-morbidity, Barrowclough et al (2006) observed that the evidence basis for specific interventions remains quite small, possibly because of the difficulties associated with utilising randomised controlled trials with people with co-morbidity; however, consensus opinion appears to emphasise the need for integrated treatment. Specifically, motivational strategies and cognitive-behavioural therapy are considered to have potential in developing effective interventions. For example, Graham et al (2003) have described a shared care model in which mainstream mental health practitioners (from assertive outreach teams) and specialist personnel work jointly to provide care to people with co-morbid severe mental health problems and substance misuse, utilising a cognitive-behavioural integrated treatment approach.

Phillips (2000) has observed that forensic mental health services should have similar collaborative relationships with substance misuse services on both a clinical and organisational level. Young (2006) notes there may be some difficulties in developing such collaboration, in that substance misuse services often look for an element of self-motivation from individuals as a crucial facet of engagement and retention in care. Some people in forensic care lack motivation to break cycles of substance use, specifically because they view their substance use positively, interpreting it as a method of coping with positive and negative symptoms, a way of rebelling against the effects of incarceration, a method of developing friendships, and having core values which reject a culture of being a mental health patient but accepting a culture of substance use. Furthermore, some people may have aspirations to return to home environments where substance use is the norm among friends and family. Being abstinent involves being the odd one out, and on balance, the negative consequences of substance misuse (that is if the individual actually believes there are any negative consequences) are considered worth the risk.

In motivational interviewing theory, Miller and Rollnick (2002) have argued that resistance to change among people in therapy can be a direct consequence of confrontational techniques employed by the practitioner. This might not just be overt security type interventions in a secure environment, but also the effect of language employed by the practitioner in interactions. The expression of critical, paternalistic views on the effects of substance misuse may actually reinforce this behaviour. Confrontational styles of counselling evoke resistance to change. The practitioner is instead encouraged to 'roll' with resistance and recognise and encourage the less resistive dialogue, termed 'change talk'. High levels of change talk are associated with less resistance to change. The core beliefs and values of the individual with respect to their substance misuse are likely to be different from that of the forensic mental health practitioner. The various interventions applied need to take due account of the individual's milieu, with realistic goals set. Young (2006) contends that forensic mental health practitioners are well placed to work with service users and their families to promote achievable change. The length and intensity of their contact affords opportunities that may not be apparent in generic mental health practice. Ford and Woods (2006) have provided an extensive discussion on the impact of research and practice on responses to co-morbidity in forensic inpatient settings. The remainder of this chapter will discuss the development of practice in community forensic mental health practitioners in relation to co-morbidity.

Working with co-morbidity and a forensic history in the community

People with co-morbidity can be cared for in a number of ways within a community setting. Historically, care for those with a serious mental health problem has been managed within community mental health teams, where care co-ordinators may have little expertise in addressing specific problems relating to substance misuse and how this might impact upon the individual's mental health. With the development of community drug and alcohol teams many individuals have been given an opportunity to address such difficulties with the expertise of specialist services. Such services, however, have often been given limited resources and therefore, provision has struggled to respond adequately to the needs of this population. Waiting lists are often lengthy and this can impact upon the individual, where the timing of engagement with services can often be crucial. Without specialist support, individuals may continue to misuse substances with deleterious consequences for their mental health. Substance misuse can be a primary concern in the care of an individual with co-morbidity as this can often lead to a deterioration in mental health and possible relapse (Manning et al, 2002) and ultimately, offending behaviour with an increased risk of reconviction (Maden et al, 2004). While cannabis use can exacerbate psychotic symptoms (Rassool, 2002), alcohol substantially increases the risk of violent offending (Snowden, 2001). These, together with the effect of other substances, a chaotic lifestyle, fragmentation of supportive relationships, possible homelessness and financial difficulties can increase the likelihood of involvement with the criminal justice system.

High rates of co-morbidity are problematic within forensic mental health settings and continue to be somewhat of a challenge to both inpatient and community services (Ford and Woods, 2006). Some individuals' mental health might improve rapidly following admission to a medium secure unit when their access to substances is restricted (Scott et al, 2004). This can offer an opportunity to engage in substance misuse work and clarify aspects of the risk assessment (Snowden, 2001), which might be more beneficial while these issues are current. However, due to a stabilisation in mental health, these individuals might be discharged relatively quickly without having completed this work, which suggests both a missed opportunity and a poorer prognosis. In many circumstances, work in this area ceases upon discharge, when relapse is most likely.

Length of stay in medium secure units is often longer than in acute services. However, while the necessary focus on addressing substance misuse needs to occur, access to expert help can be limited. In a study exploring the adequacy of substance misuse treatment in English medium secure units, 67% of consultants and 81% of unit managers believed that specialist drug and alcohol services were best placed in taking a greater role both in inpatient care and following discharge (Scott et al, 2004). In another survey of medium secure care in England, only four units (15%) believed their staff had received adequate training to work with individuals who misuse substances (Durand et al, 2006). Mental health practitioners in such units often find themselves as the main, and sometimes sole person providing education in addressing substance misuse in those with co-morbidity (Dolan and Kirwan, 2001) and can feel ill-equipped and lacking in confidence and expertise (Jeffery et al, 2000; Maslin et al, 2001). Although they are skilled in assessing and engaging with individuals, few have received specific training in techniques that have been found to be successful when working with those who misuse substances.

It has been suggested that practitioners might benefit from liaising with local drug and alcohol agencies (Phillips, 2000). This would enable access to specialist skills and provide an opportunity to facilitate knowledge and skill development. Currently, there are specialists in substance misuse in some medium secure units although there is limited literature describing this work. Specialists co-ordinate the care of people with co-morbidity and work on a one-to-one basis or within groups. Waiting lists can occur due to the increasing numbers of referrals but this can be partly addressed by practitioners at ward level working with individuals under close supervision. Prior to discharge, individuals should be addressing issues around their substance misuse within a clear, structured framework which will continue following their departure into the community. Within the Care Programme Approach (CPA) they should have a detailed crisis plan, where relapse indicators and triggers have been identified and contingency plans made to address any possible deterioration or relapse. Treatment plans must be thorough, effective and communicated to all involved to ensure that the individual remains well supported and the potential risks are well managed. Individuals who have been convicted of violent or sexual offences will be subject to Multi-Agency Public Protection Arrangements (MAPPA). This will ensure that the statutory bodies within the individual's local area are aware of the potential risks posed to the public and can manage them accordingly (Coffey et al, 2007).

Conditions of discharge

Some individuals leaving medium secure units might find themselves subject to restriction orders under Section 41 of the Mental Health Act 1983, due to the serious nature of their offence. Such conditions might include directions upon where they must reside or the treatment they must accept from services. Failure to abide by the restrictions could result in a recall to hospital (Jenkins and Coffey, 2002). Those with co-morbidity might additionally see conditions imposed regarding their misuse of substances, which can indicate a possible recall to hospital unless abstinence is maintained.

Such an expectation may contradict the views of those who advocate harm reduction as a more realistic option for individuals with co-morbidity and allows for little leverage within a motivational interviewing framework. Some, however, might criticise such a liberal approach, given the risks involved if substance misuse has been implicated in the individual's offending history. Abstinence could be seen as crucial in attempting to secure the safety of the public. It has been suggested that mental health services are becoming increasingly coercive (Szmukler, 2000), and that public safety is being considered over and above the human rights of the individual (Rose, 1998). There is a greater emphasis being placed upon risk assessment and management as a response to the perceived failings of community care, which has been highlighted throughout previous homicide inquiries. One such enquiry, following a homicide in Wales, in 2003, has made recommendations that have had a direct impact upon practice (ECRI, 2004).

One recommendation of this inquiry advocates that all individuals discharged from secure units, with a history of substance misuse, will be routinely, regularly and randomly tested for any such use. Where the substance misuse has impacted upon the risk of the individual, a clear management strategy should be outlined within the care plan. Monitoring is carried out with either urine or hair testing. In order for the monitoring to be as accurate as possible, the practitioner will need to carefully select the most appropriate method of testing. Substances such as amphetamines, cocaine and heroin will not be detectable in urine within several days and serum screening times are even narrower as the substances will be metabolised within several hours. In these circumstances, hair testing would be indicated, although this is a more costly option. The advantage would be an accurate profile of use over several months, dependant upon the length of the hair sample.

Difficulties encountered with hair testing include the possibility of false positives created by environmental contamination of hair and false negatives which might be caused by certain cosmetic hair treatments (McPhillips et al, 1998). Some individuals might be concerned about the possible repercussions of misusing substances, such as exclusion from services or possibly, prosecution (Wheatley, 1998) and in some circumstances, recall to hospital. This might encourage more covert behaviour so that use will remain undetected. Anecdotal evidence suggests that some people have coloured their hair to avoid detection. To counteract these difficulties, hair samples can also be obtained from the axilla, beard and pubic area but this presents its own challenges. If avoidant behaviour was to continue, then the individual could be considered to be in breach of the conditions of discharge and appropriate guidance would need to be sought from the Home Office. Urine testing would be the choice if attempting to identify cannabis misuse, as this substance remains in the urine for a longer period and is not so easily detected in hair samples. Overall, urine testing is a cheaper screening tool with more rapid results but has a much smaller window of opportunity. An important additional aspect of hair testing is that it can clearly demonstrate abstinence over several months (Mieczhowski, 2006).

Monitoring for alcohol use is more complicated as this cannot be unequivocally confirmed by any conventional laboratory tests. Breathalysers can be used, possibly in the case of individuals living in supported accommodation, but otherwise alcohol use is unlikely to occur prior to arranged appointments with practitioners and is therefore likely to go undetected. Monitoring of blood screening can be a useful tool in detecting longer-term alcohol misuse but only when other physical causes can be excluded.

Collaboration

There are many challenges to working with someone with co-morbidity, particularly if they have a forensic history. Returning to the community can be a challenge as individuals have to face the stigma of having a mental illness, being an offender and having a substance addiction (Young, 2006). In addition, those on a restriction order may be resentful of services as their liberty has been curtailed. Although restriction orders with clear conditions of discharge might be viewed as powerful tools in achieving compliance with treatment, many believe that a collaborative relationship is a key factor in the success of restriction orders (Jenkins and Coffey, 2002). Szmukler (2000) questions whether compulsory treatment is a safer option than a therapeutic relationship with a professional whom the individual contacts in times of crisis.

Collaboration is fundamental within any therapeutic relationship and individuals with co-morbidity are no different. Effective collaborative working is based upon honest and respectful relationships and promotes individuals as partners in their own care (Watkins, 2001). This facilitates an opportunity for recognition that there is a problem and a desire to work towards alleviating it, which will, in turn, improve quality of life. Cognitive-behavioural therapy appears to have had the most success in working with those with co-morbidity and motivational interviewing techniques are well placed within such approaches. This is of particular relevance while exploring ambivalence to making changes, attempting to raise awareness and enhancing decision-making skills. Health promotion is a fundamental element of working with those with co-morbidity and is seen as a process for enabling individuals to have some control over their health, with both prevention and education being recognised as integral components. The provision of information and education for both individuals and any significant others can assist in the making of informed choices and can facilitate empowerment resulting in a greater control over their lives (MIND, 1999).

Conclusion

This chapter has briefly explored the concept of co-morbid mental health and substance misuse problems. The increased prevalence of substance use among service users in forensic settings shows that co-morbidity has a particular relevance to forensic mental health practitioners. Additionally, the various deleterious outcomes, including increased risk of suicide and homicide associated with the condition, enhance this relevance to practice. Increased security and vigilance in inpatient settings and screening for substance misuse in individuals subject to conditional discharge have a place in practice, but also, there are limitations to such interventions. Recent developments in models of care offer potential, but systematic evaluation of treatment approaches is required. Working with individuals with co-morbidity requires a creative approach and practitioners need to be mindful that where possible, approaches adopted should reflect the individual milieu of the service user rather than utilising a paternalistic 'top down' approach. Within forensic care, issues of risk management will be paramount, yet even with these considerations, there remain opportunities to utilise a collaborative approach and apply expertise from other areas of practice. Difficulties are often complex and multifaceted, and while treatment plans can be carefully drawn up within the structure of CPA documents, practitioners can often find their skills and confidence being challenged. As well as being knowledgeable and skilled, practitioners need to be flexible with an ability to adapt to individual circumstances without necessarily being over-reactive. Clear communication with service users, families, the responsible medical officer and other stakeholders within the care package is critical to ensure best practice and to minimise risk.

References

Barrowclough C, Haddock G, Fitzsimmons M, Johnson R (2006) Treatment development for psychosis and co-occurring substance misuse: A descriptive review. *J Ment Health* **15**(6): 619–32

Barry KR, Tudway JA, Blissett J (2002) Staff drug knowledge and attitudes towards drug use among the mentally ill within a medium secure psychiatric hospital. *J Substance Use* **7**: 50–6

Carey KB, Purnine DM, Maisto SA, Carey MP, Simons JS (2000) Treating substance abuse in the context of severe and persistent mental illness. Clinicians' perspectives. *J Substance Abuse Treat* **19**: 189–98

Chaloner C (2000) Characteristics, skills, knowledge and inquiry. In: Chaloner C, Coffey M (eds) *Forensic Mental Health Nursing. Current Approaches* (pp 1–20) Blackwell Science, Oxford

Chappel JN, Veach TL, Krug RS (1985) The Substance Abuse Attitude Survey: An instrument for measuring attitudes. *J Studies in Alcohol* **46**(1): 48–51

Coffey M, Morgan J, Gronow T (2007) Forensic aspects of discharge planning from acute care: Transition to community. In Kettle A, Woods P, Byrt R, Addo M, Coffey M, Doyle M (eds) *Forensic Mental Health Nursing: Forensic Aspects of Acute Care* (pp 175–85) London, Quay Books Division

Department for Culture, Media and Sport; Home Office and Office of the Deputy Prime Minister (2005) *Drinking Responsibly: The Government's Proposals* [On-line] Available from: http://www.homeoffice.gov.uk/documents/2005-cons-drinking/2205-

cons-drinking-doc?view=Binary [Accessed 5 November 2007]

Department of Health (2002) *Mental Health Policy Implementation Guide: Dual Diagnosis Good Practice Guide.* Department of Health, London

Department of Health (2006) *Dual Diagnosis in Mental Health Inpatient and Day Hospital Settings: Guidance on the assessment and management of patients in mental health inpatient and day hospital settings who have mental ill–health and substance use problems.* Department of Health, London

Dolan M, Kirwan H (2001) Survey of staff perceptions of illicit drug use among patients in a medium secure unit. *Psychiatric Bull* **25**: 14–17

Durand MA, Lelliott P, Coyle N (2006) Availability of treatment for substance misuse in medium secure psychiatric care in England: A national survey. *J Forensic Psychiatry Psychol* **17**(4): 611–25

ECRI (2004) *Independent External Review into a Homicide at Prestatyn Wales on 25th March 2003.* ECRI, Welwyn Garden City

Ford P, Woods P (2006) Dual diagnosis in a forensic setting. In: Rassool GH (ed) *Dual Diagnosis Nursing* (pp 161–8) Blackwell, Oxford

Foster JH, Onyeukwu C (2003) The attitudes of forensic nurses to substance using service users. *J Psychiatric Ment Health Nurs* **10**: 578–84

Graham HL, Copello A, Birchwood J, Orford J, McGovern D, Georgiou G, Godfrey E (2003) Co-existing severe mental health and substance use problems: Developing integrated services in the UK. *Psychiatric Bull* **27**: 183–6

Jeffery D, Ley A, Bennun I, Mclaren S (2000) Delphi survey of opinion on interventions, service principles and service organisation for severe mental illness and substance misuse problems. *J Ment Health* **9**(4): 371–80

Jenkins E, Coffey M (2002) Compelled to interact: forensic community mental health nurses' and service users' relationships. *J Psychiatric and Ment Health Nurs* **9**:553–62

Maden A, Scott F, Burnett R, Lewis GH, Skapinakis P (2004) Offending in psychiatric patients after discharge from Medium Secure Units: prospective national cohort study. *Brit Med J* **328**: 1534

Manning VC, Strathdee G, Best D, Keaney F, McGillivray L, Witton J (2002) Dual Diagnosis Screening: Preliminary findings on the comparison of 50 clients attending community mental health services and 50 clients attending substance misuse services. *J Substance Use* **7**: 221–8

Maslin J, Graham H, Cawley M, Copello A, Birchwood M, Georgiou G, McGovern D Mueser K, Oxford J (2001) Combined severe mental ill health and substance use problems: What are the training and support needs of staff working with this client group? *J Ment Health* **10**(2): 131–40

McKeown M, Liebling H (1995) Staff perception of illicit drug use within a special hospital. *J Psychiatric Ment Health Nurs* **2**: 343-350

McPhillips MA, Strang J, Barnes TRE (1998) Hair analysis: New laboratory ability to test for substance use. Brit J Psychiatry **173**(10): 287–90

Menezes PR, Johnson S, Thornicroft G, Marshall J, Prosser D, Bebbington P, Kuipers E (1996) Drug and alcohol problems among individuals with severe mental illness in south London. Brit J Psychiatry **168**: 612–19

Mieczkowski T (2006) Hair analysis for detection of psychotropic drug use (Letters to the

Editor). *Mayo Clinic Proc* **81**(4): 568–9

Miller WR, Rollnick S (2002) *Motivational Interviewing: Preparing People for Change.* Guilford Press, New York

MIND (1999) *Creating Accepting Communities: Report of the Mind Inquiry into Social Exclusion and Mental Health Problems 1999.* Mind Publications, London

Nash M (2005) Who let the dogs in? The use of drug sniffer dogs in mental health settings. *J Psychiatric Ment Health Nurs* **12**: 745–9

Phillips P (2000) Substance misuse, offending and mental illness: a review. *J Psychiatric Ment Health Nurs* **7**: 483–9

Phillips P, Labrow J (2000) Dual diagnosis - does harm reduction have a role? *Int J Drug Policy* **11**: 279–83

Rassool GH (2002) Substance misuse and mental health: an overview. *Nurs Stand* **16**(50): 47–55

Richmond IC, Foster JH (2003) Negative attitudes towards people with co-morbid mental health and substance misuse problems: An investigation of mental health professionals. *J Ment Health* **12**(4): 393–403

Rose N (1998) Living dangerously: risk-thinking and risk management in mental health care. *Ment Health Care* **1**(8): 263–6

Saunders W, Marsh A (1999) Harm reduction and the use of current illegal drugs: some assumptions and dilemmas. *J Substance Use* **4:** 3–9

Scott F, Whyte S, Burnett R, Hawley C, Maden T (2004) A national survey of substance misuse and treatment outcome in psychiatric patients in medium security. *J Forensic Psychiatry Psychol* **15**(4) 595–605

Snowden P (2001) Substance misuse and violence: the scope and limitations of forensic psychiatry's role. *Adv Psychiatric Treat* **7**: 189–97

Soyka M (2000) Substance misuse, psychiatric disorder and violent and disturbed behaviour. *Brit J Psychiatry* **176**: 345–50

Szmukler G (2000) Homicide inquiries: What sense do they make? *Psychiatric Bull* **24**: 6–10

University of Manchester (2006) *Five year report of the national confidential inquiry into suicide and homicide by people with mental illness.* [On-line] Available from: http://www.medicine.manchester.ac.uk/suicideprevention/nci/Useful/avoidable_deaths_full_report.pdf [Accessed 5 November 2007]

Watkins P (2001) *Mental Health Nursing: The Art of Compassionate Care.* Butterworth-Heinemann, Oxford

Weaver T, Madden P, Charles V, Stimson G, Renton A, Tyrer P, Barnes T, Bench C, Middleton H, Wright N, Paterson S, Shanahan W, Seivewright N, Ford C (2003) Co-morbidity of substance misuse and mental illness in community mental health and substance misuse services. *Brit J Psychiatry* **183**: 304–13

Welsh Assembly Government (2004) *Substance Misuse Treatment Framework.* Welsh Assembly Government, Cardiff

Wheatley M (1998) Assessment of substance misuse in detained mentally ill patients. *J Substance Misuse* **3**: 67–72

Young A (2006) Dual diagnosis and forensic care. Are needs of service users being met? *J Psychiatric Ment Health Nurs* **13**: 117–124

CHAPTER 14

Forensic community mental health nursing

Michael Coffey and Richard Jones

Introduction

Providing care for people leaving forensic mental health services is a most challenging but growing reality for mental health nurses working in the community. Achieving positive aftercare and sustained community living with its potential for integration, rehabilitation and the hope of recovery are fundamental aspects of forensic community mental health nursing (FCMHN) practice. Doing so in the face of competing tensions of policy and risk aversive thinking, versus the important drivers of values and evidenced-based practice, remains a difficult balancing act. FCMHNs therefore have to be one part of a complex system delivering aftercare which is comprehensive in addressing the full range of mental health needs of people who have often required significant periods of detention in secure facilities.

This chapter briefly reviews the literature on forensic community mental health nursing as a precursor to an examination of the benefits of providing crisis-orientated services. This is one element of the comprehensive provision necessary to address the needs of people living in the community. We will not attempt to address the breadth of FCMHN practice here and the reader is directed towards chapters in companion volumes (Coffey, 2006a; Coffey et al, 2007) and elsewhere (Coffey, 2000a; Buchanan, 2002) for examples of the range of service provision in forensic community mental health.

Background

For people receiving forensic mental health services, their preparation for discharge and eventual return to community living is potentially fraught with difficulty. For many, there is the stark reality of discrimination and social exclusion which can limit opportunities for recovery and reintegration. It should be recognised at the outset that mental health nurses are only one of the multi-disciplines making up the aftercare team. These teams provide a range of services and support for people living in the community with complex needs arising from mental health problems and co-occurring criminal offending behaviour. What makes teams succeed or fail is the ability of all participants to successfully communicate with each other and the person receiving the service. Thoughtful, considered and compassionate aftercare is not the sole preserve of nursing and remains a challenge for all professions working in this field. The role of FCMHNs is to contribute to what is, in effect, a dialogue between the team, the community, the people receiving the services and their families.

Most forensic community services in England and Wales operate from regional secure services and in parallel to generic community mental health teams (Judge et al, 2004). In most cases, FCMHNs support and monitor people post-discharge from forensic services. These nurses are often the largest single professional group and their work for the most part remains poorly described. Where descriptions of the work do exist it often alludes to a case management style approach to service delivery (Coffey, 2000a; Kelly et al, 2002; Judge et al, 2004). This is based upon the rationale that comprehensive provision of services may help to reduce, delay or lessen the impact of relapse and any associated re-offending, as well as providing opportunities for sustained community tenure and rehabilitation.

We still know relatively little about the work of FCMHNs. More than a decade ago, Brooker and White's survey (1997) estimated there were 228 FCMHNs in the England and Wales with just half responding to the survey; they were more likely to be men and working in Regional Secure services or courts. Compared to generic community mental health nurses, they were unsurprisingly, working with a client group who demonstrated enduring and severe mental health problems complicated with offending histories, 27% of whom were subject to restriction orders.

Forensic community mental health nurses themselves have offered descriptions of their work in attempts to define what it is they do. Evans (1996: 35) believes, 'A forensic community mental health nurse provides... care for patients both inside and outside the secure environment, dependent upon the individuals needs' and involves 'collating information as an integral member of the multidisciplinary clinical team to develop a comprehensive risk assessment leading to a risk management strategy'.

Evans suggests that there is some value for the community nurse in seeing the person throughout their stay in hospital. The person can be seen when unwell and as they start to improve. This will give the nurse a greater understanding of how the person presents when unwell and will facilitate identification of early signs of relapse. This process may even help later engagement strategies. It is not, however, a ubiquitous state for many nurses that they have this experience of all people for whom they provide services and therefore this advantage should not be overstated.

Many FCMHNs are also involved in other aspects of forensic work including liaison with the criminal justice system through court and police cell liaison schemes, as well as multi-agency risk assessment committees (Coffey et al, 2007) and less commonly, offence-related work with sex offenders.

The focus on defining the profession appears to be a curiously nursing one and not so apparent in the literature of other professions. Definitions are by their nature, descriptive, based on individual authors' experience and frequently not based upon the results of empirical research. It may be that delineating and defining elements of the profession will open up opportunities for research on aspects of forensic community mental health nursing. Mason (2002) has made a useful and informative analysis of the literature on forensic nursing more generally, which provides recognition of what he refers to as 'binary oppositions' or tensions in the roles of these nurses.

Most research on forensic nursing is unsurprisingly focused on inpatient services and in particular, nurses' perceptions of relationships and the interventions they report delivering. Although not directly transferable to community aftercare and follow-up, there are some important lessons to be learned from this material.

For instance, Rask and Levander's (2001) survey noted the most commonly used interventions by nurses working in a forensic mental health setting were 'social interaction', 'regular communication' and 'social skills training'. The salient findings included that nurses often used confronting interventions. This is despite the fact that we have known for some time that hostility and critical remarks may provoke a worsening of mental illness symptoms (Wearden et al, 2000). Consequently little correspondence between actual practice and theoretical models of practice were noted by Rask and Levander (2001). The ability of the profession to generate evidence for practice and disseminate it is one challenge but it is also salutary to consider how the profession itself makes use of this evidence.

Research on forensic community mental health nursing is limited in both the range of topics covered and the methods used to study them. There is however an increasing literature which is set to grow as this area of practice extends its reach and scope.

It would seem that the professional project of forensic community mental health nursing is articulated in terms of the social division of labour at the micro level of professional interaction in aftercare provision. For instance Coffey and Jenkins' (2002) survey of FCMHNs in England and Wales noted concerns expressed by nurses with regard to involvement in decision-making and formal reporting mechanisms to the Home Office in regard to conditionally discharged patients.

Kelly et al (2002) describe nurses employing a risk management model within a case management approach in Australia aimed at intervening and reducing violence among people discharged from forensic services. They advocate support for the role of the therapeutic relationship as a fundamental focus for community care but highlight concerns about clinician fatigue when working with people with complex needs.

The concern about occupational pressures on this group of nurses is well founded. One study discovered that as a group, 44.3% of FCMHNs were experiencing high burnout in relation to emotional exhaustion and 31.2% met criteria for psychiatric caseness (Coffey, 1999). The multi-agency, multi-disciplinary model of working that offers so many benefits for the care of people with complex needs can come at a heavy price. Conflicts with other professionals and anxieties about vicarious liability are continuing concerns for FCMHNs (Coffey, 2000b). It has also been noted there is an association between the most stressed nurses and the number of people they have on their caseloads (Coffey and Coleman, 2001).

Listening to people who use services

An emphasis on accessing the perspectives of forensic mental health services users is a relatively unexplored area of research (Banongo et al, 2005). The potential is that people can tell their stories in their own words and focus upon what is important to them. To date, we have very limited accounts from people leaving forensic inpatient services and subsequent follow-up and aftercare and as a result we remain largely ignorant of their perspective. In practice, many nurses may subscribe to notions of involvement and partnership but good quality studies from which the wider profession can draw lessons are rare.

A recent review of research claiming to access views of people using forensic mental health services has noted the need for improved theoretical and methodologically designed studies of service user experiences in the broader multi-disciplinary context within which mental health nurses practice (Coffey, 2006b). Many studies have significant limitations that make it difficult to determine precisely how people experience services. Studies in this area have also failed to articulate the significant ethical complexities of researching a largely captive population. In terms of community provision, what is clear is that people want to be adequately prepared for discharge and receive sensitive and caring follow-up. FCMHNs must therefore actively engage with people to provide this care.

Conditional discharge and aftercare

Reports by Kershaw et al (1997), Street (1998) and Johnson and Taylor (2002) have indicated the number of recalls, admissions and conditional discharges from forensic services in England and Wales. These findings suggest a consensus from a system perspective that conditional discharge works, in that it protects the public and ensures problem behaviours are detected and addressed promptly. This finding is observable in literature from research in a number of different cultural settings. For instance, Feder's (1991) study of an 18 month post-discharge follow-up compared mentally ill offenders ($n = 147$) with those from the general prison population ($n = 400$) in relation to their community adjustment and found no significant differences in re-arrests between the groups. Bailey and MacCulloch (1992) followed up 112 people discharged from a special hospital and found that those given a conditional discharge were less likely to be reconvicted.

Although there appears to be significant focus upon risk and recidivism in the literature, there have been some attempts at evaluative research. Dell and Grounds' (1995) Home Office funded interview study of 46 people on conditional discharge found that the orders were viewed positively by service users although a third of respondents indicated that they wished to see the conditions ease off with time.

Steels et al (1998) found no difference in outcomes between mentally ill and personality disordered offenders subject to conditional discharge but note a discordant relationship between re-offending and psycho-social adjustment.

Differences in the perspectives of service users and professionals have been reported by Riordan et al (2002) who found that discharged people valued practical support and human relationships, whereas responsible medical officers valued the legal framework provided by conditional discharge arrangements. Although not thoroughly examined, the researchers noted that both stigma and vulnerability were features of life for those subject to aftercare. The likelihood of discriminatory treatment, however, is not confined to the community and can occur within services themselves (Porporino and Motiuk, 1995). It has been found that people with a diagnosis of schizophrenia are more likely than people with personality disorder to have conditions placed on their discharge (Renzaglia et al, 2004). This therefore subjects them to continued scrutiny and control by services long after they have left the confines of the institution.

This quick overview of the field is revealing in that few if any of these studies on conditional discharge are conducted by or involve FCMHNs, suggesting that evaluating interventions in this field is long overdue. What has been noted is that significant anxiety and concern exists among FCMHNs with regard to emergency responses to mental health crises among people on their caseloads (Coffey, 1999). This is one rationale for the need to focus on crisis intervention as an important element in providing aftercare for people leaving forensic inpatient services. There is also distinct value in exploring this specific area of practice in relation to people for whom relapse is such a potentially volatile situation requiring pre-emptive planning and urgent response.

Crisis intervention

People will inevitably experience crises in their lives. These crises are often initiated by changing social circumstances, perhaps by bereavement, a loss of employment or a breakdown of a relationship, and can have a dramatic effect on health and social functioning. Where individuals suffer with mental health problems, the likelihood of experiencing a crisis is significantly increased (Rosen, 1997).

Managing mental health crises or 'crisis resolution' is a subject that has gained significant prominence in the past decade. Mental health policy in England and Wales (Department of Health, 2001; Welsh Assembly Government, 2005) has demanded the introduction of crisis resolution and home treatment (CRHT) teams to serve the adult population of the nations. Such was the perceived need, that in 2000 the Government issued a statement that 335 CRHT teams should be established across England (Department of Health, 2000) and the evidence suggests that this figure has now been surpassed (McGlynn, 2006).

CRHT teams are designed to provide intensive, flexible, short-term treatment for individuals experiencing an acute mental health crisis. They also aim to reduce the number of admissions, length of stay of admissions, and need for hospital beds within the adult population (McGlynn, 2006). The flexibility of the service should allow it to respond to the service user's needs rather than fitting the service user into a system of care (National Institute for Mental Health in England, 2007).

Despite the recent emphasis on the creation of CRHT teams, it should be recognised that mental health crises have always occurred. It remains the role of the FCMHN to act prima facie to resolve these crises as the professional who has the greatest knowledge about the person. Indeed within the sphere of forensic mental health nursing, it could be argued that the FCMHN has perhaps been afforded a greater opportunity to gain knowledge of the client, due to the slower transition from inpatient to community services.

Roberts (2005a:13) argues that 'there is a general consensus among professionals that the following represents a crisis':

- *Perceiving a precipitating event as being meaningful and threatening.*
- *Appearing unable to modify or lessen the impact of stressful events with traditional coping methods.*

- *Experiencing increased fear, tension and/or confusion.*
- *Exhibiting a high level of subjective discomfort.*
- *Proceeding rapidly to an active status of crisis – a state of disequilibrium.*

Roberts (2005a:13)

Perhaps the most widely quoted author on crisis intervention is Gerald Caplan, who wrote about individuals moving from a state of equilibrium to disequilibrium and how practitioners should adapt to meet these changing needs (Caplan, 1964). However, it has been suggested that Caplan's work is now dated (Sainsbury Centre for Mental Health, 2001) and other authors have proposed definitions. Parad and Parad (2005: 3–4) suggest that 'a crisis is an upset in a steady state, a turning point leading to better or worse, a disruption or breakdown in a person's or family's normal or usual pattern of functioning. The upset, or disequilibrium, is usually acute in the sense that it is of recent origin.' Rosen (1997: 44) offers the description, 'a psychological crisis is a brief, non-illness response to severe stress. When maladaptive responses to a crisis are detected, crisis intervention is employed to achieve a more adaptive resolution and a more effective learning experience.'

It may be argued that the purpose of crisis intervention is to assist the individual in returning to a state of equilibrium with greater coping skills than before, using the crisis as an opportunity to develop and enhance existing strengths (Roberts, 2005b). In forensic mental health nursing in particular, this necessarily includes addressing the increased perceptions of risk and recidivism that might surround such a crisis.

As the inclusion of home treatment in the name suggests, CRHT teams are designed to offer a safe and effective alternative to hospital-based care, by managing mental health care needs in people's homes. This is supported by the 10 high impact changes for mental health services (Care Services Improvement Partnership, 2006), which demand that home treatment becomes the norm.

Due to the dramatic effects that mental health crises can have on individuals it is important to plan for crises and their management before they occur. The increased engagement time afforded to the FCMHN may be utilised effectively here.

The introduction of the Care Programme Approach in England and Wales (Welsh Assembly Government, 2003) has addressed this issue with the requirement that every service user has a contingency and crisis plan, agreed with their care co-ordinator and carer, that sets out all the actions that need to be taken in the event of a relapse of a client's mental health. These plans should routinely include previous successful methods of intervention and relapse indicators (Coffey and Bishop, 2000).

A crisis plan should be agreed with the client in conjunction with the standard care plan. This plan should include the actions to be taken if clients begin to experience a relapse in their illness, and should consider who individual clients are most responsive to, how to contact that person, previous strategies that have been successful and early warning signs or indicators (Care Programme Approach Association, 2004). Where CRHT teams may become involved, they should not necessarily assume the care co-ordinating role of the FCMHN. This responsibility may remain with the care co-ordinator, and the CRHT team's actions form a part of the overall care plan. The FCMHN, as care co-ordinator, should increase the intensity of their intervention at these times and work closely with the CRHT team.

The relapse prevention process is a useful approach to identify early warning signs, a relapse signature, action plans and monitoring systems (Knight, 2002). Early signs of illness or prodromal signs may be used to elicit signs of deterioration in an individual's mental health (Birchwood, 1996). The process of creating a relapse plan is extremely useful in identifying stages of relapse and how to respond to them. This plan may be shared in advance and agreed with other agencies likely to be involved in any crisis or contingency response. This should include the management of risk to the client, others and wider public, and the circumstances under which a defined action should be taken. Anticipating the potential of a crisis and identifying early methods of response may reduce the likelihood of such an event occurring.

What do CRHT teams do?

There appears to be a consensus among the literature that the elements proposed by Smyth and Hoult (2000) fulfil the essential elements of a CRHT team. These have been adapted and introduced into the policy implementation guidelines for England and Wales (Department of Health, 2001; Welsh Assembly Government, 2005). The CRHT team should be:

- *Available 24 hours a day, seven days a week.*
- *Capable of rapid response...*
- *Able to spend time flexibly with patients and their social network, including several visits daily if required.*
- *Address the social issues surrounding the crisis right from the beginning.*
- *Able to administer and supervise medication.*
- *Provide practical, problem solving help.*
- *Able to provide explanation, advice and support for carers...*

The CRHT team also:

- *Acts as a gate-keeper to inpatient care.*
- *Remains involved throughout the crisis until its resolution.*
- *Ensures that patients are linked up to further, continuing care.*

(Smythe and Hoult, 2000:306)

In addition, it is essential that CRHT teams adopt multi-disciplinary ways of working and learn from crisis situations.

FCMHNs should, where possible, make contact and ready use of CRHT team services to assist them in managing complex crises and to facilitate their own skill development. Issues such as gate-keeping provide a fundamental role in CRHT team services, in order to provide a genuine alternative to hospital-based care and reduce pressure on inpatient units (Sainsbury Centre for Mental Health, 2001); however, heightened sensitivities around risk and recidivism in forensic services may lower the threshold for decisions on admission.

Review of effectiveness

There appears to be a degree of consensus about the advantages of providing crisis services. Smyth and Hoult (2000) state that they reduce admissions by approximately 66% and influence a reduction in length of stay by up to 80%. Patients and relatives prefer home treatment and there remains little evidence for a preference for inpatient care. CRHT teams offer equal clinical outcomes to inpatient care, carers are more willing to care for an individual at home if they know that they have immediate assistance at hand and it is suggested that there is increased engagement where home treatment is provided. As Kelly et al (2002) have noted, there may be concerns about clinician fatigue in providing crisis services, although this remains largely unexplored.

Johnson et al (2005) conducted a randomised controlled trial of a CRHT team in north Islington, London and concluded that the evidence supported reduced admissions and increased patient satisfaction. People who received the service were generally more satisfied with their care and there were no significant differences in rates of suicide or violence. Similarly, Joy et al (2004) found that home treatment reduced repeat admission rates, reduced family burden, and was a more satisfactory form of care for both patients and families.

Introducing crisis services in forensic care

There remain clear opportunities to develop crisis intervention services in forensic mental health services, although adequately resourcing such developments remain a concern. The evidence for crisis and home treatment clearly demonstrates effectiveness in reducing admissions and length of stay of inpatients, increasing sense of satisfaction from service users, while contributing no recorded increase in homicides or suicides.

There are financial constraints around providing out-of-hours forensic services (Coffey, 1998) and generic crisis teams continue to experience difficulties in funding fully functional teams seven years after official guidance required their introduction. In order to achieve a successful crisis service, it is necessary to provide adequate resources to achieve the impact required. Lack of staffing is frequently cited as the key obstacle to effectiveness (Onyett et al, 2006). There would be a requirement to demonstrate that the need exists within forensic services to justify the cost. However the Reed Report (Department of Health and Home Office, 1992) specifically mentions that forensic services should consider the need for out-of-hours services.

A practical approach might be for FCMHNs to access existing generic CRHT team services. It should be recognised that generic CRHT teams are required to intervene with people in crisis and not all individuals with a forensic history and mental health problems are necessarily treated by these services. There is, perhaps, scope for closer inter-agency working between forensic services and generic CRHT teams. Making available clear crisis and contingency plans with relapse indicators and actions to be taken at certain events, might serve to alleviate any heightened concerns surrounding risk. Increased sensitivities surrounding risk and recidivism may reduce the ability to provide home-based care. An individual with a risk assessment that suggests a history of violence or aggression, or living in accommodation that is considered unsafe to visit out of hours, is unlikely to receive home visits on a 24-hour basis. These issues may be addressed through offering face-to-face intervention at 'safe' venues such as GP out-of-hours suites, accident and emergency departments, or in some cases police stations, all of which are currently used by CRHT teams where need dictates.

FCMHNs themselves may have concerns around the ability of generic services to respond appropriately and skilfully with their clients. However, as highlighted earlier, the use of a crisis service should provide an extension to an existing care plan with the focus of care remaining with the FCMHN. Greater collaborative working including sharing of care plans, crisis and contingency plans should help alleviate these concerns.

Conclusion

Accessing generic crisis teams may be a solution for forensic services due to the costs of setting up an out-of-hours service, however there may be concerns over the generic service's abilities to engage with such clients. Such a system is more likely to occur in urban areas as rural teams appear to be less well established.

We know that establishing social supports and social networks can do much to help people reintegrate into the community following discharge and that people who are conditionally discharged report this as an important element of their rehabilitation. FCMHNs therefore have an important responsibility in ensuring that they provide the necessary support to facilitate sustained reintegration of people discharged from forensic mental health services. Intervening and preventing relapse and associated offending behaviours by using the range of available community mental health resources at their disposal is an important and crucial step in providing people with the hope that their condition can be managed safely and that recovery is a realistic target.

References

Bailey J, MacCulloch M (1992) Patterns of reconviction in patients discharged directly to the community from a special hospital: implications for aftercare. *J Forensic Psychiatry* **3**(3): 445–61

Banongo E, Davies J, Godin P, Thompson JB, Lohneis C, Denys C, Floyd M, Fuller S, Heyman B, Reynolds L, Simpson A (2005) *Engaging Service Users in the Evaluation and Development of Forensic Mental Health Care Services.* Forensic Mental Health Research Programme, Department of Health, London

Birchwood M (1996) Early intervention in psychotic relapse. In Haddock G, Slade P (Eds) *Cognitive-Behavioural Interventions with Psychotic Disorders.* Routledge, London

Brooker C, White E (1997) *The Fourth Quinquennial National Community Mental Health Nursing Census of England and Wales.* Universities of Manchester and Keele, Manchester and Keele

Buchanan A (Ed) (2002) *Care of the Mentally Disordered Offender in the Community.* Oxford University Press, Oxford

Caplan G (1964) *Principles of Preventive Psychiatry.* Basic Books, New York

Care Programme Approach Association (2004) *The CPA Handbook.* Care Programme Approach Association, Chesterfield

Care Services Improvement Partnership (2006) *10 High Impact Changes for Mental Health Services.* Care Services Improvement Partnership, London

Coffey M (1998) Provision of out-of-hours support to a forensic population: Strategies and research potential. *J Psychiat Ment Health Nurs* **5**(5): 367–78

Coffey M (1999) Stress and burnout in forensic community mental health nurses: an investigation of its causes and effects. *J Psychiat Ment Health Nurs* **6**(6): 433–44

Coffey M (2000a) Developing Community Services. In: Chaloner C, Coffey M (Eds) *Forensic Mental Health Nursing: Current Approaches* (pp 171–90) Blackwell Science, Oxford

Coffey M (2000b) Stress and coping in forensic community mental health nurses: demographic information and qualitative findings. *NT Research* **5**(1): 5–16

Coffey M (2006a). Community interventions in forensic. In National Forensic Nurses' Research and Development Group (Eds) *Mental Health Nursing: Interventions with*

People with 'Personality Disorder' (pp 123–34) Quay Books, Salisbury

Coffey M (2006b) Researching service user views of forensic mental health services: a literature review. *J Forensic Psychiatry Psychol* **17**(1): 73–107

Coffey M (2006). Community interventions in forensic. In: National Forensic Nurses' Research and Development Group (Eds) *Mental Health Nursing: Interventions with People with 'Personality Disorder'* (pp 123–34) Quay Books, Salisbury

Coffey M, Bishop N (2000) Crisis plans in forensic mental health nursing. *Ment Health Pract* **4**(4): 22–5

Coffey M, Coleman M (2001) The relationship between support and stress in forensic community mental health nursing. *J Adv Nurs* **34**(3): 397–407

Coffey M, Jenkins E (2002) Power and control: forensic community mental health nurses' perceptions of teamworking, legal sanction and compliance. *J Psychiat Ment Health Nurs* **9**(5): 521–9

Coffey M, Morgan J, Gronow T (2007) Forensic aspects of discharge planning from acute care: Transition to community. In: National Forensic Nurses' Research and Development Group (Eds) *Forensic Mental Health Nursing: Forensic Aspects of Acute Care* (pp 175–85) Quay Books, Salisbury

Dell S, Grounds A (1995) *The Discharge and Supervision of Restricted Patients: Report to the Home Office.* Institute of Criminology University of Cambridge, Cambridge

Department of Health (2000) *The NHS Plan: A Plan for Investment, A Plan for Reform.* Department of Health, London

Department of Health (2001) *The Mental Health Policy Implementation Guide.* Department of Health, London

Department of Health, Home Office (1992) *Review of Health and Social Services for Mentally Disordered Offenders and Others Requiring Similar Services. Final Summary Report.* Department of Health and Home Office, London

Evans N (1996) Defining the role of the forensic community mental health nurse. *Nurs Stand* **10**(49): 35–7

Feder L (1991) A comparison of the community adjustment of mentally ill offenders with those from the general prison population: an 18-month follow-up. *Law and Human Behav* **15**(5): 477–93

Johnson S, Nolan F, Pilling S, Sandor A, Hoult J, McKenzie N, White I, Thompson M, Bebbington P (2005) Randomised controlled trial of acute mental health care by a crisis resolution team: the north Islington crisis study. *Brit Med J* **331**: 599–602

Johnson S, Taylor R (2002) *Statistics of Mentally Disordered Offenders 2001: England and Wales. Home Office Statistical Bulletin 13/02.* Home Office. London

Joy CB, Adams CE, Rice K (2004) Crisis intervention for people with severe mental illnesses. *The Cochrane Database of Systematic Reviews 4.* John Wiley & Sons Ltd, London

Judge J, Harty MA, Fahy T (2004) Survey of community forensic psychiatry services in England and Wales. *J Forensic Psychiatry Psychol* **15**(2): 244–53

Kelly T, Simmons W, Gregory E (2002) Risk assessment and management: A community forensic mental health practice model. *Int J Ment Health Nurs* **11**(4): 206–13

Kershaw C, Dowdeswell P, Goodman J (1997) *Restricted Patients – Reconvictions and Recalls by the End of 1995: England and Wales.* Home Office Statistical bulletin 1/97. Home Office, London.

Knight A (2002) Relapse prevention intervention in psychosis. In: Harris N, Williams S, Bradshaw T (Eds) *Psychosocial Interventions for People with Schizophrenia.* Palgrave Macmillan, Basingstoke

Mason T (2002) Forensic psychiatric nursing: a literature review and thematic analysis of role tensions. *J Psychiat Ment Health Nurs* **9**(5): 511–20

McGlynn P (2006) *Crisis Resolution and Home Treatment: A Practical Guide.* Sainsbury Centre for Mental Health, London

National Institute for Mental Health for England (2007) *Crisis Resolution and Home Treatment.* National Institute for Mental Health, Redditch, West Midlands

Onyett S, Linde K, Glover G, Floyd S, Bradley S, Middleton H (2006) *A National Survey of Crisis Resolution Teams in England. Executive Summary.* Care Services Improvement Partnership, London

Parad H, Parad L (2005) *Crisis Intervention Book 2. The Practitioner's Sourcebook for Brief Therapy.* Fenestra Books, Tucson, Arizona

Porporino FJ, Motiuk LL (1995) The prison careers of mentally disordered offenders. *Int J Law and Psychiatry* **18**(1): 29–44

Rask M, Levander S (2001) Interventions in the nurse–patient relationship in forensic psychiatric nursing care: a Swedish survey. *J Psychiatr Ment Health Nurs* **8**(4): 323–33

Renzaglia G, Vess J, Hodel B, McCrary L (2004) Mentally disordered offenders: From forensic state hospital to conditional release in California. *Int J Law and Psychiatry* **27**: 31–44

Riordan S, Smith H, Humphreys MS (2002). Alternative perceptions of statutory community aftercare: patient and responsible medical officer views. *J Ment Health Law* **7**: 119–29

Roberts A (2005a) Bridging the past and present to the future of crisis intervention and crisis management. In: Roberts A (Ed) *Crisis Intervention Handbook. Assessment, Treatment, and Research.* (3rd Edn) Oxford University Press, New York

Roberts A (2005b) *Crisis Intervention Handbook. Assessment, Treatment, and Research.* (3rd Edn) Oxford University Press, New York

Rosen A (1997) Crisis management in the community. *Med J Aust* **167**(11–12): 44–9

Sainsbury Centre for Mental Health (2001) *Mental Health Topics: Crisis Resolution.* Sainsbury Centre for Mental Health: London

Smyth MG, Hoult J (2000) The home treatment enigma. *Brit Med J* **320**: 305–9

Steels M, Roney G, Larkin E, Jones P, Croudace T, Duggan C (1998) Discharged from special hospital under restrictions: a comparison of the fates of psychopaths and the mentally ill. *Criminal Behav Ment Health* **8**(1): 39–55

Street R (1998) *The Restricted Hospital Order: From Court to the Community.* Home Office Research Study 186. Home Office, London

Wearden AJ, Tarrier N, Barrowclough C, Zastowny T R, Rahill AA (2000) A review of expressed emotion research in health care. *Clin Psychology Rev* **20**(5): 633–66

Welsh Assembly Government (2003) *Mental Health Policy Guidance: The Care Programme Approach for Mental Health Service Users.* Welsh Assembly Government: Cardiff

Welsh Assembly Government (2005) *Policy Implementation Guidance on the development of Crisis Resolution/Home Treatment (CR/HT) Services in Wales.* WHC (2005) 048. Welsh Assembly Government, Cardiff

CHAPTER 15

Managing a forensic mental health organisation

Gavin Garman and Fomayi Saliki

Introduction

Tell me and I'll forget, show me and I may remember, involve me and I'll understand.

Chinese Proverb

Contrary to popular belief, health services need managers to oversee, shape and lead their operation and development. Meetings and managers are not always effective, but when they are, they can not only facilitate the creation and maintenance of hugely valuable services that help the patients they care for but also provide a positive working environment for the staff making up the organisation.

Most forensic nurse managers begin their careers as staff nurses and 'make their way up' the hierarchy of an organisation before finding themselves, perhaps with some degree of surprise, responsible for the working lives of dozens of staff, budgets in the hundreds of thousands (or millions) and the caring environments for scores of challenging patients. Most managers will be nurses because most staff members are nurses and more nursing managerial positions are needed to shape and maintain the nursing workforce than the less populated disciplines.

Individuals with the skills to take on senior leadership roles are few and far between. As a result, those who do possess management potential can find themselves progressing up the career ladder rapidly. Few will have completed formal management training, other than short locally provided courses. Ask most ward managers to talk about management theory and they will smile at you wistfully and say they wish they had the time to read about that sort of thing.

This chapter outlines the careers and managerial roles that nurses take on within forensic mental health services. The challenges that nurse managers face and the rewards they can receive will be discussed. We look at the key competencies that leaders in such organisations must possess and outline what it is that makes a good forensic mental health nurse manager. We talk to a number of nurses in different types of management positions about what they do and how they would advise others seeking to follow in their footsteps. We asked patients for their experiences of the way services they are using are being managed. It will be argued that nurse managers of a forensic service must possess a core set of competencies common to managing in other settings, together with a high level of specialised knowledge of forensic mental health care.

What is management?

Some of the earliest theories applied to management will already be familiar to nurses. Maslow's hierarchy of needs argues that individuals will work for an ascending series of needs, starting with the basic need to survive, through obtaining a sense of security and up to a higher plane of self-actualisation.

From the 1950s onwards, several strands of management theory developed. These included management by objectives (Drucker, 1977), the influence of which persists in the form of performance management schemes and performance-related pay. Drucker argued that managers must set objectives, organise, motivate and communicate, and measure and develop people. His formulation recognises the importance of good communication and the existence of wider social concerns.

Change in organisations is analysed within organisational theory. Strategic management theory focuses on wider goals and the process of project team work. More recently, much has been written on the concepts of leadership and motivation. Managers in health services are almost certain to have been sent on some form of leadership training and will face questions on their leadership skills at interview.

Defining the difference between management and leadership is fairly easy. Managers hold a particular position or formal role in an organisation. They co-ordinate and organise the activities of staff. Leaders influence and guide others and motivate others to follow their vision. Leaders may not be in a formal management role. Managers may be less emotional and seek compromise during times of conflict. While it is easy to differentiate the two terms, in practice, good managers will need to show their leadership qualities on occasion and leaders may have managerial responsibilities mitigating their visions (Walton, 1997).

Managing organisations

Values, beliefs and philosophies affect the way cultures organise their activity to form nations, societies and smaller organisations such as a health service (Handy, 1999).

The culture of an organisation rests on a set of beliefs about the way work should be organised, the way authority should be exercised, the way people should be rewarded and what plans should be laid for the future. This culture is often reflected in the organisation's buildings, corporate identity, stated aims and objectives, the kind of people it employs, their career aspirations and roles and the way departments and managers are organised (Starkey, 1996).

The ability of an organisation to achieve its vision and purpose may be determined by its leaders and managers. An easy dichotomy of styles can be drawn along an authoritarian and democratic dimension of management. In an authoritarian organisation, power resides in the leader. Authority of decision-making, arbitration, control and reward or punishment is vested in the leader who alone exercises this authority (Handy, 1999).

In a democratic system, power and responsibility is shared with the group in one way or the other. Managers must have the skills to build a shared vision and foster systemic patterns of thinking throughout their organisation. Through a shared vision, managers are responsible for shaping the organisational culture and enabling it to accomplish its purpose. This also implies that managers have to be designers, teachers and stewards of the organisation. A third type of management style, 'laissez-faire', describes a hands off approach – allowing staff and systems to operate without strong guidance (Walton, 1997).

Employees may prefer to work under a democratic style of management, rather than authoritarian or laissez-faire conditions. Depending on the size and type of organisation, all three styles may have their place at different times. Contingency theorist, Brooks (2006) suggests that 'leadership behaviour interacts with the favourableness of a situation to determine effectiveness'.

Stewart (1983) describes the manager's job as being made up of constraints, choices and demands. Demands include the set minimum criteria of performance and procedures that cannot be ignored. Constraints include resource limitations, physical location, attitudes and expectations of others. Mintzberg (1973) outlines 10 roles of the manager divided into three main categories: 'interpersonal, informational and decisional roles' (see *Table 15.1*).

Management in healthcare organisations

The NHS is one of the largest organisations in the UK and has its own core values and beliefs within a complex culture. The NHS culture is articulated in Government policy documents, the recent avalanche of which began with the NHS Plan (Department of Health, 2000) and a subsequent deluge of Government papers. These papers form a core set of values and beliefs, which it is argued must be at the centre of the NHS. In 'Shifting the balance of power', the Government argued that the NHS must adopt a

Table 15.1: Mintzberg's (1973) roles of a manager

Interpersonal roles	Informational roles	Decisional roles
Figurehead	Monitor	Entrepreneur
Leader	Disseminator	Disturbance handler
Liaison	Spokesman	Resource allocation
		Negotiator

notion of shared values to foster systemic patterns of thinking throughout the organisation. This meant attempts to empower frontline staff to make decisions about patient care.

Policy imperatives can come in waves. Having done away with all matrons, in 2001 the role of the 'Modern Matron' was re-introduced to the NHS as a key means of ensuring good care on the wards (Department of Health, 2001, 2003a).

The NHS as a large organisation has many subdivisions and subcultures including the fields of general medicine, learning disabilities and adult and forensic mental health services. This chapter is concerned with the role of the nurse manager in forensic services, focusing on strategies for managing human resources, finance and clinical issues, with quality as an overriding target in all three strategies. These are the three main dimensions shaping the role of the manager (see *Figure 15.1*). We will explore management roles within each dimension via interviews with managers in forensic services.

Forensic services: Generic or specialist skills?

Forensic services operate a high cost, low volume business. They deal with comparatively few patients at a high cost per bed day. At the time of writing, the typical cost for an NHS medium secure bed is around £470 a day. A bed in a low secure service may cost around £370 while a psychiatric intensive care bed comes in at over £540. In contrast a bed in an open, acute admission ward may cost £240. Topping the price list is a bed in a high secure womens' unit, estimated at up to £880 a day (Department of Health, 2006a).

It is our contention that to fulfil the roles outlined above, managers in a forensic service must possess a set of core skills common to all managers. The South East Thames Regional Health Authority (SETRHA) interviewed 30 managers using critical incident techniques, repertory grid analysis and expert panels and identified the core competencies shown in *Table 15.2* (Perkins and Snapes, 1992).

In addition to these skills, managers must have the specialist knowledge to fully understand the nature of their forensic service.

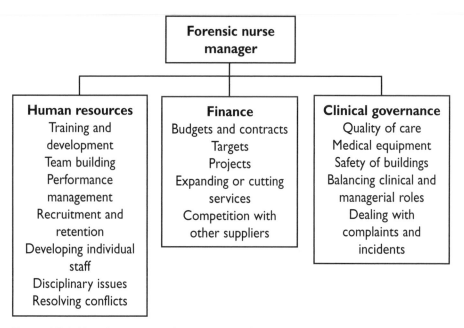

Figure 15.1: Key dimensions of managing a forensic mental health organisation.

What skills does a manager need?

A manager needs to know how to run and manage a financial budget; knowledge of the Mental Health Act, the importance of how to manage the risk assessment process and anxieties brought about by change in level of risk; and how to conduct an investigation.

Ward Manager

Managers should do a management course, especially an MBA, because it allows one to work with people from outside the NHS. A diploma in management is good as well. A good understanding of what is required by the job which includes leadership and managing finance.

Service Director

Careers in management

There are many paths that nurses can take to develop a career at the head of an organisation, although they may not seem to be very clearly laid out at times.

A manager should be chilled out and not worrying about their budget every minute of the day. He should integrate and get out of his office, but not only speak to patients to tell them off.

Forensic service user

Table 15.2: SETRHA's managerial competencies (From Perkins and Snape, 1992)

Competency	Skills required
People orientation	Promotes team working and co-operation Takes the view of others into account Supports and enables staff Establishes joint working relationships
Personal skills	Communication and interpersonal skills Clear and confident speaker with good written work Able to listen and show empathy Negotiator, able to pull threads together and reach outcome
Persuasion	Able to influence others
Leadership	Takes control. Draws on others' strengths Gives clear instructions, direction and energy
Persistence	Hard working, accepts responsibility Finishes projects and meets deadlines Confronts difficult issues Committed to personal and organisation's goals, despite setbacks
Consistent under pressure	Accepts pressure Keeps a sense of humour and resilience Accessible to staff
Creative resource management	Independent thinker, creative and original Finds new solutions, is creative in a crisis Responds to shifting priorities
Priority and objective setting	Sets clear priorities. Delegates and monitors progress
Problem analysis	Grasps problems quickly and identifies options Considers new solutions. Tackles both difficult and easy problems
Planning and organisation	Thinks ahead and plans practical actions Recognises needs and ensures staff are aware of and pursuing plans
Decision making	Makes quick decisions without unnecessary consultation or delay, recognises where further support is needed Recognises implications Willing to make unpopular decisions

Ward managers

Within in-patient services, the roles of ward manager and charge nurse (sometimes the term deputy ward manager is preferred) are the first levels of the management tree. The key responsibilities of ward managers are to ensure the safe and efficient running of their corner of the service. Their daily headaches are ensuring the ward is staffed, the staff feel supported and they have the resources to be able to perform their jobs.

A medium secure ward may have over 30 nursing staff, every one of whom (much like their patients) presents with a unique package of needs. All require supervision and appraisal. Tasks include the 'nuts and bolts, people management of running duty rotas, agreeing leave (annual, study, maternity, carers, compassionate, etc.), managing sickness, and dealing with poor performance. The ward manager needs to ensure that information is flowing in both directions from senior management to ward staff and upwards from ward staff and patients to senior management.

They have the responsibility of ensuring the ward is clean and tidy (they may line manage the ward's domestic staff) and will pass its environmental and health and safety inspections. Non-clinical risk assessments and risk management plans must be in place. An unending stream of faults must be repaired and the physical fabric of the building maintained. Incidents must be reported, investigated and learned from. Patients' complaints must be openly and fully investigated.

The ward must satisfy universities that they are good learning environments for students of various disciplines. The process of nursing and clinical care must be of the highest possible quality. Risk assessments, care plans and medical notes must all meet the required standards.

On top of all these imperatives, ward managers will face a continuing set of targets and standards to meet. Limits may be set on spending or the use of agency and bank staff. Wards can be taxed to make large-scale savings when an organisation is forced to downsize or re-structure. Ward managers may find money leaking out of their budgets to fund wider developments over which they have no control.

In addition, every day a succession of staff will be knocking on the door with requests (and gripes about each other), all expecting a sympathetic ear in the light of initiatives such as flexible working policies and improving working lives.

There are times you just have to give someone a shift although you'd rather not have them work because you suspect some staff are overworking by taking shifts somewhere else on bank and then coming to work on the ward. This affects their performance, but sometimes there is no choice but to let them work because the ward would be short of staff.

One doesn't need to be a nurse to be a ward manager but knowledge of the clinical area and the core business you are in is important.

The difference between forensic and generic services is in the awareness and management of risk of offenders. In the forensic service, admissions are long-term as compared to generic, which are short-term. Also, the forensic manager has to work within Home Office boundaries with patients, which is rarer in generic services.

Ward managers

Lead nurse/head of forensic nursing

In 2001 the role of modern matron was trumpeted as a key means of ensuring good quality nursing care and clean, efficient ward environments. Mental Health organisations took longer to assimilate how such a character, with 'Carry On' film associations, could be sensibly integrated into psychiatric care environments.

Typically, a forensic service will cover a large geographical area (in the UK for example, at least one and probably more counties). To deliver services efficiently, there is a pressure to expand (see below) and a service will typically develop to encompass multiple wards and/or units with differing levels of security or aiming to meet the needs of different patient groups.

Such a multi-faceted service requires a single point of professional leadership and accountability in the form of a lead or head nurse. The lead nurse will manage ward managers who report to him or her on the human resources, financial and clinical areas already outlined. Depending on the size and stage of development of the organisation, the head of nursing may have responsibilities beyond the forensic service and indeed, may not have worked within and developed a wide experience of forensic units.

I was on one of the wards yesterday to meet a group of patients who had asked to see me. They were very unhappy about the fact that we were planning to take away the ward's smoking room. One young woman got very annoyed and quite abusive. But to be honest, it was quite a relief to spend some time with service users. It made a change from listening to staff complain all the time, which seems to be what I do most days. Senior staff lecturing me about spending, junior staff threatening to leave.

Head of forensic nursing

Service manager

The focus of a service or business manager is finance and use of resources. Are the wards providing a good service within the limitations of their budget? Where are the cost pressures and overspends occurring? What changes may be required on the way resources are used? Service managers will have commonly risen from the ranks of qualified nurses. However, the skills of a service manager may more clearly been seen as generic and generalisable from other business or service environments.

One has to be a nurse because clinical knowledge gives you the ability to understand where you are coming from; what drives the business and motivation behind the business. Being a nurse helps because it gives a clear picture and understanding of what your staff are going through. However it takes a while to get used to being a manager from a clinician but at the end, you need to think like a manager and not like a nurse to be able to make hard decisions.

Service manager

Service director

Continuing up the managerial tree, we reach service directors. As the name implies, they give direction and overall leadership across a larger part of the organisation. Service directors may appear more distant from the front line of clinical staff and less involved in the daily mechanics of the service as they paint with a broader brush. They maintain overall accountability however, should the basic mechanics of the service break down.

Managers make mistakes all the time because in the course of the day they deal with an array of things, for example, 50 e-mails per day among other things. Therefore, you have to make decisions on your feet all the time, which gives room for mistakes because some things need to be checked and confirmed but there is no time. So decisions have to be made, either good or bad. And I can make them.

Service director

Forensic community mental health service team (CMHT) manager

Forensic community mental health services are likely to be smaller and operate differently to generic adult community teams. The forensic CMHT manager should have experience as a community psychiatric nurse or social worker within a forensic service. Health and Social Care services are increasingly working together or indeed, combining into one service. The forensic CMHT must liaise with their general counterparts as generic teams can be reluctant to take on 'forensic cases'.

One of the frustrations of managing a forensic CMHT is that there are often conflicts of interest, in that team members may be pulled different ways by their professional leads and therefore, the feeling of a cohesive team can be challenged at times. However, on the plus side having a good mix of disciplines provides a more balanced, holistic approach to providing a care package and service.

I feel that it is important to appreciate that although you have your own professional background, that when you are managing the team, you are not biased to this profession as this could limit your approach to a problem. It is beneficial to encompass the different viewpoints that a range of disciplines can bring.

Forensic CMHT manager

Other organisational roles

Within a forensic service you are likely to come across other senior roles with some managerial responsibilities. These may include job titles such as practice development nurse or clinical nurse specialist. Such roles will also have expectations on providing professional nursing leadership and helping to improve and maintain the quality of care. Post-holders may line manage some staff or control budgets. A senior dual diagnosis worker may manage a small team of dual diagnosis or substance abuse workers or nurses.

Other staff members may be in less formal leadership roles. Individuals may have taken on additional responsibilities or developed an area of local expertise. In good organisations, where the efforts of staff are recognised and valued, such individuals should receive recognition and develop into more formal lead roles.

Career paths have to be picked up through appraisals because it's important to know what your staff want to do. If interested in management, give them management tasks; there are open opportunities in management. The staff need to know what they want to achieve and when. One has to have a desire and will to go into management, not to be forced into it.

Clinical nurse manager

Challenges of management

Managers face an array of targets and needs that must be met for the organisation to function.

Human resources

Recruitment and retention

The imperative for any service is to have enough staff with the necessary skills and experience to deliver a quality service. Impending shortages must be anticipated, although in reality the recruitment process is continuous. The supply and demand of nurses ebbs and flows, from times of glut to periods of famine. Managers must be adept at workforce planning, the projection of staffing patterns and the development of new roles (such as the support time and recovery worker, Department of Health, 2003b).

Agenda for Change (Department of Health, 2005) and the introduction of the Knowledge and Skills Framework (Department of Health, 2004a) is transforming the way staff are managed and the discretion managers have in organising their workforce. Further legislation has been introduced with regard to non-discriminatory practice, including the Age Discrimination Act (2006), Disability Discrimination Act (1995) and the Work and Families Act (2006).

Managers work closely with human resources departments. Senior Management are likely to need to agree each post to be filled to ensure the money exists to pay the proposed staff. These must then be advertised, applications received and candidates short-listed and interviewed. Before staff can start, there is an increasing array of background work to be done, including a criminal records check, occupational health clearance, possible immigration and work permit issues and obtaining satisfactory references.

Once in post, we then need to hang on to our staff. Staff need to feel valued and listened to and informed of changes in the organisation. Individuals require a career path to guide their development – which should allow for horizontal as well as vertical changes in job role. Modernising Nursing Careers – Setting the Direction (Department of Health, 2006b) outlines priorities for the future development of nursing careers.

Pay is a key reward for work but not the only incentive. People work to be part of a supportive team that produces results. Resources must be found to enable staff to continue to study. These resources include the money to pay tuition fees but also to replace the staff's time while they are lost from the ward. Such resources are finite so must be seen to be allocated fairly.

I seem to spend so much of my time chasing up recruitment issues. Human resources make mistakes and you end up just doing it yourself so that things get done. But I like the process – putting people into post or giving them promotions changes peoples' lives.

Lead nurse

In this business, we deal with human beings as compared to some private industry that deals with machinery. Therefore, you should be able to say to staff that you know where they are coming from and that you can offer alternatives. You need to give people support so that they are able to deal with their problems with confidence. Then they'll stay with you.

Service director

Team building and developing individual staff

As well as developing individual staff skills, through study and work experience, a manager must maintain the cohesiveness of the team. Factors leading to positive job attitudes (motivators) such as having variety, challenge and flexibility are key to job satisfaction and improve productivity and performance. This requires the ability to articulate a shared vision of the pressures on the team and their future. A staff group will look to the manager to support them during times of change, while the manager may be under intense pressure from above to drive through unpopular initiatives.

Most clinical areas will ensure they have 'away days' for team building exercises. These can be valuable and help to identify work streams for the team. But the building of a cohesive team cannot be achieved solely during one day in a nice hotel.

As the proverb opening this chapter neatly expressed, people need to feel that they are involved and have a stake in an organisation. Management systems that rely on disembodied orders or autocratic instruction will fail to engage large portions of the workforce. Even changes that have a negative effect are more likely to be accepted if they have been fully explained and we feel we have been treated fairly.

Rewards include job satisfaction because it's challenging and when you see staff doing a good job after putting a lot of effort to take them where they are, it is satisfying and rewarding. Staff satisfaction and appreciation of working on the ward. Seeing patients getting better and moving on towards discharge. Seeing staff being promoted after working with them for a long time is rewarding and makes you feel you're making a positive change in people's lives. It is satisfying to see students on placement wanting to come back and work on the ward and giving positive comments about their experience on the ward.

Ward manager

Performance management and discipline of staff

It can seem to managers that a disproportionate amount of time is spent dealing with disciplinary and performance issues. Recognising and addressing poor performance is a key component of clinical governance, enshrined in professional 'watchdog' bodies such as the Nursing and Midwifery Council (NMC). It is hard to develop the skills necessary to work with an individual over whom there are concerns. Managers must be assertive but also seen to be fair and following local policy.

> *What are the negatives of being a manager? Staff not performing despite intensive input from the manager. Staff complaining all the time but not coming up with suggestions to improve the situation. Difficulties in managing sickness. Too many meetings.*
>
> Ward manager

> *It's got to the point that when I appear on a ward, the first thing staff say is, 'Am I in trouble?' Dealing with disciplinary issues isn't what I want to spend my time doing. But, it's my duty to the patients to ensure poor performance is picked up and something is done about it.*
>
> Head of forensic nursing

Finances

Balancing a budget

Services must be delivered on or under budget. The days of overspending in the NHS without reprisal are gone. Managers receive constant feedback on the state of their finances and must be able to account for all aspects of spending. It is the most obvious and easily summarised indicator of their performance.

The NHS is more accountable for the way it spends its money and the value that services deliver. Trusts have been expected to make cost savings year by year in addition to having penalties applied for overspend. This has had a national impact on staff either being made redundant or relocated to other jobs for which they may feel unskilled or lacking in experience. The idea that working for the NHS is a 'job for life' is no longer true and can impact negatively on the psychological contract (Rousseau and McLean Parks, 1993) between employees and organisations.

> *Financial issues always need forward planning and shifting resources around from areas of less need to areas of need. This, therefore, becomes a day-to-day exercise of resource allocation to minimise spending. Most of the activities have a cost pressure on the ward budget, for example escorting patients to court which could run for weeks, takes up a lot of*

human resources off the ward; some patients on ground and community leave needing more than one member of staff also has an implication on ward staff. Having someone in the intensive care unit means more human resources to cover the ward and more money to be paid out. The manager has to look at the patient needs first before the finances.

Ward manager

Project management

Services change constantly. New units or types of service delivery are introduced and old ones closed or changed. Managers must have an understanding of the process of managing change and project management. They must be able to organise and lead project teams tasked with delivering objectives for the organisation.

We were opening a brand new forensic unit for women. It had taken years of meetings, endless arguing over plans, budgets and operational policies. Then today, I met the new staff team on their induction programme. What had been proposals, business plans and lists of figures that didn't add up had turned into two well-equipped wards and a room full of people we had recruited to work in the service. It gave me a huge sense of satisfaction to see plans coming to fruition and a new service take shape.

Service manager

Expanding and cutting services

There is governmental pressure for services to develop greater choice for services users, including closer geographical placements, high quality care pathways, guidance on clinical standards (from the National Institute of Health and Clinical Excellence and Healthcare Commission) and introducing national reference costs for services. The larger the service, the greater the opportunity for cost savings, the smaller the risk of replication and the greater the pool of tangible (buildings, infrastructure) and intangible (staff knowledge and experience) assets to draw on.

Larger organisations should be able to develop better document management systems, a pool of shared knowledge and operating procedures, better efficiency and lower costs and more power as a buyer of services. Thus it can seem that there is a pressure to expand individual or merge existing services. Hofstede (2001) writes that within cultures, there is a varying degree of uncertainty and avoidance when the environment is seen as being unpredictable. Equally, due to cost improvement pressures, services may need to restructure and cut back.

Managing change requires an understanding of how organisations must unfreeze existing practices, introduce change and then 're-freeze' into a new way of working (Lewin, 1947).

The job is exciting because the service is expanding while other services are cutting down, hopefully it will become a quality service. It is rewarding to see the positive achievements that one day I will look back on and say that I have contributed to change and provided a quality service.

Service director

Competition

The health service operates in a competitive market. NHS managers may be in direct competition with the private sector or other NHS trusts and seek to win contracts to deliver forensic inpatient, outpatient, community or prison care. This will require the ability to prepare and submit tenders and sell services to the commissioners holding the purse strings.

I co-ordinated a multi-million pound bid to provide low secure beds for a whole county, trying to take the contract from the private sector. It felt great when we heard we had won. Mind you, it just created a whole lot more work as a result. Sometimes I wonder if we weren't better off when we were small and our work was more contained.

Senior nurse

Quality

Balancing managerial and clinical roles

Can a manager with so many demands on their time find the time to remain connected to the users of their service? The ultimate outcome of all the challenges we are outlining must be that patient care is of the highest standard or all the meetings and project documents have been for nothing.

The manager should be able to juggle clinical and management stuff because there are a lot of pressures on managing performance, sickness and finance. The pressure comes mainly when faced with clinical risk versus cost, i.e. balancing how much money to spend on clinical aspects and its implication on risk management and meeting budgetary needs. For example, the requirement of nursing observation has an implication on cost pressure as the ward needs to employ extra staff to cover the observations and reduce the level of risk and at the same time, provide the quality of care needed.

Ward manager

Resolving conflict

Conflict occurs between individuals or groups. Managers must be able to step in, halt destructive clashes and establish what lies at the root of a disagreement. Resolution may be achieved rapidly and informally or require more formal procedures, such as dealing with a grievance.

Services are run by human beings, which unfortunately, means you will always run into problems and conflict. You need to develop arbitration skills and be assertive and decisive to resolve confrontations.

Lead nurse

Meeting local and national targets

The number and range of targets that each health organisation has to meet has never been so vast and bewildering. At the time of writing, the Government's Standards for Better Health (Department of Health, 2004b) contains over 300 'fields of enquiry' that an NHS Trust may be asked to provide evidence that they are compliant on.

If the manager makes sure that they do what is expected of them, then they would not need anyone to tell them that they are doing a good job. They need to meet their targets and make them their priority task.

Service director

Conclusion: Keys to good management

The purpose of a forensic mental health service is to provide high quality care to a group of service users with complex and at times, challenging needs. Above and beyond the duty to the individual, the service provides for the community and society at large by seeking to minimise risk and reduce relapse and re-offending. In addition, there are responsibilities to the staff who deliver the service, to provide a safe and rewarding working environment in which staff can continue to develop their careers and feel valued. Government bodies seek further reassurance on the way money is spent and the nature of the service that is being paid for.

As a result, it is perhaps small wonder that managers are not universally beloved by their workforce. Demands and constraints are conflicting and intense. Rewards for the manager may not always seem obvious. Pay is not the only reward we need. A sense of achievement and the ability and space to exercise the range of skills we have discussed is required. Managers are as likely to feel unsupported as anyone else in the organisation.

There is no one way to be an effective manager. All managers can benefit by thinking about how they function and identifying other options and ways of managing that are different from those habitually used. Decisions about changing particular ways of working must be personal. They are influenced by seeing how other people do things effectively and by reviewing and reflecting on the literature and recent events to elicit clues about how to change current ways of working. After all the frustrations and hurdles, managers must have the self-belief that they are the right person to lead an organisation or team, and the strength and drive to accept the attacks that follow.

This chapter has outlined the core skills and specialist knowledge that a nurse will need to develop to successfully run a forensic mental health service. At times, they may seem far removed from the clinical skills we first wished to develop when we chose nursing as a career. However, the ultimate outcome of our working week should remain intact: working in a team to provide compassionate care to those in need.

Managers should be friendly and work co-operatively. Some don't understand the interactions between staff and how they affect patients. They need to listen, so I can trust them and feel welcome.

When a patient brings up an issue, it should be dealt with. I pulled the handset off the phone two weeks ago and it still hasn't been fixed.

Forensic service users

References

Age Discrimination Act (2006) *Employment and Training: Age Discrimination* [Online] Available from: http://www.opsi.gov.uk/SI/si2006/draft/ukdsi_0110742664_en.pdf [Accessed 2 November 2007]

Brooks I (2006) *Organisational Behaviour: Individuals, Groups and Organisation* (3rd edn) Pearson: Essex

Department of Health (2000) *The NHS Plan: A Plan for Investment, a Plan for Reform.* Department of Health, London

Department of Health (2001) *Implementing the NHS Plan – Modern Matrons: Strengthening the role of ward sisters and introducing senior sisters (Health Service Circular 2001/010).* Department of Health, London

Department of Health (2003a) *Modern Matrons – Improving the Patient Experience.* Department of Health, London

Department of Health (2003b) *Mental Health Policy Implementation Guide Support, Time and Recovery (STR) Workers.* Department of Health, London

Department of Health (2004a) *The NHS Knowledge and Skills Framework (NHS KSF) and the Development Review.* Department of Health, London

Department of Health (2004b) *Standards for Better Health.* Department of Health, London

Department of Health (2005) *Agenda for Change: NHS Terms and Conditions Handbook.* Department of Health, London

Department of Health (2006a) *NHS Reference Costs 2005–2006.* Department of Health, London

Department of Health (2006b) *Modernising Nursing Careers – Setting the Direction.* Department of Health, London

Drucker P (1977) *People and Performance.* Heinemann, London

Handy C (1999) *Understanding Organisations.* (4th edn) Penguin Books: London

HM Government (1995) *Disability Discrimination Act:* HSMO [Online] Available from: http://www.opsi.gov.uk/acts/acts1995/1995050.htm [Accessed 2 November 2007]

HM Government (2006) *Work and Families Act* HSMO [Online] Available from: http://www.opsi.gov.uk/acts/en2006/2006en18.htm [Accessed 2 November 2007]

Hofstede G (2001) *Culture Consequences: Comparing Values, Behaviours, Institutions and Organisations Across Nations.* (2nd edn) Sage, London

Lewin K (1947) Group Decision and Social Change. Cited in: Schein E (ed) (2004) *Organisational Culture and Leadership* (3rd edn) Wiley: San Fransisco

Mintzberg H (1973) *The Nature of Managerial Work.* Harper and Row, New York

Perkins D, Snapes T (1992) Developing the Best Managers. In: Vickerstaff S (ed) *Human Resource Management in Europe.* Chapman and Hall, London

Rousseau DM, McLean Parks J (1993) The contracts of individuals and organizations. In: Cummings LL, Staw BM (eds) *Research in Organizational Behavior.* JAI Press, Greenwich, CT

Starkey K (1996) *How Organizations Learn.* International Thomson Business Press, London.

Stewart R (1983) *Choices for the Manager.* McGraw-Hill, Maidenhead

Walton M (1997) *Management and Managing: Leadership in the NHS.* (2nd edn) Stanley Thomas, London.

CHAPTER 16

Mental health nursing in prison: A time for change in role

Graham Durcan

Introduction

This chapter, parts of which are directly quoted from, or based on Durcan (2008), concerns prison mental health nursing and divides it into two forms, one that does exist and one that by and large does not. The former, the Mental Health Inreach Nurse (MHIN), has spread across the English and Welsh Prison estate with the introduction of specialist mental health inreach teams that are largely staffed by nurses (Her Majesty's Inspectorate of Prisons, 2007a). The latter, the Primary Mental Health Care Nurse (PMHCN), which much of this chapter will be given over to discussing, is a role within a service that desperately needs to be developed across the prison estate for the majority of prisoners with mental health problems who do not have severe mental illness.

It is possible that these two distinct nursing roles might be combined in some settings or even further sub-divided in others. Some mental health nursing in some prisons could well be performed by nurses from non-prison based services such as Community Mental Health Teams (CMHTs), Crisis Resolution Teams, Assertive Outreach Teams and Early Intervention in Psychosis Teams. However, as both roles require 'specialist' skills, I would envisage in most cases the roles being discrete ones and practised by nurses dedicated to working in the prison setting. It is also perfectly possible that one could substitute the word 'nurse' for 'practitioner' as other skilled mental health professionals could perform many, if not all, the functions within these roles. But as this is a book on nursing and more importantly, because nurses are most likely to fill these roles, I shall throughout the chapter refer to these roles as nursing ones.

Rather paradoxically, this chapter is both overdue and comes a little too early. The mental health of prisoners has long been neglected, but because there is little experience of providing mental health services to prisoners, there is also little in the way of an evidence base to draw upon when attempting to define and describe the nurses' role. So much of what is raised in the pages that follow is 'up for discussion' and will not be the last word on prison mental health nursing.

In 2005 the Sainsbury Centre for Mental Health conducted a review of London prison mental health services (Durcan and Knowles, 2006). In 2006 we conducted another study in the West Midlands of the mental health provision in five quite different prison setting (Durcan, 2006, 2008). This study included 173 in-depth interviews, including 98 with prisoners. Some of these were unsentenced (remand) prisoners, most were adult men, but we interviewed women prisoners too and male juveniles (under 17 years of age) and young people (18–21 years of age). All had mental health problems, some moderate and some severe, but all had experienced a complicated range of social and health challenges of which their mental health problem was just a part. The Sainsbury Centre also supported the All Party Parliamentary Group on Prison Health's (2006) review of prison mental health. These studies and others and the many visits we have made to prisons have influenced the contents of this chapter.

Prisons and the mental health of prisoners

Prison health care is going through a period of change; responsibility for prison health care has transferred from the Prison Service to the NHS and this was completed in April 2006 (in most areas it had taken place by April 2005). Perhaps the greatest change has been to mental health provision within prisons. It is unrealistic to ever expect our prisons to be mental illness-free zones: depriving people of their liberty and the conditions of incarceration are always likely to have an impact on the mental well-being of people in prisons. The World Health Organization and International Red Cross (2005) jointly released a briefing paper on the negative impact of imprisonment on mental health. The Joint House of Commons and House of Lords Committee on Human Rights (Joint Committee on Human Rights, 2004) reached similar conclusions, as did the International Centre for Prison Studies (2004). Prisoners also report this (e.g. Nurse et al, 2003) and in our West Midlands Prisons study, prisoners reported a number of factors that negatively impacted on their mental health; these were:

- *Bullying (by other inmates).*
- *Concerns about family and difficulty in communicating with [them].*
- *Having no one they can trust to talk to.*
- *Having little meaningful activity and the monotony of the regime.*
- *Worries and concerns over their release.*
- *Substance misuse.*
- *Incompatibility with cell mates.*
- *Poor diet.*
- *Limited access to physical activity such as the gym.*

Table 16.1: Prevalence of mental illness among prisoners and the general population (From Singleton et al, 1998, 2001)

	Prevalence among prisoners (%)	*Prevalence in general population (%)*
Schizophrenia and delusional disorder	6–13	0.5
Personality disorder	50–78	3.4–5.4
Neurotic disorder	40–76	16.5
Drug dependency	34–52	0.4
Alcohol dependency	19–30	0.3–1.2

- *Unresolved past life traumas.*
- *Difficulty in accessing services, particularly health care and counselling.*

(Durcan, 2008:18)

Prisoners with severe mental health problems can and should be transferred to a more appropriate facility for care and management of their illness, and in the UK context, this will be an NHS mental health facility. Compulsory treatment under the Mental Health Act (1983) (in England and Wales) is not possible as prison-enhanced care units or hospitals are not recognised as places of safety under the Act. Therefore treatment against the person's will is rarely possible and then only under common law and exceptional circumstances. Prisons have not been designed as therapeutic environments and providing therapy in them is a challenge (Durcan and Knowles, 2006). There has been a recent concerted effort to speed up transfers (Department of Health, 2005a), but there are still significant delays (Rutherford and Duggan, 2007) and average waiting times in one London prison have been cited as 53 days (Sales and McKenzie, 2007).

'The most recent exhaustive study of mental illness in English prisons, that conducted by the Office of National Statistics (ONS)... is now a decade old' (Durcan, 2008: 13 quoting Singleton et al, 1998; Lader et al, 2000), but remains the best information we have on prevalence rates. For some populations, there is more recent and updated information (but all from smaller scale studies), such as that produced by Chitsabesan et al (2006) on young offenders. The ONS statistics are presented in *Tables 16.1 and 16.2*. But all studies have consistently shown the high rates of psychiatric morbidity among prisoners (for example see the review by Brooker et al, 2002).

Table 16.2: Prevalence across different prison populations (From Singleton et al, 1998 and adapted from Brooker et al, 2002)

	Sentenced		Remand	
	Male (%)	*Female (%)*	*Male (%)*	*Female (%)*
Personality disorder	64	50	78	50
Neurotic disorder	40	63	59	76
Drug dependence	34	36	43	52
Alcohol dependence	30	19	30	20
Suicide attempt in last year	7	16	15	27
Any schizophrenic or delusional disorder	6	13	9	13
Self-harm (not suicide attempt)	7	10	5	9
Affective psychosis	1	2	2	2

The complexity of prisoners' problems

Prisoners are particularly socially excluded (Durcan, 2008:22):

- 67% are unemployed before going to prison (Social Exclusion Unit, 2002).
- 70% will have no employment or placement in training/education on release (Niven and Stewart, 2005).
- 42% of released prisoners have no fixed abode (cited in Williamson, 2006).
- 65% of prisoners have numeracy skills at or below the level of an 11-year-old.
- 48% have reading skills at or below this level (Social Exclusion Unit, 2002).
- 50% are not registered with a GP before coming into prison (cited in Williamson, 2006).

Many prisoners have experienced abuse and many have concurrent substance misuse problems and live chaotic lifestyles prior to and in between spells in prison. This 'package' of problems and vulnerabilities poses challenges for mental health services in prisons (and of course, other services) and means that the type of provision, even for those with moderate mental health problems, needs to address these.

Growth in the prison population

Overcrowding is a relative term and in other parts of the world, the concentration of prisoners in a prison is far greater than ours. But there is a trend for continued and marked growth in our prison population and our prisons are holding more people than they were designed for. The English and Welsh prison population rose to 81 133 (National Offender Management Service, 2007) in September 2007 and is predicted to continue rising to somewhere in the region of 116 550 by 2013 (Home Office, 2006). It is reasonable to assume that the prevalence of mental health problems remains at least the same as when last measured a decade ago, but of course the absolute numbers of prisoners with mental health problems will have risen.

Pressure on prison spaces means that transfers around the prison estate are necessary to create spaces in the right places and in the year up to March 2007 there were over 71 000 prison transfers (House of Commons, 2007). Even when accounting for prisoners with multiple transfers in a year, the above statistic still indicates a significant number of prisoners will move between prisons in any given year.

Current health care in the English prison system

A description follows of the English prison system, the current nature of health care provided within it and an overview of the workforce.

English and Welsh prisons are categorised by the level of security they provide, category 'A' being the most secure and housing those who pose the greatest security risk, although some category 'A' prisons also serve local courts and will house remand and sentenced prisoners who do not pose this level of risk. Most prisons that serve courts are category 'B', these are often called 'local prisons' and are still very secure but are a step down from the category 'A' level. Some category B prisons have only sentenced prisoners and may have a specialist function such as providing programmes for those on life sentences. Category 'C' prisons will normally house sentenced prisoners who, while still posing an escape risk, warrant lower security. Category 'C' prisons may also provide training and workshops. The lowest level of security is category 'D'. These prisons will often allow prisoners some movement outside the prison, usually for the purposes of work or training, and considerable freedom of movement within the establishment. This categorisation largely applies to adult men's prisons, but while not following the same categorisation system, prisons for juveniles and women will likewise vary in security level.

There are currently 143 prisons in England and Wales. The vast majority are public sector prisons, although there are 11 'contracted out' or private sector prisons. All prisons have some form of health care provision, at least consisting of GP clinics, prison nurses and visiting primary and secondary care clinicians (e.g. dentists, chiropodists, mental health inreach). Approximately half of the prisons have what are known as enhanced health care units (formerly known as prison hospitals) and have on site access to a health care professional (usually a prison nurse) 24 hours a day, 7 days a week (Dale and Woods, 2001).

The vast majority of prisoners occupying beds or cells in the enhanced health care units are there for reasons associated with poor mental health (Reed and Lynne, 2000). In our West Midlands study, two prisons had enhanced health care units and these were almost exclusively used for prisoners admitted for reasons of poor mental health. Often the reason for admission would be related to incidences of self-harm and attempted suicide but there were a small number of prisoners with acute and severe mental health problems (e.g. psychotic episodes) awaiting assessment for transfer to the NHS.

All prisons have access to GP services and in most cases, there is a daily clinic. Prisons by and large still work on what most resembles a 'sick parade' basis. Prisoners complete application forms ('apps') for a health care appointment and these are collected from the prison wings on most days. Many prisons then escort all the prisoners with an 'appointment' (typically all those with a morning appointment or all those with an afternoon appointment) from a wing to the health care department. In some cases, all prisoners will remain there until all the appointments are complete and are then escorted back to their wing or workplace in the prison. Understandably security considerations around prisoner movements and prison officer staff shortages all have an influence on the nature of prisoner escorts to the prison's health care department. In most cases, seeing a GP in the prison involves long waits in what are usually large and bare holding cells. Prisons with less security restrictions do attempt to run a more conventional primary care appointment system, with prisoners able to come at their specific appointment time; and as was the case for one prison in our West Midlands study, a semi-open women's prison, there was considerable freedom of movement within the establishment.

While GPs form an important part of the prison health care service, the most frequent health contact in a prison is with a member of the prison nursing staff, who will visit the wings daily, dispense medication, provide nurse-led clinics, deal with 'health' crises and in some prisons, triage GP referrals and are generally the 'first port of call'. In those prisons with 24 hour onsite access to health care, this is usually access to a nurse.

It is worth noting that offenders, as a group, generally fall outside the system of health care when not in prison but when incarcerated, choose to consult with health care professions considerably more frequently than do the general public (see Williamson, 2006). There are a variety of reasons, including the general poor health of offenders, some prisoners seeking opportunities to break the monotonous prison regime, others seeking alternatives to illicit substances, many prisoners wanting help with the symptoms of drug addiction and withdrawal from drugs, and many wanting help with mental health issues. Therefore there are great demands placed on prison health services. In the West Midlands, we observed that GP consultations tended to be much shorter than those in the wider community, perhaps two to three minutes, with few lasting longer; indeed we noted that all contacts with health professionals (including nurses) tended to be short exchanges (with the exception of mental health inreach contacts).

In addition to MHINs other mental health trained nurses do work in prisons as part of the prison health care department. However, few prisons currently deploy them in a specific mental health role. Most prison nurses, regardless of training, are employed in a generic health role. Prison health care departments vary considerably to the degree that generically employed mental health trained nurses are able to utilise their mental health skills. Some prisons encourage staff to use some clinical time in a primary mental health care role, in others there is less such opportunity. However, where there is no dedicated mental health staff within the health care department, the role is vulnerable to staff shortages in other clinical areas. This is also a finding of Her Majesty Inspectorate of Prisons' (2007a) most recent thematic review on Mental Health.

Recent prison service statistics indicate there are somewhere in the region of 1100 prison health care staff (Her Majesty Inspectorate of Prisons, 2006), most of whom will be nurses. Perhaps a third of these nurses are mental health trained (NHS Executive and Her Majesty's Prison Service, 2000). Additionally, some health care departments have prison officers specifically trained to work in prison health care, known as health care officers (HCOs). HCOs provide some health interventions and also have a security role with the department. Some have taken the opportunity to train as nurses. The primary care trusts (PCTs) in the West Midlands decided not to continue funding the HCO role in the public sector prisons we studied.

Most prison health care nurses are now employed by NHS organisations, as opposed to the prison service, as would have been the case in the past.

Virtually all prisons have access to a mental health inreach team. *Changing the Outlook* (Department of Health and Her Majesty's Prison Service, 2001) envisaged these teams as having the same role and function as community mental health teams (CMHTs) but for a prison 'community'. Unlike CMHTs and the range of new mental health services that recent reforms in mental health provision in England has introduced, inreach services have not been launched with implementation guidance and a published evidence base. Consequently, there is considerable variation in the make-up and how these teams are integrated with prison services, as well as with wider mental health services. These teams largely consist of mental health nurses (Her Majesty's Inspectorate of Prisons, 2007a) and there is a question as to how truly multidisciplinary these teams are. Not all teams have clinical psychology staff, occupational health staff or social workers and a small number of teams do not have psychiatry as an integral part of the team (psychiatry may be provided under a separate arrangement).

The teams can be embedded within the prison and fully based there; others have external bases and are more fully integrated with an external NHS mental health care provider. There has been no academic work on which is the better arrangement and under which circumstances, but we have collected much anecdotal evidence to suggest that good integration with mental health services in the community is a preferred arrangement. Prisons are powerful institutional cultures that are not designed around the principles of care. It may be more difficult for an embedded team to resist the pressures of the prison culture than a team well linked in mainstream mental health care. Inreach staff in both the London and the West Midlands described the challenges of working in a prison and the differences between the ethos of the NHS and the prison service (Durcan, 2006; Durcan and Knowles, 2006).

Mental health services and nursing in prisons: The state of the art

There can be no disputing that the mental well-being of prisoners in English goals has until very recently been largely neglected. Prison inspectorate reports and research consistently report on the poor state of prison mental health services (e.g. Guite and Field, 1997; Her Majesty's Inspectorate of Prisons, 1997, 2003, 2005, 2006a, b, 2007a, b; Reed and Lyne, 2000; Reed, 2003; Rickford, 2003; Rickford and Edgar, 2005; Durcan, 2006; Durcan and Knowles, 2006; Sainsbury Centre for Mental Health, 2007). Arguably, a critical point in movement towards improvements in mental health provision came when the then Chief Inspector of Prisons, Sir David Ramsbotham, published *Prisoner or Patient* (Her Majesty's Inspectorate of Prisons, 1996). This seminal report had a major influence on Government thinking (e.g. see Department of Health, 1999). More recently, the criticism has focused in on primary mental health care (e.g. Durcan, 2006; Durcan and Knowles, 2006; Sainsbury Centre for Mental Health, 2007), seen as part of the function of prison health care departments, of which nurses form the most significant part of the workforce.

The level of mental health provision to prisons until recently was variable, but for many there was very little (Smith et al, 2002). A small number of prisons did contract for psychiatry sessions and these were provided by a few forensic psychiatrists (then the only psychiatrists with prison-related training) (Birmingham, 2002).

While the introduction of inreach teams can be criticised for being separate from the broader programme of mental health service reforms such as proposed in the NHS Plan (Department of Health, 2000) and for providing no guidance for commissioners, providers or practitioners (as was provided with the wider reform programme), it does represent the most significant investment in prison mental health care ever. Funding was provided for 360 mental health staff across the prison estate.

The new guiding principle for prison mental health care and indeed, all health care, is that it be equivalent with that provided in the community (Department of Health and Her Majesty's Prison Service, 2001). This is an important concept for prison health practitioners and especially nurses, who are the largest single group of practitioners. It is also a debated concept; offenders access less and have less access to health care services in the community; it is clear that they suffer from complex problems and some would argue that equivalent provision is not enough: '…equivalence is a minimal standard, rather than one that satisfies the legal or health obligations of States' (Lines, 2006).

Research has shown that mental health provision falls well short of equivalent and therefore, below a minimal standard. Primary mental health care is thin on the ground and where it does exist, unless it has a dedicated resource, it struggles to achieve anything (see *Box 16.1*)

The 'traditional' prison nurse

Prison nursing has a limited literature and evidence base, most of which consists of descriptions of the role with little in the way of an exhausting critique (Gannon, 2002, is an exception). The prison nurse is seen as the 'jack of all trades' (e.g. Norman and Parrish, 1999, 2002), a generic nurse who, regardless of training, is supposed to cater to both the physical and mental well-being of the patient, this despite the fact that prisoners tend to have a complex range of problems. As has been detailed earlier, prison health care is heavily criticised both in research and Her Majesty's Inspectorate of Prisons' reports, yet this criticism is largely absent from the very limited literature on prison nursing. This is a curious omission given that nurses form the largest single group in the prison health care workforce.

The generic prison nurse has a wide range of duties from dispensing medication, triaging prisoner-patients to providing 'inpatient' care. There is an expectation that nurses will set-up and run 'nurse-led' clinics for a

---

Box 16.1: Key findings from Sainsbury Centre for Mental Health's West Midlands prisons study (Durcan, 2008)

- The vast majority of prisoners with mental health problems received little or no mental health service at all
- Screening for poor mental health was far from robust and was mostly a 'one off' effort on the prisoners' arrival
- Occasionally prisoners with what appeared quite marked and severe mental health problems were not identified at screening
- Continuity of care between community services and prison health services was poor
- Continuity of care between prisons was often poor with no or little medical information being transferred with the prisoner (e.g. in West Midland prison half the prisoners arriving came with no medical information and many more with missing information)
- Most reported a history of co-morbid substance misuse and mental health problems
- Joint working between mental health and substance misuse teams was at best limited
- Many prisoners told SCMH that what they needed most in prison was someone to talk to, but what concerned them more was leaving the prison. All of those prisoners we spoke to with a release date within 12 months of the interview were anxious about leaving and many predicted their return. In particular they were concerned about having appropriate accommodation and support for substance misuse and mental health problems on release

---

variety of chronic illnesses and that they will support prisoners with issues around their mental health and substance misuse and help those wishing to stop smoking. They are most likely to be first on the scene for any accidents occurring in workshops or wings and most likely to be called to assess prisoners appearing to undergo an acute mental health crisis. At the reception area of the prison, where prisoners first arrive at the prison or return from court, prison nurses will provide a general health screening (including mental health) and will complete part of a cell sharing risk assessment. Not only is much expected of prison nurses but they are expected to perform in a regime that has not been designed with health care in mind. Prisons are designed for deprivation of liberty and public protection. Because of the nature of the clientele and the regime, there are restrictions on what health staff can and cannot do. Prisoners, in some form of distress or crisis in their cell, may not be unlocked until there are sufficient members of staff in place to meet security requirements.

In the West Midlands we observed that much of the activity of the prison nurse was not health related and that considerable potential clinical time was instead spent on duties such as non-health related clerical tasks, escorting prisoners and chaperoning GPs or other visiting clinicians.

Bar some pilot programmes, training specifically designed to help nurses work in prisons does not exist and for almost a decade this lack of professional development has been acknowledged (e.g. Department of Health, 1999; UKCC, 1999). Clinical supervision is also something of a rarity and has been described as patchy (e.g. Freshwater et al, 2001; Her Majesty's Inspectorate of Prisons, 2006b, 2007b). Where there have been attempts to introduce it there have been barriers and even attempts to sabotage it (Walsh, 2005).

The primary mental health care nurse (PMHCN)

A small number of prisons across England and Wales have recognised the need and established a service for prisoners with mild to moderate mental health problems in addition to those served by inreach teams. But most prisons do not have such a service and it is even questionable to just what extent inreach teams do, and are able to, see those meeting the criteria for their service (Her Majesty's Inspectorate of Prisons, 2007a).

In a workshop conducted at the end of the West Midlands study, participants concluded that the generic nurse's role did not work for prisoners with mental health problems and that within prison health care teams there was a need for dedicated primary care level mental health nurses. Also, as most 'inpatients' in the enhanced health care units were there for reasons of poor mental health, most staff supporting inpatients ought to be dedicated mental health staff too. The role of the PMHCN was described by participants and included the following:

- 'Supporting screening for mental health problems' (Durcan, 2008:67) (but all health care nurses, mental health trained or not, should continue to have a role
  in this).
- 'More detailed assessment of all those identified with mental health problems' (Durcan, 2008:67).
- 'Working with a small caseload using brief interventions (e.g. cognitive-behavioural therapy)' (Durcan, 2008:67).
- 'Supporting GP in medication reviews' (Durcan, 2008:67).
- 'Crisis assessment and support' (Durcan, 2008:67).
- Onward referral and signposting.
- Health promotion.
- Joint work with inreach.
- Group work.

- 'Liaison with internal and external agencies' (Durcan, 2008:67).
- Support and liaison for prison/NHS transfer and resettlement.

This is a far from exhaustive list and the role would need to vary according to the particular population served. However, skills in working with mental health and substance misuse co-morbidity would be essential, as would some knowledge and skill in working with people with personality disorder. What should be clear is that the PMHCN role is itself a 'specialist' role just like that of the MHIN.

The mental health inreach nurse

This chapter is being written before a national review of mental health inreach is published. This will doubtless provide pointers for developing the MHIN role. In a small number of prisons, mental health inreach has been present for years (e.g. see Polczyk-Przybyla and Gournay, 1999) but for most prisons, inreach is a very recent arrival. The teams were set up with no guidance for commissioners or providers and consequently their size, structure, makeup and management arrangements vary considerably.

Inreach teams have been established with a very limited resource base, given the level of need. Many teams report that they have been overwhelmed by referrals (e.g. Durcan and Knowles, 2006). Her Majesty's Inspectorate of Prisons (2007a) reports that the average practitioner caseload is 33 prisoners. If it is assumed that all 360 proposed new staff were employed then around 15% of the total prison population is on an inreach caseload. Early reporting of the national review of inreach (Steel et al, 2007) suggests that the need for inreach is considerably higher than this. By comparison, CMHT guidance (Department of Health, 2002) suggests a caseload similar to the current reported inreach average, but for communities with the national average deprivation levels. Prisoners invariably come from the most deprived communities and, as has been stated, it is the norm for them to have a complex range of problems. The CMHT guidance does not give a precise formula for accounting for other factors such as deprivation when calculating caseload size, but it does state that caseloads should be lower to account for higher deprivation and greater complexity. We profiled two teams in the West Midlands study and compared them to 40 or so CMHTs we had profiled in the previous three years. The inreach teams' caseloads were very similar in profile to those of CMHTs working in deprived inner city communities and even to some assertive outreach teams. Given that at best a full-time inreach nurse will struggle to provide 22 hours per week clinical time, it is questionable what can be done, meaningfully, with caseloads exceeding 30 complex patients. Inreach workers in local prisons (those receiving remanded prisoners) often have larger caseloads (Her Majesty's Inspectorate of Prisons, 2007a).

There is not yet any published evidence of the impact of mental health inreach but research with just a few teams suggests some positive impact. For example, prisoners in contact with the West Midlands inreach teams were almost universally very positive about it and reported that their inreach worker (usually a MHIN) had encouraged more proactive planning for their release, including finding appropriate accommodation, employment/training, support for substance misuse problems, as well as continuity of care for their mental health problem. This was in contrast to prisoners with mental health problems not in contact with inreach who reported receiving little or no help in the prison and had greater concerns about their release and resettlement. Prisoners interviewed described feeling 'ejected' from prisons on previous occasions, with little support and sometimes to homelessness. For these MHINs at least, liaison with resettlement agencies was seen as a key part of the role.

Inreach teams and MHINs also appear to have played a significant role in speeding up transfers to the NHS from prison for prisoners with severe mental health problems (Mohan and Fahey, 2006). This role is likely to continue, not least because court liaison and diversion services are still thin on the ground and vary greatly in the services they offer. Additionally, there are likely to be some prisoners who will not exhibit severe mental health problems until within a prison.

The Sainsbury Centre has identified another potential role for the MHIN. A significant number of prisoners will have suffered traumatic events in their past, such as loss of significant others during critical life stages and sexual and physical abuse. Most felt they had unresolved issues, and most wanted to be able to talk about these or at least find a means of living with their past 'less painfully'. Some prisoners have reported that they built a trusting relationship with a member of health care staff in the past and disclosed their experiences, only to be transferred before any further work could be done. This means caution must be taken in approaching these issues and it may not be possible to embark on this with remand and short-term prisoners. But perhaps MHINs need to develop specialist skills in supporting prisoners with these needs.

Few of the teams we have encountered report anything approaching integrated working with prison substance misuse agencies. This needs to develop, given the high proportion of prisoners with substance misuse. Equally, so-called dual diagnosis skills should be part of the MHIN's armoury: indeed it should be seen as a 'default' skill.

Many prisoners are labelled with personality disorder and some of these present a management challenge within prisons. MHINs need to develop skills in working with these prisoners and also in consulting and supporting prison staff in finding ways of working effectively with this group.

It has been reported that assessment and liaison are the primary interventions of MHINs (Durcan and Knowles, 2006). While there is a need to go beyond this, these are two crucial skills and for a significant proportion of the prison population (remanded prisoners) little more can be done. Effective assessment and liaison can at least be crucial in ensuring that the right community resources are in place when prisoners are released.

It is important for both MHINs and PMHCNs to be familiar with the Offender Mental Health Care Pathway (Department of Health, 2005b). This is essentially a series of templates to guide practitioners and commissioners in decision making on how to intervene with prisoners and other offenders suffering from mental health problems. And, as in the community, an important vehicle for that intervention is the Care Programme Approach (CPA). Mental health nurses in prisons need to consider how CPA integrates with other systems of case management and in England and Wales, that includes the new system of 'end to end' offender management run by the National Offender Management Service. *Changing the Outlook* saw CPA as playing a key role in ensuring continuity of care between prisons and the community. However, there is little evidence that this is happening. Instead, there is some evidence suggesting inconsistency in how it is applied within the prison system and also of a lack of engagement in it by prison health care staff (Durcan, 2006).

Conclusion

At this point in time, the MHIN role is embryonic and PMHCN still just a 'twinkle in the eye', so it is not really possible to go much further in defining either role. Further research on both is required and doubtless there will be different 'solutions' for different prison settings (e.g. the two roles merging into one). What we can say for sure is that investment is needed in both, and in their absence, prisoners will continue to experience unnecessary distress and face an uncertain outlook in life.

References

All Party Parliamentary Group on Prison Health (2006) *The Mental Health Problem in UK HM prisons: A Report from the All-Party Parliamentary Group on Prison Health. London. House of Commons.* [Online]. Available from: http://www.scmh.org. uk/80256FBD004F3555/vWeb/flKHAL6VBJQE/$file/allparty_prison_health_report_nov06.pdf [Accessed 16 November 2007]

Birmingham L (2002) Commentary. *Adv Psychiatr Treat* **8**: 125–7

Brooker C, Repper J, Beverley C, Ferriter M, Brewer Nl (2002) *Mental Health Services and*

Prisoners: A Review. Commissioned by Prison Healthcare Taskforce. Department of Health/Home Office. Sheffield: ScHARR, University of Sheffield

Chitsabesan P, Kroll L, Bailey S, Kenning C, Sneider S, Macdonald W, Theodosiou L (2006) Mental health needs of young offenders in custody and in the community. *Brit J Psychiatry* **188**: 534–40

Dale C, Woods P (2001) *Caring for Prisoners: RCN Prison Nurses' Forum Roles and Boundaries Project. Royal College of Nursing: London* [Online] Available from: http://www.rcn.org.uk/members/downloads/prison_nurses_final_report.pdf#search=%2 2Caring%20for%20Prisoners%3A%20RCN%20Prison%20Nurses%20Forum%20Roles %20and%20Boundaries%20Project%20Colin%20Dale%20and%20Phil%20Woods%22 [Accessed 16 November 2007]

Department of Health (1999) *The Future Organisation of Prison Health Care.* Department of Health, London

Department of Health (2000) *The NHS Plan.* Department of Health, London

Department of Health (2002) *Mental Health Policy Implementation Guide: Community Mental Health Teams.* Department of Health, London

Department of Health (2005a) *Procedure for the Transfer of Prisoners To and From Hospital Under Sections 47 and 48 of the Mental Health Act (1983).* Department of Health, London

Department for Health (2005b) *Offender Mental Health Care Pathway.* Department of Health, London

Department of Health, Her Majesty's Prison Service (2001) *Changing the Outlook: A Strategy for Developing and Modernising Mental Health Services in Prisons* Department of Health, London

Durcan G (2006) Equivalent to what? Mental health care in Britain's prisons. *J Ment Health Workforce Development* **1**(4): 36–44

Durcan G (2008) *From the Inside: Experiences of Prison Mental Health Care.* Sainsbury Centre for Mental Health, London.

Durcan G, Knowles K (2006) *London's Prison Mental Health Services: A Review. SCMH: London.* [Online]. Available from: http://www.scmh.org.uk/80256FBD004F3555/ vWeb/flKHAL6N3GV4/$file/policy5_prison_mental_health_services.pdf [Accessed 16 November 2007]

Freshwater D, Walsh L, Storey L (2001) Prison health care: Developing leadership through clinical supervision. *Nurs Manag* **8**(8): 10–13

Gannon S (2002) A reflective view. In: Norman A, Parrish A (Eds) *Prison Nursing.* Blackwell: Oxford

Guite H, Field V (1997) Services for mentally disordered offenders. In: Johnson S, Ramsey R, Thornicroft G, Brooks L, Lelliott P, Peck E, Smith H, Chisholm D, Audini B, Knapp M, Gooldberg D (Eds) *London's Mental Health: The report to the Kings Fund London Commission.* Kings Fund, London

Her Majesty's Inspectorate of Prisons (1996) *Patient or Prisoner.* HMSO, London

Her Majesty's Inspectorate of Prisons (1997) *Women in Prison: A Thematic Review.* HMSO, London

Her Majesty's Inspectorate of Prisons (2003) *Report on Full Announced Inspection of HM Prison Lewes – 10–14 March 2003.* HMSO, London

Her Majesty's Inspectorate of Prisons (2005) *Report on a Full Announced Inspection of HM Young Offender Institution, Feltham: 15–20 May 2005*. HMSO, London

Her Majesty's Inspectorate of Prisons (2006a) *Report on an Unannounced Full Follow-up Inspection of HMP Pentonville – 7–16 June 2006*. HMSO, London

Her Majesty's Inspectorate of Prisons (2006b) *Report on an Unannounced Full Follow-up Inspection of HMP Brixton – 22 February–3 March 2006*. HMSO, London

Her Majesty's Inspectorate of Prisons (2007a) T*he Mental Health of Prisoners: A Thematic Review of the Care and Support of Prisoners with Mental Health Needs*. HMSO, London

Her Majesty's Inspectorate of Prisons (2007b) *Annual Report 2005–2006*. HMSO, London

Home Office (2006) *Prison Population Projections 2006–2013. England and Wales 11/06*. Home Office, London

House of Commons (2007) *Hansard Written Answers. 16 April 2007: Column 482W. House of Commons: London*. [Online]. Available from: http://www.publications.parliament. uk/pa/cm200607/cmhansrd/cm070416/text/70416w0106.htm [Accessed 16 November 2007]

International Centre for Prison Studies (2004) *Guidance Note 10: Improving Prison Health Care. In Guidance Notes for Prison Reform*. Kings College, London

Joint Committee on Human Rights (2004) *Joint Committee On Human Rights – Minutes of Evidence – Examination of Witnesses (Questions 140–159) – Monday 9 February 2004. House of Lords/House of Commons: London*. [Online]. Available from: http://www.publications.parliament.uk/pa/jt200405/jtselect/jtrights/15/4020903.htm [Accessed 16 November 2007]

Lader D, Singleton N, Meltzer H (2000) *Psychiatric Morbidity Amongst Young Offenders in England and Wales*. Office for National Statistics, London

Lines R (2006) From equivalence of standards to equivalence of objectives: The entitlement of prisoners to health care standards higher than those outside prisons. *Int J Prisoner Health* 2(4): 269–80

Mohan R, Fahey T (2006) Is there a need for community forensic mental health services? *J Forensic Psychiatry Psychol* 17(3): 365–71

National Offender Management Service (2007) *Prison Population and Accommodation Briefing, 28 September 2007* [Online] Available from: www.hmprisonservice.gov.uk/ resourcecentre/publicationsdocuments/index.asp?cat=85 [Accessed 16 November 2007]

NHS Executive HM Prison Service (2000) *Nursing in Prisons: Report by the Working Group Considering the Development of Prison Nursing, With Particular Reference to Health Care Officers*. Department of Health, London

NHS Executive HM Prison Service (1999) *The Future Organisation of Prison Health Care*. Department of Health, London

Niven S, Stewart D (2005) *Findings 248: Resettlement Outcomes on Release from Prison in 2003*. Home Office, London

Norman A, Parrish A (1999) Nursing in prisons is a poorly understood area of health care. *Nurs Manag* 6(6): 8–9

Norman A, Parrish A (2002) The role of the nurse in prison healthcare. In: Norman A, Parrish A (Eds) *Prison Nursing*. Blackwell, Oxford

Nurse J, Woodcock P, Ormsby J (2003) Influence of environmental factors on mental health within prisons: focus group study. *Brit Med J* **327**: 480–4

Polczyk-Przybla M, Gournay K (1999) Psychiatric nursing in prison: the state of the art? *J Adv Nurs* **30**(4): 893–900

Reed J (2003) Mental health care in prisons. *Brit J Psychiatry* **182**: 287–8

Reed J, Lyne M (2000) Inpatient care of mentally ill people in prison: results of a year's programme of semi-structured inspections. *Brit Med J* **320**: 1031–4

Rickford D (2003) *Troubled Inside: Responding to the Mental Health Needs of Women in Prison*. Prison Reform Trust, London

Rickford D, Edgar K (2005) *Troubled Inside: Responding to the Mental Health Needs of Men in Prison*. Prison Reform Trust, London

Rutherford M, Duggan S (2007) *Forensic Mental Health Services: Facts and Figures on Current Provision*. Sainsbury Centre for Mental Health, London

Sainsbury Centre for Mental Health (2007) *Mental Health Care in Prisons*. Sainsbury Centre for Mental Health, London

Sales B, McKenzie N (2007) Time to act on behalf of mentally disordered offenders. *Brit Med J* **334**: 1222

Singleton N, Bumpstead R, O'Brien M, Lee A, Meltzer H (2001) *Psychiatric Morbidity among Adults Living in Private Households, 2000*. London: Office of National Statistics.

Singleton N, Meltzer H, Gatward R (1998) *Psychiatric Morbidity Among Prisoners in England and Wales*. Office of National Statistics, London

Smith S, Baxter V, Humphreys M (2002) The interface between general and prison psychiatry – the consultants perception. *Psychiatr Bull* **26**: 130–2

Social Exclusion Unit (2002) *Reducing Re-offending by Ex-prisoners*. Social Exclusion Unit, London

Steel J, Thornicroft G, Birmingham L, Brooker C, Mills A, Harty M, Shaw J (2007) Prison mental health inreach services. *Brit J Psychiatry* **190**: 373–4

UKCC (1999) *Nursing in Secure Environments: A Scoping Study Conducted on Behalf of the UKCC by the Faculty of Health, University of Central Lancashire*. UKCC, London

Walsh L (2005) Developing prison health care through reflective practice. In: Freshwater D, Johns C (Eds) T*ransforming Nursing Through Reflective Practice* (2nd edn) Blackwell, Oxford

Williamson M (2006) *Improving the health and social outcomes of people recently released from prisons in the UK: A perspective from primary care*. SCMH: London. [Online]. Available from: http://www.scmh.org.uk/80256FBD004F3555/vWeb/flKHAL6SFKML/$file/scmh_health_care_after_prison.pdf [Accessed 16 November 2007]

World Health Organisation, International Red Cross (2005) *Information Sheet Mental Health and Prisons* [Online] Available from: http://www.who.int/mental_health/policy/mh_in_prison.pdf [Accessed 16 November 2007]

CHAPTER 17

Management of therapeutic boundaries

Cindy Peternelj-Taylor and Penny Schafer

Introduction

The ability to create and maintain therapeutic relationships with forensic clients has frequently been described as one of the most important competencies required by nurses working in secure environments. Relationships that are established are often tenuous and fraught with trials and tribulations unique to the forensic milieu. Nurses who work in forensic settings are often warned about getting 'too close' to their clients; an edict that is rarely coupled with guidance regarding how to become engaged in a manner that safely promotes the achievement of treatment goals.

Epstein (1994: 2) states 'any behaviour that infringes upon the primary goal of providing care' can be considered a boundary violation. Forensic nurses are frequently exposed to a multitude of clinical situations where threats to the integrity of the therapeutic relationship are present, as illustrated in their multiple roles and responsibilities, the complexity of the treatment needs experienced by forensic clients, the seductive pull of helping, the inherent power differential that exists between forensic clients and nurses, and the influence of the interpersonal climate unique to most forensic settings. In our quest to better understand the therapeutic relationship with forensic clients, we have previously explored issues related to boundary violations (Schafer, 1997, 2000; Peternelj-Taylor, 1998, 2002, 2003; Peternelj-Taylor and Yonge, 2003; Schafer and Peternelj-Taylor, 2003), and we have concluded that the creation and maintenance of therapeutic boundaries represents a complex interplay of treatment and ethical dilemmas, for which there are no easy answers.

In writing this chapter, we draw upon our clinical and educational experiences, our previous research and publications, and contemporary literature and ethical standards. We hope that readers will find our personal insights and recommendations to be helpful and thought provoking. Readers will not, however, find a 'how to' manual in this chapter, as we agree with Pope et al (1993: 179) who state, in reference to boundaries in the therapeutic relationship 'there are no clear one-size-fits-all answers'. Likewise, we do not expect that readers will agree with all we have to say, but we anticipate that what we say will invite further discourse on this sensitive topic. Ultimately, it is our hope that nurses will be challenged to reflect on their practice, when creating a therapeutic space for the forensic clients in their care.

The language of therapeutic boundaries

The importance of respecting boundaries in therapeutic relationships is widely recognised by mental health professionals (Herlihy and Corey, 2006). Everett and Gallop (2002: 299) have concluded that 'boundaries define the helping pathway – for both clients and professionals – and as such are integral to therapeutic effectiveness'. It is through the establishment of boundaries that a relational space is created whereby the nurse working with the client, is able to explore the client's treatment needs within the safety of the therapeutic relationship. By its very nature, the nurse–client relationship is asymmetrical, and the inherent power differential that exists between a nurse and a client cannot be overlooked; as those seeking help are automatically placed in a position of vulnerability. The vulnerability experienced by forensic clients is profound, and the power differential between nurses and clients exceeds that which is typically associated with the therapeutic relationship in general. As such, the creation and maintenance of therapeutic boundaries is recognised as a significant clinical challenge (Melia et al, 1999; Peternelj-Taylor, 2002; Schafer and Peternelj-Taylor, 2003).

Othering

The discourses of security, safety, risk, dangerousness, caring, and the language used to refer to clients, have the potential to shape relationships, to perpetuate binary conceptualisations of 'us and them', and, ultimately promote othering. Othering is about the way one perceives and engages with another person. Considering someone the other is not typically a negative act, as differences are inevitable (Derrida and Caputo, 1997). Othering can be inclusionary, based upon a recognition and appreciation of the other's differences, or exclusionary, whereby the other's differences are perceived in a hierarchical fashion, as we cast them into a position of less than (Canales, 2000). Most often though, othering tends towards negative sentiments and is often exclusionary in nature; it is how we engage those perceived to be different from the self that is potentially a negative act (Pagels, 1995; Canales, 2000). The other is unknowable to us, and thus is vulnerable to being reduced to that which is presented, such as social position, accomplishments (Burggraeve, 1999), or legal status. In the context of forensic mental health, clients are often cast into the role of 'other', as they are referred to in terms of their legal status of 'offender', 'inmate,' or 'prisoner' (Peternelj-Taylor, 2004).

Although a full discussion of othering is beyond the scope of this chapter, it is included here as a way of expanding our understanding of boundaries in therapeutic relationships, as othering is often associated with under-involvement, or a failure of engagement. Engagement, according to Bergum (2004: 496), is 'located in the shared moment when people have found a way to look at something together'. For Gadow (2003: 164), 'engagement involves openness to the possible validity of the other's perspective and vulnerability to being altered by that perspective'. However, when a forensic client is accused (or convicted) of committing a morally reprehensible act, the ability to commit to engagement in the therapeutic relationship can be especially difficult (Chaloner, 2000). This begs the questions: How do nurses engage clients perceived as different? How do they avoid othering and develop therapeutic relationships? Can nurses who work in secure environments be open to facing their own vulnerabilities in their relationships with clients? Or will acknowledgement of one's vulnerabilities be seen as one's downfall given the custodial philosophies that permeate most correctional and forensic environments?

Under-involvement

Under-involvement occurs when nurses fail to engage therapeutically with clients in their care. Unfortunately, in the forensic environment, under-involvement is often the accepted norm; as Maeve (1997) has observed, attempts to engage the 'other' empathetically may be viewed as one's downfall. When nurses engage in 'othering' in their work with clients, they fail to fulfil not only their ethical obligations, but also the conditions of the therapeutic relationship. Nurses rarely consider under-involvement as a boundary violation (Peternelj-Taylor, 2002). In fact in some situations, under-involvement is often justified as necessary for individual and institutional safety, as opposed to an unwillingness, or inability to risk the vulnerability necessary for engagement. It is our position that under-involvement is as offensive as over-involvement, and equally harmful to our clients, and to our profession.

Under-involvement is often the result of exclusionary othering in practice. When this type of othering occurs there is no space for the other. It is not our intention to imply that nurses should never experience strong reactions to their clients. On the contrary, strong emotional responses are inevitable.

Box 17.1: Strategies to identify and avoid under-involvement

- *Red flags of under-involvement*
  - Do you avoid scheduled interviews with your client?
  - Are treatment goals mutually established?
  - Are you present for significant milestones in your client's treatment?
  - When clients ask you personal information, are your responses based solely on policy (e.g. nurses should not engage in self-disclosure), or are you guided by a commitment to the client and his or her treatment goals?
  - How do you refer to the clients in your care? What labels do you use? Are you engaging in othering?
  - Do you provide meaningful feedback to your client?
- *Promote a sense of partnership with your clients.* Consider and acknowledge their perspectives; it lets them know they have been heard. Be sure to discuss alternative perspectives, including your own. Acknowledge differences.
- *Avoid othering.* Look beyond the legal status of your clients; they are more than prisoners, mentally disordered offenders, or criminals. Challenge your own and others tendencies to think in binary terms, such as, 'us' and 'them', 'good' or 'bad'.
- *Provide specific feedback.* Nonspecific positive feedback lacks meaning; specific constructive feedback related to treatment goals demonstrates your interest in the client's progress in treatment. Failing to respond following a client's significant self-disclosure during treatment may increase the vulnerability clients feel in their working relationship.
- *Be congruent.* Clients sense when you are incongruent, or when you are modifying your approach to avoid an anticipated negative reaction from them. Use a team approach when it is expected that clients will have a strong reaction to feedback. Share the rationale for the team approach with clients.
- *Have mutually developed treatment goals.* A common objective and direction helps to define roles and the relationship. Uncertainty regarding the objectives of the therapeutic relationship or the direction that you are taking in treatment, not only increases their confusion, but contributes to the vulnerability they experience.
- *Practice cultural safety.* Consider cultural differences in planning treatment.
- *Seek out clinical supervision and professional development opportunities.* Developing competence to work with forensic clients and being engaged in their care is challenging.
- *Develop personal resources.* Engaging a client group and considering the other, requires significant personal resources. It is easier to avoid engagement and be under-involved than risk the vulnerability that is required of engagement.

(For further information see Schafer, 2000)

As Haynes (2006) has observed, it is not uncommon to experience feelings of disgust, dislike, or repulsion, particularly in response to the criminal acts committed by some forensic clients. Nurses will experience strong emotional responses to their clients. Such reactions are often a reflection of the perceived difference between 'them' and 'us'. However, instead of thinking in such binary terms, the point we are trying to make here is that perceived or identified difference should be used to promote understanding, and such strong emotional responses to clients pursued and processed within the safety of clinical supervision. Strategies to facilitate the identification and avoidance of under-involvement are summarised in *Box 17.1*. Readers are encouraged to consider the relevance of these strategies within their own practice context.

Over-involvement

Over-involvement occurs when nurses fail to establish or maintain therapeutic boundaries, and instead use their relationship with the client to meet personal needs. Over-involvement in practice is frequently conceptualised as boundary violations, transgressions that are clearly harmful or exploitive. Simply stated: 'A boundary violation is a serious breach that causes harm. When a therapist's actions are harmful to or exploitive of a client, a violation has taken place' (Herlihy and Corey, 2006: 10). Over-involvement with forensic clients is often seen in the form of a romantic or sexual relationship; such relationships are perceived by most as an extreme boundary violation. Questions for further reflection are presented in *Box 17.2*.

Other forms of boundary violations can be equally damaging for the client. For example, artistic clients may be seen as a means for nurses to acquire a piece of unique artwork, something that they may not be able to afford otherwise. Nurses may also collect stories of violence and sensational cases, to fulfil personal curiosity, or to use for publication and professional recognition (Mercer and Richman, 2006). Other behaviours commonly

---

Box 17.2: Clinical contemplation

Sexual attraction to clients is a subject that is rarely discussed in the nursing literature. Consider how this phenomenon may apply to you.

- Have you experienced struggles with sexual attraction in your relationships with your forensic clients?
- If so, how did you deal with your feelings?
- What would you do if you found yourself attracted to a particular client?
- What would you do if a client was demonstrating attraction to you?

---

interpreted as boundary violations are articulated in relation to satisfaction of personal needs, self-disclosure, engaging in dual roles, the giving and receiving of gifts, and touch (Baer and Murdock, 1995). Boundaries are also described as the limits of the fiduciary relationship, 'one in which a person with particular knowledge and abilities accepts the trust and confidence of another to act in that person's best interest' (Penfold, 1998: 19). When forensic nurses are over-involved in their clients' care, the boundaries of the therapeutic relationship have been violated and nurses have failed to fulfil their fiduciary responsibilities. Given the multitude of issues experienced by forensic clients, coupled with their inherent vulnerability, we wonder if nurses should he held to a higher fiduciary responsibility with this population. Peplau (1989: 57) has concluded that regardless of the setting, or the problems experienced by the clientele: 'The professional is the keeper of the purpose of the therapeutic relationship which is to produce whatever improvements in health status possible for the client by suggesting pathways toward that end.'

The potential for boundary violations exists in all relationships; however, it is the intensity of the forensic environment that contributes to the immediacy of complicated relationships. Nurses are clearly influenced by the organisational context in which they find themselves, and thus, the impact of the physical and interpersonal environment on the therapeutic relationship cannot be ignored. Holmes and Federman (2006: 27) conclude that 'forensic psychiatric settings do not constitute a neutral institutional setting in which care takes place from the larger influences that operate within society'.

Impact of boundary violations

The potential harm that results from boundary violations in clinical practice is profound, not only for those clients and nurses directly involved, but also for those who bear witness.

Risks to forensic clients

Influential contextual factors of time, power, and gender were identified by the forensic clients in one study (Schafer, 2000; Schafer and Peternelj-Taylor, 2003). Clients in secure settings owe time, have time, and may use time as a way to assert themselves. Making time for a client was viewed as valuable by the participants. However, spending 'too much time' with a client could be perceived as a boundary violation (or over-involvement) by clients and management alike. In the case of the latter, this could lead to inappropriate policy development whereby time spent with clients is prescribed as a way of preventing boundary violations, as opposed to the clients' treatment needs determining the appropriate amount of time needed for therapeutic engagement.

Likewise, the power inequality between forensic clients and nurses is ever present, yet rarely understood as vulnerability. Nurses report on their clients' progress and influence decisions about placement, parole, and freedom. Furthermore, nurses hold the power to grant feelings. As a participant in a recent study declared, 'I don't have empathy, guilt, or remorse until such a time as a report says I do' (Schafer and Peternelj-Taylor, 2003: 614). This power differential may result in manipulative behaviours on the part of the clients, in order to avoid getting on the 'bad side' of their nurses. Yet, within the dominant discourses common to secure environments, manipulation is often seen as a defining characteristic of the client, as opposed to a way of retaining a sense of power, and managing the vulnerability associated with being in a relationship where a power differential exists.

Forensic clients are ill prepared for the intimacy of a therapeutic relationship, and they are seldom advised what is considered appropriate or inappropriate behaviour with staff. Even though they recognise the dangerousness of over-involvement, they experience uncertainties regarding how minor transgressions might be addressed. Boundary maintenance has been conceptualised here as a dynamic process, one that requires nurses to gain an appreciation of those behaviours that clients experience as boundary violations. Rarely do we afford our clients this opportunity. Instead, forensic clients are expected to know what is appropriate behaviour, and when they do not, they may be accused of testing limits or pushing the boundaries.

It is not uncommon for forensic clients to be positioned in terms of the threat they pose to nurses; clients are seen as perpetrators, nurses as victims. This is particularly so when the client is a male and the nurse female, and the boundary violation is of a sexual nature. Regrettably, this view of the nurse as a victim is one that is perpetuated in the forensic nursing literature, and by forensic mental health nurses themselves (Melia et al, 1999; Peternelj-Taylor and Yonge, 2003). Forensic clients have expressed confusion and vulnerability in regard to mixed messages regarding boundary violations. As one participant revealed, 'No one has ever told me what my boundaries are.' Like others in the study, he too feared that he could be blamed for any boundary transgressions that might occur during the course of treatment (Schafer, 2000; Schafer and Peternelj-Taylor, 2003). As such, those who experience boundary violations, are in essence, re-victimised when they are blamed and held responsible for the transgressions of the nurse; sadly, this may result in lost opportunities that treatment presents.

When boundaries are not clear, clients are reluctant to trust the nurse to manage transgressions professionally, and the vulnerability they experience is exacerbated, and their willingness to take risks, and to be open and honest within the therapeutic relationship, is reduced. Subsequently, their potential to benefit from treatment is limited. Instead they may just go with the flow, attempt not to make any waves, and hope for a good treatment report (Schafer and Peternelj-Taylor, 2003).

Boundary crossings are also relevant to this discussion. Boundary crossings such as nurses' self-disclosures or the use of touch may be conceptualised as a way of promoting the therapeutic relationship. Herlihy and Corey (2006: 10) stated, 'A boundary crossing is a departure from commonly accepted practice that might benefit the client.' However, boundary crossings may also lead to confusion on the part of the client, contribute to deterioration of the therapeutic relationship, and ultimately lead to boundary violations, especially if there is an increase in frequency and severity. Self-disclosure on the part of a nurse may facilitate client understanding and promote the therapeutic relationship; however, disclosures that mirror the nurse's needs may burden the client, and provoke a desire to help, as illustrated in role reversals (Schafer and Peternelj-Taylor, 2003).

Similarly, the use of touch can be equally confusing for clients, and although touch has been promoted as a therapeutic intervention in nursing in general, Wysoker (2000) has cautioned nurses to be cognisant of the fact that touch can be easily misinterpreted by clients. When contemplating the use of touch with forensic clients, nurses need to be aware of whose needs are being met, the nurse's or the client's? The following two case studies illustrate further the use of touch in practice. Readers are encouraged to reflect upon the following questions as they examine the issues raised by these cases:

- What are the needs of the client?
- Is the nurse's behaviour therapeutic for the client? Why/Why not?
- Does the nurse's behaviours make it more or less likely that the needs of all the clients will be met? Why/Why not?
- Are there boundary signs that might alert the nurse to a possible boundary violation?
- Should boundary issues such as these be addressed by agency policy? The nurse's professional judgement? Why/Why not?

(College of Registered Nurses of Alberta, 2005: 3).

Case study: Clinical illustrations of touch

Karen's dilemma

Karen, a registered nurse, worked on a forensic unit for clients with personality disorders. Touch, apart from a handshake was generally frowned upon on the unit, as it was often seen as a precursor to boundary violations in practice.

Peter, a client on the unit, had recently learned of the death of a close relative. During an interview with Karen, he broke down sobbing. His sobs, and obvious grief, provoked a strong desire in Karen to comfort and relieve not only Peter's distress, but her personal discomfort as well. Karen struggled with how to best respond. She had learned in nursing that touch can be therapeutic, especially during times of grief. She thought that by using touch, she would at least be demonstrating a desire to help Peter, and thereby avoid her own distress of not responding. Peter was sitting in a chair with his head tipped up to the ceiling and legs stretched out in front of him. He was covering his face with his arms, making it impossible for Karen to touch his hand therapeutically without stretching out over his body. Instead, in an attempt to comfort Peter she briefly touched his knee.

Later that day, Peter was scheduled to meet with another member of his treatment team. However, he insisted that Karen was the only one who could help him. Following a meeting with more experienced team members, Karen learned that her use of touch was not interpreted by Peter as an act of comfort, but instead he was confused by her gesture, and thought that she was attracted to him. For Peter, Karen's touch had been experienced as a violation of the therapeutic relationship.

Karen apologised to Peter, and clarified with him that her intention had been to offer comfort in a time of distress, and was not meant to be a demonstration of affection.

Sandra's need for touch

The treatment team on a forensic unit designed to meet the needs of female forensic clients, identified that Sandra, a patient with a long history of impulsive behaviour, often resulting in assaults on staff, was deteriorating. Described as dangerous, staff were advised to approach her with caution.

Morgan, a registered psychiatric nurse, was facilitating a social skills group, and although Sandra was not a regular member, she joined the group. There were times in the group where she experienced difficulty managing herself, and the other group members were aware of this tension. Following termination of the group, Sandra stayed in the room to talk further with Morgan. Morgan suggested to her that she was vulnerable. When Sandra asked Morgan what she meant, Morgan told her that she thought she was vulnerable to use violence. Sandra visibly relaxed as noted by her posture, and agreed with Morgan that she was in fact having a difficult time. Morgan continued to talk with Sandra, and as their discussion was drawing to a close, Sandra asked Morgan for a hug. Morgan remembered reading that for touch to be perceived as therapeutic, it is often best initiated by the client, as the client remains in control of the touch; and that touch should always be followed up by therapeutic dialogue.

Following this brief review, Morgan decided to give Sandra a hug (with the intention to let go as soon as she did). As Morgan hugged her, she shared her observation that she was now holding her, in order to initiate a dialogue about the touch. She responded by saying, 'I know. It is what I need.' Following, this encounter, Morgan sought out clinical supervision, and documented this encounter in Sandra's chart. Feedback received during clinical supervision, coupled with Sandra's comment, confirmed for Morgan that the touch had been perceived as therapeutic, and not a boundary violation. With the support of Morgan and the treatment team, Sandra made it through a very difficult time in her life without resorting to violence.

Risks to other forensic clients

In addition to the clients who experience the victimisation of boundary violations, other clients on the unit may also experience negative consequences, as a 'ripple effect' can result, especially in closed systems (Herlihy and Corey, 2006), such as hospitals, forensic psychiatric units, and prisons.

In our experiences, clients are very aware of boundary violations that occur in practice, particularly in regard to sexual transgressions that may occur between a nurse and a client (Peternelj-Taylor, 2002; Schafer and Peternelj-Taylor, 2003). It is not uncommon for clients, not directly involved in the boundary violation, to experience resentment to those with 'special' relationships. In the case of over-involvement, the context of the therapeutic relationship is impacted at a system level, and there may be a reluctance to speak out for fear of negative reprisals (Herlihy and Corey, 2006). Furthermore, access to one-to-one interview time may be restricted, and the dynamics of the treatment groups and therapeutic ambiance in the environment altered. In secure environments over-involvement may be further conceptualised as a security concern, as opposed to an issue of clinical supervision. In such cases, clients on the unit may find themselves being interviewed for the purpose of an investigation, losing treatment time, and spending more time engaged in the pathology producing sub-culture that exists in many forensic settings (particularly prison settings).

Risks to nurses

When a nurse's boundary transgressions are exposed, the therapeutic relationship is damaged. An over-involved nurse is less likely to be able to remain objective, and may form alliances with particular clients, or groups of clients. When this occurs, the safety of the nurse, other clients, and other staff is jeopardised. Love (2001) has reported that staff who have become romantically involved with forensic clients have, in many situations, become victims of violent crimes.

Moreover, it is not uncommon for nurses to experience embarrassment, loss of professional integrity, and loss of professional friends and colleagues. In forensic settings, nurses who become over-involved in their client's care often have their contracts terminated (as their behaviours are frequently perceived as a safety issue), resign under the threat of an internal investigation (or before they are found out), and/or they may move out of the jurisdiction altogether (Peternelj-Taylor, 1998, 2003). And although, nurses may be reported to their professional licensing bodies, and have their licenses to practise suspended (or revoked), in our experiences, employers have not consistently reported offending nurses. It is almost as though a double standard exists, when forensic clients are involved, particularly when the client is male and the nurse female.

Effects on other nurses and the profession

Collins (1989) has noted, once a boundary violation is exposed in practice, there is always someone ready to declare, 'I could have told you so!' or 'I could see that coming!' However, if boundary erosion is in fact, so obvious, what stops nurses (and others) from intervening to prevent such violations from occurring in the first place? Twemlow (1997) observes that in all instances of serious boundary violations (i.e. sexual exploitation), warning signs indicating problems in the relationship had been present, but normally only perceived by others after the fact. It is not uncommon for colleagues to be in shock or disbelief following the disclosure of a significant boundary violation, especially when the nurse involved is a respected colleague. Those bearing witness often experience they own insecurities, in part due to the anxiety manifested in the thought, 'There but for the grace of God go I' (Gabbard, 1995). Herlihy and Corey (2006) have observed that when therapists learn of a colleague's involvement in a boundary violation, they are often torn between speaking up, or retreating in silence.

Clearly, confronting a colleague is never an easy or comfortable task, and a schism often exists between what one should do and what one actually does (Peternelj-Taylor, 2003). Frais (2001) has acknowledged that 'a powerful culture of loyalty' typically exists among practitioners, which fuels a 'conspiracy of silence' as described by Penfold (1998). For example, in practice, it is not uncommon for nurses (and others) to secretly hope that by avoiding speaking out, the issue just might go away. In doing so, they adopt a variety of rationalisations in an attempt to cope with the discomfort experienced by a colleague's unethical behaviour. They avoid seeing what is going on around them, they ignore

---

Box 17.3: Clinical contemplation

In recent years the nursing profession has become more attune to the importance of boundaries in the therapeutic relationship. Boundary violations that occur in practice can be particularly difficult for other health professionals.
- How would you approach a colleague who you suspected was struggling to maintain therapeutic boundaries with a client in his or her care?
- How would you like to be approached if you were the one struggling?

---

their gut feelings, they dismiss rumours as gossip (without exploring their underlying message further), and they minimise the impact of the offending nurse's behaviour, especially in relation to under-involvement (Dwyer, 1994; Plaut, 1997; Peternelj-Taylor, 2002, 2003). The reader is encouraged to reflect on the questions presented in *Box 17.3*, and to discuss these further with colleagues.

Nurses may consciously choose not to speak up for fear of being labelled a whistleblower. McDonald and Ahern (2000: 314), have defined a whistleblower as one 'who identifies an incompetent, unethical, or illegal situation in the workplace, and reports it to someone who may have the power to stop the wrong'. In the forensic setting, whistleblowing can generate turmoil within the workplace and disrupt the status quo, it can undermine the morale and trust within a particular team or health care agency, and it can lead to an ambiance of mutual suspicion where all staff members' behaviours are viewed as suspect (Peternelj-Taylor, 2003). In an earlier study, Fisher (1995), found that when working with clients with a known history of violence, getting along with colleagues often took precedence over speaking up and doing what might be perceived as the right thing to do, as members of staff depended upon one another for their own personal safety. Such factors are indeed powerful deterrents to speaking up. However, both the Canadian Nurses Association (CNA) (2008) and Nursing and Midwifery Council (NMC) (2008) address the responsibilities required of professional nurses. For example, the CNA (2008: 9) in its Code of Ethics for Registered Nurses states:

Nurses question and intervene to address unsafe, non-compassionate, unethical or incompetent practice or conditions that interfere with their ability to provide safe, compassionate, competent and ethical care to those to whom they are providing care, and they support those who do the same.

Likewise, the Nursing and Midwifery Council (2008: 11) in its Code states, in relation to managing risk that nurses must act without delay if they believe that they, a colleague or anyone else may be putting someone at risk.

Box 17.4: Clinical contemplation

- How does one find an appropriate balance between over-involvement and under-involvement in the forensic milieu?
- What potential risks might be associated with coming to know the forensic client, given the inherent vulnerability that resides within engagement?

Transforming practice through nursing leadership

The implications for nursing practice, education, and research, are discussed from a perspective of nursing leadership, one in which leadership is viewed as a collective responsibility of individual nurses, managers, professional bodies, and educators.

Individual leadership

Given the complex and multifaceted clinical challenges our clients experience, the development of clinical competence is essential to effective nursing practice. Engagement requires the ability to be vulnerable. Putting our identities at risk in our interactions with others, is the kind of vulnerability we must develop the capacity for. We must avoid the tendency to think in dual opposites of 'good' and 'bad,' and the temptation to attribute to the other, characteristics we find unacceptable in ourselves, in order to regard ourselves as good (Kitzinger and Wilkinson, 1996). Recognising that this is a shared vulnerability and that others are dependent on us for recognition, awakens us to our responsibility to the other, reduces the power difference in our relationships with clients, and, ultimately promotes engagement. Two critical reflection questions are presented in *Box 17.4*, for the reader to think about and discuss with colleagues

When the establishment and maintenance of boundaries are not enacted in practice, then rules are often outlined. The development of rules or guidelines may on the surface appear as an attractive solution to complex practice issues. However, the potential also exists for the implementation of rules and guidelines to hinder the development of therapeutic relationships, as strict adherence to rules and guidelines can result in a de-contextualisation of the relationship, thereby fostering a cookie cutter approach that denies nurses the opportunity to develop clinical judgement. Austin et al (2006: 83) have concluded that 'strict rules can perpetuate the idea that professionals need to rely primarily on external constraints to do what is right'. This is especially problematic if a standard response to unethical behaviour results. Instead, the establishment and maintenance of therapeutic boundaries is a dynamic process. Nurses need to be able to draw upon their ongoing

Box 17.5: Strategies to promote boundary maintenance

- Be aware of red flags such as:
  - Sharing and keeping secrets with your client
  - Spending more time with your client (e.g. starting early, staying late, extending interviews)
  - Disclosing personal information to your client
  - Believing that you are the only one who can meet the client's needs
  - Engaging in flirtations or sexual banter
  - Be cautious of the client who pays special attention to you:
    'You are such a good nurse'
    'You are the only one who understands me'
    'I would never have gotten into trouble if I had someone like you in my life'
- Do not become dependent on your clients to meet your social needs. Have a good, intact, and separate social life.
- Avoid inappropriate self-disclosure. If used appropriately, self-disclosure can be very therapeutic. Self-disclosure that meets the needs of the nurse, not the client, can burden the client and lead to role reversal.
- Examine potential boundary violations by engaging in routine 'spot checks'. Ask yourself the following questions:
  - 'Am I treating this client differently?'
  - 'What do I do when I am attracted to a client, or when a client is attracted to me? How do I set the boundaries?'
  - 'Am I having my intimacy needs met through my relationship with my clients?'
  - 'How might my actions be viewed by other clients? My colleagues? My supervisor? My profession?'
  - 'Am I doing this for the client's benefit or to meet a need of my own? And if I think I am doing this for the client's benefit, am I fooling myself?'
  - 'When in doubt about my actions, do I note my concerns? Seek out clinical supervision? Consult with more experienced colleagues?'
- Talk to trusted colleagues. Be honest with yourself regarding your feelings about clients. Talking to trusted colleagues and supervisors will assist you in sorting out complex dilemmas, and will promote effective boundary maintenance.
- Seek out clinical supervision. This is an effective risk management strategy, one that can assist with the management of feelings related to the nurse–client relationship, and prevent the gradual erosion of boundaries.
- Contribute to meaningful practice guidelines. Realistically, guidelines for every situation are unlikely. However, hypothetical scenarios can be used to educate team members and invite differing views and recommendations for practice.

(For further information see Peternelj-Taylor and Yonge, 2003)

knowledge of the client, their past experiences, and their interpersonal skills to engage the client in the establishment of mutually defined treatment goals, and together determine a course of action that is based on the client's best interests. Strategies to promote boundary maintenance are highlighted in *Box 17.5*. Readers are once again encouraged to consider the relevance of these strategies within the context of their own practice.

Nursing management

Nursing management has a critical role to play in fostering a culture that promotes a supportive work environment where staff of all disciplines can acknowledge, discuss and examine their feelings in relation to boundary dilemmas that will inevitably occur in practice. However, in an attempt to reduce the potential for boundary violations with forensic clients, resulting from either over- or under-involvement, a more rigid approach often prevails. Managers may create and enforce policy dictating the frequency and length of interviews, self-disclosure, and touch. When policy, as opposed to treatment needs, frame nurse–client interactions, therapeutic relationships may take longer to develop, and nurses may become over-reliant on policies to establish and maintain boundaries. Inexperienced nurses (including students) may find it easier to explain a reluctance to self-disclose in terms of policy, versus developing clinical competence in practice. For example, referring to a given policy as the rationale for not disclosing personal information, is significantly different than asking clients what it would mean to them, to know more about the nurse. The former communicates that adherence to policy is a priority, for if not for policy, the nurse would disclose. The latter communicates that the client's needs are central to the developing relationship, and, as such fosters the development and maintenance of boundaries, and the therapeutic relationship.

Developing a culture that promotes clinical competence in all practitioners is a collective responsibility of nurses and managers alike. And although well-crafted policies and clinical guidelines complement good practice, they alone cannot take the place of clinical supervision. Peplau (1952) was an early advocate of clinical supervision in nursing. Unfortunately, clinical supervision is rarely formalised in nursing, when compared to other disciplines, and is often left to the direct line manager who is also responsible for the completion of annual performance appraisals. For supervision to be truly effective, it should be undertaken by someone other than the nurse's direct line supervisor, for the power differential that exists between a manager and a nurse by design places the nurse in a position of vulnerability (Peternelj-Taylor and Yonge, 2003). Instead, clinical supervision should be undertaken as a formal process whereby the supervisee–supervisor relationship is embraced to assist the supervisee in managing how to deal with the emotions of caregiving and the complexities of boundary maintenance. Staff who are uncertain about their professional responsibilities and ethical obligations, may seek out the advice of others, or simply keep their dilemmas to themselves. In our work, we have often recommended that in the absence of formalised clinical supervision, nurses should seek out trusted colleagues for guidance. Unfortunately, the resources that they seek out independently may lack the competence to provide effective clinical supervision, and as such, we remain staunch advocates of formal clinical supervision in forensic nursing practice.

Furthermore, nurse managers who are open to thinking laterally are more likely to support new or alternative approaches that would complement clinical supervision. In addressing the potential problems and ethical dilemmas that may arise in the course of one's work, a variety of approaches have been proposed and implemented in practice. For example, Rushton et al (1996) have promoted the adoption of accountability partners in practice, while Baron (2001), on the other hand, has advocated for group supervision. The most novel approach documented in the literature however, is the triumvirate model proposed by Melia et al (1999). All three approaches are designed to provide staff with supportive feedback and clinical guidance, and can easily be adapted to a variety of settings.

When determining client assignments, nurse managers need to find the appropriate match between clients and nurses, and ensure that the most clinically challenging clients are assigned to work with the most experienced and competent staff. In so doing, they need to recognise that errors will be made, even among experienced staff. All too often, nurses have learned about boundaries through trial and error. Boundary creation and maintenance needs to be seen as a dynamic process embedded within the therapeutic relationship. Given the complexities inherent in the therapeutic relationship, all staff will require support and assistance to grow and mature as forensic nurses. Managers, through the inherent power within their roles, are responsible for providing time for professional development sessions, and for clinical supervision.

Finally, nurse managers are responsible for fostering a culture where therapeutic involvement is the expected norm and under- or over-involvement considered unacceptable. Embracing an attitude of working *with* staff, through the creation of a culture that supports mentoring at all levels of the organisation, will contribute to the transformation of the workplace. Such an approach will see novice nurses being coached as they embrace new roles and experience clinical challenges, while seasoned nurses will be engaged in a meaningful way through their contribution to the professional development of less experienced nurses. This is a win-win situation for all involved, one in which retention of nurses in practice is promoted (Bally, 2007).

Role of professional codes and standards for practice

Herlihy and Corey (2006) have observed that professions themselves can be damaged by the unethical conduct of their individual members, which has resulted in further attention being directed to the intricacies of the therapeutic relationship in various codes of ethics guiding health professionals. Storch (2007), in a review of professional codes, has concluded that codes of ethics: (1) provide guidance to nurses regarding their ethical responsibilities (including relationships, behaviours, and decision making); (2) inform others (health care professionals, providers, and the public) about the moral obligations of nurses; (3) provide a tool for self-reflection and evaluation of nursing within an ethical framework; and (4) offer directives for the development of standards and policies. Codes of ethics for nursing, such as the Code of Ethics for Registered Nurses (CNA, 2008) and the NMC Code of Professional Conduct: Standards for Conduct, Performance and Ethics (NMC, 2004), are invaluable to nursing practice. For example, consider the following excerpts:

Nurses maintain appropriate professional boundaries and ensure their relationships are always for the benefit of the persons they serve. They recognize the potential vulnerability of personas and do not exploit their trust and dependency in a way that might compromise the therapeutic relationship. They do not abuse their relationship for personal or financial gain, and do not enter into personal relationships (romantic, sexual, or other) with persons in their care.

(CNA, 2008: 13)

You must establish and actively maintain clear sexual boundaries at all times with people in your care, their families and carers.

(NMC, 2008: 5)

Critics of codes of ethics contend that codes alone are not sufficient in promoting ethical practice, and such declarative statements as those cited above may be viewed as rigid prescriptions. However, codes have generally been designed to provide practitioners with a broad or general framework, and rarely address the idiosyncrasies of particular practice areas, or specific dilemmas. Instead, they are intended to be used in conjunction with professional judgement within clinical practice which takes into account such variables as context, theoretical orientation, standards for practice, and culture. In short, codes alone do not promote ethical practice; instead they provide a springboard or a platform for further education and dialogue regarding matters of concern (Storch, 2007). Forensic nurses need to be ongoing participants in this dialogue.

Role of nursing education

It is the responsibility of nursing education programmes to ensure that the next generation of nurses has the background to approach boundary maintenance in a competent and self-assured manner. Issues surrounding the creation and maintenance of boundaries and the prevention of boundary violations must be an integral component of all nursing curricula (theory, practice, and supervision in practice) (Herlihy and Corey, 2006; Hughes and Farrow, 2005; Peternelj-Taylor and Yonge, 2003).

Hughes and Farrow (2005) believe that boundary workshops should be provided for all nurses, whereby increased awareness and open dialogue contribute to discussion and professional debate. Education surrounding treatment boundaries also promotes competence in clinical practice. The National Council's Sexual Misconduct Task Force (1996: 6) has concluded,

> *Nursing faculty have the opportunity to nurture the growth of professionalism among their students. This kind of foundation for caring, within appropriate professional boundaries, will serve students well throughout their nursing careers.*

Utilising the therapeutic relationship as a foundation for learning, Gallop (1998) has concluded that education surrounding the appropriate management of therapeutic boundaries is not a one-time venture, rather it needs to occur at varying points in the educational process (undergraduate, graduate, and continuing professional development), and reinforced in practice.

Research that addresses issues in practice, education, and administration is required as a way of gaining further insight into boundaries within the therapeutic relationship and to guide forensic nursing practice.

As we bring this chapter to a close, we would like to share the words of forensic clients who candidly shared their thoughts, feelings, and experiences of boundary maintenance in the therapeutic relationship in a qualitative study designed specifically to access their perspectives. The following hypothetical letter, composed by Schafer (2000), represents the participants' collective experiences and is included herein as a way of furthering reflective thought regarding the establishment and maintenance of therapeutic boundaries.

Clients' views of boundary maintenance

Dear Forensic Mental Health Nurse,

Adjusting to the treatment environment and the therapeutic relationship is a challenge for us. Initially the friendliness of all staff is confusing and reason for suspicion. For many of us, such frequently friendly contact with staff, particularly attractive attentive females, is new, and, although not unwelcome, is awkward. With time we come to see that we are not being set up and that no one means us harm. We come to believe in your good intentions. We are, however, afraid to be vulnerable with you, while recognising that trusting you is the only way to complete treatment. The intention of the following suggestion is not to make you feel bad or to insult your professional integrity. Instead, it is our hope to enlighten you regarding our perspective. Let our words be a gift to you, given in recognition of all you do to help us, and with an awareness of your commitment to continually improve the treatment you provide.

Recognise the power you hold. You hold the key to our futures. We may not act or look like we are vulnerable but we are. Our desire to return to our communities and families colours our worlds. We are likely to do what it takes to get a good report, one that will take us one step closer to home. We trust in you to lead us in the right direction. When the direction is not clear we may assume that being respectful and not causing you trouble is what it takes to get a good report, but we are not sure. It is demeaning, when we don't know what we are aiming for, or where we are going. Be sure to let us know when we are on track, and give us meaningful feedback. It is nice to hear we are doing 'awesome', but when everything is awesome to you, we worry that we are not receiving the feedback we need to reach our goals and stay out of prison.

We recognise that we may not always seem grateful for the feedback we receive. However, we ask that you take a risk and be direct with us. It is frustrating when we can see that you are not being direct. It tells us that you have little confidence in our ability to consider what you have to say, that you may be afraid of us, that you think we are fragile, or that perhaps you are overly concerned about being nice. Know that we are not made of glass, we will not break.

Recognise that although we have irrational thoughts, we are not totally irrational. If we cross the line, believing that the relationship we have with you goes beyond our roles (as client and nurse), recognise your influence on the relationship that has emerged. Let us know that we have crossed the line, and, by all means, set us straight. No one tells us where our boundaries are, or where the line is drawn. Not knowing, we assume the responsibility is yours. Yet it seems we are held responsible to maintain a line we cannot see. Betrayal and confusion are the least of the consequences that we face when a line is crossed. We know of others before us who have been shipped out (e.g. returned to prison) and lost the opportunity to complete their treatment. We also know of romantic relationships between nurses and clients that have developed. Generally, we know the risk is not worth the consequences, but the opportunity to be someone other than an inmate, or a forensic client – to be a gentleman – can be a seductive pull for some of us.

Even the prospect of intelligent conversation is appealing. Relationships where we can be equals with you and talk about something other than drugs and crime is what we may want. And although some us may protest when you insist on keeping the focus on our treatment, know that by being consistent you show us that window of opportunity that treatment can be. We come to welcome a relationship where nothing is expected of us, other than to use the time together to help ourselves. It sounds selfish, but it feels wonderful. Here we learn more than how to challenge our distorted thoughts, you show us a way of being with others, that we want to take to our future relationships.

Remember that touch is foreign to some of us. If your shoulder brushes my chest as you lean towards me making a funny comment, it is nice but awkward. Who is watching, how will it be interpreted, and who can initiate touch, are all questions that touch raises for us. Yes, our perceptions may be distorted; knowing this about us, is it not advisable to limit touching to shaking our hands? Or at least be prepared to discuss touch with us, and if we have misinterpreted it, assist us to understand.

Some of us like to know a little about you. It helps to reduce the inequality we feel in our relationships. Even sharing a past personal experience may help us, but sharing your current problems with us may provoke a desire in us to be your hero. Conversely, it may diminish our perception of you as able to help. Be careful, some of you play with fire, and are crossing the line when you disclose too much. There are a few among us who are playing the game, and may be looking to exploit you.

Listening and being there for the significant periods in our treatment tells us you are interested in us, and not just your pay cheque. Know that if you are not present, we may not challenge you to work with us. We are not all here out of a genuine desire to change. However, feeling coerced and fearing a negative report we may just go with the flow, stay out of your way, not cause you too much trouble, and hope for the best. When you listen to us, we feel like we have a voice, when you include our perspective in your reports we know we have been heard and that our interests in the treatment processes recognised. To have no voice is to be nobody. Listen to us; let us know that we are more than a number to you.

Be sensitive to cultural differences. Accept that for some of us a traditional approach to healing is more comfortable. We benefit from your treatment programmes, but struggle to find a balance between your programme, cultural programmes, and ourselves. Show us that you are prepared to meet us half way. It helps us to accept you.

Lastly, remember always that you are a nurse and not a guard. Know too that we watch you to see if you are consistent with what you say. Your credibility with us is reduced when you tell us one thing, yet do another.

Thank you for your consideration. Respectfully submitted.

Sincerely,

Forensic patients

Conclusion

In this chapter we invited you to consider how our professional insights might be applied to your practice with forensic clients. In our experiences, the creation and maintenance of boundaries with forensic clients represents a complex and dynamic process for which there are no easy answers, and we often feel we have more questions than answers. Finally, we wish to reaffirm our beliefs that the vulnerability experienced by forensic clients engaged in therapeutic relationships is extreme. As such, nurses have the responsibility to develop interpersonal competence in working with forensic patients, and not take the nature of the therapeutic relationship for granted. Finally, readers are encouraged to think about their own clients, consider their own clinical experiences, and ultimately, draw their own conclusions regarding the management of therapeutic boundaries in the forensic milieu.

References

Austin W, Bergum V, Nuttgens S, and Peternelj-Taylor C (2006) A re-visioning of boundaries in professional helping relationsips: Exploring other metaphors. *Ethics Behav* **16**(2): 77–94

Baer BE, Murdoch NL (1995) Nonerotic dual relationships between therapists and clients: The effects of sex, theoretical orientation, and interpersonal boundaries. *Ethics and Behavior* **5**:131–45

Bally JMG (2007)The role of nursing leadership in creating a mentoring culture in acute care environments. *Nurs Econ* **25**(3): 143–8

Baron S (2001) Boundaries in professional relationships. *J Amer Psychiatric Nurses Assoc* **7**(1): 32–4

Bergum V (2004) Relational ethics in nursing. In Storch JL, Rodney P, Starsomski R (Eds) *Toward a Moral Horizon: Nursing Ethics for Leadership and Practice* (pp. 485–503). Pearson Prentice Hall, Toronto

Burggraeve R (1999) Violence and the vulnerable face of the other: The vision of Emanuel Levinas on moral evil and our responsibility. *J Soc Philos* **30**(1): 29–45

Canadian Nurses Association (2008) *Code of Ethics for Registered Nurses.* Canadian Nurses Association, Ottawa

Canales M (2000) Othering: Toward an understanding of difference. *Adv Nurs Sci* **22**(4): 16–31

Chaloner C (2000) Ethics and morality. In: Chaloner C, Coffey M (Eds) *Forensic Mental Health Nursing: Current Approaches* (pp 269–87) Blackwell Science, Oxford

College and Association of Registered Nurses of Alberta (2005) *Professional Boundaries: A Discussion Guide and Teaching Tool.* College and Association of Registered Nurses of

Alberta, Edmonton

Collins DT (1989) Sexual involvement between psychiatric hospital staff and their patients In: Gabbard GO (Ed) *Sexual Exploitation in Professional Relationships* (pp 151–62) American Psychiatric Press, Washington

Derrida J, Caputo JD (1997) *Deconstruction in a Nutshell: A Conversation With Jacques Derrida*. Fordham University Press, New York

Dwyer J (1994) Primum non tacere: An ethics of speaking up. *Hastings Centre Report* **24**(1): 13–18

Epstein RS (1994) *Keeping Boundaries: Maintaining Safety and Integrity in the Psychotherapeutic Process*. American Psychiatric Press, Washington, DC

Everett B, Gallop R (2001) *The Link Between Childhood Trauma and Mental Illness*. Sage Publications, Thousand Oaks, CA

Fisher A (1995) The ethical problems encountered in psychiatric nursing practice with dangerous mentally ill persons. *Scholarly Inquiry for Nurs Pract* **9**(2): 193–208

Frais A (2001) Whistleblowing: Heroes – boon or burden? *Bull Med Ethics* **170**: 13–19

Gabbard GO (1995) Transference and countertransference in the psychotherapy of therapists charged with sexual misconduct. *Psychiatric Annals* 35(2): 100–5

Gadow S (2003) Restorative nursing: Toward a philosophy of postmodern punishment. *Nurs Philos* **4**: 161–7

Gallop R (1998) Post discharge social contact: A potential area for boundary violation. *J Amer PsychiatrNurses Assoc* **4**(4): 105–9

Haynes R (2006) Managing multiple relationships in a forensic setting. In: Herlihy B, Corey G (Eds) *Boundary Issues in Counseling: Multiple Roles and Responsibilities* (2nd edn) (Ch 9 pp 170–3) American Counseling Association, Alexandria, VA

Herlihy B, Corey B (2006) *Boundary Issues in Counseling: Multiple Roles and Responsibilities* (2nd edn). American Counseling Association, Alexandria

Holmes D, Federman G (2006) Organisations as Evil Structures. In: Mason T (Ed) *Forensic Psychiatry: Influences of Evil* (pp 15–30) The Humana Press Inc, Totowa

Hughes M, Farrow T (2005) Invisible borders: Sexual misconduct in nursing. *Nurs Praxis NZ* **21**(2): 15–25

Kitzinger C, Wilkinson S (1996) *Representing the Other: A feminism and psychology Reader*. Sage, London

Love CC (2001) Staff–patient erotic boundary violations: Part one – staff factors. *On the Edge: The Official Newsletter of the International Association of Forensic Nurses* **7**(3): 4–7

Maeve MK (1997) Nursing practice with incarcerated women: Caring within mandated (sic) alienation. *Issues in Ment Health Nurs* **18**: 495–519

McDonald S, Ahern K (2000) The professional consequences of whistleblowing by nurses. *J Prof Nurs* **16**(6): 313–21

Melia P, Moran T, Mason T (1999) Triumvirate nursing for personality disordered patients: Crossing the boundaries safely. *J Psychiatr Ment Health Nurs* **6**(1): 15–20

Mercer D, Richman J (2006) Scapegoat, spectacle and confessional: Close encounters with sex offenders and other species of dangerous individuals. In: Mason T (Ed) *Forensic Psychiatry: Influences of Evil*. The Humana Press Inc, Totowa

National Council's Sexual Misconduct Task Force (1996) Raising awareness of professional boundaries and sexual misconduct. Nursing faculty are encouraged to take a proactive role.

National Council Publications **17**(2): 1–7

Nursing and Midwifery Council (2008) *The Code: Standards of Conduct, Performance and Ethics for Nurses and Midwives.* Nursing and Midwifery Council, London

Pagels E (1995) *The Origin of Satan.* Ramdon House, New York

Penfold PS (1998) *Sexual Abuse by Health Professionals.* University of Toronto Press: Toronto, ON

Peplau HE (1952) *Interpersonal Relations in Nursing.* GP Putnam's Sons: New York, NY

Peplau HE (1989) Interpersonal constructs for nursing practice. In: O'Toole AW, Welt SR (Eds) *Interpersonal Rheory in Nursing Practice: Selected Works of Hildegard E Peplau* (pp 42–55) Springer Publishing Company, New York, NY

Peternelj-Taylor C (1998) Forbidden love: Sexual exploitation in the forensic milieu. *J Psychosoc Nurs Ment Health Serv* **36**(6): 17–23

Peternelj-Taylor C (2002) Professional boundaries: A matter of therapeutic integrity. *J Psychosoc Nurs Ment Health Serv* **40**(4): 22–9

Peternelj-Taylor C (2003) Whistleblowing and boundary violations: Exposing a colleague in the Forensic Milieu. Nurs Ethics **10**(5): 526–537

Peternelj-Taylor C (2004) An exploration of othering in forensic psychiatric and correctional nursing. Can J Nurs Res **36**(4): 130–46

Peternelj-Taylor C, Yonge O (2003) Exploring boundaries in the nurse–client relationship: Professional roles and responsibilities. *Perspectives in Psychiatric Care* **39**(2): 55–66

Plaut SM (1997) Boundary violations in professional–client relationships: Overview and guidelines for prevention. *Sexual and Marital Ther* **12**(1): 77–94

Pope KS, Sonne JL, Holroyd J (1993) *Sexual Feelings in Psychotherapy.* American Psychological Association, Washington

Rushton CH, Armstrong L, McEnhill M (1996) Establishing therapeutic boundaries as patient advocates. *Pediatr Nurs* **22**: 185–9

Schafer PE (1997) When a client develops an attraction: Successful boundary resolution versus boundary violation. *J Psychiatr Ment Health Nurs* **4**: 203–11

Schafer P (2000) *Therapeutic Relationships and Boundary Maintenance: The Perspective of Forensic Patients Enrolled in the Aggressive Behaviour Control Program.* Masters Thesis, University of Saskatchewan: Saskatoon, Saskatchewan, Canada

Schafer P, Peternelj-Taylor C (2003) Therapeutic relationship and boundary maintenance: The perspective of forensic patients enrolled in a treatment program for violent offenders. *Issues in Ment Health Nurs* **24**: 605–25

Storch JL (2007) Enduring values in changing times: The CNA code of ethics. *Can Nurse* **103**(4): 29–37

Twemlow SW (1997) Exploitation of patients: Themes in the psychopathology of their therapists. *Amer J Psychother* **51**(3): 357–75

Wysoker A (2000) Legal and ethical considerations: Sexual misconduct. *J Amer Psychiatr Assoc* **6**(4): 131–2

CHAPTER 18

Conclusions: Themes, action and research for the future

Richard Byrt, Alyson McGregor Kettles and Phil Woods

Introduction

In this final chapter, we aim to consider briefly some principal themes that have been explored by the authors contributing to this book. Some of these themes are the same as, or similar to, those identified in the first two books in this sub-series on forensic mental health nursing (National Forensic Nurses' Research and Development Group, 2006, 2007) and some material is reproduced, with kind permission of Mark Allen Publishing, Quay Books, from Byrt et al (2007a). As identified by Byrt et al (2007a: 291): 'Insights from practice and related writing in this area can provide a basis for the development of ideas, thinking and future research related to ways that nurses' roles and interventions can enable the best possible care to be given to the person in this situation'. In addition, there is a need to focus, not only on the diverse needs of the individual, but on specialist issues related to risk assessment, risk management and offending behaviours (Byrt et al, 2007b), without stigmatising the individual or ignoring the cultural context. (This is considered further under Theme 6 in this chapter.)

Emerging themes

The wide variety of topics covered by the chapter authors in this book indicates the many areas of nursing and multi-disciplinary role, and the capability and competence relevant to forensic nursing. However, as with any text, there is space for only so much material and this is the case here. Relevant issues that have been considered in this book include the following:

Theme 1: Aims

All nursing and multi-disciplinary roles, capabilities and competence for forensic patients are concerned with the overlapping aims of:

- Ensuring safety and prevention and reduction of risk of harm to self and others.
- Relieving distress.
- Respecting individuals' unique needs and their shared humanity and diversity.
- Ensuring social inclusion.

These aims (Kettles et al, 2007) are considered by various authors throughout this book.

Theme 2: Models and therapeutic frameworks of care

There is a need for nursing and multi-disciplinary interventions for forensic patients to be informed by models and therapeutic frameworks of care which achieve the aims highlighted in Theme 1, above. Capabilities related to models include those identified in *Chapter 4* (individuals with learning disability), *Chapters 5–7* (patient empowerment and participation), *Chapter 8* (nutrition provision), *Chapter 9* (assessment, management and treatment of sex offenders), *Chapter 10* (risk assessment), *Chapters 11 and 12* (managing anger), *Chapter 13* (dealing with substance misuse problems) and *Chapter 14* (working in the community).

Theme 3: System change

We would reiterate that, in the future, staff need to begin working towards changes given in the timetables from the National Reviews of Mental Health Nursing, including the following measures that could benefit forensic patients and enhance nurses' professional development:

- Staff rotation between different services, in order to learn skills and perspectives.
- The opportunity to follow patients through their journey from the onset of a mental health problem to recovery in the community. (See *Chapter 14*.)
- Improved educational opportunities.
- The use of models of care specific to forensic mental health, as well as the adaptation, where appropriate, of models used elsewhere, but which appear to be applicable to forensic settings.

Theme 4: Staff attitudes

Chapters 4–7 and 17 all deal with some of the major issues involved in this vitally important part of care, including reviews of the views of forensic service users, for whom staff attitudes have been vitally important. There is research evidence that positive staff attitudes are particularly crucial to effective nursing interventions with individuals with personality disorder in secure hospitals (Mercer et al, 1999; Bowers, 2002; Schafer and Peternelj-Taylor, 2003).

Theme 5: Therapeutic communication

As with previous volumes in this forensic mental health nursing sub-series, therapeutic communication has been emphasised by several authors in the present book, who refer to the importance of this area to forensic patients, with reference to research-based and other literature (see, for example, *Chapters 7, 11–14 and 17*). However, there appears to be a lack of research-based evidence to indicate the most effective ways of using empathy and other communication skills in relation to forensic patients. (Bowers, 2002; Kirby and Cross, 2002 are notable exceptions.) For example, how does a nurse develop and maintain empathy with an individual who is hostile and rejecting towards her/him over a long period of time (Bowers, 2002)?

Theme 6: Risk assessment and management

The importance of valid and reliable risk assessment and management in increasing the safety of the individual and others is stressed by Phil Woods in *Chapter 10* and Paul Burberry and Mohammed Khoshdel in *Chapter 9*. The findings of some inquiries suggest that the risk posed by the offending behaviours of forensic patients have sometimes been ignored (Byrt et al, 2007b). At the same time, efforts need to be made to avoid stigmatisation, to assess risk in its cultural context; and to consider the individual's 'health and social functioning' (Woods and Kettles, 2007: 123). As far as possible, nurses and other professionals should work in collaboration with the patient, in some instances, with informal carers and with a variety of agencies, in identifying and managing risk (Morgan and Wetherell, 2004; Department of Health, 2007). There is also a need for forensic nurses to be aware of the social and political factors impinging on ideas about risk: a point considered in *Chapter 10*, as well as in *Chapters 5, 6 and 7* on power.

Theme 7: Cultural and diversity issues

As in a previous volume (National Forensic Nurses' Research and Development Group, 2007), several authors have indicated the need for increased understanding of diversity issues; and implementation of culturally sensitive and culturally competent care. Aspects of cultural and diversity issues, including cultural sensitivity and cultural competence, are considered in *Chapters 4, 6 and 7*. In particular, there is a consideration in these chapters of specific issues concerning individuals with learning disabilities, women, people from minority ethnic groups, and gays and lesbians.

Theme 8: Social inclusion and recovery

Concepts of social inclusion and recovery are relevant to the care of all forensic patients, and these are considered in various parts of the book, for example, at the end of *Chapter 7*, where steps to increase social inclusion are outlined. Social inclusion and recovery can be particularly problematic for individuals with the roles of both 'offender' and 'mental health patient'; and result in particular stigmatisation, discrimination and a lack of life opportunities in wider society (Bartlett, 2004).

Theme 9: Provision of a safe and therapeutic ward environment

The provision of safe, therapeutic ward environments is considered in *Chapter 6*, with an examination of the all-pervasive, and potentially harmful effects of institutions (Foucault, 1991; Fox, 1999). Besides a concern for safety, it is argued that professionals, managers and commissioners of services have a responsibility to be aware of, and attempt to ameliorate the negative effects of, and enhance the positive consequences of living in secure environments, often for long periods of time, and with various deprivations (Byrt with James, 2007). More research is needed in this area.

Theme 10: Ethical awareness

Staff ethical awareness, with an emphasis on values-based, as well as evidence-based practice (Fulford, 2004) is crucial, particularly in view of the considerable power disparities between forensic patients and staff, as identified in *Chapter 6*. As the authors of *Chapters 5 to 7* conclude, unnecessary disempowerment may be overcome by steps to increase social inclusion and increase patients' empowerment and participation in practical ways, within the parameters of safety, with the avoidance of local health service and central Government policies which unnecessarily restrict forensic patients' freedoms, without contributing to public safety (Lester and Glasby, 2006).

Theme 11: Political role

Related to issues of power is a possible political role for the forensic nurse (Kettles et al, 2006), and this is considered at the end of *Chapter 7*. This could include working within trade unions and professional associations; with groups concerned with the rights and interests of service users, and with other professionals, in order to positively influence Government policy and legislation. It can be argued that such action is particularly crucial when Governments attempt to implement measures which unnecessarily infringe service users' freedoms (commensurate with assessed levels of risk), while failing to contribute to public safety (Kettles et al, 2006; Lester and Glasby, 2006).

Theme 12: Partnership working

Partnership working with the patient, his/her carers and community-based and other professionals and agencies is expected to increase, in line with Government policy. *Chapter 7* by Richard Byrt, Linda Hart and Linnette James-Sow and *Chapter 12* by participants in anger management groups remind us of the crucial need to consider service users' views and to enable their participation. Helen Walker considers the importance of multi-professional education in *Chapter 2*.

Theme 13: Specialist assessment and intervention

There is a need for the development of specialist nursing and multi-disciplinary assessments and interventions, including those concerned with:

- Individuals with needs related to specific mental health problems, including:
  - People with nutrition problems (whose needs have often not been met in generic mental health services: see *Chapter 8*).
  - Individuals with problematic substance use (*Chapter 13*).
  - Individuals with histories of sex offending (*Chapter 9*).
- The application of community and specialist approaches (*Chapters 8, 9 and 14*), including:
  - Specific aspects of community forensic nursing (*Chapter 14*).
  - The nursing of individuals in prison health services (*Chapter 16*).
  - The therapeutic use of self and the maintenance of therapeutic boundaries (*Chapter 17*).
  - Preventing and reducing violence and aggression (*Chapters 11 and 12*).

Theme 14: Health promotion and prevention of ill health

It can be argued that the forensic nurse has a role in health promotion and prevention of ill health, in liaison with a variety of agencies and other professionals. Examples include measures to improve forensic patients' physical health, as outlined in *Chapter 8*, and the work of nurses, as part of wide-ranging multidisciplinary/inter-agency teams, in preventing violence in the home and in wider communities (Riner and Flynn, 1999; World Health Organisation, 2002).

Theme 15: Education, support and clinical supervision

Helen Walker (*Chapter 2*) and several other authors in the book have emphasised the need for high quality education, support and clinical supervision to enable nurses to work with forensic patients.

Theme 16: Development of research and evidence-based practice

It has emerged either directly or indirectly through many of the chapters in this text that there is a continuing need for evaluative studies in forensic services. There is also an argument for some research that crosses boundaries, to enable understanding of the meaning of care for both staff and patients in the different settings and how transition through different settings affects people. According to Peternelj-Taylor (2005: 356) 'Nursing has a pivotal role to play in the correctional milieu. Embracing a research agenda with offenders will guide nursing practice in this highly specialised area, provide new insights into primary, secondary and tertiary health care (including reintegration into the community), and contribute to nursing science through the advancement of nursing knowledge regarding vulnerable populations.' The need for those at nurse consultant level (*Chapter 3*) to be engaged in research and development activities is now an imperative. Also of crucial importance are opportunities for the participation of forensic patients at all stages of research and quality projects (Coffey, 2006b): an area considered in *Chapter 7*. Moreover, nurses are now increasingly being trained in research methods and skills, both at the undergraduate and the postgraduate level. Therefore, it could almost be assumed that nurses, including forensic mental health nurses, are poised to have a more active role in research and evidence-based practice.

Theme 17: Further practice development

Finally, in line with recommendations of the Mental Health Nursing Reviews for Scotland, England and Wales (Department of Health, 2006a; Scottish Executive Health Department, 2006), developments in nursing policy are needed to further practice development and care of people who are forensic patients, as described by David Langton in *Chapter 3*.

In *Chapter 1* the arguments for and against there being a forensic role are introduced and the idea that forensic nursing is not a single entity is discussed. In the current socio-political climate, it is not so much role as capabilities that are being addressed in clinical practice and to that end *Table 18.1* illustrates the various themes and capabilities that this series of texts on forensic mental health nursing have specifically identified. What is noticeable is that when these themes are compared to the *10 Essential Shared Capabilities* (ESCs) (Sainsbury Centre for Mental Health, 2004) not only are the 10 ESCs identified but also there are more than 10 for forensic mental health nursing practice. Forensic nursing requires the same fundamental practice as mental health nursing in general, but then it requires more, such as the specialist practice identified by Paul Burberry and Mohammed Khoshdel in *Chapter 9*.

If we refer back to both Burrow's (1993) study and to the case presented for forensic mental health nursing in *Chapter 1*, it can be seen that the need for a 'formidable and accelerating knowledge base' is as true today as it was in 1993. Indeed, the need for sound evidence in practice is more imperative than ever to ensure that our patients receive forensic mental health nursing that is safe, effective, caring, sensitive and therapeutic. In addition, forensic nursing needs to be value-based (Fulford, 2004) and incorporate the effective and therapeutic use of professional relationships and communication with patients, based on ethical issues and self-awareness (Kirby and Cross, 2002).

Forensic mental health nurses' involvement in both primary and secondary research can only help to develop the evidence base for our specialised area of practice. Woods et al (2002: 244–5) set forth what could really be viewed as a challenge for forensic mental health nurses in the final chapter of their text on therapeutic interventions – a challenge that still exists today:

> *If forensic mental health nurses are to develop their unique evidence base, consideration needs to be given to researching the effectiveness of the interventions they utilise. In the current climate, where only best evidence will do, it is no longer acceptable practice to publish the effectiveness of care with no systematic research to support this. Without such systematic review, evidence provided can only be viewed at best as the author's opinion.*
>
> *This, however, is not to say that forensic nurses should be moving towards only using interventions that have been shown to be effective through randomised controlled trials. Consideration should be given to utilising more pragmatic yet well-designed research approaches. For example: (1) multiple interrupted baseline measures (with patients acting as their own controls); (2) single- or multiple-case studies utilising before*

Table 18.1: An illustration of the themes from the forensic mental health nursing series so far and their relationship to the Ten Essential Shared Capabilities for England and Scotland

10 Essential Shared Capabilities*	'Personality Disorder' Book Themes	'Forensic Aspects of Acute Care' Book Themes	'Roles, Capabilities and Competence' Book Themes
Working in partnership	The nurse—patient relationship	All nursing and MDT assessments and interventions concerned with overlapping aims of safety/prevention and reduction of harm/relieving distress/respecting individual's unique needs	All nursing and MDT roles, capabilities and competence concerned with overlapping aims of safety prevention and reduction of harm/relieving distress/respecting individual's unique needs
Respecting diversity	Attitudes	Models to inform care	Models to inform care
Practising ethically	Stigma	System change	System change
Challenging inequality	Risk assessment and management	Attitude change	Attitude change
Promoting recovery	Nursing policy	Engagement and communication	Engagement and communication
Identifying people's needs and strengths	A political role	Risk assessment and management	Risk assessment and management

*From: National Health Service Education for Scotland (2007) and Department of Heath et al (2004)

Table 18.1 (continued)

	A political role		
Identifying people's needs and strengths		Risk assessment and management	Risk assessment and management
Providing service user-centred care		Diversity issues	The need for increased understanding of diversity issues and implementation of culturally sensitive and culturally competent care
Making a difference		Safe and therapeutic environments	Social inclusion and recovery
Promoting safety and positive risk taking		Partnership working	Safe and therapeutic environments
Personal development and learning		Social inclusion Improvements in crisis care Specialist interventions High quality education, support and clinical supervision Research Nursing policy	Staff ethical awareness, with an emphasis on values-based, as well as evidence-based practice Partnership working Specialist interventions Health promotion, ill heath prevention and liaison with other agencies High quality education, support and clinical supervision Research Nursing policy

and after measures with long-term follow-up; or (3) observational studies with a battery of before-and-after measures with long-term follow-up.

In essence, the way the evidence-based practice develops depends on how the forensic service sees the role of forensic nursing practice. Does this involve all forensic nurses drawing on an advanced knowledge base, using best available evidence, standardised assessments, positive risk taking, offence-focused work, and so on; or is this relying on one or two clinical nurse specialists or nurse consultants using their advanced clinical skills in a narrowly focused way?

We suggest that in order for forensic nursing practice to develop its own clear evidence base this has to involve interrogating current practice, adding an advanced knowledge base, synthesising and evaluating – so that practice will be teased and steered to only that which is evidence-based. This would encourage nurses to challenge their existing practice, encourage positive risk-taking, but more importantly, would ensure their practice was outcome driven.

Forensic nursing needs to develop its evidence in relation to the day-to-day management of patients to compensate for very specific specialist intervention from other members of the multidisciplinary team. But the mistake should not be made in assuming that this is any less valuable. Fundamentally, this would develop the knowledge base around just how forensic nurses intervene and meet the individual needs of the patients under their care. Indeed, it would help to ensure that care was simplistic yet effective, maximising benefits, thus improving quality. All this would help to develop practice in a meaningful and sustainable way to define forensic nursing and its role, skills and competencies.

(Woods et al, 2002:244–5)

We hope that you have enjoyed this book and found it useful. Forensic nursing has expanded rapidly over the past 20 years, and is continuing to develop. It is an area that presents particular challenges because of the considerable ethical issues involved, for example, those concerned with issues of social control and the weighing up of the rights and needs of the individual patient, including those related to autonomy, and the rights and needs of the public. More than most, if not all, areas of nursing, forensic nursing appears to be particularly influenced by political and social factors (Barker and Stevenson, 2000), which are certain to change over time. As forensic nurses, it can be salutary to remind ourselves that what are, at present, seen as acceptable practices, may be viewed as barbaric or questionable in a few decades' time (Barker and Stevenson, 2000). On a hectic ward, or working within a busy forensic community mental health team, it can be hard to 'reflect on action' (Schon, 1991). But such reflection, with a 'standing back' to review our work, although difficult, is crucial to questioning and subsequent development of ethical, caring and safe nursing and multidisciplinary practice (Clark et al, 2001). The experiences of both staff and patients may enable this reflection (Ramsay et al, 2002). The following comments are examples:

> *There was one nurse who taught me something very important really, which was to actually meet with the individual, and to get to know the individual before reading their case notes. And what I find with doing that is that it's... easier then to put into perspective their past psychiatric history or offending history, when you actually know the person for who they are today.*
>
> (Bowers, 2002:72, quoting a forensic nurse working in a high secure hospital)

> *It was strange because there was a great amount of hatred in me for all screws, yet some of the unit staff would approach me in a way that was so natural, it made it difficult for me to tell them to f*** off. Something inside me, in spite of all the pent up hatred, would tell me there was something genuine about them.*
>
> (Boyle, 1977, quoted in Smith, 1984, referring to his experience of a prison therapeutic community)

> *[Clients] consistently described the importance of relationships in terms of hope, recovery and survival. People described how the most significant support they received was from people whom they could trust, and who, as Carol said, 'treat you as a person, rather than a diagnosis...' Carol felt that 'it's about getting the right support around you...even so far as the way they speak to you.'*
>
> (Horn et al, 2007: 263)

'Hope, recovery and survival' (Horn et al, 2007:263) – how can we, as forensic nurses, ensure this in relation to the individual patient and his or her needs and the safety of others? We hope this book has provided some answers, as well as questions and ideas for further research.

References

Barker P, Stevenson C (Eds) (2000) *The Construction of Power and Authority in Psychiatry.* Butterworth Heinemann: Oxford

Bartlett A (2004) Fashions in Psychiatric Care: Implications for Sense of Self. In: Crisp AH (Ed) *Every Family in the Land: Understanding Prejudice and Discrimination Against People with Mental Illness* (Ch 49) Royal Society of Medicine Press, London

Bowers L (2002) *Dangerous and Severe Personality Disorder: Response and Role of the Psychiatric Team.* Routledge, London

Boyle J (1977) *A Sense of Freedom*. Pan Books, London

Burrow S (1993) An outline of the forensic nursing role. *Brit J Nurs* **2**(18): 899–904

Byrt R, Aiyegbusi A, Hardie T, Addo A (2007b) Cultural and Diversity Issues. In: National Forensic Nurses' Research and Development Group: Kettles AM, Woods P, Byrt R, Addo M, Coffey M, Doyle M (Eds) *Forensic Mental Health: Forensic Aspects of Acute Care*. Quay Books, MA Healthcare, London

Byrt R, James L (2007) Towards therapeutic environments: Challenges and problems. In: National Forensic Nurses' Research and Development Group: Kettles AM, Woods P, Byrt R, Addo M, Coffey M, Doyle M (Eds) (2007) *Forensic Mental Health: Forensic Aspects of Acute Care*. Quay Books, MA Healthcare, London

Byrt R, Kettles AM, Woods P (2007a) Conclusions: 15 Themes, Action and Research for the Future. In: National Forensic Nurses' Research and Development Group: Kettles AM, Woods P, Byrt R, Addo M, Coffey M, Doyle M (Eds) *Forensic Mental Health: Forensic Aspects of Acute Care*. Quay Books, MA Healthcare, London

Clark A, Dooher J, Fowler J (Eds) (2001) *The Handbook of Practice Development*. Quay Books, Dinton, Salisbury

Coffey M (2006a) Community Interventions. In: National Forensic Nurses' Research and Development Group: Woods P, Kettles AM, Byrt R, Addo M, Aiyegbusi A, Coffey M, Collins M, Doyle M, Garman G, Watson C (Eds) *Forensic Mental Health Nursing: Interventions with People with 'Personality Disorder'*. Quay Books, MA Healthcare Ltd, London

Coffey M (2006b) Researching service user views in forensic mental health: A literature review. *J Forensic Psychiatry Psychol* **17**(1): 73–107

Department of Health (2005) *Delivering Race Equality in Mental Health Care. An Action Plan for Reform. Inside and Outside Services and the Government's Response to the Independent Inquiry Into the Death of David Bennett*. Department of Health, London

Department of Health (2006a) *From Values to Action: The Chief Nursing Officer's Review of Mental Health Nursing*. Department of Health, London

Department of Health (2006b) *Supporting Women into the Mainstream: Commissioning Women Only Community Day Services*. Department of Health, London

Department of Health (2007) *Best Practice in Managing Risk*. Department of Health, London

Department of Health, NHSU, Sainsbury Centre for Mental Health, National Institute for Mental Health in England (2004) *The Ten Essential Shared Capabilities. A Framework for the Whole Mental Health Workforce*. Department of Health, London

Foucault M (1991) *Discipline and Punishment: The Birth of the Prison*. Translated from the French by Alan Sheridan Penguin Books, Harmondsworth

Fox KJ (1999) Changing violent minds: discursive correction and resistance in the cognitive treatment of violent offenders in prison. *Soc Problems* **46**(1): 88–103

Fulford KWM (2004) Facts/values: ten principles of values-based medicine. In: Radden J (Ed) *The Philosophy of Psychiatry: A Companion*. Oxford University Press, Oxford

Horn N, Johnstone L, Brooke S (2007) Some service user perspectives on the diagnosis of borderline personality disorder. *J Ment Health* **16**(2): 255–69

Kettles AM, Byrt R, Woods P (2007) Introduction. In: National Forensic Nurses' Research and Development Group: Kettles AM, Woods P, Byrt R, Addo M, Coffey M, Doyle M (Eds) *Forensic Mental Health: Forensic Aspects of Acute Care*. Quay Books, MA Healthcare, London

Kettles AM, Woods P, Byrt R (2006) Conclusions. In: National Forensic Nurses' Research and Development Group: Woods P, Kettles AM, Byrt R, Addo M, Aiyegbusi A, Coffey M, Collins M, Doyle M, Garman G, Watson C (Eds) *Forensic Mental Health Nursing: Interventions with People with 'Personality Disorder'*. Quay Books, MA Healthcare Ltd, London

Kirby SD, Cross D (2002) Socially Constructed Narrative Interventions: A Foundation for Therapeutic Alliances. In: Kettles AM, Woods P, Collins M (Eds) *Therapeutic Interventions for Forensic Mental Health Nurses* (Ch 12). Jessica Kingsley, London

Lester H, Glasby J (2006) *Mental Health Policy and Practice*. Palgrave Macmillan: Basingstoke

Mercer D, Mason T, Richman J (1999) Good and evil in the crusade of care. *J Psychosoc Nurs Ment Health Services* **37**(9): 13–17

Morgan S, Wetherell A (2004) Assessing and managing risk. In: Norman I, Ryrie I (Eds) *The Art and Science of Mental Health Nursing: A Textbook of Principles and Practice*. Open University Press, Maidenhead

National Forensic Nurses' Research and Development Group: Woods P, Kettles AM, Byrt R, Addo M, Aiyegbusi A, Coffey M, Collins M, Doyle M, Garman G, Watson C (Eds) (2006) *Forensic Mental Health Nursing: Interventions with People with 'Personality Disorder'*. Quay Books, MA Healthcare Ltd, London

National Forensic Nurses' Research and Development Group: Kettles AM, Woods P, Byrt R, Addo M, Coffey M, Doyle M (Eds) (2007) *Forensic Mental Health: Forensic Aspects of Acute Care*. Quay Books, MA Healthcare, London

NHS Education for Scotland (2007) *Educational Solutions for Workforce Development,Values Based Practice. The 10 Essential Shared Capabilities for Mental HealthPractice, Learning Materials (Scotland)*. NHS Education for Scotland: Edinburgh

Peternelj-Taylor C (2005) Conceptualizing nursing research with offenders: Another look at vulnerability. *Int J Law Psychiatry* **28**: 348–59

Ramsay R, Page A, Goodman T, Hart D (Eds) (2002) *Changing Minds: Our Lives and Mental Illness*. Gaskell/Royal College of Psychiatrists, London

Riner ME, Flynn BC (1999) Creating violence-free cities for our youth. *Holistic Nursing Practice* **14**(1): 1–11

Sainsbury Centre for Mental Health (2004) *The Ten Essential Shared Capabilities: A Framework for the Whole Mental Health Workforce (England)*. Sainsbury Centre for Mental Health, London

Schafer P, Peternelj-Taylor C (2003) Therapeutic relationships and boundary maintenance: the perspective of forensic patients enrolled in a treatment program for violent offenders. *Issues in Ment Health Nurs* **24**: 605–25

Schon DA (1991) *The Reflective Practitioner: How Professionals Think in Action*. Avebury, Aldershot

Scottish Executive Health Department (2006) *Rights, Relationships and Recovery: The Report of the National Review of Mental Health Nursing in Scotland*. Scottish Executive, Edinburgh

Skelly C (2001) Managing the Transition from Higher to Lower Levels of Security. In: Dale C, Thompson T, Woods P (Eds) *Forensic Mental Health: Issues in Practice* (Ch 23) Bailliere Tindall/Royal College of Nursing, Edinburgh

Smith R (1984) *Prison Health Care*. British Medical Association, London

Woods P, Collins M, Kettles A (2002) Forensic nursing interventions and future directions for forensic mental health practice. In: Kettles A, Woods P, Collins M (Eds) *Therapeutic Interventions for Forensic Mental Health Nurses* (pp 240–5) Jessica Kingsley, London

Woods P, Kettles AM (2007) Measurement of Health and Social Functioning. In: National Forensic Nurses' Research and Development Group: Kettles AM, Woods P, Byrt R, Addo M, Coffey M, Doyle M (Eds) (2007) *Forensic Mental Health: Forensic Aspects of Acute Care*. Quay Books, MA Healthcare, London

World Health Organization (2002) *World Report on Violence and Health*. World Health Organization, Geneva

Index